E-commerce: Business Models and Service Management

E-commerce: Business Models and Service Management

Edited by Anthony Rocus

CLANRYE
INTERNATIONAL
www.clanryeinternational.com

Clanrye International,
750 Third Avenue, 9ᵗʰ Floor,
New York, NY 10017, USA

ISBN: 978-1-63240-588-3

Cataloging-in-publication Data

E-commerce : business models and service management / edited by Anthony Rocus.
    p. cm.
Includes bibliographical references and index.
ISBN 978-1-63240-588-3
1. Electronic commerce. 2. Electronic commerce--Management. 3. Business planning. I. Rocus, Anthony.
HF5548.32 .E36 2017
658.872--dc23

For information on all Clanrye International publications
visit our website at www.clanryeinternational.com

Printed in the United States of America.

Contents

Preface

E-commerce is a relatively nascent yet swiftly expanding field of study. It is concerned with trading via computer networks, primarily internet. The aim of this book is to present researches that have transformed this discipline and aided its advancement. This book strives to put across a plethora of tools and techniques that e-commerce business specialists employ like online shopping websites, online marketplaces and electronic data interchange, etc. The text also lays forth multiple business applications of e-commerce that are prevalent across the globe. As this field is emerging at a rapid pace, the contents of this book will help the readers understand the modern concepts and applications of the subject. For all readers who are interested in E-commerce, the case studies included herein will serve as an excellent guide to develop a comprehensive understanding of the field.

This book has been an outcome of determined endeavour from a group of educationists in the field. The primary objective was to involve a broad spectrum of professionals from diverse cultural background involved in the field for developing new researches. The book not only targets students but also scholars pursuing higher research for further enhancement of the theoretical and practical applications of the subject.

It was an honour to edit such a profound book and also a challenging task to compile and examine all the relevant data for accuracy and originality. I wish to acknowledge the efforts of the contributors for submitting such brilliant and diverse chapters in the field and for endlessly working for the completion of the book. Last, but not the least; I thank my family for being a constant source of support in all my research endeavours.

Editor

A Structural Equation Model of Customer Satisfaction and Future Purchase of Mail-Order Speciality Food

Li-Wei Mai, University of Westminster
Westminster Business School,
University of Westminster, 35 Marylebone Rd, London NW1 5LS, UK,

Email: d.l.mai@wmin.ac.uk

Mitchell R. Ness, Newcastle University
School of Agriculture Food and Rural Development
Newcastle University, Newcastle upon Tyne, NE1 7RU, UK,

Email: mitchell.ness@ncl.ac.uk

Abstract

Analyses the relationship between satisfaction with mail-order speciality food attributes, overall satisfaction, and likelihood of future purchase using a structural equation model. The results indicate that customer satisfaction is associated with both service and product features of mail order speciality food.

Keywords: customer satisfaction, re-purchase intentions, speciality mail order food, structural equation modelling

1 INTRODUCTION

In the UK the market for mail-order speciality foods has evolved in line with the growth of direct marketing in response to changes in modern lifestyles and customer expectations. These changes have paved the way for the exploitation of in-home shopping systems (The Economist, 1994; Victor, 1995). The issues faced by speciality food marketers concern the identification and satisfaction of customers' needs in the context of key elements of direct marketing such as targeting, interaction, continuity and control with an emphasis on customer retention (McCorkell, 1997).

In this context direct marketing emphasises the importance of building a long-term relationship with customers through quality, value and service. In this respect there is a shift in emphasis from pure transactions-based marketing to give at least equal attention to relationship marketing. Thus in the face of increasing competition firms pursue objectives of survival, prosperity and competitive advantage by building products and customers through the delivery of high value (Kotler et al., 1996).

The consumer is assumed to have an objective of maximising value; the difference between the benefits conferred in relation to the costs of acquisition, including costs of decision making, relative to alternative products or suppliers. According to Kotler et al. (1996), maximisation of customer value is translated into maximisation of customer satisfaction relative to expectations and product performance.

From the firm's perspective, delivery of value may be related to the notion of the value chain (Porter, 1985). Porter emphasises that value is not just delivered by products but through all primary activities (in-born logistics, operations, out-bound logistics, marketing and sales, and service) in association with support activities (infrastructure, human resources, technological development and procurement).

The problem facing mail-order speciality food companies is consistent with this particular area of research. Although, in what constitutes a relatively new sector, these firms face the traditional transactions-based task of recruiting new customers, they also need to engage customers in a long-term relationship; to encourage repeat business and loyalty through the delivery of value. Thus the focus of this paper is to identify whether and to what extent such firms deliver satisfaction across the transactions aspects of their operations and whether this creates a positive response in terms of overall satisfaction and intentions to repeat purchases.

The structure of the paper is as follows. It begins with a discussion of the background literature and is followed by an explanation and discussion of the research methodology. This is followed by the presentation of the empirical results. Finally the paper closes with some summary and concluding comments.

2 BACKGROUND ISSUES

According to Dick and Basu (1994), consumer loyalty plays a central role in marketing strategy, and marketing planning in the achievement of brand loyalty, vendor loyalty in industrial marketing, service loyalty in the service sector and store loyalty in the retail sector. The marketing literature defines loyalty as an attitude or a behavioural intention (Hallowell, 1996). Attitudinal loyalty reflects an individual's overall attachment to a product, service or organisation (Fornier, 1994). Behavioural loyalty is expressed in terms of intentions to re-purchase, to increase the scale and scope of a relationship, brand-switching or the act of recommendation (Yi, 1990; Selnes, 1993; Biong, 1993).

The widest perspective of behavioural loyalty is set within the context of the quality-value-satisfaction (Q-V-S) literature. In a review of this literature Cronin et al. (2000) report that research interest in Q-V-S has proceeded from a focus on perceived quality to satisfaction and hence to value according to national awards or paradigm shifts such as total quality management, customer satisfaction measurement, and customer value measurement. Research studies have paid attention to the measurement of the constructs (Dabolkar et al., 2000), the relationships between them (Cronin et al., 2000) and how they affect behavioural intentions (Bou-Llusar et al., 2001).

The elements within the Q-V-S framework tend to be defined as constructs with multiple measures. Typically a construct of 'Sacrifice' is specified to depict the sacrifice in terms of price, time and effort to accomplish the transaction. An independent construct of 'Perceived Quality' along with 'Sacrifice' is linked to a construct of 'Perceived Value'. 'Perceived Value' thus reflects the influence of the trade-off between 'Sacrifice' and 'Perceived Quality'. Three alternative forms of measurement have been applied to the perceived quality construct. One approach has been to address perceived quality (Very poor, Very good). Another has been to employ disconfirmation measures that are related to expectations (Much worse than expected, Much better than expected). A third approach employs computed disconfirmation that employs measures of perceived quality and expectations and computes disconfirmation by subtraction. A further issue is whether disconfirmation is more suitable measured in a cross-section study or longitudinal study. In the latter approach expectations are measured prior to service delivery while service quality is measured afterwards.

The need for firms to measure customer satisfaction has led to the use of instruments such as customer satisfaction and purchase intentions surveys, analysis of complaints and suggestions, ghost shopping and lost customer analysis. A study by Wilson (2002) researched the use of customer satisfaction measurement within the retail sector. The research reveals a high degree of usage for monitoring customer attitudes, the overall performance of the firm and to identify problem areas. Yet more than two-thirds of firms indicated that satisfaction measures are most useful when combined with complementary measures. Hausknecht (1990), in a review of methods of measuring customer satisfaction/dissatisfaction, provides a taxonomy of measurement scales, which are classified as evaluative or cognitive, emotional or affective and, behavioural or conative approaches. However, Halstead (1989) makes the point that satisfaction is not desirable as an end but rather as a means to understand future customer responses. Hence interest in satisfaction is linked to customer loyalty and retention. However, satisfaction is regarded as a necessary but not a sufficient condition to lead to repeat purchase behaviour (Van Looy et al., 1998; Bloemer and Kasper, 1995).

Satisfaction is typically measured as an overall feeling or as satisfaction with elements of the transaction in terms of its ability to meet customers' needs and expectations (Fornell, 1992; Zeithaml and Bitner, 2000). Another approach employs a disconfirmation paradigm, which examines deviations of performance from customer expectations and norms (Bearden et al., 1981).

A series of studies has further elaborated the satisfaction-loyalty relationship for products and services, brands and retailers and considered the interaction between these (Bloemer and Lemmink, 1992). For example, Dabholkar and Thorpe (1994) employ multiple measures of both overall satisfaction and loyalty. Bloemer and Kasper (1995) distinguish between spurious and true (brand) loyalty and between manifest and latent satisfaction. They also provide explicit treatment of the situation in which purchase takes place. In a study of customers of a car dealership Bloemer and Lemmink (1992) distinguish between the satisfaction-loyalty relationship for both dealers and brands. La Barbera and Mazursky (1983) employ a longitudinal study, which enables them to consider the analysis of satisfaction over time, including brand-switching behaviour.

A further issue within the Q-V-S framework is the nature of the interactions between its component constructs including direct and indirect links to behavioural intentions. In their review of the applications Cronin et al. (2000) identify three broad approaches that reflect researchers' interests in different perspectives. The Value Model is typical of service value studies and specifies that behavioural intentions are directly influenced by service value and where service value is influenced independently by sacrifice, service quality and satisfaction or a subset of these constructs (Zeithaml, 1988; Cronin et al., 1997).

In the Satisfaction Model behavioural intentions are directly influenced by satisfaction and where this construct is simultaneously influenced by service value and service quality, and where service value is simultaneously influenced by sacrifice and service quality (Cronin and Taylor, 1992; Hallowell, 1996; Oliver 1999).

A third model, the Indirect Model reflects a focus on the interaction between service quality, value and satisfaction. Hence there are direct effects on behavioural intentions from value and satisfaction constructs. Value is influenced directly by quality and in turn, has a direct effect on satisfaction. Hence there are indirect effects on behavioural intentions by quality, via value and also via value and satisfaction, and value, via satisfaction (Ennew and Binks, 1999).

Anderson et al. (1994) provide a framework for the estimation of the economic returns arising from the delivery of consumer satisfaction. Evidence in support of the satisfaction-loyalty-profitability relationship is provided by Heskett et al. (1994) and Hallowell (1996). Apart from the application to individual firms, the concept has been extended, for example in the form of the American Consumer Satisfaction Index (ACSI), to industrial sectors or economies (Fornell, 1992). Subsequently, the ACSI inspired the development of the European Consumer Satisfaction Index (ECSI) in association with the European Foundation for Quality Management (EFQM) and the European Academic Network for Customer Oriented Quality Analysis (IFCF). In 1999 a pilot study was implemented in 12 European countries (Kristensen et al., 2001; Cassel and Eklöf, 2001)).

A related development extends the satisfaction-loyalty relationship to include profitability. Loyalty enhances profitability through an increase in the scale and scope of the relationship with loyal customers, lower customer recruitment costs, reduced customer price sensitivity and lower customer servicing costs (Hallowell, 1996). However, Reinartz and Kumar (2002) warn against the assumption that loyalty automatically promotes greater profitability. These authors test four assertions from the customer relationship marketing paradigm, that loyal customers: are more profitable, cost less to serve, pay higher prices; and, act as word-of-mouth marketers. They established that the respective associations between bivariate measures of loyalty with profit, costs, price and marketing activity were generally 'weak' to 'moderate'.

The authors attribute these results to the 'crude' nature of loyalty measurement that typically employs recency-frequency-monetary value criteria. Alternatively, they propose the use of event history modelling, which establishes the probability of purchase over future time periods and subsequently segments customers into four categories ('Buterflies': short term loyalty/high profitability; 'Strangers': short-term loyalty/low profitability; 'True-friends': long-term loyalty/high profitability; and 'Barnacles': long-term loyalty/low profitability) according to profitability (high/low) and loyalty (short-term/long-term). Hence they are able to propose management strategies for each segment.

3 METHODOLOGY

The research methodology employed a mail survey to investigate mail-order shoppers' characteristics, attitudes, preferences and behaviour. It was implemented as a national (UK) survey of (3,052) customer contacts supplied by five mail-order speciality food companies located in Cumbria, Northumberland and the Scottish Borders region. The sample frame consisted of names and addresses supplied by these companies. The sampling method employed a stratified random sample based upon the relative sizes of the firms' contact lists. Subsequently the survey yielded 1,639 valid responses, representing a response rate of 54 per cent.

It should be emphasised that the sample frame consisted of names and addresses of contacts, comprising existing customers and potential customer contacts from various sources such as exhibitions, trade fairs and from general enquiries. The firms did not have access to the type of customer databases that are recognised in the direct marketing literature as a key aspect of direct marketing and which would typically contain demographic, lifestyle and behavioural information to provide for detailed analysis (McCorkell, 1997).

The respondents were classified as "Active" or "Non-active" mail-order customers according to the recency of their last orders. The "Active" group comprised 1,030 respondents who had shopped for speciality food using mail-order during the previous 12 months whilst the "Non-active" group comprised 609 respondents who had not purchased food by mail-order during the same period. Whilst the questionnaire design incorporated questions addressed to both groups, the research reported within this study focuses only on the "Active" group, since this group had experience of speciality mail-order products and were thus equipped to express their evaluations on the various scales. This approach follows the notion that customer experience is an essential requirement in the analysis of satisfaction assessments (Bolton and Drew, 1991; Cronin and Taylor, 1994; Parasuraman et al., 1988).

4 MEASURES

Although there are no directly comparable studies, this study is broadly consistent with existing satisfaction literature (Cronin and Taylor, 1992; Anderson and Fornell, 1994; Hallowell, 1996; Bolton, 1998; Oliver, 1999; Garbarino and Johnson, 1999; Bolton and Lemon, 1999; Bernhardt et al., 2000). Hence it takes a conventional approach in that re-purchase likelihood is directly influenced by a measure of overall satisfaction that in turn is influenced by a construct to represent transaction satisfaction associated with the attributes of mail order speciality foods. The measures of the attribute satisfaction construct were identified from in-depth discussions with managers and proprietors of mail-order firms and follow the approach of Biong (1993) in principle. The approach is parsimonious in that in likelihood of purchase can be traced to actionable attributes associated with mail-order speciality food and that are relevant to customers' encounters with mail-order transactions within the speciality food sector. The structural model is presented in Figure 1.

The eight effective indicators of the transaction satisfaction construct are concerned respectively with enquiry service (satis1), product selection (satis2), product quality (satis3), price (satis4), catalogue presentation (satis5), delivery service (satis6), ordering process (satis7) and payment terms (satis8). The response measures are defined as overall satisfaction (ovsat) with mail-order and the likelihood of future purchase (likbuy).

The levels of transaction satisfactions are measured as five-point scales (1 = Very satisfied, 5 = Very dissatisfied) for each of the eight satisfaction variables. Overall satisfaction is measured as a separate entity on the same basis. Likelihood of future purchase is measured on a 5 point scale (1 = Definitely would buy, 5 = Definitely would not buy).

Figure 1: Structural Equation Model

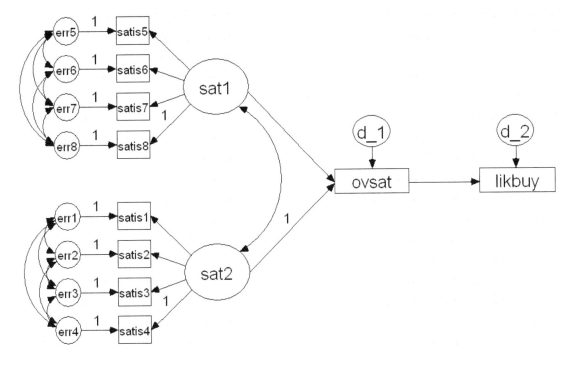

5 EMPIRICAL RESULTS

Each of the measures are analysed in the first instance using univariate analysis of the 10 measures in terms of frequencies and mean scores. Following this correlation analysis of the measures is presented. Exploratory factor analysis is applied to the eight measures that comprise the transactions satisfaction construct and the resulting factor structure is assessed using confirmatory factor analysis. Finally a structural equation model to analyse the relationships between the construct and measures is estimated. Univariate analysis, correlation analysis and exploratory factor analysis are conducted using SPSS (2003) while confirmatory factor analysis and structural equation modelling are conducted using AMOS (Amos, 2005).

Analysis of satisfaction attributes
The percentage distributions of responses for the eight satisfaction attributes are presented in Table 1. From the perspective of the proportion of customers who are very satisfied mail-order speciality food firms have been relatively more successful in delivering satisfaction with respect to product quality, delivery service, enquiry service and selection of products available. They have been least successful with respect to the order process, payment terms, catalogue presentation and price. Price is the least satisfactory aspect with only 10 per cent of customers who are very satisfied. However, this is not surprising, given the nature of these foods, which generally carry price premia, and with respect to the high levels of satisfaction with quality that indicates that it is value for money which customers evaluate.

Table 1: Frequencies and Means for Satisfaction and Purchase Likelihood Measures

Satisfaction	Satisfaction (Percentage response)						Mean rating
	Very satisfied	Satisfied	Somewhat satisfied	Dissatisfied	Very dissatisfied	Total	
Enquiry service	38.7	52.2	8.4	0.7	0.0	100	1.71
Product selection	37.6	55.1	6.9	0.4	0.0	100	1.70
Product quality	51.4	42.3	5.9	0.3	0.1	100	1.55
Price	10.0	52.8	29.4	7.2	0.6	100	2.36
Catalogue presentation	23.4	58.4	16.5	1.6	0.2	100	1.97
Delivery service	43.6	44.5	9.2	2.2	0.6	100	1.72
Ordering process	37.3	55.0	7.2	0.4	0.1	100	1.71
Payment terms	27.6	60.5	10.8	0.9	0.1	100	1.85
Overall satisfaction	36.5	56.3	6.6	0.3	0.3	100	1.72
	Purchase likelihood (Percentage response)						
Future purchase likelihood	Definitely	Likely	Not sure	Not likely	Definitely not	Total	Mean rating
Likelihood rating:	58.5	35.0	4.7	1.7	0.1	100	1.50

Notes: Sample size (N) = 1028-1030 according to the presence of missing values in the data

Consideration of the two most favourable rating categories (Satisfied and Very satisfied) indicates that for each item the major proportion of customers are at least satisfied with all eight aspects of satisfaction. For example, 94 per cent of respondents are either satisfied or very satisfied with product quality and 93 per cent are at least satisfied with product selection. The least satisfactory aspect is associated with price where 63 per cent of respondents are at least satisfied but this still represents a majority attitude. On the basis of mean scores it is product quality, product selection and the order process which are more highly rated.

Analysis of overall satisfaction and likelihood of purchase

Following from this, consideration of overall satisfaction reveals that whilst a little more than one third of mail-order speciality food customers are very satisfied, 93 per cent are either satisfied or very satisfied (Table 1).

With respect to future purchase intentions, nearly 60 per cent of mail-order food shoppers definitely intend to repeat their purchases of mail order speciality food in the future while 35 per cent indicate they are likely to purchase again (Table 1). Consequently, the results indicate that mail-order appears to deliver high levels of satisfaction to match or exceed customers' expectations and that a high proportion of customers intend to repurchase.

Correlation analysis

The ultimate aim of the analysis is to examine the rationale of assuming that future purchase intentions can be associated with overall satisfaction and in turn, that overall satisfaction is associated with a satisfaction (with the features of mail-order) construct that is composed of eight indicators. Thus as a preliminary step the simple correlation coefficients for these sets of variables are examined (Table 2). Statistical tests, based upon the null hypothesis that the population correlation coefficient is equal to zero, indicate that all correlations are significantly different from zero at the 1 per cent significance level.

There is a significant positive association between overall satisfaction and purchase likelihood. Furthermore, there are significant correlations between overall satisfaction and all eight satisfaction attribute variables but, in descending order of magnitude, it is associated with the order process, product quality, deliver service, payment terms, product selection, enquiry service, price and catalogue presentation. The correlations between future purchase intentions and the satisfaction attributes are generally weaker, though significant, but it is more strongly associated with product quality, enquiry service, order process and price.

Table 2: Correlation Matrix

Variable	Variable[1]									
	satis1	satis2	satis3	satis4	satis5	satis6	satis7	satis8	ovsat	likbuy
satis1	1.000									
satis2	0.480**	1.000								
satis3	0.390**	0.581**	1.000							
satis4	0.297**	0.366**	0.412**	1.000						
satis5	0.363**	0.348**	0.257**	0.363**	1.000					
satis6	0.318**	0.254**	0.317**	0.304**	0.340**	1.000				
satis7	0.480**	0.356**	0.353**	0.297**	0.409**	0.588**	1.000			
satis8	0.377**	0.266**	0.258**	0.374**	0.396**	0.456**	0.627**	1.000		
ovsat	0.465**	0.466**	0.517**	0.437**	0.425**	0.500**	0.550**	0.492**	1.000	
likbuy	0.309**	0.286**	0.376**	0.299**	0.235**	0.217**	0.298**	0.208**	0.452**	1.000

Notes:
1. Variables are defined as follows:
   satis1 = enquiry service; satis2 = product selection; satis3 = product quality; satis4 = price;
   satis5 = catalogue presentation; satis6 = delivery service; satis7 = ordering process; satis8 = payment terms
   ovsat = overall satisfaction; likbuy = likelihood of future purchase.
2. ** Indicates correlation is significant at the 0.01 level (two-tailed test)
3. Sample size (N) = 1028Exploratory Factor Analysis of the Satisfaction Construct

Exploratory Factor Analysis of the Satisfaction Construct

Factor analysis of the eight-item satisfaction construct employed the extraction procedure of principal components with Varimax rotation. The criterion used to determine the number of factors was based upon the derivation of factors with an eigenvalue greater than unity.

A two-factor solution was derived (Table 3). Bartlett's test of sphericity lead to a rejection of the null hypothesis, that the data are not correlated ($\chi 2$ (28) = 2225.463, p < .001), while the KMO index of 0.827 is, according to Kaiser's classification, 'meritorious' (Kaiser 1974). The two factors account for 59% of total variance and the communalities are generally respectable although those associated with catalogue presentation (0.410) and price (0.411) is rather low. The first factor (sat1) is associated with ordering process (0.819), payment terms (0.801), delivery service (0.762) and catalogue presentation (0.537) and is defined as service satisfaction. The second factor (sat2) is associated with product selection (0.833), product quality (0.827), price (0.553) and enquiry service (0.520) and is defined as product satisfaction.

Table 3: Satisfaction Construct: Exploratory Factor Analysis

Attribute	Factor Number		h2
	1	2	
Enquiry service	.442	.520	.466
Product selection	.135	.833	.712
Product quality	.124	.827	.699
Price	.324	.553	.411
Catalogue presentation	.537	.350	.410
Delivery service	.762	.121	.596
Ordering process	.819	.252	.734
Payment terms	.801	.161	.667
Eigenvalue	2.514	2.180	
Variance (%)	31.429	27.253	
Cumulative variance (%)	31.249	58.682	

Notes:
1. h2 refers to communality
2. Sample size (N) = 1028

Confirmatory Factor Analysis of the Satisfaction Construct

The results of confirmatory factor analysis are presented in Table 4. The non-constrained regression weights linking the sub-constructs or factors and their associated measures are all statistically significant. The covariance between the two sub-constructs service satisfaction (sat1) and product satisfaction (sat2) is positive and significant and is associated with a correlation of 0.674.

Table 4: Satisfaction Construct: Confirmatory Factor Analysis

Structural Relation	Regression Weight	Standard Error	Critical Ratio	Standard Weight	Squared Multiple Correlation
satis1 ← sat2	0.921	0.069	13.444	0.615	0.378
satis2 ← sat2	1.027	0.070	14.761	0.727	0.528
satis3 ← sat2	1.053	0.071	14.796	0.726	0.527
satis4 ← sat2	1.000	na	na	0.554	0.307
satis5 ← sat1	0.786	0.053	14.924	0.529	0.279
satis6 ← sat1	1.113	0.058	19.034	0.673	0.453
satis7 ← sat1	1.146	0.052	22.164	0.855	0.730
satis8 ← sat1	1.000	na	na	0.727	0.528
sat1 ↔ sat2	0.136	0.012	10.978	0.674	na
Chi-Square	$\chi2(19) = 216.179, P = 0.000$				
Model	**RMSEA**	**TLI**	**IFI**	**CFI**	
Default	0.080	0.848	0.921	0.920	
Saturated	na	na	1.000	1.000	
Independence	0.205	0.000	0.000	0.000	

Notes:
1. Variables are defined as follows:
    satis1 = enquiry service; satis2 = product selection; satis3 = product quality; satis4 = price; satis5 = catalogue presentation; satis6 = delivery service; satis7 = ordering process; satis8 = payment terms; sat1 = factor 1 (service satisfaction), sat2 = factor 2 (product satisfaction)
2. Sample size (N) = 1028.

Structural Equation Model

The structural equation model follows conventional linkages between satisfaction constructs, overall satisfaction and likelihood of future purchase. The model employed maximum likelihood estimation because of the presence of missing values in the data. Two versions of the model were estimated. Version 1 revealed a significant covariance between service and product satisfaction constructs of 0.136 so that Version 2 imposed a constraint between them. The estimated relationships are presented in Table 5

Table 5: Estimated Structural Equation Model

Structural Relation	Regression Weight	Standard Error	Critical Ratio	Standard Weight	Squared Multiple Correlation
ovsat ← sat1	1.605	0.108	14.904	0.891	0.794
ovsat ← sat2	1.000	na	na	0.608	na
satis1 ← sat2	1.032	0.061	16.807	0.624	0.291
satis2 ← sat2	1.089	0.058	18.645	0.697	0.279
satis3 ← sat2	1.158	0.060	19.298	0.721	0.342
satis4 ← sat2	1.000	na	na	0.517	0.254
satis5 ← sat1	0.788	0.049	15.984	0.543	0.239
satis6 ← sat1	1.111	0.054	20.745	0.688	0.322
satis7 ← sat1	1.110	0.045	24.932	0.845	0.393
satis8 ← sat1	1.000	na	na	0.739	0.464
sat1 < -- > sat2	0.136	na	na	0.719	na
likbuy ← ovsat	0.497	0.029	16.950	0.473	0.215
Goodness of Fit Measures					
Absolute	**Incremental**				
Chi-Square	**Model**	**RMSEA**	**TLI**	**IFI**	**CFI**
$\chi2 = 69.359$	Def	0.069	0.877	0.922	0.922
df =17	Sat	na	na	1.000	1.000
P = 0.000	Indep	0.196	0.000	0.000	0.000

Notes:
  1. Variables are defined as follows:
      satis1 = enquiry service; satis2 = product selection; satis3 = product quality; satis4 = price;
      satis5 = catalogue presentation; satis6 = delivery service; satis7 = ordering process;
      satis8 = payment terms; ovsat = overall satisfaction; likbuy = likelihood of future purchase;
      sat1 = service satisfaction; sat2 = product satisfaction.
  2. Sample size (N) = 1028

The goodness of fit measures presented in the table generally follow the recommendations of Hoyle and Panter (1995) except for the inclusion of root mean square error of approximation (RMSEA). The chi-square measure of discrepancy tests how much the implied and sample covariance matrices differ under the null hypothesis that they do not. The results of the test indicate a rejection of the null hypothesis, which does not auger well for the proposed model. However, Hu and Bentler (1995: 78) suggest that the test may not be a good enough guide to model adequacy because of model mis-specification, the power of the test, or violation of some technical assumptions underlying the test (Hu and Bentler 1995: 77-8).

In the case of the model examined here it is highly likely that this is associated with the large sample size (1028). Hair et al. (1998) report that if the sample size becomes large enough significant differences will be found for any specified model. Hence they suggest that the test is not reliable outside the sample range of 100-200 observations. However, it is also likely that the technical assumptions underlying the test have been violated.

Given this situation, goodness of fit is also indicated by root mean square error of association (RMSEA) that is recommended as an alternative to the chi-square test in the case of large samples (Hair et al. 1998), and three type 2 indices suggested by Hoyle and Panter (1995); Tucker-Lewis index (TLI), incremental fit index (IFI), and comparative fit index (CFI). RMSEA lies below the upper threshold value of .080 regarded as 'reasonable' by Brown and Cudeck (1993) while values of TLI, IFI and CFI approximate to the lower threshold of 0.9 suggested by Hair et al. (1998).

For the measurement models, the reliability of the indicators of the satisfaction sub-constructs is conducted using the Reliability procedure within SPSS (SPSS, 2005). This yielded Cronbach alpha coefficients of 0.768 for service satisfaction (sat1) and 0.723 for product satisfaction' (sat2). Both coefficients exceed the acceptable threshold level of 0.7 suggested by Nunally (1978). The respective construct reliabilities (CR) of these sub-constructs are 0.801 and 0.737, which are above the threshold level of 0.7 suggested by Hair et al. (1998). The respective variances extracted (VE) are 0.507 and 0.416 compared to a threshold value 0.5 suggested by the same authors, so that the VE for product satisfaction is disappointing.

With respect to the structural model service satisfaction (sat1) and product satisfaction (sat2) have a strong positive effect on overall satisfaction (ovsat) and explain 79 per cent of the variance of this measure. The regression weight of product satisfaction (sat2) was constrained to unity to achieve identification of the model but the coefficient of service satisfaction (sat1) is highly significant. Overall satisfaction (ovsat) has a moderately positive effect on future purchase intentions (likbuy) but only manages to explain 22 per cent of the variance of this dependent measure. The coefficient is also highly significant. Examination of the standard coefficients reveals that service satisfaction (sat1) has a stronger impact on overall satisfaction (ovsat) compared to product satisfaction (sat2) and that overall satisfaction (ovsat) has a comparatively weaker impact on future purchase intentions (likbuy).

Examination of the relations between the two satisfaction constructs and their respective measures reveals that all non-constrained coefficients are highly significant. For service satisfaction (sat1) the relative importance of measure's coefficients indicates that the highest associations in descending order of importance are product quality, product selection, enquiry service, and price. For product satisfaction (sat2) the highest associations are ranked in descending order as ordering processes, payment terms, delivery service and, catalogue presentation.

6 SUMMARY AND CONCLUSIONS

The study set out to analyse customer satisfaction in terms of eight satisfaction attributes, a measure of overall satisfaction and likelihood of future purchase.

The initial analysis considered analysis of individual scale items. The implications of this analysis for mail-order speciality food businesses depend very much on the perspective that is taken. From the perspective of the proportion of customers who are very satisfied there is concern because only in the case of product quality are a majority of customers very satisfied. Thus it appears that mail-order speciality food firms should pay attention to all other aspects of mail-order operations.

On the other hand, if the criterion is to consider customers who are at least satisfied, satisfied or very satisfied, there is more cause for an optimistic stance. Analysis of the eight-item satisfaction scale reveals high levels of satisfaction with the eight attributes, especially with respect to product quality, delivery service and enquiry service.

Thus it is not surprising that consideration of overall satisfaction reveals that 93 per cent of mail-order speciality food shoppers are either satisfied or very satisfied. With respect to future purchase intentions, nearly 60 per cent of mail-order food shoppers definitely intend to repeat their purchases in the future. Consequently, the results indicate that mail-order appears to deliver high levels of satisfaction that matches or exceeds customers' expectations and that a high proportion of customers intend to purchase in the future.

Simple correlation analysis reveals that there are significant correlations between overall satisfaction and likelihood of future purchase and that each of these variables are significantly correlated with each of the eight items of the satisfaction attributes.

The results of the SEM show that it is possible to establish credible inter-relationships between the sub-constructs of transaction satisfaction with mail order, overall satisfaction, and re-purchase intentions. The measures of fit are acceptable and all free parameters are strongly significant. Satisfaction with the transactions of mail order has a strong association with overall satisfaction. However, higher levels of overall satisfaction have a weaker association with intentions to re-purchase. The structural relations indicate that both product and service aspects of the mail-order transaction have strong associations with overall satisfaction, but satisfaction with the service transaction is more important. Consequently, the message to mail-order firms is that they need to expand their vision of their respective businesses beyond that of a food delivered by post. After all, some speciality food products are available in speciality stores but it is the high level of customer care and service that differentiates the mail-order product from the in-store equivalent. The most important message is that satisfaction and hence re-purchase likelihood are dependent on integrated features of both product and service aspects of the mail order business.

The results are consistent with current emphasis on building customer satisfaction and loyalty, which is envisaged as a goal and a key element in the achievement of company objectives, through service aspects of the marketing mix. They are broadly compatible with the results of other studies applied to other sectors that identify the positive link between satisfaction and response (Hallowell, 1996; Bolton, 1998; Oliver, 1999; Garbarino and Johnson, 1999; Bolton and Lemon, 1999; Bernhardt et al., 2000). Hence the most important aspects of customer satisfaction revealed in this study can be associated with those service marketing elements concerned with physical evidence (catalogue presentation, product quality, product selection), process (order process, delivery service, payment terms) and people (enquiry service).

The study reported here is regarded as an exploratory study which could be elaborated in further work that focuses uniquely on the issue of satisfaction and loyalty. The model is set in the context of the satisfaction literature rather than a more general Q-V-S framework. The model excluded constructs of sacrifice, quality, and value and so assumes that these issues are incorporated in the transactions and overall measures of satisfaction. Further extensions of this approach could employ multiple measures of both overall satisfaction and behavioural intentions.

There would appear to be some justification for the exclusion of the perceived quality and perceived value constructs. Some studies have questioned whether they are synonymous or distinct, since they tend to be highly correlated such that some studies have failed to establish discriminant validity between them (Dabhollkar, 1993; Oliver, 1993). However it should be noted that Dabhollkar et al. (2000) regard them as distinct but highly correlated.

According to Cronin et al. (2000), the omission of the constructs of sacrifice, quality and value excludes the possibility of exploring the impact that these constructs have on behavioural intentions, and more complex relations that emerge from both indirect and direct effects. Hence, a more ambitious extension in further work could employ a more comprehensive framework to include the constructs of sacrifice, perceived risk and perceived quality in addition to satisfaction.

REFERENCES

Amos. 2005. Amos Version 6, (PA., USA: Amos Development Corporation)

Anderson, E. W., Fornell, C. 1994. A customer satisfaction research prospectus. In Rust, R. T., and Oliver R. L. (Eds.), Service quality: New directions in theory and practice, 241-268 (Thousand Oaks, CA, Sage Publications.

Anderson, E. W., Fornell, C., Lehmann, D. R. 1994. Customer satisfaction, market share, and profitability: findings from Sweden. Journal of Marketing 58 (3), 53-66.

Beardon, W.O., Crockett, M., Teel, J. E. 1981. Disconfirmation of purchase expectations and subsequent consumer attitudes and patronage intentions. Paper delivered at the American Marketing Association conference on Retail Patronage, May 1981.

Bernhardt, K. L., Donthu, N., Kennett, P. A. 2000. A longitudinal analysis of satisfaction and profitability. Journal of Business Research, 47, 161-171.

Biong, H. 1993. Satisfaction and loyalty to suppliers within the grocery trade. European Journal of Marketing 27 (7), 21-38.

Bloemer, J. M. M., Kasper, H. D. P. 1995. The complex relationship between customer satisfaction and brand loyalty. Journal of Economic Psychology, 16, 311-29.

Bloemer, J. M. M., Lemmink, G. A. M. 1992. The importance of customer satisfaction in explaining brand and dealer loyalty. Journal of Marketing Management, 8, 351-364.

Bolton, R. N. 1998. A dynamic model of the duration of the customer's relationship with a continuous service provider: the role of satisfaction. Marketing Science 17 (1), 45-65.

Bolton, R. N., Drew, J. H. 1991. A longitudinal analysis of the impact of service changes on consumer attitudes. Journal of Marketing, 55 (1), 1-9.

Bolton, R. N., Lemon, K. N. 1999. A dynamic model of customers' usage of services: usage as an antecedent and consequence of satisfaction. Journal of Marketing Research, 36 (May), 171-186.

Bou-Llusar, J. C., Camisón-Zornoza, C., Escrig-Tena, A. B. 2001. Measuring the relationship between firm perceived quality and customer satisfaction and its influence on purchase intentions. Total Quality Management, 12 (6), 719-734.

Browne, M. W., Cudeck, R. 1993. Alternative ways of assessing model fit. In K. A. Bollen, K. A., Long, J. S. (Eds.), Testing structural equation models, 136-162 (Newbury Park, CA, Sage Publications)

Cassel. C., Eklöf, J. A. 2001. Modelling customer satisfaction and loyalty on aggregate levels: Experience from the ECSI pilot study. Total Quality Management, 12 (7-8), 834-841.

Cronin, J. J., Brady, M. K., Brand, R. R., Hightower Jr., R., Shenwell, D. J. 1997. A cross-sectional test of the effect and conceptualization of service value. The Journal of Service Marketing, 11 (6), 375-391.

Cronin, J. J., Brady, M. K., Hult, G. M. 2000. Assessing the effects of quality, value and customer satisfaction on consumer behavioural intentions in service environments. Journal of Retailing, 76 (2), 193-218.

Cronin, J. J., Taylor, S. A. 1992. Measuring service quality: a re-examination and extension. Journal of Marketing, 56 (3), 55-68.

Cronin, J. J., Taylor, S. A. 1994. SERVPERF versus SERVQUAL: reconciling performance based and perception based - minus - expectation measurements of service quality. Journal of Marketing, 58 (1), 125-31.

Dabholkar, P. A. 1993. Customer Satisfaction and service quality: Two constructs or one? In Cravens, D. W. and Dickson, P. R. (Eds.), Enhancing knowledge development in marketing, 10-18 (Chicago, IL, American Marketing Association).

Dabolkar, P. A., Shepherd, C. D., Thorpe, D. I. 2000. A comprehensive framework for service quality: an investigation of critical, conceptual and measurement issues though a longitudinal study. Journal of Retailing, 76 (2), 139-173.

Dabholkar, P. A., Thorpe, D.I. 1994. Does customer satisfaction predict shopper intentions? Journal of Consumer Satisfaction, 7, 161-71.

Dick, A. S., Basu, K. 1994. Customer loyalty: toward an integrated conceptual framework. Journal of the Academy of Marketing Science, 22 (2), 99-113.

The Economist 1994. A survey of television-feeling for the future. February, 12-18.

Ennew, C. T., Binks, M. R. 1999. Impact of participative service relationships on quality, satisfaction and retention: an exploratory study. Journal of Business Research, 46, 121-123.

Food from Britain 1987. Specialist foods study: market overview (Watford, UK, Institute of Grocery Distribution)

Fornell, C. 1992. A national customer satisfaction barometer: the Swedish experience. Journal of Marketing, 56 (1), 1-21.

Fornier, S. 1994. A consumer-based relationship framework for strategic brand management, Unpublished PhD dissertation, University of Florida.

Garbarino, E., Johnson, M. S. 1999. The different roles of satisfaction, trust and commitment in customer relationships. Journal of Marketing, 63 (April), 70-87.

Hair, J. R., Anderson, R. E., Tatham, R. L., Black, W. C. (1998). Multivariate data analysis (5th edition) (New Jersey, Prentice Hall International Inc).

Hallowell, R. 1996. The relationships of customer satisfaction, customer loyalty, and profitability: an empirical study. International Journal of Service Industry Management, 7 (1), 27-42.

Halstead, D. 1989. Expectations and disconfirmation beliefs as predictors of consumer satisfaction, repurchase intention and complaining behaviour: an empirical study. Journal of Consumer Satisfaction, Dissatisfaction and Complaining Behaviour, 5, 1-11.

Hausknecht, D. R. 1990. Measurement scales in consumer satisfaction/dissatisfaction. Journal of Consumer Satisfaction, Dissatisfaction and Complaining Behaviour, 3, 1-11.

Heskett, J. I., Jones, T. O., Loveman, G. W., Sasser, W. E. Jr., Schlesinger, L. A. 1994. Putting the service profit chain to work. Harvard Business Review, March-April, 105-11.

Hoyle, R. H., Panter, A. T. (1995). Writing about structural equation models. In Hoyle, R. H. (Ed.), Structural equation modeling: Concepts issues and applications, 158-176 (London, Sage Publications).

Hu, Li-Tze., Bentler, P. M. 1995. Evaluating model fit. In Hoyle, R. H. (Ed.), Structural equation modeling: Concepts issues and applications, 76-90 (London: Sage Publications).

A Structural Equation Model of Customer Satisfaction and Future Purchase of Mail-Order...

13

Kaiser, H. F. 1974. An index of factorial simplicity. Psychometrika, 39, 31-36.

Kondo, Y. 2001. Customer satisfaction: how can I measure it? Total Quality Management, 12 (7-8), 867-872.

Kotler, P., Armstrong, G., Saunders, S., Wong, V. 1996. Principles of marketing (European Edition) (Hemel Hempstead: Prentice Hall).

Kristensen, K., Juhl, H. J., Østergaard, P. 2001. Customer satisfaction: Some results for European retailing. Total Quality Management, 12 (7-8), 890-897.

La Barbara, P. A., Mazursky, D. 1983. A longitudinal assessment of consumer satisfaction/dissatisfaction: the dynamic aspect of the cognitive process. Journal of Marketing Research, November, 393-404.

McCorkell, G. 1997. Direct and data base marketing (London: Kogan Page).

Nunally, J. C. 1978. Psychometric Theory (2nd Edition) (New York: McGraw Hill).

Oliver, R. L. 1999. Whence consumer loyalty? Journal of Marketing, 63 Special Issue, 33-44.

Parasuraman, A. Zeithaml, V. A., Berry L. L. 1988. SERVQUAL: a multiple item scale for measuring consumer perceptions of service quality. Journal of Retailing, 64 (1), 12-40.

Porter, M. 1985. Competitive advantage: creating and sustaining superior performance (New York: Free Press).

Reinartz, W., Kumar, V. 2002. Mis-customer loyalty. Harvard Business Review, 80 (7) July, 86-94.

Selnes, F. 1993. An examination of the effect of product performance on brand reputation, satisfaction and loyalty. European Journal of Marketing, 27 (9), 19-23

SPSS. 2003, SPSS for Windows Version 12, (Chicago, IL: SPSS Inc)

Van Looy, B., Gemmel, P., Desmet S., Van Dierdonck. R, Serneels S. 1998. Dealing with productivity and quality indicators in a service environment: some field experiences. International journal of service industry management 9 (4): 359-376.

Victor, P. 1995. Tele-shops to take 20 per cent of high street sales. Independent on Sunday, June 4th.

Wilson, A. 2002. Attitudes towards customer satisfaction measurement in the retail sector. International Journal of Marketing Research, 44 (2), 213-222.

Yi, Y. 1990. A critical review of consumer satisfaction. In Zeithaml, V. (Ed.), Review of Marketing 1990, 213-222 (Chicago, IL: American Marketing Association).

Zeithaml, V. A. 1988. Consumer perceptions of price, quality and value: a means-end model and synthesis of evidence. Journal of Marketing, 52 (July), 2-22.

Zeithaml, V. and Bitner, M. J. 2000. Services marketing (New York: McGraw-Hill).

2

Game design as marketing: How game mechanics create demand for virtual goods

Juho Hamari
Helsinki Institute for Information Technology
HIIT P.O. Box 9800, FI-02015 TKK, Finland

Email: juho.hamari@hiit.fi

Vili Lehdonvirta
Helsinki Institute for Information Technology
HIIT P.O. Box 9800, FI-02015 TKK, Finland

Email: vili.lehdonvirta@hiit.fi

Abstract

Selling virtual goods for real money is an increasingly popular revenue model for massively-multiplayer online games (MMOs), social networking sites (SNSs) and other online hangouts. In this paper, we argue that the marketing of virtual goods currently falls short of what it could be. Game developers have long created compelling game designs, but having to market virtual goods to players is a relatively new situation to them. Professional marketers, on the other hand, tend to overlook the internal design of games and hangouts and focus on marketing the services as a whole. To begin bridging the gap, we propose that the design patterns and game mechanics commonly used in games and online hangouts should be viewed as a set of marketing techniques designed to sell virtual goods. Based on a review of a number of MMOs, we describe some of the most common patterns and game mechanics and show how their effects can be explained in terms of analogous techniques from marketing science. The results provide a new perspective to game design with interesting implications to developers. Moreover, they also suggest a radically new perspective to marketers of ordinary goods and services: viewing marketing as a form of game design.

Keywords: online games, social networking, virtual world, virtual goods, business model, sustainability, captology

1 INTRODUCTION

Selling virtual goods has become a major new revenue model for consumer-oriented online services, social networking sites, massively-multiplayer online games (MMOs) and virtual worlds in particular. This is especially true in the East Asian market. In September 2005, 32% of titles surveyed by Nojima (2007) in Japan used virtual item sales as their main revenue model. In October 2006, the share had grown to 60%. The global volume of real-money trade of virtual goods was estimated at 2.1 billion USD per year in 2006 (Lehtiniemi & Lehdonvirta 2007). This dramatic rise of the virtual good model arguably merits increased attention from the disciplines of marketing and technology management.

In practice, the so-called virtual good sales or microtransactions revenue model involves selling some form of virtual items, "avatars" or currencies to the users of an online service. Perhaps most frequently, the object sold for real money is a virtual currency, which is then exchanged for virtual items. The items can range from weapons and armour in online games to clothes in virtual worlds and simple two-dimensional graphical badges in social networking sites. The items are used as part of gameplay or to fulfil similar social and aesthetic functions as physical commodities are used for elsewhere in consumer culture (Lehdonvirta, Wilska & Johnsson 2009).

In this paper, we consider the question of what leads consumers to purchase virtual goods. Previous studies on the topic mostly focus on the consumer, considering what motivations and decision processes lead individuals into purchasing virtual goods (Guo and Barnes 2007; Lehdonvirta 2005; Nojima 2007; Lehdonvirta, Wilska & Johnsson 2009). We adopt a different, complementary approach, focusing on how the rules and mechanics that developers build into their MMOs lead to virtual good purchases. Our theoretical perspective is based on marketing: we view game design as one aspect in the company's marketing process that aims to create demand for virtual goods that can be sold for real money. This way, we are able to offer new explanations as to how certain designs and patterns create demand and to suggest designs that could still be explored further. Moreover, learning can happen in the other direction as well, from game design to marketing. Insights built into game designs, based on the collective experience of generations of game designers, can potentially teach traditional marketers new things about how people's behaviour is shaped.

In the second section of this paper, we discuss the virtual good sales revenue model in more detail and review related literature. We also provide a review of basic marketing literature that acts as a conceptual framework for the rest of the discussion. In the third section, we outline the research design of the empirical part of this paper. In sections 4 and 5, we present empirical analyses of design and game mechanics in a number of MMOs. In section 6 we summarise the results, and in the final section, present conclusions and discuss the implications and limitations of the study.

2 BACKGROUND

2.1 Virtual Good Sales As a Revenue Model

Real-money trade of virtual goods first emerged in 1999 in the form of player-to-player trade in MMOs such as *Ultima Online* and *EverQuest*. Users would list their hard-earned game possessions on eBay and let other users bid for them (Lehdonvirta 2008). In recent years, the growth of the market has increasingly been driven by operators selling goods directly to their users. Instead of requiring users to pay a monthly subscription fee, operators allow users enter the service for free, with the expectation that some users will nevertheless spend money on virtual good microtransactions (Nojima 2007). For this reason, virtual good sales-based games like *MapleStory* are occasionally called "free-to-play" games. One example of a virtual world that follows the same model is *Habbo*. *Second Life* follows a similar but more complicated model, where users are the primary actors in virtual good production and sales.

Successful subscription-based MMOs charge around $10-$15 per month from their users, while Liew (2008a) estimates that successful "free-to-play" operators earn around $1-2 in monthly ARPU (average revenue per user). The estimate is based on figures pertaining to *Second Life*, *Club Penguin*, *Habbo* and *RuneScape*. Korean-based *MapleStory* is estimated to have a monthly ARPU of $20 in the United States (Liew 2008b), while Hyatt (2008) estimates the average ARPU of "free-to-play" titles being around $5 per month. At first glance it would therefore seem that the subscription model is often the more attractive option, but if we consider other metrics such as registered users, active users, conversion rates and costs, the situation may change. Users that are willing to pay a subscription fee belong to a fairly limited segment of hardcore users, while "free-to-play" services have the potential to court much larger audiences.

For these and other reasons, operators are increasingly applying the virtual good sales revenue model in virtual worlds, MMOs as well as other online services. Understanding how to create and maintain demand for virtual goods is therefore an increasingly pertinent question. How does a service entice users into virtual good spending? How can sales be sustained over time without saturating the demand? To begin answering these questions, in the following part we review relevant literature from MMO related studies.

2.2 Understanding Virtual Good Purchases

In the academic literature pertaining to MMOs, the majority of works focus on fascinating legal and philosophical questions that virtual worlds and real-money trade of virtual goods give rise to (e.g. Fairfield 2005; Lastowka and Hunter 2004). Works that deal with virtual goods from a business perspective are relatively scarce.

MacInnes (2004) and Lehdonvirta (2008) discuss different approaches that MMO and virtual world operators can take towards real-money trade of virtual goods on a strategic level, without going into detail about what creates demand for the virtual goods. Nojima (2007), Lehdonvirta (2005) and Guo and Barnes (2007) focus on the individual user, examining motivations and decision processes that lead into virtual good purchases. Nojima (2007) examines relationships between the revenue models and players' motivations for play. The motivations are based on a model by Yee (2005). Nojima finds that players who buy items report higher levels of immersion in a game. One explanation offered is that it takes a certain amount of immersion before virtual objects begin to feel desirable enough to purchase. Using a similar approach, Lehdonvirta (2005) examines different motivations that players have for purchasing virtual goods: advancement in a status hierarchy, advantage in competitive settings, keeping up with co-players, experiencing new content, customisation, and self-expression, among others. According to Lehdonvirta, users' attitudes towards virtual good purchases are linked to their general motivations for participating in the service and the activities they engage in. Guo and Barnes (2007) use a technology acceptance model in developing a preliminary model for virtual good purchase acceptance.

Lehdonvirta (2009) approaches the question of why people buy virtual goods from the point of view of attributes pertaining to the goods themselves. Lehdonvirta categorises these attributes to functional, hedonic and social attributes. Lehdonvirta, Wilska and Johansson (2009) examine "virtual consumption" from a sociological perspective, documenting the way in which virtual goods are used as social markers to draw distinctions between "haves" and "have-nots" and to build and communicate self-identity to other members of the community.

Table 1: Explanations offered for virtual good purchases in previous literature

Work	Perspective	Explanations offered
Lehdonvirta 2005	individual/psychological	(various)
Nojima 2007	individual/psychological	high immersion
Guo & Barnes 2007	individual/psychological	psychometric model
Oh & Ryu 2007	game design	(various)
Lehdonvirta 2009	virtual item attributes	functional/hedonic/social
Lehdonvirta, Wilska & Johansson 2009	community/sociological	social distinctions, identity, self-expression

The different approaches to understanding virtual good purchases in previous literature are summarised in Table 1. Most studies adopt the individual user as their unit of analysis, focusing on the individual's motivations and decision processes that lead into virtual good purchases. In contrast, Oh and Ryu (2007) examine ways in which game design can successfully accommodate and enhance virtual item sales. Based on observations from two Korean online games, *KartRider* and *Special Force*, they present examples of how design and game mechanics built by developers can be used to create and sustain demand for virtual goods; a fact fairly obvious to gamers but little explored in literature. Oh and Ryu's paper is a start in analysing these mechanics, but it lacks ties to any previous body of knowledge that could be used to put the observations in perspective. In the following part of this paper, we outline a perspective from marketing that can be used to examine efforts aimed at promoting virtual good sales.

2.3 A Marketing Based Approach

Traditional authorities in marketing emphasise that marketing is about identifying and meeting human and social needs (Kotler and Keller 2006; Drucker 1993). In the ideal case, marketing results in a customer who is willing to buy. Thus the aim is to understand the customer (Durcker 1993). On the other hand, marketing can also be seen as an activity that *creates* needs. This view is particularly pertinent in the context of MMOs, where designers create the rules and mechanics that determine to a large extent the activities and specific needs of the participants.

In traditional marketing activities, products are offered in an already-existing market and customers are segmented mostly based on existing segmentation attributes, such as socio-demographic variables. When designing a virtual world, its rules and internal economy can be regarded as marketing activities concerned with creating the underlying needs and conditions for customers to become incentivised to buying virtual goods. The design and creation of virtual goods can then be regarded as separate design iterations that address the needs created in the previous stage (see e.g. Stabell & Fjeldstad 1998 and Porter 1980 on value configuration). This sets value creation through virtual goods somewhat apart from traditional marketing, as the value for the goods has to be first created through designing the context for the goods. Next we will present some examples of value creation from traditional marketing science that will be linked with game design patterns in the next section.

Segmentation is one of the basic and central concepts of marketing. Its purpose is to identify and divide populations into strategically relevant homogeneous segments based on segmentation variables and customer needs. This enables companies to target their marketing efforts according to the defining attributes of the segment (Day 1981; Jonker et al. 2004; Kotler and Keller 2006). Segmentation in game design can be used in forming segments to which sell virtual goods to: for example, in-game classes and professions. Game design -derived player demographics have also been covered in literature (e.g. Bartle 1996; Bartle 2003; Yee 2007).

Differentiation is another basic concept in marketing. The aim of product differentiation is to attain higher desirability, and therefore promote sales, by being distinguishable from rival products (Kotler and Keller 2006; Sharp and Dawes 2001). Differentiation can take place in relation to a multitude of product attributes, but it can be divided into two general subsets: vertical and horizontal differentiation. Vertical differentiation refers to the differentiation of product attributes that are comparable to rival products' attributes. Horizontal differentiation refers to differentiation by offering a completely different set of attributes, as in a different product (Piana 2003; Vandenbosch and Weinberg 1995). Both of these dimensions will be further discussed in the context of game design.

In product life cycle management, the concept of *planned obsolescence* is particularly pertinent. It can be divided into two subcategories: 1) contrived durability and 2) actual planned obsolescence (Orbach 2004). Contrived durability refers to the intentional shortening of a product's lifetime in the production process, leading to quality deterioration. Planned obsolescence refers to an artificial shortening of a product's useful lifetime by means of fashion cycles or technological developments (Kotler and Keller 2006). The purpose of these strategies is to encourage customers to make repeated purchases and to enables sales to be sustained over a long period of time (Bulow 1986; Choi 1994; Orbach 2004). These strategies are interesting in the context of virtual items, since they are digital products: whatever their durability, it is always rather artificial.

Finally, various cognitive and psychological biases are frequently studied and exploited in marketing. Hsee et al. (2003) found that introducing points as a medium of exchange had a clear effect on people's behaviour in a setting where no effect should have been observed under an assumption of rational choice. According to the study, the medium caused an illusion of advantage, certainty and linearity and led test subjects to change their preferences and select the options that were originally less desirable. Subjects were willing to pay more effort when points were used as a medium between the effort and the outcome, compared to a situation with no mediating factor. These results are interesting, because most MMO operators use a virtual currency as a medium of exchange between real money and virtual items. Virtual currency as a medium also enables other psychological pricing possibilities, such as odd-pricing.

In summary, basic approaches in marketing include segmentation and differentiation on one hand, and a large variety of devices for enhancing the perceived desirability of purchases on the other hand. In the following sections, we examine how game mechanics and design patterns found in MMOs can be mapped to these marketing techniques.

3 DATA AND METHODS

This empirical part of the paper is based on an exploratory study of how existing MMOs, especially massively-multiplayer online role-playing games (MMORPGs), are currently creating and sustaining demand for virtual goods through their design and game mechanics. These design patterns and game mechanics are then compared with concepts and techniques outlined in the previous section to examine how design can be linked with marketing science.

Table 2: Games, virtual worlds and other online hangouts referenced in the study

Title	Publisher
Cyworld	SK Telecom, Korea
Entropia Universe	MindArk, Sweden
EverQuest	Sony Online Entertainment, U.S.
Habbo	Sulake, Finland
IMVU	IMVU, U.S.
KartRider	Nexon, Korea
MapleStory	Nexon, Korea
Puzzle Pirates	Three Rings, U.S.
Special Force	Neowiz, Korea
Travian	Travian Games, Germany
World of Warcraft	Blizzard, U.S.
ZT Online	Giant Interactive, China

The virtual good platforms referenced in the study are listed in Table 2. Most of the titles are performance-oriented games as opposed to socialising-oriented hangouts, which is somewhat visible in the scoping of our study. Many of the game elements analysed below are connected to performance-oriented game rules. A few of the above titles do not actually use the virtual good sales revenue model. They can nevertheless be equally informative cases, because demand for virtual goods exists and varies regardless of whether the operator harnesses it as a revenue stream or whether the demand is simply part of the internal mechanics of the game.

We studied each title through first-hand use experience and/or related literature and online materials. The data was collected during 2007-2008. We then analysed our observations with assistance from MMO design literature (Bartle 2003; Pardew et al. 2004; Alexander 2003, 2005) to identify generalisable design patterns and game mechanics that contribute towards creating or sustaining demand for virtual goods. In the following sections, we report the findings, examples from our observations and references to literature that were used as sources.

The selection of titles discussed in this study is based on their popularity, relative variety in mechanics and availability of information. This information-oriented sampling, as opposed to random sampling, is appropriate for exploratory studies and situations where depth of information is valued over breadth (Flyvbjerg 2006). No claim is made as to how representative the identified patterns are of virtual worlds and MMOs in general; only that such patterns have been used by designers in several cases. The actual identification and abstraction of relevant design patterns and game mechanics from the cases is necessarily a somewhat subjective step, although grounded in design and marketing literature.

4 SEGMENTATION AND DIFFERENTIATION – CREATING NEEDS ON MULTIPLE DIMENSIONS

While segmentation itself does not make products more desirable to customers, it enables identification of strategically relevant customer groups and enables differentiation of products to address the needs of customer segments, resulting in more desirable products (Day 1981; Jonker et al. 2004; Kotler & Keller 2006). This section focuses on how MMO design can generate and enforce user segments and create targeted offerings for them.

Companies offer different products according to customers' usage rate and status, which are behavioural segmentation variables (Kotler and Keller 2006). For example, an amateur might require lesser products than a professional. This enables companies to sell new products as a customer's skill or interest increases. In the real world, an amateur might directly buy the high-end products and thus bypass the entry-level products. Alternatively, a consumer might settle for the entry-level products and leave higher quality products on the shelves.

4.1 Stratified content

Usage rate and status in MMOs is typically reflected in stratified content (Figure 1). The most common example of this is found in MMORPGs, where a player's avatar starts from level one and gradually through gameplay progresses through the game content and gains levels, rising in status. This mechanism can be used to segment players vertically and then differentiated items can be targeted accordingly.

Figure 1: Content stratification based on avatar levels

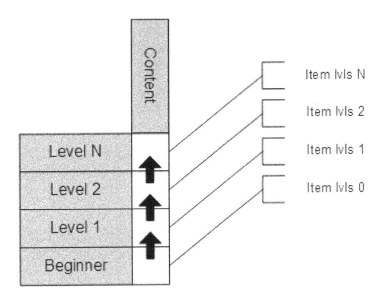

In practice, while most users progress through stratified content, the segments might not be as clear cut. Users go through the content with differing time investments and thus it might be reasoned to offer even more differentiated items in smaller increments as players are differently price sensitive and have varying amounts of time at their disposal. The levels represent a game design -derived segmentation, whereas differentiation within these level tiers (black blocks in Figure 2) addresses users' real-world behavioural segmentation attributes. For example, in *World of Warcraft* there are items of several quality rankings inside each level tier (Figure 2), which can be seen as addressing sub-segments within each tier that invest differing amounts of time in the game. The degree of vertical differentiation is determined by the operator according to its business strategy.

Figure 2: Differentiation within levels

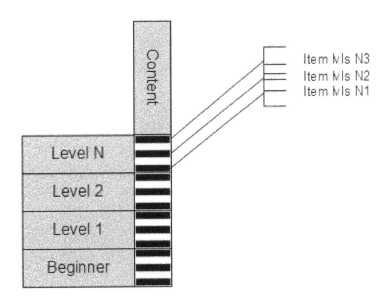

4.2 Status restrictions

Programming status restrictions into items is one way of enforcing the differentiation of items. This way, the operator forces players to obtain new items iteratively if they wish to maintain the same relative performance or status. This mechanism could be compared to regulations in karate belts, which can officially be worn only when the karateka has achieved the appropriate status. A karateka iteratively progresses through the different skill stages and has to purchase a new belt on every stage.

Status restrictions in items also bear a resemblance to contrived durability, as the restrictions are designed into the products themselves. On the other hand, it also has similarities to planned obsolescence, as the players' progression in the game gradually renders old items useless.

Vertical status restrictions have been implemented in at least two ways: 1) an item cannot be used if the avatar's level is too high (e.g., *ZT Online*), and 2) an item cannot be used if the avatar's level is too low (e.g., *World of Warcraft*). This way, the avatar has a sliding window of usable items at a given time depending on the avatar's level, thus iteratively directing buying behaviour. According to Davis (2007), in *ZT Online* players essentially have to renew their inventory every five levels. Status restrictions are also implemented horizontally, e.g., via avatar type restrictions, offering goods that are only usable by a certain avatar type.

Online hangouts such as *Cyworld* and *Habbo* lack explicit level systems, but similar item tiers could perhaps be designed around more socially oriented measures. For example, in many services participants either implicitly or explicitly compete for fame. In *MapleStory,* there are explicit lists of "most famous" players.

4.3 Increasingly challenging content

Content that gradually turns more challenging is a design pattern that has many of the same implications as status restricted items, discussed above. The difference is that the measures implemented are directed towards the game environment, avatar, and rules. When the game content becomes increasingly difficult, it requires the user to obtain better items to maintain the same relative level of performance or status, as old items gradually become useless. Thus the operator is able to differentiate items in terms of quality and item effectiveness in differing content difficulty. This is a very common game design pattern and is implemented in almost every MMO, but rarely as a marketing device to support virtual good sales.

In other types of services, the concept of "game content" is more ambiguous. In socially-oriented online hangouts, gameplay could be understood as the user-to-user interactions aimed at establishing social distinctions and hierarchies. For example, in *IMVU*, participants rate each other "cool", "smart", "fun", "hot" or "lame". The difficulty of the "competitive gameplay" thus depends on other users and their behaviour. Introducing explicit measures in this way might further help the operator in identifying segments and selling items accordingly.

4.4 Horizontal gameplay

While the mechanics discussed above enabled vertical segmentation and differentiation, horizontal segmentation is an equally important marketing device. In MMOs, horizontal segmentation is achieved via multiple content or gameplay dimensions (e.g., performance-oriented, socialising, trading), which can be used in designing differentiated virtual goods that are mutually non-rivalrous and not explicitly comparable. The dimensions can be further divided into smaller horizontal modes of play. For example, performance-oriented content might require the user to have several types of items to address varying needs derived from content; social status of an avatar could be rated on multiple scales (e.g., IMVU, see black blocks in Figure 3). Such dimensions must have meaningful content, however; otherwise they risk being seen as blatant profiteering.

For example, a simple form of horizontal differentiation is offering many types of avatar clothing (e.g. shirts, trousers, vests), which are not mutually rivalrous. These can then be seen inside a larger horizontal dimension covering gameplay concerned with avatar clothing in general. For example, in *Maplestory*, it might not be well reasoned to add more clothing categories for the avatar itself, but the addition of *pets* creates another meaningful context for offering more (pet)clothes for sale.

Figure 3: Horizontal dimensions of content

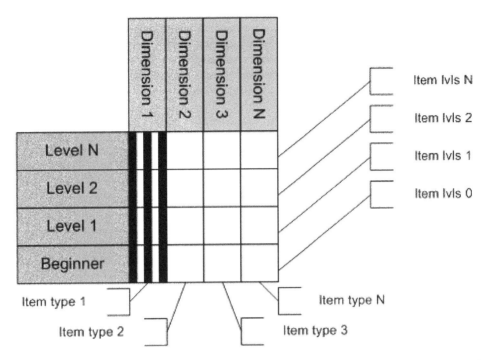

In Figure 2 and Figure 3, the dimensions are simple examples from actual implementations. In practice, the design of vertical and horizontal dimensions is specific to each MMO: there are no fixed sets of dimensions. There are no explicit limits on how many nested dimensions can be designed, but it considerations of usability, compelling gameplay and business strategy that set practical limits.

4.5 Avatar types

While segmentation and differentiation can be achieved through game design patters presented above, a further overarching way of creating segmentation is avatar types. Most performance-oriented MMOs have avatar "classes", which determine avatars' core competencies, items they can use, and their play style in the gameworld. In more socialising-oriented MMOs, appearance-related avatar attributes such as gender, hair colour, and style might be more relevant avatar-defining attributes.

In terms of Figure 3 above, avatar types can be said to create avatar-specific gameplay dimensions. Additionally, avatar types are implemented to further create nested segments inside larger segmentation blocks. For example, for slaying monsters in a MMORPG, a hunter might require a bow, whereas a mage requires a magic wand. This way, avatar type is one of the determinants of differentiation of virtual goods.

In essence, designing avatar types and attributes is equal to designing game-based behavioural and demographic segmentation factors. Whereas in traditional marketing, independent customer attributes are examined to segment customers into strategically relevant groups, the design of avatar attributes is actually a process of deciding and forming some of those factors beforehand. This is not say that real-world segmentation factors would not apply, but both have a role in determining and creating user segmentation and differentiation of virtual goods.

5 MECHANICS THAT DRIVE DESIRABILITY OF VIRTUAL GOODS

5.1 Item Degradation

In some virtual worlds, virtual items *degrade* with time or usage, sometimes to the extent of vanishing completely. In performance-oriented MMOs such as *World of Warcraft* and *EverQuest*, item degradation by use is frequently implemented by items degrading due to combat. Items may also degrade gradually with time, or alternatively, item can have a set expiration date after which they vanish or become useless (e.g., in *Puzzle Pirates* and *MapleStory*). Items vanishing can also prevent "rich" players from giving items away to "poorer" players and thus encourage players to purchase items by themselves. Item degradation through destroying items or by rendering them useless creates the possibility of selling replacement items over and over again. In marketing terms, degradation is closely analogous to contrived durability, as the operator controls exactly when and how the item ceases to function or exist.

Unlike with material goods, there is no technical reason why virtual items could not last indefinitely, so the marketer may have to justify why such a mechanism is implemented. Degradation through usage is easily justified in terms of the background fiction in performance-oriented MMOs such as *World of Warcraft*. Items usually break gradually when used in combat. Repairing costs currency, which can also be harnessed as a revenue stream, as is done by the operator of *Entropia Universe*. In online hangouts such as *Habbo*, item degradation is more difficult to implement in a way acceptable to users. In these contexts, degrading could perhaps be justified using more mundane scenarios such as items becoming dirty and requiring washing.

One way of implementing item degradation is to have "charges" in items, that is, setting a limit to the number of times an item can be used. This is often the case with consumable items. For example, a player can drink from a magic potion five times. Consumable items can have many purposes for players in a given game or service. For example, in *World of Warcraft*, there are many performance-enhancing consumables. In *MapleStory*, players can purchase a wide variety of performance-enhancing and functional consumables, such as a bonus that prevents players from losing experience points when killed. Time-based degradation is used in *Cyworld*, a socially oriented online hangout.

Habbo does not use degradation at all. As a result, some users have accumulated massive amounts of items in the service, and it is not unheard of for older users to give away substantial goods to new users for free, essentially cannibalising the operator's sales. On the other hand, very old items that are no longer available for purchase have become highly valued content among *Habbo* users. Lack of items with interesting histories and provenance (Lehdonvirta 2009) is a drawback of services utilising the degradation model.

In summary, degradation works in the same way as contrived durability, forcing customers to buy replacement products after a certain time. On the other hand, rational players should factor potential degradation into their value assessment of a new good, lessening its appeal. Implementing degradation is thus essentially an optimisation problem between initial sales potential and sustained sales potential, with game mechanics and background stories being applied to nudge players' economic reasoning towards the desired outcome.

5.2 Inconvenient Gameplay Elements

Several free-to-play MMO operators sell user interface (UI) enhancements to generate revenues. This implies that some gameplay or interface elements have been intentionally designed to be somewhat inconvenient, at least from the point of view of an advanced user. The enhancements range from actual virtual items to non-item power-ups and UI upgrades. Some services provide additional advantages over other players, others merely ease the use of UI. Below, we discuss a few examples of such implementations.

A "Travian Plus" account in *Travian* provides users with several UI and performance enhancements. For example, users can make shortcuts to more easily manage their civilisation. Other purchasable user interface enhancements include a larger map view, construction queues, information sorting and statistics. In *Special Force*, a Korean first-person shooter game, the default colour of the weapons' crosshair can be difficult to recognise on some backgrounds. To address this inconvenience, players can purchase new crosshairs (Oh and Ryu 2007). In *MapleStory*, there is only limited space available for storing friends' contact information. Once the limit is reached, users have to buy more "friend slots". *MapleStory* also sells avatar facial expressions to help players communicate in more varied ways.

The virtual landscape of many MMO worlds is so large as to make travel between places time-consuming. In most MMOs, distance is countered by teleportation or other instant means of travel. These instant travel mechanics can come with a price. In many games, such as *World of Warcraft*, they are paid using in-game money. In *MapleStory*, some travelling requires a currency that must be purchased with real money.

Gathering "loot" left behind by vanquished enemies is a common mechanic in MMOs. For high-performing players, it can become a significant inconvenience factor, as it takes time away from "productive" gameplay. In *MapleStory*, a pet can be taught to collect loot for the player, but the ability costs money. Limited storage space for items is a related inconvenience factor that will be discussed further below.

Operators might also seek to take advantage of the always-on nature of virtual worlds, and the fact that players have limited time to be online. In *MapleStory*, users can buy an automated merchant character that will conduct trade on their behalf while they are offline. Players' scarce time resources are also harnessed as a business opportunity by the so-called secondary market service providers that offer unsanctioned "power levelling" services and virtual currency sales in MMORPG games.

Unlike many other game mechanics that can be compared with marketing techniques, many of the inconvenient gameplay elements are clearly intentional parts of the design from the start, implying that they are understood as a form of marketing by the developers. A game-specific need is created, to which a virtual good that addresses the need is offered as a solution. In marketing terms, this is similar to how a generic product might be sold with certain limitations, to which augmenting products are offered as a solution.

5.3 Mediums of Exchange

In MMOs and other online hangouts, various points, credits and currencies are used as mediums of exchange in purchases and transactions, and also as rewards for accomplishments. In most free-to-play games, users first buy credits with which they buy the actual virtual items. Credits can also sometimes act as a status indicator and thus can be a desirable virtual asset themselves. In this section, we concentrate on the use of credits as a medium of exchange, and how they can be used to encourage demand.

Besides the possible economic-psychological advantages of virtual currency as medium (see section 2), a virtual currency also enables more pricing possibilities, allows the operator to sell larger amounts at a time compared to single items, and adds one more layer to maintaining the virtual economy. Operators can sell currency in amounts that are not quite divisible by the item prices. As a consequence, the users are left with change, which by itself is not sufficient for additional purchases, suggesting that the user should buy more currency. These tricks are used by most virtual item sales - based MMO operators examined in this study.

In *Puzzle Pirates,* two currencies are implemented to indirectly monetise otherwise non-paying users. This is achieved via two mutually tradable currencies, one of which is bought with real money and the other earned through gameplay. The rationale is that paying users will buy more of the paid-for currency in order to trade it for the earned currency, in order to be able to buy items which can only be purchased with the earned currency. This design could also alleviate perceived problems of unfairness relating to the use of real-money purchases that give gameplay advantages, because it allows both "money-rich" and "time-rich" users to access all goods through exchange.

5.4 Inventory Mechanics

In a typical MMO, users store their items in several types of inventories. Most commonly, users have separate spaces for items that are in use and for items that are in storage. One model is to have separate inventory categories for different types of items. Typically, all types of inventory slots are limited in number, which means that when obtaining new items, users might have to either dispose of some less needed older items or purchase additional inventory slots.

Limited inventory space is often used as a gameplay element, but it can also be a means to increase sales. In *MapleStory,* users store different item types to different inventories, which enables the operator to sell additional slots separately to each of the various inventory types. Buying four more slots to one of the inventories costs approximately 4 € in the European version of the game. Moreover, new inventory types can be introduced through gameplay. Virtual pets are a common example: they come with a set of empty inventory spaces for new clothing and other accessories.

Limited inventory slots have an obvious drawback from a sales point of view: a full inventory can prevent a user from buying more items. To make the disposal of old items easier to the user, the operator can offer to buy items back from the user for a fraction of the original purchase price in virtual money, or provide some other means of compensation. For example, *Habbo* contains a recycling machine where users can exchange 20 old items (originally purchased for real money) for a single new item.

5.5 Special Occasions

Christmas, Halloween, birthdays and other special occasions have been actively used by virtual world operators to promote virtual item sales. Occasions that traditionally provoke buying behaviour are simulated and referenced so that the same effect may be achieved in the virtual setting. For example, Christmas and Valentine's Day are used in services such as *Habbo* as they encourage gift giving and offer a natural context for selling new types of items. This strategy can further be extended to birthdays of users and their avatars, a technique used in some social networking sites.

World of Warcraft has an event calendar containing all in-game events, such as competitions. It also includes traditional seasonal occasions, which are usually modified slightly to better suit the lore of the game. For example, winter holidays are named "Feast of Winter Veil" and Halloween is "Hallow's End".

Besides real-world occasions, operators can also create their own special occasions based on the fiction of the game. One major example of a fiction-based special occasion was the release of the "Ahn'Qiraj" dungeon in *World of Warcraft*. Blizzard Entertainment designed several quests that required a server's population to collect millions of items to open the "Gates of Ahn'Qiraj". Ostensibly, the main motivation for players to collect all the items was to progress in the game faster, as the Gates were to be opened later in any case. This event caused the player populations of many *World of Warcraft* server clusters to organise co-operative attempts to amass all the required items, even before the quests were actually released into the game (WoWWiki Contibutors 2009).

5.6 Artificial Scarcity

Scarcity is a common strategy in traditional marketing. It has been used as an indicator of high quality and thus to justify premium prices (Kotler and Keller 2006). Another way of utilising scarcity without sacrificing sales quantity is to create an illusion of it through marketing communications. In essence, this means giving customers the impression that the product is almost sold out when it is in fact not, a common if somewhat questionable marketing technique. A perception of scarcity can also be achieved through exclusiveness, making a product in one way or the other challenging to obtain without necessarily altering the price.

In *Habbo*, some items exist in abundance while others are circulated in very small quantities. For example, a limited number of DJ style record players were distributed for free by Sulake in 2002 as part of an advertising campaign. In 2006, users were trading them for around 250 "Plastyk", which equals a re-purchase cost of approximately 200 € (Lehdonvirta, Wilska & Johansson 2009). Considering that the record player cannot actually play music, it is no different functionally from many other much less valuable items. Thus a large part of the record players' high value can no doubt be attributed to its scarcity.

Around mid-2006, the Habbo record player was again distributed as part of a new promotion (ibid.). This multiplied its supply on the user-to-user marketplaces, leading to a drastic decrease in its price and the prestige associated with owning one. As a consequence, its position as a top luxury good was taken over by other items, and status-conscious users had to purchase new items to maintain prestige.

Sulake also introduces collectible items, which are sold only for a limited time. This time varies from few hours to weeks. Sulake suggests that buying these items is an investment, saying that their value will rise as the same item will not be sold again after the limited sales period is over (Sulake Corporation 2009).

In most performance-oriented MMOs, scarcity is more commonly achieved by making certain items difficult to obtain through gameplay. Most commonly, these rare items drop from slain monsters. Either the rate at which the rare items are dropped is small, or the monsters that have to be slain are hard to come by and slay. These items are most commonly not purchasable and thus do not represent a revenue stream to the operator. However, users may well be incentivised to spend money on purchasable items that help them to reach the rare and desirable items. An example is found in *ZT Online*, where players use real money to buy keys that are used to open boxes dropped by slain monsters. Opening a box is designed to be similar in experience to a slot machine: superior items are shown to the user, but rarely given. The implementation thus also has elements of gambling. There is moreover a ranking of players who have opened most boxes on a given day. This ranking can be regarded as another horizontal gameplay dimension, where the ranking provides the competitive context that encourages players to keep buying the keys.

5.7 Alterations to Existing Content

One way of addressing the long-term attractiveness of an MMO and the items sold inside it is to introduce regular updates and to add new, meaningful content. At the same time, the new content devalues the existing content and items, hence making the new content and items more desirable to obtain. Updates are also used to fine-tune game rules to keep the game and its internal economy in balance.

The underlying design and rules are not perceived as intentional alterations to the service and can be more easily incorporated to the game lore, thus supporting user acceptance. On the other hand frequent upgrades are necessary to address promotional needs and in-game balance issues. Therefore, the operator might actively seek to adjust rules, items and environment, or arrange events to promote new or seasonal items. For this reason, it is important to design the initial mechanics and platform carefully and flexibly to facilitate further updates.

In traditional marketing, it may be difficult to modify tangible elements of a product after a customer has already purchased it. Virtual world operators have this possibility to some degree, but it is limited by user acceptance. This is especially the case with items that have been bought with real money, even if the modifications are necessary to balance gameplay.

Modifications do not have to be directed towards the items themselves to achieve the same effect. An item's functional effectiveness is a function of its potency as well as the game environment and its rules. By modifying the environment and the rules, the effectiveness of certain items or item types can be affected without touching the items themselves. However, despite the fact that operators have considerable power to make such adjustments, this power should be used cautiously. Modifying the specifications of a product that has already been sold simply for the reason of promoting additional sales may be ethically questionable if not illegal.

Alterations to existing content are commonly introduced through patches and upgrades, frequently rolled out by the developer. Upgrades or expansion commonly expand the gameplay by introducing new gameplay dimensions as well as building on top of the existing ones. In terms of the view introduced in Figure 3, upgrades are commonly implemented to add additional segment blocks vertically and horizontally, providing new contexts for differentiated goods to be sold.

6 SUMMARY OF RESULTS

The patterns identified in sections 4 and 5, above, can be divided into two categories. The first category consists of mechanics that in marketing terms create segmentation of users and enable differentiation of virtual goods; in other words, game mechanics that divide service content into differentiated contexts along vertical and horizontal lines, and in the process create a need for corresponding virtual goods. These mechanics are summarised in Table 3.

Table 3: Segmentation-related game mechanics that promote virtual goods purchases

Design pattern	*In marketing terms*	*Towards*	*Aims to*
Stratified content	Segmentation, differentiation	Rules, environment	Create segmentation, enable differentiation and generate incentives for repeated purchases
Status restricted items	Differentiation, planned obsolescence	Items	Enforce segmentation and generate incentives for repeated purchases
Increasingly challenging content	Segmentation, differentiation, planned obsolescence	Rules, environment	Enforce segmentation and generate incentives for repeated purchases
Multidimensional gameplay	Segmentation, differentiation	Gameplay	Create segmentation and enable differentiation and create differentiated additional settings for virtual goods
Avatar types	Segmentation, differentiation	Avatar	Create segmentation and enable differentiation

The second category includes mechanics that are used to create demand for virtual goods and encourage repeated purchases. Inconvenient user interface elements and similar gameplay factors have also been used as means to create need for complementary and value-added services that augment the core product. Special occasions related to real-world culture as well as to virtual world -specific contexts have been used in the seasonal promotion of virtual goods. These mechanics are summarised in Table 4.

Table 4: Other game mechanics that promote virtual goods purchases

Design	In marketing terms	Towards	Aims to
Item degradation	Planned obsolescence	Items, rules, environment	Create incentives for repeated purchases
Inconvenient gameplay elements	Core product -> Augmented product	User interface, gameplay	Create settings for additional virtual goods and services
Currency as medium	Psychological pricing	-	Create incentives for (repeated) purchases
Inventory mechanics	-	Items, avatar	Create incentives for repeated purchases
Special occasions	Promotional	Environment, items	Benefit from cultural patterns that encourage buying behaviour and create settings for additional virtual goods
Artificial scarcity	Exclusiveness	Items, environment, rules	Make selected virtual goods more desirable
Alterations to existing content	-	Environment, items, rules, gameplay	Create new settings for virtual goods to have value

7 CONCLUSIONS AND DISCUSSION

In this paper, we considered the question of what leads consumers to purchase virtual goods. Most previous studies adopt the individual user as their unit of analysis, focusing on motivations and decision processes that lead to virtual good purchases. We adopted a complementary approach, focusing on how the rules and mechanics developers build into MMOs encourage virtual good purchases. The theoretical perspective was based on marketing: viewing game design as one aspect in a company's marketing process aiming to create demand for virtual goods. We focused on performance-oriented gameplay elements in MMO games, as their gameplay conventions are quite established. Our objective was, firstly, to identify game design patterns that create and sustain demand for virtual goods, and secondly, to associate and compare them with analogous marketing concepts to obtain new insights about both game design and marketing. The identified patterns are summarised in the previous section. In this section, we discuss their implications for managers and policy makers, and consider potential directions for future research.

7.1 Game design as part of business planning

Based on the findings, we assert that game designers, by creating and modifying the rules and mechanics of the game, SNS or other online hangout, have an essential, but sometimes unrecognised role in planning the marketing of virtual goods. MMO operators are able to adjust the environment in which their products are sold and marketed, and the rules according to which the products are used, not to mention their role in creating the environment to begin with. This uniquely wide and flexible position the company occupies in the life cycle of the products requires a wide approach to marketing.

Even though virtual world operators have been forerunners in coordinating the efforts of game design and marketing, there still seems to be way to go before game design is harmonised with overall business logic. Many virtual world operators find themselves in a situation where revenue generation logic is distanced from the design of the service itself. If an operator was to change their revenue generation logic, it would also require drastic changes to the service itself. For example, *Chronicles of Spellborn*, operated by Acclaim Games, had to undergo a costly re-development due to a change of revenue model from subscription to free-to-play. One potential direction for future research could thus be found in examining how business models and service design, including game design, could be integrated and aligned from the start. As a first step, this could entail theoretical work that combines game mechanics with business model literature.

From a policy perspective, the findings of this study can be problematic. One cornerstone of media regulation in many countries is the conceptual distinction between content and advertising (although in film and television, this distinction has recently been challenged by product placement and multi-channel concepts). This study suggests that in games and online services that utilise the virtual good sales revenue model, it may be conceptually impossible to distinguish between "innocent" game mechanics and content that has a marketing purpose. Some other rule than the separation of "content" and "advertising" may thus be necessary if commercial online services are to be regulated in the future.

7.2 Marketing as game design

An important conclusion that can be drawn from the results is that it is possible to see many traditional marketing techniques as the equivalent of game design patterns. From this perspective, the task of planning a marketing strategy for a traditional product or service could be approached as a task of creating a game design: a structure of choices, restrictions and incentives that engage the player-consumer in an interactive relationship with the product or service. Marketers already use terms and devices reminiscent of game design: progressions, levels, prizes, collectibles, memberships and points, among others. As game design patterns, these devices are not very advanced, however. Some problems with these real-life "marketing games" are arguably the following: the game is too simplistic, the game fails to engage for more than a short period of time, the game is too easy to provide excitement or too difficult to be rewarding, or the marketer's commercial motive is blatantly obvious, preventing immersion in the game.

Our suggestion to marketing managers is, therefore, to approach the marketing task as a serious game design challenge: to hire professional game designers, to consult the large body of literature on game design, and to strive to create engaging games around their products and services. The whole customer relationship, from acquisition through retention to monetisation, could be modelled as an interactive game. This approach would be especially suited for businesses where customer interaction is mostly computer-mediated (including automatic telephone services) and the variety of possible interactions is restricted. On the other hand, businesses with face-to-face interactions and a complex variety of possible interactions could perhaps apply game design on a suitably abstract layer, and also make use of techniques and patterns in so-called *pervasive gaming*: games that are layered into everyday life as opposed to being played on a distinct device at a distinct time (Montola & Stenros 2009).

One challenge in implementing advanced game design patterns in more traditional forms of business is the obvious lack of "gameness" in such services. Complex rules and achievements might be difficult to articulate in marketing communications without an explicit agreement that there is a game in progress. One potential direction for further research could thus be to examine ways in which marketers could build game mechanics into marketing strategies in contexts where there is no explicit agreement that a "game" is being played; in other words, research on "business game design".

7.3 Patterns of persuasion

Finally, one more possible link for the patterns identified in this study is so-called *captology* or *persuasive technology*: the notion of using technology to persuade people to change their behavior towards some desired goal (Fogg 2003). These patterns can be seen as one branch or subset of persuasive techniques that could be applied in a variety of areas. Applications for persuasive technology are diverse, ranging from promoting environmentally friendly behavior (Nakajima et al. 2008) to motivating exercise (Toscos et al. 2006) or house cleaning (Strengers 2008). Selling products or services could be seen as one application area, linking game design, persuasive technology and marketing.

Malaby (2007) suggests that if we look at games as domains of artificial outcomes, of "contrived contingency", we find that society is full of games: ones associated with business risk, others associated with political risk, and still others that relate to cool consumption styles, popularity and friends. Increasingly, the distinction between computer games and these other "games" in the society is blurring, with MMOs and SNSs blazing the trail. It should perhaps not be surprising, then, that we can find similarity in the rules and structures of these domains, even if the study of those rules takes different names, such as marketing and game design. A promising direction of research, pioneered in this study, is to take what we have learned in one domain and adapt it to others.

REFERENCES

Alexander, T. (ed.) (2003). *Massively Multiplayer Game Development*. Boston, MA: Charles River Media.

Alexander, T. (ed.) (2005). *Massively Multiplayer Game Development 2*. Boston, MA: Charles River Media.

Bartle, R. (1996). *Hearts, Clubs, Diamonds, Spades: Players Who Suit Muds*. Retrieved from http://www.mud.co.uk/richard/hcds.htm.

Bartle, R. (2003). *Designing Virtual Worlds.* New Riders Games.

Bulow, J. (1986). An Economic Theory of Planned Obsolescence. *The Quarterly Journal of Economics*, 101(4), 729-49.

Choi, J. (1994). Network Externality, Compatibility Choice, and Planned Obsolescence. *Journal of Industrial Economics*, 42(2), 167-182.

Davis, S. (2007). Gold Farming + RMT + Power-Leveling + PvP + Gambling = The Most Popular Game in China - ZT Online. *PlayNoEvil Game Security News & Analysis*. Retrieved from http://www.playnoevil.com/serendipity/index.php?/archives/1818-Gold-Farming-+-RMT-+-Power-Leveling-+-PvP-+-Gambling-The-Most-Popular-Game-in-China-ZT-Online.html.

Day, G. S. (1981). Strategic Market Analysis and Definition: An Integrated Approach. *Strategic Management Journal*, 2(3), 281-299.

Drucker, P. F. (1993). Management: Tasks, Responsibilities, Practices. Collins Business.

Fairfield, J. (2005). Virtual Property. *Boston University Law Review*, 85(4), 1047-1102.

Flyvbjerg, B. (2006). Five Misunderstandings About Case-Study Research. *Qualitative Inquiry*, 12(2), 219-245.

Fogg, B. (2003). *Persuasive technology: using computers to change what we think and do*. Morgan Kaufmann Publishers, Boston.

Guo, Y., & Barnes, S. (2007). Why People Buy Virtual Items in Virtual Worlds With Real Money. *SIGMIS Database*, 38(4), 69-76.

Hsee, C. K., Yu, F., Zhang, J., & Zhang, Y. (2003). Medium Maximization. *Journal of Consumer Research: An Interdisciplinary Quarterly*, 30(1), 1-14.

Hyatt, N. (2008). Successful MMOGs can see $1-2 in monthly ARPU. *Lightspeed Venture Partners Blog*. Retrieved from http://lsvp.wordpress.com/2008/06/09/successful-mmogs-can-see-1-2-in-monthly-arpu/.

Jonker, J., Piersma, N., & Van den Poel. (2004). Joint optimization of customer segmentation and marketing policy to maximize long-term profitability. *Expert Systems with Applications*, 27(2), 159-168.

Kotler, P., & Keller, K. (2006). *Marketing Management (Twelfth Edition.)*. NJ: Prentice Hall.

Lastowka, F. G., & Hunter, D. (2004). The Laws of the Virtual Worlds. *California Law Review*, 92(1).

Lehdonvirta, V. (2005). Real-Money Trade of Virtual Assets: Ten Different User Perceptions. In *Proceedings of Digital Arts and Culture (DAC 2005)*. Copenhagan, Denmark, December 1-3, pp. 52-58.

Lehdonvirta, V. (2008). Real-Money Trade of Virtual Assets: New Strategies for Virtual World Operators. In Mary Ipe (Ed.) *Virtual Worlds* (pp. 138-156). Hyderabad: Icfai University Press.

Lehdonvirta, V. (2009). Virtual Item Sales as a Revenue Model: Identifying Attributes That Drive Purchase Decisions. *Electronic Commerce Research*, 9(1-2), 97-113.

Lehdonvirta, V., Wilska, T., & Johansson, M. (2009). Virtual Consumerism: Case Habbo Hotel. *Information, Communication & Society*, 12(7). (Forthcoming in September 2009)

Lehtiniemi, T., & Lehdonvirta, V. (2007). How big is the RMT market anyway? *Virtual Economy Research Network*. Retrieved from http://virtual-economy.org/blog/how_big_is_the_rmt_market_anyw.

Liew, J. (2008a). Successful MMOGs can see $1-2 in monthly ARPU. *Lightspeed Venture Partners Blog*. Retrieved from http://lsvp.wordpress.com/2008/06/09/successful-mmogs-can-see-1-2-in-monthly-arpu/.

Liew, J. (2008b). Nexon's Maplestory sold $30m of digital goods in the US in 2007. *Lightspeed Venture Partners Blog*. Retrieved from http://lsvp.wordpress.com/2008/05/27/nexons-maplestory-sold-30m-of-digital-goods-in-the-us-in-2007/.

MacInnes, I. (2004). The Implications of Property Rights in Virtual Worlds. *In Proceedings of Tenth Americas Conference of Information Systems (AMCIS 2004)*.

Malaby, T. M. (2007). Beyond Play A New Approach to Games. *Games and Culture* 2(2), 95-113.

Montola, M. & Stenros, J. (2009). *Pervasive Games: Theory and Design*. Morgan Kaufmann Publishers, Boston.

Nakajima, T., Lehdonvirta, V., Tokunaga, E., & Kimura, H. (2008). Reflecting human behavior to motivate desirable lifestyle. In *DIS '08: Proceedings of the 7th ACM conference on Designing interactive systems* (pp. 405–414).

Nojima, M. (2007). Pricing models and Motivations for MMO play. In *Proceedings of DiGRA 2007: Situated Play* (pp. 672-681). Tokyo, Japan.

Oh, G., & Ryu, T. (2007). Game Design on Item-selling Based Payment Model in Korean Online Games. In *Proceedings of DiGRA 2007: Situated Play* (pp. 650-657). Tokyo, Japan.

Orbach, B. (2004). The Durapolist Puzzle: Monopoly Power in Durable-Goods Market. *Yale Journal on Regulation*, 21, 67-118.

Pardew, L., Pugh, S., Nunamaker, E., Iverson, B. L., & Wolfley, R. (2004). *Game Design for Teens (1st ed.)*. Course Technology PTR.

Piana, V. (2003). *Product differentiation*. Economic Web Institute. Retrieved from http://www.economicswebinstitute.org/glossary/product.htm.

Porter, M. E. (1980). *Competitive Strategy: Techniques for Analyzing Industries and Competitors (1st ed.)*. Free Press.

Sharp, B., & Dawes, J. (2001). What is Differentiation and How Does it Work? *Journal of Marketing Management*, 17(7-8), 739-759.

Stabell, C. B., & Fjeldstad, D. (1998). Configuring Value for Competitive Advantage: On Chains, Shops, and Networks. *Strategic Management Journal*, 19(5), 413-437.

Strengers, Y. (2008). Challenging comfort & cleanliness norms through interactive in-home feedback systems. In *Pervasive 2008 Workshop Proceedings* (pp. 104-108). Sydney, Australia.

Sulake Corporation 2009. "*Habbo Keräilytavat*," Sulake Corporation. Retrieved from: http://www.habbo.fi/credits/collectibles

Toscos, T. A., Faber, S. An., & Gandhi, M. P. (2006). Chick clique: persuasive technology to motivate teenage girls to exercise. In *CHI '06: CHI '06 extended abstracts on Human factors in computing systems* (pp. 1873-1878). New York, USA.

Vandenbosch, M. B., & Weinberg, C. B. (1995). Product and Price Competition in a Two-Dimensional Vertical Differentiation Model. *Marketing Science*, 14(2), 224-249.

WoWWiki contributors 2009. "Gates of Ahn'Qiraj," *WoWWiki*. Retrieved from: http://www.wowwiki.com/Ahn%27Qiraj_War_Effort

Yee, N. (2007). Motivations of Play in Online Games. *Journal of CyberPsychology and Behavior*, 9, 772-775.

3

Driving online shopping: Spending and behavioral differences among women in Saudi Arabia

Talal Al-maghrabi
Brunel Business School, Brunel University
West London, UB8 3PH, United Kingdom

Email: talal.almaghrabi@brunel.ac.uk

Charles Dennis
Brunel Business School, Brunel University
West London, UB8 3PH, United Kingdom

Email: charles.dennis@brunel.ac.uk

Abstract

This study proposes a revised technology acceptance model that integrates expectation confirmation theory to measure gender differences with regard to continuance online shopping intentions in Saudi Arabia. The sample consists of 650 female respondents. A structural equation model confirms model fit. Perceived enjoyment, usefulness, and subjective norms are determinants of online shopping continuance in Saudi Arabia. High and low online spenders among women in Saudi Arabia are equivalent. The structural weights are also largely equivalent, but the regression paths from perceived site quality to perceived usefulness is not invariant between high and low e-shoppers in Saudi Arabia. This research moves beyond online shopping intentions and includes factors affecting online shopping continuance. The research model explains 60% of the female respondents' intention to continue shopping online. Online strategies cannot ignore either the direct and indirect spending differences on continuance intentions, and the model can be generalized across Saudi Arabia.

Keywords: internet shopping, e-shopping, technology acceptance, male and female examination, continuance online shopping, Saudi Arabia

Acknowledgements: The authors thank the respondents, the editors, and the anonymous reviewers for their many helpful suggestions. Special thanks for their families for their continued support.

1 STUDY MOTIVATION

Globalization continues to drive the rapid growth of international trade, global corporations, and non-local consumption alternatives (Alden et al. 2006; Holt et al. 2004), and advances of the Internet and e-commerce have diminished trade boundaries. E-commerce and e-shopping create opportunities for businesses to reach to consumers globally and directly, and in turn, business and social science research now focuses specifically on cross-national and cross-cultural Internet marketing (Griffith et al. 2006).

The Internet had changed how businesses and customers customize, distribute, and consume products. Its low cost gives both businesses and consumers a new and powerful channel for information and communication. In 1991, the Internet had less than 3 million users worldwide and no e-commerce applications; by 1999, about 250 million users appeared online, and 63 million of them engaged in online transactions, which produced a total value of $110 billion (Coppel 2000). Business-to-consumer online sales in the United States grew by 120% between 1998 and 1999 (Shop.org and Boston Consulting Group, 2000). According to a U.K. payment association, the number of consumers who shop online has increased by more than 157%, from 11 million in 2001 to more than 28 million in 2006 (cited in Alsajjan and Dennis, 2009). E-commerce transactions also are growing in the Middle East (19.5 million Internet users) and in the Gulf States. In Saudi Arabia, online transactions have increased by 100%, from $278 million in 2002 to $556 million in 2005 (*Al Riyadh* 2006). In 2007, Internet sales increased to more than $1.2 billion worldwide and are expected to continue to rise (World Internet Users and Population Stats 2007).

An unpublished study by the Centre for Customer Driven Quality also highlights some potential savings: For one retailer, the cost of an in-store customer contact was estimated to be $10, the cost of a phone contact $5, and the cost of a Web contact $0.01 (Feinberg, et al. 2002). In the airline industry, the savings are similar. According to the International Air Transport Association, airlines currently issue approximately 300 million paper tickets per year at a cost of $10 per ticket to process (Arab News Newspaper, 2007). One e-ticket process costs only $1(Arab News Newspaper, 2007).

Despite the impressive online purchasing growth rates though, compelling evidence indicates that many consumers who search different online retail sites abandon their purchases. This trend and the proliferation of business-to-consumer e-shopping activities require that online businesses understand which factors encourage consumers to complete their purchases. Acquiring new customers also can cost as much as five times more than retaining existing ones (Bhattacherjee 2001b; Crego and Schiffrin 1995; Petrissans 1999). For example, a 5% increase in customer retention in the insurance industry typically translates into an 18% reduction in operating costs (Bhattacherjee, 2001a; Crego et al, 1995).

Online customer retention is particularly difficult. Modern customers demand that their needs be met immediately, perfectly, and for free, and they are empowered with more information to make decisions (Bhattacherjee 2001b; Crego and Schiffrin 1995). They also have various online and offline options from which to choose, and without a compelling reason to choose one retailer over another, they experiment or rotate purchases among multiple firms (Bhattacherjee 2001b; Crego and Schiffrin 1995).

To employ the savings derived from e-businesses, companies might engage in tactics to increase switching costs and thereby retain more customers. E-retailers might recall details about the customer that reduce the customer effort demanded in future transactions; they could also learn more about the customer to tailor those future interactions to the customer's needs (Straub and Watson 2001). Better product quality, lower prices, better services, and increased outcome value should help companies build sustainable relationships with their customers.

Theoretical explanations of online shopping intentions suggest several important factors. For example, Rogers (1995) suggests that consumers reevaluate their acceptance decisions during a final confirmation stage and decide to continue or discontinue. Continuance may be an extension of acceptance behavior that covaries with acceptance (e.g., Bhattercherjee 2001a; Davis et al. 1989; Karahanna et al. 1999). We adopt the extended expectation confirmation theory (ECT; Bhattacherjee 2001b) and the technology acceptance model (TAM; Davis et al. 1989) as a theoretical basis, integrating ECT from consumer behavior literature to propose a model of e-shopping continuance intentions, similar to the way in which the TAM adapts the theory of reasoned action (TRA) from social psychology to postulate a model of technology acceptance.

The TAM, as expanded by Davis and colleagues (1992) and Gefen (2003), and the ECT (Bhattacherjee 2001a; Oliver 1980) have been used widely in research in the industrialized world, but they are less commonly applied to developing countries. Moreover, the TAM stops at intention and does not investigate continuance intentions or behavior.

As another issue in prior research, no widely acceptable definition for e-commerce exists. Coppel (2000) calls it doing business over the Internet, including both business-to-business and business-to-consumer markets. For the purpose of this research, we adopt the following definition: E-shopping, electronic shopping, online shopping, and Internet shopping are the same. All these activities include the activity of searching, buying, and selling products and services through the Internet. In recent years, the Internet has grown to include a wider range of potential commercial activities and information exchanges, such as the transaction and exchange of information between government agencies, governments and businesses, businesses and consumers, and among consumers. We focus mainly on the business-to-consumer (B2C) arena, which has been the source of most online progress and development.

Previous research also finds that gender differences significantly affect new technology decision-making processes (Van Slyke et al. 2002; Venkatesh et al. 2000). Venkatesh and colleagues (2000) report that women tend to accept information technology when others have high opinions of it and are more influenced by ease of use. Men rely more on their evaluations of the usefulness of the technology. However, in many cultures, women represent the primary decision makers in families and households' main shoppers. Greater e-commerce exposure and decision-making power may imply that women can attain greater satisfaction from online shopping (Alreck and Settle 2002).

Finally, no previous research considers Internet shopping in Saudi Arabia or, specifically, continuance intentions for online shopping in Saudi Arabia, nor do studies address gender-based differences in shopping behavior online in Saudi Arabia. This research attempts to provide a validated conceptual model that integrates different factors, including gender, and clarifies the theoretical problems of continuance intentions in the unique context of Saudi Arabia.

The remainder of this article proceeds as follows: We offer a review of existing literature, and then detail our proposed model, hypotheses, and methodology. After describing the structural equation model and analysis, we provide our results. We conclude with some limitations and recommendations for further research.

2 THEORETICAL BACKGROUND

The TAM (Davis 1989) represents an adaptation of the TRA, tailored to users' acceptance of information systems. It helps explain determinants of computer acceptance and can explicate user behaviors across a broad range of computing technologies and populations; it also is parsimonious and theoretically justified (Davis et al. 1989). The major determinants are perceived usefulness and ease of use. Perceived usefulness significantly influences attitude formation (Agarwal and Prasad 1999; Davis 1989; Dishaw and Strong 1999; Gefen and Keil 1998; Igbaria et al. 1996; Moon and Kim 2001; Taylor and Todd 1995; Venkatesh 2000; Venkatesh and Davis 2000), but evidence regarding perceived ease of use remains inconsistent. Many studies simplify the original TAM by dropping attitude and studying just the effect of perceived usefulness and ease of use on intention to use (Gefen and Straub 2000; Leader et al. 2000; Teo et al. 1999).

Updates to the TAM add antecedents of perceived usefulness and ease of use (Venkatesh and Davis 2000), such as subjective norms, experience, trust, and output quality. Ample evidence confirms that both usefulness (i.e., external motivation) and intrinsic enjoyment (i.e., internal motivation) offer direct determinants of user acceptance online (Davis et al. 1992; Leader et al. 2000; Moon and Kim 2001; Teo et al. 1999; Venkatesh 1999).

Expectation confirmation theory (ECT) in turn helps predict consumer behavior before, during, and after a purchase in various contexts, in terms of both product and service repurchases (Anderson and Sullivan 1993; Dabholkar et al., 2000; Oliver, 1980, 1993; Patterson et al. 1997; Spreng et al. 1996; Swan and Trawick 1981; Tse and Wilton 1988). According to ECT, consumers define their repurchase intentions by determining whether the product or service meets their initial expectations. Their comparison of perceived usefulness versus their original expectation of usefulness influences their continuance intentions (Bhattacherjee 2001a; Oliver 1980). Their repurchase intentions depend on their satisfaction with the product or service (Anderson and Sullivan 1993; Oliver 1980).

However, the ECT ignores potential changes in initial expectations following the consumption experience and the effect of these expectation changes on subsequent cognitive processes (Bhattacherjee 2001a). Pre-purchase expectations typically are based on others' opinions or information from mass media, whereas post-purchase expectations derive from first-hand experience, which appears more realistic (Fazio and Zanna 1981). After such first-hand experience, expectations may increase if consumers believe the product or service is useful or contains new benefits and features that were not part their initial expectation.

Venkatesh and colleagues (2003) suggest that usage and intentions to continue usage may depend on cognitive beliefs about perceived usefulness. Gefen (2003) also indicates that perceived usefulness reinforces an online shopper's intention to continue using a Web site, such that when a person accepts a new information system, he or she is more willing to alter practices and expend time and effort to use it (Succi and Walter 1999). However, consumers may continue using an e-commerce service if they consider it useful, even if they are dissatisfied with its prior use (Bhattacherjee 2001a).

Site quality and good interface design enhance the formation of consumer trust (McKnight et al. 2002a), and if a consumer perceives a vendor's Web site to be of high quality, he or she should trust that vendor's competence, integrity, and benevolence (McKnight et al. 2002a). Gefen and colleagues (2003) integrate trust into the TAM in a B2C e-shopping context and find trust positively affects consumers' intention to use a Web site. Building trust with consumers is an essential mission for e-retailers, because purchasing decisions represent trust-related behaviors (Jarvenpaa et al. 2000; McKnight et al. 2002b; Urban et al. 2000).

A person's beliefs about what important others think about the behavior also should directly influence subjective norms. Therefore, if e-shopping is a socially desirable behavior, a person is more likely to e-shop (George 2002).

Childers and colleagues (2001) also find that enjoyment can predict attitude towards e-shopping, just as much as usefulness can. However, usefulness was the better predictor for grocery items, whereas enjoyment offered better results for hedonic purchases. With regard to e-shopping, the hedonic enjoyment constructs in the TAM may reflect the pleasure users obtain from shopping online, which reinforces continuance intentions.

3 PROPOSED MODEL AND HYPOTHESES

3.1 Site Quality

Initial trust forms quickly on the basis of available information (Meyerson et al. 1996). If consumers perceive a Web site as high quality, they trust it and will depend on that vendor (McKnight et al. 2002a). Site information quality and a good interface design enhance consumer trust (Fung and Lee, 1999). Web site quality helps predict behavior (Business Wire 1999; Carl 1995; Meltzer 1999). Perceptions of Web site quality affect trust and perceptions of usefulness. In addition, e-shoppers should perceive a Web site as more trustworthy if it appears more attractive because of its contents, layout, and colors, which represent site quality. On the basis of previous research, we therefore predict:

H1a. Perceived site quality relates positively to perceived usefulness.

H1b. Perceived site quality relates positively to customer trust to use online shopping.

3.2 Trust

Trust refers to an expectation that others will not behave opportunistically (Gefen 2003). Trust therefore implies a belief that the vendor will provide what has been promised (Ganesan 1994). In turn, perceived usefulness should occur only for an e-vendor that can be trusted (Festinger 1975). Thus:

H2. Perceived trust relates positively to perceived usefulness.

3.3 Perceived Usefulness

According to Burke (1997), perceived usefulness is the primary prerequisite for mass market technology acceptance, which depends on consumers' expectations about how technology can improve and simplify their lives (Peterson et al. 1997). A Web site is useful if it delivers services to a customer but not if the customers' delivery expectations are not met (Barnes and Vidgen 2000). The usefulness and accuracy of the site also influence customer attitudes. Users may continue using an e-commerce service if they consider it useful, even if they may be dissatisfied with their prior use (Bhattacherjee 2001a). Consumers likely evaluate and consider product-related information prior to purchase, and perceived usefulness thus may be more important than the hedonic aspect of the shopping experience (Babin et al. 1994). In a robust TAM, perceived usefulness predicts IT use and intention to use (e.g., Adams et al. 1992; Agarwal and Prasad, 1999; Gefen and Keil 1998; Gefen and Straub 1997; Hendrickson et al. 1993; Igabria et al. 1995; Subramanian 1994), including e-commerce adoption (Gefen and Straub 2000). Therefore:

H3a. Perceived usefulness relates positively to increasing customer subjective norms.

H3b. Perceived usefulness relates positively to increasing customer enjoyment.

H3c. Perceived usefulness relates positively to increasing customer continuance intentions.

3.4 Subjective Norms

According to Venkatesh and colleagues (2003), social influences result from subject norms, which relate to consumers' perceptions of the beliefs of other consumers. Shim and colleagues (2001) consider subjective norms only marginally significant on e-shopping intentions, whereas Foucault and Scheufele (2005) confirm a significant link between talking about e-shopping with friends and intention to e-shop. Enjoyment also is relevant to social norms, because involving Web sites facilitate e-friendship and enforce e-shopping as a subjective norm. Thus,

H4a. Perceived subjective norms relate positively to increasing customer enjoyment.

H4b. Perceived subjective norms relate positively to increasing customer continuance intentions.

3.5 Enjoyment

Enjoyment in using a Web site significantly affects intentions to use (Davis et al. 1992; Igbaria et al. 1995; Teo et al. 1999; Venkatesh et al. 2002). Shopping enjoyment (Koufaris 2002), perceived entertainment value of the Web site (O'Keefe et al. 1998), and perceived visual attractiveness have positive impacts on perceived enjoyment and continuance intentions (van der Heijden 2003). Thus:

H5. Perceived enjoyment relates positively to increasing customer continuance intentions.

4 METHODOLOGY

To validate the conceptual model and the proposed research hypotheses, we developed an online survey, which is suitable for collecting data from large geographical areas. In addition, compared with traditional surveys, online surveys offer lower costs, faster responses, and less data entry effort.

4.1 Measures

The measures of the various constructs come from previous literature, adapted to the context of online shopping if necessary. All online survey items use 1–7 Likert scales, on which 1 indicates strongly disagree and 7 is strongly agree. The site quality and trust items come from McKnight and colleagues (2002a, 2002b). The perceived usefulness items derive from Gefen (2003). Perceived enjoyment is a measure from Childers (2001). Shih and Fang (2004) provide the subjective norm items. The continuance intention items were adapted from Yang (2004).

The pilot study suggested some clarifications to the survey. Both Arabic and English language versions were available. The Arabic questionnaire employed Brislin's (1986) back-translation method to ensure that the questionnaires have the same meaning in both languages.

5 DATA ANALYSIS

Survey respondents were people who were actively engaged in Internet and online shopping in Saudi Arabia, including undergraduate and postgraduate students and professionals. As we show in Table 1, the sample consists of 650 female participants in Saudi Arabia. This somewhat surprising participation level illustrates the high rate of Internet use among women in Saudi Arabia. Most respondents are in their late 30s (2.5% younger than 18 years of age, 26.6% between 18 and 25, 42.8% are 26–35, 22% are 36–45, and 6.2% are older than 46 years). Similarly, 60% of the Saudi population is younger than 30 years of age. The vast majority (92.6%) of participants came from the three main regions in Saudi Arabia: 24.6% from the east, 27.8% from the central region, and 40.2% from the western region. The education levels indicate 1.5% of respondents earned less than a high school degree, 10.9% attended high school, 12.9% had diplomas, 52.9% had bachelor's degrees, and 21.7% were postgraduates. Most respondents thus are well-educated. Moreover, 36% of them work in the public sector (government employee), 35.4% in the private sector, 6.5% were businesspeople, and 22.22% were students.

As we show in Table 2, 52.2% of the respondents visited at least five different online sites to purchase each month, and 66.9% used the Internet for actual shopping. The western region reveals the highest percentages in most categories, such that 31.1% spend £100–£500 per year online, and 51.3% spend more than £501 per year. Furthermore, 49.7% of the respondents used the Internet in the prior six months to make flight booking or purchase airline tickets, 37.5% made hotel reservations, 35.2% purchased clothing, 58.6% bought books, and 37.8% purchased CD-DVDs or video tapes. To indicate why they used the Internet, as we summarize in Table 3, 82% referred to information search, 56.8% to social communication, 52.5% to banking, 64.8% to entertainment, 51% to work-related tasks, and 69% used it for study-related tasks.

Table 1: Demographic Items

Question	Count	Percentage
Gender		
Total Female Participants	650	100
Age		
Less than 18	16	2.5
Between 18-25	173	26.6
Between 26-35	278	42.8
Between 36-45	143	22.0
Above 46	40	6.2
Education Level		
Less than high school	10	1.5
High school	71	10.9
Diploma	84	12.9
Bachelor	344	52.9
Post-graduate	141	21.7
Occupation		
Government employee	234	36.0
Private sector	230	35.4
Business people	42	6.5
Student	144	22.22
Income Level		
<SR4,000 (£1,000)	105	16.2
SR4,000-SR6,000 (£1,000-2,000)	78	12.0
SR6,001-SR8,000 (£2,001-4,000)	89	13.7
SR8,001-SR10,000 (£4,001-7,000)	77	11.8
SR10,001-SR15,000 (£7,001-10,000)	128	19.7
>SR15,001 (>£10,000)	123	18.9
Dependent on others	50	7.7
Region		
East region	160	24.6
West region	261	40.2
Central region	181	27.8
North region	29	4.5
South Region	19	2.9

Table 2: Items Purchased Online and Reasons

Items purchased in the last six months	Region in Saudi Arabia		
	East	West	Middle
Buying Books	47	71	45
	16.9%	25.5%	16.2%
Music CD, DVD, Videotape	34	34	28
	12.2%	15.5%	10.1%
Cloth	37	41	20
	13.3%	14.7%	7.2%
Sports equip	22	18	10
	7.9%	6.5%	3.6%
Travel reservation and ticketing	43	64	31
	15.5%	23.0%	11.2%
Hotel booking	31	50	23
	11.2%	18.0%	8.3%
Reason for using the Internet			
Info. Search	72	100	56
	25.9%	36.0%	20.1%
Entertainment	60	78	42
	21.6%	28.1%	15.1%
Social Communication	47	76	35
	16.9%	27.3%	12.6%
Work	39	71	32
	14.0%	25.5%	11.5%
Study	44	74	45
	15.8%	26.6%	16.2%
Purchasing	55	90	41
	19.8%	32.4%	14.7%
Banking	36	72	38
	12.9%	25.9%	13.7%

Table 3: Important Issues when Shopping Online

Important issues to e-shoppers	Region in Saudi Arabia		
	East	West	Middle
Security	74	100	57
	27%	36%	21%
Price	75	104	56
	27%	37%	20%
Service, Delivery	75	97	58
	27%	35%	21%
Quality	75	102	60
	27%	37%	22%
Payment	73	100	57
	26%	36%	21%
Language Barrier	62	81	41
	22%	29%	15%

6 ANALYSIS

The Cronbach's alphas (Table 4) are all greater than 0.7 (Bagozzi and Yi 1988). The squared multiple correlation cut-off point is 0.7, and the average variance extracted cut off-point is 0.5 or higher (Bagozzi 1994; Byrne 2001; Hair et al. 2006) (Table 5). We thus confirm the convergent reliability and discriminant validity.

Table 4: Scale Properties and Correlations

Model Constructs	Mean	Std. Dev.	Cronbach's alpha	Factor Correlations					
				SQ	PU	Trust	SN	Enj	CIU
SQ	26.92	6.38	0.927	1.000					
PU	32.97	7-86	0.946	.749	1.000				
Trust	21.74	5.03	0.947	.655	.695	1.000			
SN	18.73	6.19	0.943	.259	.275	.395	1.000		
Enj	28.39	8.61	0.931	.438	.465	.668	.536	1.000	
CIU	31.48	7.98	0.961	.397	.421	.606	.533	.745	1.000

Table 5: Measurement Model

Constructs/Indicators	S. Factor Loading	S.E	C.R.	AVE	Squared Multiple Correlation
Site Quality (SQ)				0.757	
SQ 1	0.922	0.039	26.510		0.85
SQ 2	0.844	0.038	26.414		0.71
SQ 3	0.855	0.035	26.972		0.73
SQ 4	0.857	—	—		0.74
Perceived usefulness				0.813	
PU 3	0.911	0.039	37.788		0.83
PU 4	0.909	0.027	37.135		0.83
PU 5	0.914	—	—		0.84
PU 6	0.871	0.029	33.487		0.76
Trust				0.804	
Trusting Beliefs Integrity 1	0.896	0.028	35.069		0.80
Trusting Beliefs Integrity 2	0.886	0.023	42.297		0.79
Trusting Beliefs Integrity 3	0.896	0.027	35.167		0.80
Trusting Beliefs Integrity 4	0.909	—	—		0.83
Subjective Norm				0.804	
SN 3	0.731	—	—		0.53
SN 4	0.973	0.054	25.507		0.95
SN 5	0.955	0.057	24.647		0.91
SN 6	0.908	0.055	23.875		0.82
Enjoyment				0.744	
Enj 4	0.705	—	—		0.50
Enj 5	0.94	0.055	22.934		0.88
Enj 6	0.925	0.055	22.918		0.86
Enj 8	0.858	0.052	20.672		0.74
Continuance Intention				0.864	
CIU 1	0.827	0.024	35.466		0.69
CIU 2	0.928	0.017	55.752		0.86
CIU 3	0.981	—	—		0.96
CIU 4	0.974	0.012	78.936		0.95

6.1 Structural Equation Model

As the first step in testing the proposed model, which operationalizes the hypotheses and the factors involved in continuance e-shopping intentions in Saudi Arabia, we estimate the goodness-of-fit indices (Figure 1). Bentler and Bonnett (1980) suggest the Chi-square/Degrees-of-freedom (CMIN/DF) ratio as an appropriate measure of model fit, which should not exceed 5 (Bentler 1989).

A structural equation model (SEM) with AMOS 5.0 software determines additional goodness-of-fit indices, including critical ratio (CR), chi-square (CMIN), degrees of freedom (df), chi-square/degrees of freedom (CMIN/DF), root mean square residual (RMR), root mean square error of approximate (RMSEA), goodness-of-fit index (GFI), comparative fit index (CFI), normal fit index (NFI), incremental fit index (NFI), and the relative fit index (RFI). In general, GFI, NFI, RFI, IFI, and CFI values greater than 0.90 indicate good model fit (Bentler 1989). As we illustrate in Table 6, all the hypotheses are statistically significant and supported, with CRs ranging from 20.318 to 4.888, which are greater than 1.96 and thus indicate acceptable results (Hair et al. 2006; Holmes-Smith 2000). As illustrated in Table 7, the goodness-of-fit indices of the proposed model of continuance intentions fit the data reasonably well, as confirmed by the chi-square CMIN = 875.370, df = 236, CMIN/DF = 3.709, RMR = 0.231, GFI = 0.905, CFI = 0.964, RMSEA = 0.065, NFI = 0.952, IFI = 0.965, and RFI = 0.944.

Table 6: Regression Weights

Hypotheses	Paths			Standardized Regression Weights (B)	Standard Error S.E.	Critical Ratio C.R.	P Value	Hypotheses Findings
H1 a	PU	<---	SQ	.305	.051	6.262	***	Supported
H1 b	Trust	<---	SQ	.749	.036	20.318	***	Supported
H2	PU	<---	Trust	.467	.053	9.324	***	Supported
H3 a	SN	<---	PU	.395	.037	9.580	***	Supported
H3 b	Enj	<---	PU	.541	.032	13.473	***	Supported
H3 c	CIU	<---	PU	.183	.040	4.888	***	Supported
H4 a	Enj	<---	SN	.322	.032	8.876	***	Supported
H4 b	CIU	<---	SN	.178	.039	5.521	***	Supported
H5	CIU	<---	Enj	.527	.062	11.481	***	Supported

*** $p < 0.001$.

Table 7: Goodness-of-Fit Indices

Confirmatory Factor Analysis CFA (Goodness-of-fit measure)	Acceptable Values	Value
Chi-Square CMIN	NA	875.370
Degree of freedom	NA	236
CMIN/DF	Chi square/ df ≤5 (Bentler and Bonnett, 1989)	3.709
P value	p≤0.05 (Hair et al., 2006)	0.000
Root mean square residual (RMR)	No established thresholds (the smaller the better) (Hair et al., 2006)	0.231
Goodness-of-fit (GFI)	≥ 0.90 (the higher the better) (Hair et al., 2006)	0.905
Comparative fit index (CFI)	≥ 0.90 (Hair et al., 2006)	0.964
Root mean square error of approximate (RMSEA)	< 0.08 (Hair et al., 2006)	0.065
Normal fit index (NFI)	≥ 0.90 (Hair et al., 2006)	0.952
Incremental fit index (IFI)	≥ 0.90 (Hair et al., 2006)	0.965
Relative fit index (RFI)	≥ 0.90 (Hair et al., 2006)	0.944

Next, we examine the regression weights (path significance) of each relationship in our research model and the variance explained (R^2 value) by each path. The AMOS software reports the standardized regression weights, standard error, and CR for each path, which we provide in Table 6. The hypothesized associations are strongly significant at $p = 0.000$. Perceived enjoyment is the strongest predictor of continuance intention ($B = 0.53$), followed by perceived usefulness ($B = 0.18$), and then subjective norms ($B = 0.18$). The model explains 60% of the variance in continuance intentions (Figure 1).

Figure 1: Internet Continuance Intention Shopping Model

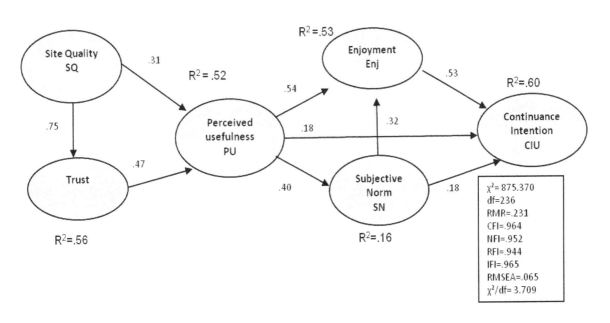

6.2 Invariance Analysis

When comparing cultures or groups, research participants may not recognize the same meaning of survey items. To minimize the bias in cross-national and cross-cultural research derived from the data collection, we applied back-translation (Brislin 1986; Yi et al. 2008). In addition, we assessed the measurement invariance across the groups to consider the constructs' factorial invariance (Cheung et al. 1999).

The invariance analysis indicates whether any differences occur between high and low online spenders among women. If we find that the annual online spending effect on the measurement invariance of the construct and the score of the group analysis is significant, the construct measurement differs for the two groups, and they cannot be compared directly.

To compare the annual spending (low and high spending) among female respondents, we use factorial invariance to assess the extent to which measures from both groups have the same meaning (Hair et al. 2006). The CMIN = 1404.966, df = 499, CMIN/DF = 2.816, RMR = 0.249, GFI = 0.855, CFI = 0.951, RMSEA = 0.053, NFI = 0.925, IFI = 0.951, and RFI = 0.918 indicate outstanding goodness-of-fit indices across the groups (Table 8).

Table 8: Goodness-of-Fit Indices

Confirmatory Factor Analysis CFA (Goodness-of-fit measure)	Acceptable Values	Value
Chi-Square CMIN	NA	1404.966
Degree of freedom	NA	499
CMIN/DF	Chi square/ df ≤ 5 (Bentler and Bonnett, 1989)	2.816
P value	$p \leq 0.05$ (Hair et al., 2006)	0.000
Root mean square residual (RMR)	No established thresholds (the smaller the better) (Hair et al., 2006)	0.249
Goodness-of-fit (GFI)	≥ 0.90 (the higher the better) (Hair et al., 2006)	0.855
Comparative fit index (CFI)	≥ 0.90 (Hair et al., 2006)	0.951
Root mean square error of approximate (RMSEA)	< 0.08 (Hair et al., 2006)	0.053
Normal fit index (NFI)	≥ 0.90 (Hair et al., 2006)	0.925
Incremental fit index (IFI)	≥ 0.90 (Hair et al., 2006)	0.951
Relative fit index (RFI)	≥ 0.90 (Hair et al., 2006)	0.918

Assuming the unconstrained model is correct, rather than constraining all factorial paths, the result across groups indicates changes in df (Δdf) = 18, chi-square ($\Delta\chi^2$) = 21.721, and p = 0.245, which is greater than Byrne's (2001) 0.05 cut-off. Tests of this measurement invariance appear in Table 9, which shows that changes in the chi-square and df are insignificant (p = 0.245). Therefore, the goodness-of-fit indices are comparable across low and high online spending groups, which justifies the invariance of the unconstrained and constrained models. Thus, we establish metric equivalence and can proceed in our analysis to regression paths.

Table 9: Invariance Analysis

Model	Δdf	$\Delta\chi^2$	p
Measurement weights	18	21.721	.245
Structural weights	9	20.273	.016

The coefficient (regression paths) invariance analysis determines if high and low spenders among female respondents have the same relationships with same variables in the research model. The findings in Table 9 suggest coefficient non-invariance between low and high online spending among women across the research model with all regression paths constrained ($\Delta\chi^2$ = 20.273, Δdf = 9, p = 0.016). To consider the relationships between model constructs for the source of non-invariance differences, we conducted an invariance analysis between low and high online spenders.

The findings in Table 10 indicate that low and high online spenders are non-invariant for certain relational paths. Differences in their behavior in the context of online shopping continuance in Saudi Arabia result from different coefficients of perceived site quality → perceived usefulness (change in chi-square = 5.033, p = 0.025). For the high spenders, this influence is greater than that for low spenders.

Table 10: Structural Factorial Analysis: High and Low Online Spending by Women

Hypotheses	Paths			Low Online Spenders			High Online Spenders			Invariance		
				RW	C.R.	P value	RW	C.R.	P Value	Δ DF	Δ CMIN	P Value
H1 a	PU	<---	SQ	.185	.070	2.641	.412	.073	5.665	1	5.033	.025
H1 b	Trust	<---	SQ	.790	.052	15.310	.692	.050	13.815	1	1.853	.173
H2	PU	<---	Trust	.570	.073	7.849	.436	.077	5.638	1	1.604	.205
H3 a	SN	<---	PU	.393	.054	7.253	.321	.050	6.362	1	.953	.329
H3 b	Enj	<---	PU	.477	.050	9.515	.402	.042	9.558	1	1.310	.252
H3 c	CIU	<---	PU	.208	.063	3.292	.196	.053	3.699	1	.021	.886
H4 a	Enj	<---	SN	.228	.047	4.883	.323	.045	7.253	1	2.118	.146
H4 b	CIU	<---	SN	.239	.058	4.143	.202	.053	3.807	1	.223	.637
H5	CIU	<---	Enj	.741	.095	7.772	.689	.082	8.399	1	.166	.683

The results of the latent mean online spending analysis appear in Table 11. The group analysis between the low and high spender samples exhibits latent mean invariance for the research constructs.

Table 11: Means: Annual Spending Sample (Low Spender – High Spender)

	Latent mean	S.E.	C.R.	P Value
PU	-.113	.102	-1.110	.267
Trust	-.077	.104	-.744	.457
Enj	.065	.105	.618	.537
CIU	-.093	.107	-.868	.386
SQ	-.040	.105	-.380	.704
SN	-.004	.088	-.050	.960

6.3 Direct and Indirect Effect Analysis

The direct and indirect effects in Table 12 reveal that the greatest total influences of direct and indirect (mediated) effects on continuance intentions come from perceived enjoyment for both the low online spenders (0.741) and high online spenders (0.689) samples. The next greatest influences derive from perceived usefulness for low (0.721) and high (0.610) online spenders. Trust has a greater influence on low online spenders' (0.411) than on high online spenders' (0.266) continuance intentions. Thus, site quality, trust, perceived usefulness, and subjective norms all play significant roles for continuance intentions toward online shopping in Saudi Arabia among women with both low and high online spending habits.

Table 12: Direct and Indirect Influences on Continuance Intentions (Low Spender – High Spender)

Construct	CIU (Low Spender)			CIU (High Spender)		
	Direct	Indirect	Total	Direct	Indirect	Total
SQ	--------	.458	.458	--------	.435	.435
TRUST	--------	.411	.411	--------	.266	.266
PU	.208	.513	.721	.196	.414	.610
SN	.239	.169	.408	.202	.223	.424
ENJ	.741	--------	.741	.689	--------	.689
$R^2 = 0.60$						

7 DISCUSSION

This research attempts to provide a validated conceptual model that integrates different factors and clarifies the theoretical problems of continuance e-shopping intentions and behavioral differences among women on online annual spending in Saudi Arabia. The online field survey validates the hypothesized model, and the model findings confirm that perceived enjoyment, perceived usefulness, and subjective norms are the main determinants of continuance intentions in Saudi Arabia, explaining 60% of continuance e-shopping intentions. However, enjoyment is more influential (see Table 6; srw = 0.527, cr = 11.481), followed by subjective norms (srw = 0.178, cr = 5.521), and then perceived usefulness (srw = 0.183, cr = 4.888). These findings are consistent with previous research (e.g., Bhattacherjee 2001a; Childers 2001; Davis et al. 1989; George 2002; Shih and Fang 2004; Taylor and Todd 1995; Teo et al. 1999; Venkatesh et al. 2003). Enjoyment, perceived usefulness, and subjective norms have positive influences (direct and indirect) on consumers' continuance e-shopping intentions.

The measurement weights of low and high online spending among female shoppers, based on metric invariance, are invariant. Testing for factorial regression paths invariance, we find that relationship path between site quality → trust; trust → perceived usefulness; perceived usefulness → subjective norms; perceived usefulness →enjoyment; subjective norms → enjoyment; perceived usefulness → continuance intentions; subjective norms → continuance intentions; and enjoyment → continuance intentions are similar for both low and high online spenders among women in Saudi Arabia. However, the site quality → perceived usefulness relationship path is non-invariant (high spenders rw = 5.665; low spenders rw = 2.641). That is, higher online spenders tend to accept technology, because these women perceive high quality content, good design, simple navigation, ease in finding necessary information, and ease of communication (utilitarian and hedonic experiences), which in turn increase the level of usefulness they perceive.

The model factorial paths for site quality and trust indicate strong antecedents of perceived usefulness on the regression weights (site quality srw = 0.361, cr = 5.804; trust srw = 0.430, cr = 6.754) (see Table 6). Both site quality (east = 0.438; west = 0.413; central = 0.415) and trust (east = 0.266; west = 0.284; central = 0.280) have great indirect effects on continuance intentions (see Tables 17–19). These findings match the collectivist culture of Saudi Arabia, where people tend to trust only those within their in-group (Yamagishi and Yamagishi 1994). They similarly may apply to other collectivist cultures or other nations in the Gulf States that appear similar to Saudi Arabia in various traits.

Trust and site quality do not have direct effects on continuance intentions toward the online retailer. Rather, significant indirect effects from trust and site quality move through perceived usefulness, subjective norms, and enjoyment. This model pertains to post-purchase behavior after a first-hand experience and provides confirmation of the effects of consumer initial trust and usefulness expectations, which lead to greater usefulness and put more pressure on social contacts to use and enjoy the site.

8 CONCLUSION AND CONTRIBUTIONS

From a theoretical standpoint, these results contribute to existing literature in several ways. First, we enhance e-shopping literature by providing insights into the factors that seem to affect online shopping continuance intentions for women with high and low spending habits in Saudi Arabia. We also posit that enjoyment, subjective norms, and perceived usefulness have direct and indirect effects on continuance intention. Furthermore, the greater positive indirect effects of site quality on perceived usefulness, subjective norms, and enjoyment and that of trust on enjoyment and subjective norms suggest that online retailers should increase the positive perceptions of trust and site quality to make their e-shopping environment more useful and enjoyable. To have a significant effect on e-shopping continuance intentions, any e-shopping environment should encourage a shopping experience that is useful and enjoyable.

Second, the results support previous research that shows perceived usefulness reflects the utilitarian aspects of online shopping, and perceived enjoyment reflects its hedonic aspects. In our study, enjoyment has the strongest effect on e-shopping continuance intentions, which confirms that enjoyment in an online shopping environment is important and has a direct effect for women with either high or low online spending habits in Saudi Arabia. Moreover, this result demonstrates that perceived enjoyment has a stronger direct and indirect effect on e-shopping continuance intentions. Usefulness came next as it is an important criterion for female consumers when they select online stores; it can increase their satisfaction. Consumers may continue using an e-commerce service they consider useful, even if they are dissatisfied with it (Bhattacherjee 2001a).

Third, few prior studies use SEM as their methodological approach, and even fewer apply invariance analysis to verify behavioral online spending differences with a sample obtained from Saudi Arabia. This study addresses this knowledge gap.

9 RESEARCH LIMITATIONS AND FURTHER RESEARCH

Typical of most field surveys, this study suffers some limitations. First, the novelty associated with using an online survey in the Saudi Arabian market indicates the empirical data may be biased by a novelty effect. Second, the online survey was posted with permission on Saudi universities' online forums. The survey may suffer a non-response bias, but there is no systematic way to test for the response rate.

More research should address the online context in Saudi Arabia, including ways to appeal to both hedonic and utilitarian shoppers, especially its youth population. Researchers also could extend and apply this approach in other cultures, whether those similar to Saudi Arabia, to confirm that the findings generalize to other collectivist cultures, or to cultures very unlike the Gulf states, to determine whether women in other nations behave differently when shopping online. This research shows that the well-established TAM can be integrated with ECT, which should prompt additional research related to continuance intentions, such as comparisons of new e-shoppers with continuing users, who have Internet knowledge and experience.

The continuance intention antecedents reveal direct and indirect effects, as well as online spending differences. The impact of additional factors, such as satisfaction, loyalty, and interactivity, and the moderating effect of different demographic factors, such as income, age, gender, regional and e-shopping experience, should be considered in further research.

9.1 Managerial Implications

This study provides managers with useful and important information about planning their Web sites and marketing strategies. Managers and site developers should focus on quality and informative content, which reflect usefulness and enjoyment. Knowing consumer behavioral patterns is critical for improving customer acquisition, retention, and relationship penetration. Managers should work to minimize churn, because customers who never return reduce the firm's customer base and revenues and require substantial expenditures to lure them back from competitors. According to the Pareto principle 80% of revenue from a customer base comes from 20% of the customers. Therefore, managers must identify and focus on higher spenders to retain them and generate more revenue.

To build sustainable, continued e-shopping relationships, managers cannot ignore either direct (perceived usefulness, enjoyment, subjective norms) or indirect (site quality, trust, perceived usefulness, subjective norms) influences on continuance intentions. Moreover, they should build positive word of mouth to enhance the perceptions of friends and family members of current customers about the Web site's usefulness, site quality, interactivity, and enjoyment, which can increase perceptions of the firm's trustworthiness. The return will maximize the value of customer expenditures for mutual company/customer gain.

This study draws attention to the direct and indirect differences among high and low female e-shoppers' spenders in Saudi Arabia, which should influence any Web site development and marketing strategy. Understanding the online spending differences between consumers can help managers identify high spenders and shift consumers from single visits to ongoing, trusted, useful, and enjoyable relationships, which should produce more stable, long-run business for online firms in Saudi Arabia.

REFERENCES

Adams, D. A., Nelson, P. R., and Todd, P. A., (1992). Perceived usefulness, ease of use and usage of information technology: a replication. *MIS Quarterly*, 16(2), 227-47.

Agarwal, R. And Prasad, J. (1999). Are individual differences germane to the acceptance of new information technologies? *Decision Sciences*, 30(2) 361-391.

Al Riyadh, (2006). Challenge bad the future of e-com in Saudi Arabia. Issue 13943, year 43, 27\8\2006. Retrieved April 4, 2007, from http://www.alriyadh.com/2006/08/27/article182047.html

Alden, Dana L., Jan-Benedict E. M. Steenkamp, and Rajeev Batra (2006). Consumer Attitudes Toward Marketing Globalization: Antecedent, Consequent and Structural Factors. *International of Research in Marketing*, 23 (3), 227-39.

Alreck, P., & Settle, R.A. (2002). Gender Effects on Internet, Catalog and Store Shopping. *Journal of Database Marketing*, 9(2), 150-162.

Alsajjan, B., Dennis, C., (2009). Internet banking acceptance model: cross-market examination", *Journal of Business Research*, forthcoming.

Anderson, E. W., and Sullivan, M. W., (2993). The Antecedents and Consequences of Customer Satisfaction for Firms. *Marketing Science*, 12(2), 125-143.

Arab News Newspaper (2007), Airlines Initiate E-Ticketing Process to Meet Deadline, Retrieved July 10, 2007, from
http://www.arabnews.com/?page=9&section=0&article=96844&d=30&m=5&y=2007

Babin, B. J., Darden, W. R., and Griffen, M. (1994). Work and/or fun: measuring hedonic and utilitarian shopping value. *Journal of Consumer Research*, 49 (2), 91-99.

Bagozzi R. Yi Y., (1988). On the evaluation of structural equation models. *Journal of the Academy of Marketing Science*, 16, 74-94.

Bagozzi, R (1994). *Principles of Marketing Research*. Blackwell Publishers Inc. Massachusetts

Barnes, S. J. and Vidgen, Richard, (2000). Information and Interaction quality: Evaluating Internet Bookshop Web sites with SERVQUAL. Proceedings of the 13th International E-Commerce Conference, BLED.

Bentler, P.M., (1989). *EQS Structural Equations Program Manual*", BMDP Statistical Software, Los Angeles.

Bentler, P.M., D.G. Bonett, (1980). Significance tests and goodness of fit in the analysis of covariance structures. *Psychological Bulletin,* 88(3), 588-606.

Bhattacherjee, A. (2001). Understanding Information Systems Continuance: An Expectation-Confirmation Model. *MIS Quarterly*, (25)3, pp. 351-370

Bhattacherjee, A. (2001a). An empirical analysis of the antecedents of electronic commerce service continuance. *Decision Support Systems*, 32(2), 201-214.

Brislin R. (1986). *The Wording and Translation of Research Instruments, in: Field Methods in Cross-Cultural Research*. Beverly Hills: W. Lonner and J. Berry, eds, Sage.

Burke, R. R. (1996). Virtual shopping breakthrough in marketing research. *Harvard Business Review*, 74 (2), 120-131.

Business Wire (1999), Online Investing Market Grows by 37% in 1998; online Investors Expect Impact to be felt by Full Service and Discount Firms, Retrieved Feb. 2009, from http://www.businesswire.com/webbox/bw.021199/1100662.html.

Byrne, B. (2001). SEM with AMOS: *Basic concepts, applications, and programming*. Routledge.

Carl, J., (1995). Online service users: loyal as alley cats? *Web Week*, 1(7).

Cheung, G. W., & Rensvold, R. B. (1999). Testing factorial invariance across groups: a reconceptualization and proposed new method. *Journal of Management* **25**(1), 1–27.

Childers, T., Carr, C., Peck, J., & Carson, S. (2001). Hedonic and utilitarian motivations for online retail shopping behavior. *Journal of Retailing*, 77(4), 511-535.

Coppel, J. (2000). E-commerce: impacts and policy challenges. OECD Economics Department Working Papers, No. 252, OECD Publishing. Doi: 10.1787\801315684632

Crego, E. T., Jr., and Schiffrin, P. D., (1995). *Customer-Centered Reengineering: Remapping for Total Customer Value*, Irwin, Burr Ridge, IL.

Dabholkar, P. A.; Shepard, C. D.; and Thorpe, D. I. (2000). A Comprehensive Framework for Service Quality: an investigation of critical conceptual and measurement issues through a longitudinal study. *Journal of Retailing,* 76(2), 139-173.

Davis, F. D., (1989). Perceived Usefulness, Perceived Ease of Use and User Acceptance of Information Technology. *MIS Quarterly*, 13(3) 319-340.

Davis, F. D., Bagozzi, R. P., and Warshaw, P. R., (1989). User Acceptance of Computer Technology: A Comparison of Two Theoretical Models. *Management Science*, 35(8) 982-1003.

Davis, F. D., R. P. Bagozzi and P. R. Warshaw (1992). Extrinsic and Intrinsic Motivation to Use Computers in the Workplace. *Journal of Applied Social Psychology*, (22)1111-1132.

Dishaw, M. T., and Strong, D. M. (1999). Extending the technology acceptance model with task-technology fit constructs. *Information and management*, 36(1), 9-21.

Fazio, R. H., and Zanna, M. P., (1981). Direct Experience and Attitude Behavior Consistency in Advances in Experimental Social Psychology. L. Berkowitz (ed.), *Academic Press*, New York, 6, 161-202.

Feinberg, R. A., R. Kadam, et al. (2002). The state of electronic customer relationship management in retailing. *International Journal of Retail &amp* 30(10).

Festinger, L. A., (1975), "*A Theory of Cognitive Dissonance*", Row and Peterson, Evanston, IL.

Foucault B E and Scheufele Laroche, M., Yang, Z., McDougall, G. H. G. and Bergeron, J. (2005). Internet versus bricks and mortar retailers: an investigation into intangibility and its consequences. *Journal of Retailing*, 81(4), 251-267.

Fung, R.K.K., Lee, M.K.O., (1999). EC-trust (trust in electronic commerce): exploring the antecedent factors. In Haseman, W.D., Nazareth, D.L. (Eds.), Proceedings of the Fifth *Americas Conference on Information Systems*, August 13–15, 517–519.

Ganesan, S. (1994). Determinants for Long-Term Orientation in Buyer-Seller Relationships. *Journal of Marketing,* 58 pp. 1-19.

Gefen, D. and Straub, D. W. (1997), "The relative importance of perceived and adoption of email: an extension to the technology acceptance model", *MIS Quarterly*, 21(4), 389-400.

Gefen, D., and Keil, M. (1998). The impact of developer responsiveness on perceptions of usefulness and ease of use: An extension of the technology acceptance model. *The DATA BASE for advances in information Systems*, 29(2), 35-49

Gefen, D., and Straub, D. W., (2000). The Relative Importance of Perceived Ease-of-Use in IS Adoption: A Study of E-Commerce Adoption. *Journal of the Association for Information Systems*, 1(8), 1-30

Gefen, D., Karahanna, E. and Straub, D.W. (2003). Trust and TAM in online shopping: An integrated model. *MIS Quarterly*, 27(1), pp. 51-90.

George, H. F., (2002). Influences on the Internet to make purchases. *Internet Research*, 1(2) 165-80.

Griffith, Davis A., Matthew B. Myers, and Michael G. Harvey (2006). An Investigation of National Culture's Influence on Relationship and Knowledge Resources in Interorganizational Relationships between Japan and the United States. *Journal of International Marketing*, 14(3), 1-32.

Hair J. Black W. Babin B. Anderson R. Tatham R. (2006). *Multivariate Data Analysis*, (6th) Pearson Education.

Hendrickson, A. R., Massey, P. D., and Cronan, T. P. (1993). On the test-retest reliability of perceived usefulness and perceived ease of use scales. *MIS Quarterly*, 17 (2), 227-230.

Holmes-Smith, P. (2000). *Intoduction to Stractural Equation Modelling Using AMOS 4.0 and LISREL 8.30*. School Research, Evaluation and Meaurement Services, Canberra.

Holt, Douglas B., John A., Quelch, and Earl L. Taylor (2004). How Global Brands Compete. *Harvard Business Review*, 82(9) 68-75.

Igbaria, M., Livari, J., and Maragahh, H. (1995). Why do individuals use computer technology? A finish case study. *Information and Management*, 29, 227-38.

Igbaria, M., Parasuraman, S., and Baroudi, J. J. (1996). A motivational model of microcomputer usage. *Journal of Management Information Systems*, 13(1), 127-143.

Jarvenpaa, S.L., Tractinsky, N., & Vitale, M, (2000). Consumer trust in an Internet store. *Information Technology & Management*, 7(1-2), 45-71.

Karahanna, E.; Straub, D. W.; and Chervany, N. L. (1999). Information Technology Adoption Across Time: A Cross-Sectional Comparison of Pre-Adoption and Post-Adoption Beliefs. *MIS Quarterly*, 23(2) 183-213

Koufaris, M. L., (2002). Applying the technology acceptance model and flow theory to online consumer behaviour. *Information System Research*, 13(2) 205-23.

Lai V. Li H., (2005). Technology acceptance model for Internet banking: an invariance analysis. *Information & Management*, 42, 373-386.

Leader, A. L., Maupin, D. J., Sena, M. P., and Zhuange, Y. (2000). The technology acceptance model and the World Wide Web. *Decision Support Systems*, 29(3), 269-282.

McKnight, D.H., Choudhury, V. and Kacmar, C., (2002a). The impact of initial consumer trust on intentions to transact with a web site: a trust building model. *Journal of Strategic Information Systems*, 11(3-4) 297-323.

McKnight, D.H., Choudhury, V., & Kacmar, C. (2002b). Developing and validating trust measures for e-commerce: An integrative typology. *Information Systems Research*, 13(3), 334-359.

Meltzer, M., Customer Profitability: Information Just Isn't Enough, CRM Forum. Reterived Feb. 2009, from http://www.crm-forum.com/crm_forum_white_papers/cpie/ppr.htm.

Meyerson, D., Weick, K.E., Kramer, R.M. (1996). Swift trust and temporary groups. In: Kramer, R.M., Tyler, T.R. (Eds.), *Trust in Organizations: Frontiers of Theory and Research*, Sage, Thousand Oaks, CA, 166–195.

Moon, J. W., and Kim, Y. G., (2001). Extending the TAM for a world-wide-web context. *Information and Management*, 38(4), 217-230.

O'Keefe, R., O'Connor, G. And Kung, H. J. (1998). Early adopters of the Web as a retail medium: small company winners and losers. *European Journal of Marketing*, 32(7/8), 629-643.

Oliver, R. L. (1980). A Cognitive Model for the Antecedents and Consequences of Satisfaction. *Journal of Marketing Research*, 17 460-469.

Oliver, R. L. (1993). Cognitive, Affective, and Attribute Bases of the Satisfaction Response", *Journal of Consumer Research*, CRM Forum, 20, 418-430.

Patterson, P. G.; Johnson, L. W.; and Spreng, R. A. (1997). Modeling the Determinants of Customer Satisfaction for Business-to-Business Professional Services. *Journal of the Academy of Marketing Science*, 25(1) 4-17.

Peterson, R. A., Balasubramanian, S, and Bronnenberg, B. J. (1997). Exploring the implications of the Internet for consumer marketing", *Journal of the Academy of Marketing Science*, 25(4) 329-46.

Petrissans, A., (1999). Customer Relationship Management: The changing economics of customer relationship. *IDC and Gap Gemini*, white paper.

Rogers, E. M. (1995). *Diffusion of Innovations* (4th ed), Free Press, New York.

Shih, Y. Y., Fang, K. (2004). The use of decomposed theory of planned behavior to study Internet Banking in Taiwan, *Internet Research*, 14(3) 213-223

Shim S, Eastlick M A, Lotz S L and Warrington P (2001). An online prepurchase intentions model: the role of intention to search. *Journal of Retailing*, 77: 397-416.

Shop.org & Boston Consulting Group, (2000). State of Online Retailing 3.0. Washington, D. C., National Retail Federation. [http://www.shop.org].

Spreng, R. A.; MacKenzie, S. B.; and Olshavsky, R. W., (1996). A Reexamination of the Determinants of Consumer Satisfaction", *Journal of Marketing,* 60, 15-32.

Straub, D. W. and Watson, R. T. (2001). Research commentary: transformational issues in researching IS and net-enabled organizations. Information Systems Research, 12(4), 337-345.

Subramanian, G. H., A. (1994). Replication of perceived usefulness and perceived ease of use measurement, *Decision Sciences,* 25 (5/6), 863-874.

Succi, M. J., and Walter, Z. D. (1999). Theory of user acceptance of information technologies: an examination of health care professionals. Proceedings of the 32nd Hawaii *International Conference on System Sciences* (HICSS), 1-7.

Swan, J. E., and Trawick, I. F. (1981). Disconfirmation of Expectations and Satisfaction with a Retail Service. *Journal of Retailing,* 57, 49-67.

Taylor, S., and Todd, P. A., (1995b). Understanding Information Technology Usage: A Test of Competing Models. *Information Systems Research*, 6(2) 144-176.

Teo, T. S. H., Lim, V. K. G., and Lai, R. Y. C. (1999). Intrinsic and extrinsic motivation in Internet usage. *Omega*, 27(1), 25-37.

Tse, D. K., and Wilton, P. C., (1988). Models of Consumer Satisfaction: An Extension. *Journal of Marketing Research*, 25, 204-212

Urban, G.L., Sultan, F., and Qualls, W.J. (2000). Placing trust at the center of your Internet strategy. *Sloan Management Review,* 42(1), 39.

van der Heijden, H. (2003). Factors Influencing the Usage of Websites - the Case of a Generic Portal in the Netherlands. *Information & Management*, (40)6, 541-549

Van Slyke, C., Comunale, C., & Belanger, F. (2002). Gender Differences in Perceptions of Web Based Shopping. *Communications of ACM*, 45(7), 82-86.

Venkatesh, V. and F. Davis (2000) "A Theoretical Extension of the Technology Acceptance Model: Four Longitudinal Field Studies", Management Science, (46)2, pp. 186-204.

Venkatesh, V., (1999). Creation of favorable user perceptions: exploring the role of intrinsic motivation. *MIS Quarterly*, 23(2), 239-260.

Venkatesh, V., (2000). Determinants of Perceived Ease of Use: Integrating Control, Intrinsic Motivation, and Emotion into the Technology Acceptance Model. *Information Systems Research*, 11(4), 342-365.

Venkatesh, V., C. Speier and M. G. Morris (2002). User Acceptance Enablers in Individual Decision Making About Technology: Toward an Integrated Model. *Decision Sciences*, (33)2, 297

Venkatesh, V., M. G. Morris, G. B. Davis and F. D. Davis (2003). User Acceptance of Information Technology: Toward a Unified View. *MIS Quarterly*, (27)3, 425-478

Venkatesh, V., Morris, M., & Ackerman, P. (2000). A Longitudinal Field Investigation of Gender Differences in Individual Technology Adoption Decision Making Processes. *Organizational Behavior and Human Decision Processes*, 83(1), 33-60.

World Internet Users and Population Stats. Areterived April 4, 2007, from http://www.internetworldstats.com/stats.htm

Yamagishi T. Yamagishi M., (1994). Trust and commitment in the United States and Japan. *Motivation and Emotion*, Vol. 18, pp 129-166.

Yang, Z. and R. T. Peterson. (2004). Customer perceived value, satisfaction, and loyalty: The role of switching costs. *Psychology & Marketing* 21(10), 799.

Yi He, Michael A. Merz, Dana L. Alden. (2008). Diffusion of Measurement Invariance Assessment in Cross-National Empirical Marketing Research: Perspectives from the Literature and a Survey of Researchers. *Journal of International Marketing* 16(2), 64 – 83

Yi, M. Y. and Y. Hwang (2003). Predicting the Use of Web-Based Information Systems: Self-Efficacy, Enjoyment, Learning Goal Orientation, and the Technology Acceptance Model. International Journal of Human-Computer Studies, 59(4), 431-449.

4

3D Product authenticity model for online retail:
An invariance analysis

Raed Algharabat
Brunel Business School, Marketing Department, Brunel University
Elliot Jaques Building, Uxbridge, Middlesex, UB8 3PH, United Kingdom

Email: raed.algharabat@brunel.ac.uk

Charles Dennis
Brunel Business School, Marketing Department, Brunel University
Elliot Jaques Building, Uxbridge, Middlesex, UB8 3PH, United Kingdom

Email: charles.dennis@brunel.ac.uk

Abstract

This study investigates the effects of different levels of invariance analysis on three dimensional (3D) product authenticity model (3DPAM) constructs in the e- retailing context. A hypothetical retailer website presents a variety of laptops using 3D product visualisations. The proposed conceptual model achieves acceptable fit and the hypothesised paths are all valid. We empirically investigate the invariance across the subgroups to validate the results of our 3DPAM. We concluded that the 3D product authenticity model construct was invariant for our sample across different gender, level of education and study backgrounds. These findings suggested that all our subgroups conceptualised the 3DPAM similarly. Also the results show some non-invariance results for the structural and latent mean models. The gender group posits a non-invariance latent mean model. Study backgrounds group reveals a non-invariance result for the structural model. These findings allowed us to understand the 3DPAMs validity in the e-retail context. Managerial implications are explained.

Keywords: 3D product authenticity, control, animated colours, value, behavioural intention, invariance analyses

1 INTRODUCTION

Scholars (e.g., Li et al., 2001, 2002, 2003) classify experiences, based on the interaction between a product or an environment and an individual, into three types. First, direct experience permits consumers to interact (e.g., physically) directly with a product. Second, indirect experience often allows consumers to interact with second-hand source such as static visual pictures. Third, virtual experience allows consumers to interact with three dimensional (3D) virtual models. According to Steuer (1992, p.78) virtual reality (VR) is *"a real or simulated environment in which a perceiver experiences telepresence"*. In contrast, virtual experience (VE) derives from VR and can be defined as *"psychological and emotional states that consumers undergo while interacting with a 3D environment"* (Li et al., 2001, p. 14). A 3D presentation enables consumers to interact with products, enriches their learning processes, and creates a sense of being in a simulated real world. Furthermore, direct and virtual experiences combine within VR, such that the latter enhances and enriches the overall experience because consumers use almost all of their senses when interacting with a 3D product visualisation (Klein, 2003; Li et al., 2001, 2002, 2003). Despite widespread discussions and various definitions of VE, we notice that previous scholars, within the online retail context, consider the notions of 3D telepresence as virtual substitutes for actual experience with the products. However, the telepresence and presence constructs are not necessarily wholly appropriate concepts for marketers since they represent a process of being mentally transported into other areas or being immersed into an illusion environment. Such notions may not be particularly helpful for marketers and website designers who are concerned with 3D product visualisation of real products. Instead, we propose the 3D product authenticity construct, which refers to simulating a real product authentically online. We therefore first discuss the notions of telepresence or presence in the immersive virtual reality (IVR) environment then proceed to explain applications of non-immersive virtual realties (NIVR i.e., an online retailer context). We also offer a new definition and measurement scale for the construct of 3D authenticity. Furthermore, we introduce the 3D product authenticity model to replace the telepresence model in the virtual reality environment. To validate our findings of the 3D product authenticity model, we investigate the effects of different levels of invariance analysis, across gender, levels of education and study backgrounds subgroups.

2 THEORETICAL BACKGROUND

2.1. 3D Product Visualisation in the Immersive and Non-Immersive VR

VR terminologies enter the vocabulary with the emergence of IVR devices, such as head-mounted display, which allow users to interact with virtual environments and to visualise different objects (Suh and Lee, 2005). As a result, the notions of telepresence or presence emerge. Notwithstanding, previous literature in the IVR area has provided readers with different classifications and conceptualisations of VR experience. For example, Steuer's (1992, p. 76) definition of VR focuses on human experience, not technological hardware, and differentiates between two types of VE; presence and telepresence. Whereas presence refers to *"the experience of one's physical environment; it refers not to one's surroundings as they exist in the physical world, but to the perception of those surroundings as mediated by both automatic and controlled mental processes"*, telepresence is *"the experience of presence in an environment by means of a communication medium"*. In turn, Sheridan (1992) distinguishes between virtual presence and telepresence, such that presence relates to the sense of being in a computer-mediated environment, whereas telepresence indicates a sense of being in any real remote location. However, Biocca (1992) defines VE (based on the telepresence construct) as users' ability to be, psychologically, transported into another area. To that end, Biocca and Delaney (1995) argue that the definition of virtual reality experience depends on technological hardware and software. The authors define VE as perceptual immersion. This type of VE depends on sensory immersion in virtual environments. To extend prior literature, Lombard and Ditton (1997) identify six taxonomies of VE: social richness, realism, transportation, immersion, social actor within medium and medium as social actor. Notwithstanding Lombard and Ditton's (1997) classification, two types of presence are identified in the NIVR area, concerning users interaction with e-retailers' websites and products using desktop or laptop computers (Suh and Lee, 2005). The first is telepresence, or the illusion of being in a place far from the physical body (Biocca, 1997; Heeter, 1992). This conceptualisation of telepresence relates to transporting a user, self, or place, to another place. The second form is telepresence in a social sense, such that other beings exist in the VR world with whom users can interact (e.g., avatars). Authors such as Heeter (1992) and Lombard and Ditton (1997) empirically test this concept, and McGoldrick and colleagues (2008) emphasise the avatar's role in enhancing virtual personal shopper capabilities. Moreover, to identify the main determinants of VE within IVR, researchers follow interactivity and vividness theories. For example, previous scholars (Biocca & Delany, 1995; Heeter, 1992; Lombard & Ditton, 1997; Sheridan, 1992; Steuer, 1992) assert that interactivity and vividness may represent the main antecedents of virtual reality experience. Interactivity appears particularly of interest since the appearance of new communication channels such as the World Wide Web, for which it represents a critical concept and primary advantage (Rafaeli & Sudweeks, 1997). Considerable research investigates and empirically tests the construct, but there is little agreement on the definition or operationalisation of the interactivity construct (e.g., Ariely, 2000; Klein, 2003; Liu & Shrum, 2002; McMillan & Hwang, 2002). For example, Steuer (1992) classifies it into three elements: speed, mapping and range. Rafaeli and Sudweeks (1997) argue interactivity relates to the communication process, and Ariely (2000) defines it on the basis of the control construct (the narrowest definition). Rowley (2008) focuses on information interactivity. Still other scholars (e.g., Lui & Shrum, 2002; McMillan & Hwang, 2002) argue that definitions of interactivity cannot be restricted to messages, human interactions or communications but rather should include multidimensional aspects. Thus speed, responsiveness and communications represent the main elements to define and measure interactivity construct. In contrast, vividness, according to Steuer (1992, p. 81) is *the way in which an environment presents information to the senses*. Steuer explains that vividness is stimulus driven and depends completely on the technical characteristics of a medium. In turn, it represents a product of two important variables: sensory breadth, and sensory depth. Most scholars use this definition of vividness.

To that end, Lee (2004) revises all the previous definitions of telepresence or presence and argues that none of the previous definitions could be used to tap the concept of using virtual environment to reflect consumers' virtual experience. The author posits two ways for an experience to become a virtual. First, using "Para-authentic objects" in which the users interact with objects in which they can find in real life aspects such as clothing. Secondly, using "Artificial objects", which simulates objects that do not exists in real life. On that basis, we claim that using the notions of 3D telepresence or presence and their definitions to define VE neither help marketers and e-retailers to understand the effect of 3D product visualisation on consumers' VE, nor suit the online retail context. Because (i) these notions represent a process of being mentally transported into other areas or being immersed into an illusion environment, such notions often reflect negative meanings such as immersion, delusion and transportation (Lee, 2004); (ii) presence and telepresence measurement scales, were originally built upon external devices, such as head-mounted display, which are not used in online retailers' 3D virtual model; and (iii) the lack of agreement upon the antecedents of telepresence and presence (interactivity and vividness) often complicates measuring the 3D product visualisation VE, and (iv) these notions measure VE based on different technologies (see Table 1). For example, to measure VE, Shih (1998) proposes a conceptual framework. Coyle and Thorson (2001) focus on videocassette movies. Klein (2003) employs a simple technology such as Authorware © 3.0 and 4.0, and Hopkins *et al.* (2004) investigate websites VE. Moreover, we notice that only few of the previous studies focused on the use of 3D product visualisation to measure VE (see Table 1). For instance, Li et al. (2001, 2002, 2003) and Fiore et al. (2005a) measured VE using 3D product visualisation. Unfortunately, both studies measured it based on the telepresence construct. Based on the above gaps, we claim that a 3D virtual experience should be an authentic representation of the direct (offline) experience. The concept of 3D authenticity of the product visualisation implies that ability of the 3D to simulate the product experience in bricks-and-clicks contexts. We felt that it is important to measure how consumers, within the online retail context, could imagine that 3D presented products. Particularly, we introduced our new construct, namely, 3D product authenticity to reflect customers' virtual experience, where customers can feel the authenticity of the 3D products.

Table 1: Previous research on online VR using 3D telepresence

Study	Sample	Stimuli	Virtual experience measurement	Virtual experience antecedents	Invariance analysis
Shih (1998)	Conceptual paper	N/A	Conceptual	Vividness (breadth and depth) and interactivity (speed and control)	N/A
Coyle and Thorson (2001)	Students	Videocassette movies. Blues music CDs. Women's golf clothing and equipment. Hot sauces.	Transporting into another place; being there.	Vividness (breadth and depth) and interactivity (speed and control)	N/A
Li et al. (2001)	Students	3D products: Bed, ring, watch, laptop computer.	Illusion and Immersion	Virtual experience is vivid, involving, active, affective and psychological states	N/A
Li et al. (2002)	Students	3D/2D bed, ring, watch, laptop advertisements	Presence: based on physical engagement, naturalness, and negative effects.	Interactivity and media richness	N/A
Li et al. (2003)	Students	3D/2D product type: wristwatch, bedding material and laptops	Telepresence and virtual affordance	Interactivity and media richness	N/A
Klein (2003)	Non-students	Authorware © 3.0 and 4.0 Study = 1, Wine Study = 2, Face cream	Telepresence: transporting into another area	User control and media richness (full-motion video and audio)	N/A
Hopkins et al. (2004)	students	Website for the National Arbor Day Foundation	Telepresence: being there	Vividness (media richness)	N/A
Fiore et al. (2005a)	Students	Clothing (3D virtual model)	Telepresence: being there	Interactivity and vividness	N/A

3D Product Authenticity (3DPA) Construct

None of the previous definitions of telepresence or presence that use 3D virtual models realistically taps consumers' virtual experiences. A 3D virtual experience should be an authentic representation of the direct (offline) experience. We therefore propose a new notion that relates to the simulation of online products and virtual experience, namely, the authenticity of the 3D product visualisation. Telepresence and presence are not particularly well suited to the online retail context, because they reflect illusion and transportation to other places. In contrast, the concept of 3D authenticity of the product visualisation implies the ability to simulate the product virtual experience in bricks-and-clicks contexts. We propose the following definition of perceived 3D product authenticity in a computer-mediated environment: 3D Product Authenticity (3DPA) is a *psychological state in which virtual objects presented in 3D in a computer-mediated environment are perceived as actual objects in a sensory way.* Furthermore, we identify users' ability to control the content and form of the 3D flash (interactivity), animated colours (vividness) and 3D authenticity as the main elements of the 3D virtual experience. Moreover, we define control and animated colours as the main antecedences of 3D authenticity.

3 RESEARCH MODEL

We demonstrate our research model in Figure 1. Our model is testing the relationships between control, animated colours, 3D product authenticity, hedonic and utilitarian value and behavioural intention. As the objective of our study is 3D product authenticity model's measurement equivalence, the focus of our model is concentrated on whether gender, education levels and study backgrounds affect participants' responses to our 3D product authenticity model.

3.1 3D Product Authenticity Antecedents and Definitions

We use the control construct to represent interactivity in an online retail context. Ariely's (2000) definition of control refers to users' abilities to customise and choose Web site contents to achieve their goals. We focus more on consumers' ability to control and easily interact with the 3D virtual model. Therefore, we define control as *users' abilities to customise and choose the contents of the virtual model (i.e., 3D product visualisation), rotate, and zoom in or out on the product in the virtual model and the ability of the virtual model (3D) to respond to participants' orders properly.* In turn, we hypothesise:

H_{1a}: *A high level of control of 3D product visualization increases 3D authenticity.*

Furthermore, 3D vividness should facilitate virtual experience by providing more sensory depth and breadth (Li et al., 2002, 2003). High-quality online animations enhance perceived reality of the 3D products (e.g., Fortin and Dholakia, 2005; Klein, 2003; Shih, 1998). Specifically, we consider vividness of the visual imagery, such that consumers can see online products with different colours (skins) just as they would see them in person. Media richness may lead to a real (authentic) experience, according to research on online shopping (Algharabat and Dennis, 2009a; Klein, 2003; Schlosser, 2003). Moreover, consumers' ability to change the animation (colours) of the 3D product might help them sense control over the product. We therefore hypothesise:

H_{1b}: *A high level of 3D animated colours increases perceived 3D authenticity.*
H_2: *A high level of 3D animated colours increases control.*

3.2 Effects of 3D products Authenticity on Utilitarian and Hedonic Value

To identify the main consequences of using authentic 3D product visualisations, and to explain cognitive and emotional experiences that consumers might have from navigating an authentic 3D product visualisation, we follow the hedonic and utilitarian value theories (based on Babin et al., 1994; Fiore et al., 2005a). Scholars (e.g., Fiore and Jin, 2003; Fiore et al., 2005a; Kim et al., 2007; Klein, 2003; Li et al., 2001, 2002, 2003; Suh and Chang 2006) explain the importance of using 3D product visualisations in enhancing consumers' understanding of product attributes, features and characteristics. 3D visualisation increases consumers' involvement and encourages them to seek more information about the products (Fiore et al., 2005a). Suh and Lee (2005) posit a positive relationship between higher levels of 3D product visualisation and seeking more information about the products' characteristics and features. Suh and Chang's (2006) empirical research of the influence of 3D product visualisation and product knowledge reveals a positive relationship between 3D and perceived product knowledge. Using 3D product visualisation helps consumers to imagine how a product may look and it gives them more details about the products' characteristics (Fortin and Dholakia, 2005; Klein, 2003; Shih, 1998). Therefore, we hypothesise:

H_{3a}: 3D authenticity in a retailer website will positively affect website use for utilitarian value.

Scholars (Fiore et al., 2005b; Kim and Forsythe, 2007; Lee et al., 2006; Schlosser, 2003) report the importance of 3D product visualisation in enhancing the experiential aspects of a virtual shopping. The above researchers find that the ability of 3D product visualisation to produce hedonic values for shoppers is greater than its ability to produce utilitarian values. Fiore et al. (2005b) assert that 3D virtual model produces hedonic value, which is highly correlated with consumers' emotional pleasure and arousal variables. Fiore et al. (2005a) posit the importance of virtual models in boosting hedonic value (enjoyment). Fiore et al. (2005a) also report the importance of 3D virtual model technology in producing more hedonic value. Many scholars in the communication field (e.g., Heeter, 1992; Lombard and Ditton, 1997; Song et al., 2007) report the importance of enjoyment as a consequence of using 3D. Consumers use 3D product visualisation to have more fun, enjoyment and entertainment (Kim and Forsythe, 2007). Such sources of fun or enjoyment come from consumers' ability to rotate, and zoom in or out on the product (Fiore et al., 2005a), seeing different animated coloured pictorial images that may enhance their mental pleasure when using 3D sites.

H_{3b}: 3D authenticity in a retailer website will positively affect website use for hedonic value.

3.3 Effects of 3D Product Authenticity, Utilitarian and Hedonic Value on Behavioural Intention

The role of 3D product visualisation in enhancing behavioural intentions appears well supported; 3D utilitarian and hedonic values improve willingness to purchase from an online retailer (Fiore et al., 2005a, 2005b), intention to buy (Schlosser, 2003) and purchase intentions (Li et al., 2001; 2003). Moreover, 3D realism improves users' beliefs and attitudes towards an online store (Klein, 2003). Therefore,

H_{3c}: *The relationship between 3D authenticity and behavioural intention is positive.*
H_{4a}: *The relationship between utilitarian value and behavioural intention is positive.*
H_{4b}: *The relationship between hedonic value and behavioural intention is positive.*

Figure 1: Conceptual framework (source: the authors)

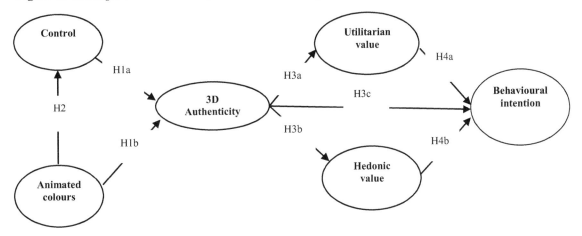

4 METHODS

4.1 *Stimuli*

A retailer's website with one stimulus was custom-designed for this study. The stimulus was illustrated in 3D product visualisation sites in which participants can see, the focal product, laptops from different angles; they can rotate it and zoom it in or out. The 3D stimulus is designed to help consumers to imagine the product in appropriate and relevant ways and it enhances consumers' virtual experiences (Li et al., 2001). Moreover, we decide to use the 3D stimulus which users can control (content and form) and see from different colours to bridge the gaps in measuring VE using the 3D product visualisation. Previous scholars measure VE based on movies, simple technology but not 3D product visualisation. Moreover, those who use the 3D product visualisation measure it based on the telepresence construct (see Table 1).

4.2 Interface Design

We designed one stimulus, a 3D flash (site), for testing the proposed hypotheses. The site allows participants to control the content and form of the 3D flash. For example, participants can zoom in or out on the product, rotate it and can see different parts of the product when clicking on it. The 3D flash permits participants to change the colour of the laptop and see it with animated colours. Also the flash allows participants to get actual and perceived information about the laptop features and attributes. Moreover, our site enhance participants' fun and enjoyment values by enabling them to control (i.e., to zoom in or out on and rotate), to change the colour of the laptop and to see more information about the product (see Appendix A). In designing this interface, we consider a comprehensive site to visualise an electrical online retailer to surpass actual experience. Moreover, this study adds more features and cases to the ones that might be found in real sites. For example, none of the national sites that sell laptops (e.g., Sony and Dell, to the best of the authors' knowledge) has a flash combining both 3D and information about laptops. The website we created for this study was not previously known to users, nor did users have any knowledge of the fictitious brands on the site. Thus, we eliminated any impact of previous experiences or attitudes (Fiore et al., 2005a). The site offers a wide variety of laptops, similar to those that many college-aged women and men currently buy and use. Therefore, site provides a suitable context for the present sample.

4.3 Participants

Student samples are well suited to online shopping research (e.g., Balabanis & Reynolds, 2001; Fiore et al., 2005a; Kim et al., 2007; Li et al., 2002, 2003), because they are computer literate and have few problems using new technology. Students also are likely consumers of electrical goods (Jahng et al., 2000). We employed a sample of 312 students to perform this study. The sample was gender balanced, consisting of 48% women and 52% men, and 90% of the sample ranged from 18 to 30 years of age. Approximately 90% reported having had prior online shopping experience.

4.4 Instrument

Participants were informed that this study pertained to consumers' evaluations of an electrical retailer's Web site. The questionnaire contained five-point Likert-type scales, anchored by "strongly disagree" and "strongly agree".

To measure the control construct, we developed a five-item scale that centres on users' ability to rotate and zoom in or out the virtual model based on Liu and Shrum's (2002); McMillan and Hwang's (2002) and Song and Zinkhan's (2008) studies. To measure animated colours, we developed a four-item animated colour scale based on Fiore and colleagues (2005a), Klein's (2003), Steuer's (1992) studies. The items tap how closely the simulated sensory information reflects the real product. We could not find an existing scale to measure 3D product authenticity so we developed a new five-item scale. We submitted the items to evaluations by academics (lecturers in online retailing and Ph.D. students); these respondents considered the items relevant for measuring the authenticity construct. We followed Churchill's (1979) procedures for developing a marketing construct scale and adopted Christodoulides and colleagues (2006) procedures for developing a scale for the online context. Each item began with "After surfing the 3D sites", and then obtained responses to the following: "3D creates a product experience similar to the one I would have when shopping in a store", "3D let me feel like if I am holding a real laptop and rotating it" (i.e. virtual affordance), "3D let me feel like I am dealing with a salesman who is responding to my orders", "3D let me see the laptop as if it was a real one", and "Being able to zoom in/out and rotate the laptop let me visualise how the laptop might look in an offline retailer". To measure hedonic values, we adopted a modified version of Babin and colleagues (1994) scale. We based the study on 4 of the 11 items. To measure utilitarian values, we adopted a modified version of Fiore and colleagues (2005a) scale. To measure Behavioural intention, we used a modified version of Fiore and colleagues (2005a) scale. See Table 2 for the purified items.

5 RESULTS

5.1 Measurement Model for the 3D Product Authenticity Model

We evaluated the measurement and structural equation models using AMOS 16. The measurement model includes 23 indicators, and we provide its results in Table 2, including the standardised factor loading, standard error (S.E), critical ratios (C.R), composite reliability, squared multiple correlation and average variance extracted (AVE) for each construct. The standardised factor loadings (λ) are all greater than .61. The composite reliabilities for control (.80), animated colours, (.782), 3D authenticity (.86), utilitarian (.85), hedonic (.86) and behavioural intention (.88) are acceptable (Hair et al., 2006). Moreover, average variance extracted by each construct exceeds the minimum value recommended by Hair et al. (2006), (i.e., exceeds .5).

Table 2: Measurement model results for hypothetical 3DPAM.

Construct Indicator	Standard-ised factor loading (λ)	S.E	C.R	Average Variance extracted	Squared multiple correlation	Composite reliability
η1 (Control)				0.50 •		0.80
- I felt that I could choose freely what I wanted to see	.78	–			0.602	
- I felt that I had a lot of control over the content of the laptop's options (i.e. angles and information)	.71	0.077	12.097		0.508	
- I felt it was easy to rotate the laptop the way I wanted.	.71	0.076	10.009		0.503	
- I felt I could control the laptop movements.	.61	0.071	8.916		0.369	
η2 (Animated colours)				.502		0.78
-There are lots of colours on 3D laptop websites.	.79	–			0.631	
- Colours brightness of the 3D laptop let me visualize how the real laptop might look.	.71	0.067	11.391		0.499	
- The laptop illustrated by 3D was very colourful	.61	0.064	10.099		0.375	
η3 (3D Authenticity)				.608		0.86
- 3D Creates a product experience similar to the one I would have when shopping in a store.	.77	–			0.598	
- 3D Let me feel like if I am holding a real laptop and rotating it (i.e. virtual affordance)	.79	0.078	14.093		0.628	
- 3D Let me feel like I am dealing with a salesman who is responding to my orders.	.81	0.078	14.581		0.656	
- 3D let me see the laptop as if it was a real one.	.74	0.076	13.293		0.550	
η4 (Hedonic value)				0.59		.86
- Would be like an escape.	.64	–			0.411	
- Would be truly enjoyable	.77	0.105	12.752		0.589	
- Would be enjoyable for its own sake, not just for the items I may have purchase.	.88	0.128	11.987		0.722	
- Would let me enjoy being immersed in an existing new product.	.79	0.144	11.123		0.618	
η5(Utilitarian value)				.582		0.85
- Help me make a better decision about the product.	.80	–			0.637	
- help me buy the right product.	.92	0.079	16.179		0.844	
- Aid me in evaluating the laptop items.	.69	0.067	12.481		0.475	
- Help me in finding what I am looking for	.61	0.066	11.002		0.375	
η6 (Behavioural intention)				0.631		.88
- After seeing the web site, how likely is it that you would buy a laptop from this online store.	.81	–				
- I would be willing to purchase a laptop through this online store.	.82	0.061	16.151			
- I intend to buy a laptop from this online store.	.82	0.075	15.323			
- I would be willing to recommend this online retailer to my friends.	.72	0.059	13.160			

5.2 Structural Equation Model for the 3D Product Authenticity Model

The hypothesised model achieves a chi-square of 350.225 (df = 219), with a goodness-of-fit index (GFI) of .911, comparative fit index (CFI) of .965, root mean square residual (RMR) of .038 and root mean square error of approximation (RMSEA) of .044, normed fit index (NFI) of .912, relative fit index (RFI) of .9, incremental fit index (IFI) of .965, and χ^2/df = 1.599. These results indicate a good fit of the data to the model (Byrne, 2001; Hair et al., 2006). Furthermore, the structural equation model confirms that control and animated colours have significant positive effects on 3D authenticity (H_{1a} t = 2.098; H_{1b} t = 7.951). Moreover, animated colour exhibits a significant positive effect on control (H_2 t = 7.888). Finally, as we hypothesized, 3D authenticity, hedonic and utilitarian values have positive effects on behavioural intention (H_{3c}: 2.465, $H4_a$: t = 2.216, $H4_b$: t= 2.454). Table 3 reports estimates, standardised estimates, and critical ratio for each hypothesized path. All the hypothesized paths are supported ($p < .05$).

Table 3: Summary of results of structural model estimation

Standardised regression paths (β)		Estimate	S.E	C.R	P	Hypothesis
H_1	Animated colours → Control	.539	.068	7.888	***	Supported
H_{2a}	Control → 3D Authenticity	.165	.079	2.098	.036	Supported
H_{2b}	Animated colours → 3D Authenticity	.672	.085	7.951	***	Supported
H_{3a}	3D Authenticity → Utilitarian	.470	.055	8.567	***	Supported
H_{3b}	3D Authenticity → Behavioural intention	.229	.093	2.465	.014	Supported
H_{3c}	3D Authenticity → Hedonic	.483	.054	8.875	***	Supported
H_{4a}	Utilitarian → Behavioural intention	.211	.086	2.454	.014	Supported
H_{4b}	Hedonic → Behavioural intention	..274	.124	2.216	.027	Supported

6 INVARIANCE ANALYSIS

We use the invariance analyses to determine the effects of gender, education levels and study backgrounds and their relationships in our conceptual framework. We start with conducting a measurement invariance analysis (measurement weight) for gender, education levels and study backgrounds to determine whether, for example, the males and females groups would use the same pattern in measuring the observed items. If the result is invariant, then the data of each group is suitable for further analysis (i.e., structural invariance analysis). However, if the two groups understood the items in different ways (i.e., non-invariance), then, we identify the source of the non-invariance. To do so, we identify the observed item(s) that caused the non-invariance. If the result of the measurement model is invariance, then, we go to the next step. However, if the results still non-invariant, then, we stop the analysis.

Secondly, after having the insignificant results in the measurement model, we conduct the invariance structural model analysis to determine if gender, education levels and study background groups have invariance or non-invariance results in perceiving the relationships between the unobserved constructs. To conduct this analysis, we follow two steps; (i) if the members of any group (e.g., the males and females groups) perceive the relationships between the constructs similarly (i.e., invariance), then, we move to the third step (i.e., latent mean invariance analysis), (ii) however, if the members of any group perceive the relationships between the constructs differently (i.e., non-invariance), then we determine the source of the non-invariance. Moreover, if the structural model analyses are non-invariance, we calculate the un-standardised direct, indirect and total effects. Thirdly, we conduct the latent mean invariance analyses among latent constructs to determine if the groups have perceived each construct similarly (invariance) or differently (non-invariance). In all the three previous steps, we report $\Delta\chi^2$ and Δdf and fit indices (TLI, CFI and RMSEA) models for the comparison purposes.

6.1. Invariance Analysis Results

The invariance analyses provide a better understanding of our conceptual model and its constructs invariance validity. Following a series of invariance analyses, we could conclude that our conceptual framework was invariant of measurement loading, structural loading and latent mean across gender, education level and study background. The following explains the invariance analysis and it reports the non-invariance models.

Gender

We classify the participants into two groups according to their gender (i.e., males or females). The measurement model results (Table 4) reveal insignificant differences between the males and females groups regarding the measurement and structural models. However, result shows a significant difference in the mean model. The females group is higher (.179) than the males group in perceiving the behavioural intention construct (Table 5).

Table 4: Results of factorial invariance analysis for gender: assuming model unconstrained to be correct.

Model	P	χ^2	df	$\Delta \chi^2$	Δdf	CFI	RAMSE
Measurement model	**.404**	635.786	455	17.761	17	.952	0.036
Structural model	**.082**	649.793	463	14.007	8	.952	0.036
Structural mean model	**.019**	650.619	464	15.136	6	.946	.950

Table 5: Means: (male-Measurement weight)

Construct (gender mean 312)	Estimate	S.E	C.R	P
Control	-.138	.088	-1.562	.118
Animation	.069	.069	.994	.320
Authenticity	.016	.097	.168	.867
Hedonic	.071	.065	1.092	.275
Utilitarian	.048	.055	.875	.382
Behavioural intention	.179	.069	2.581	.010

Education Level

The second invariance analysis classifies participants into two groups according to the participants' educational levels (undergraduates and postgraduates groups). The measurement model, structural model and latent mean model results reveal invariance differences (i.e., insignificant differences) between the undergraduates and postgraduates groups (Table 6).

Table 6: Results of factorial, structural and mean invariance analysis for education: assuming model unconstrained to be correct.

Model	P	χ^2	df	$\Delta \chi^2$	Δdf	CFI	RAMSE
Measurement model	**.562**	649.828	455	15.466	17	.949	0.37
Structural model	**.240**	660.190	463	10.363	8	.943	.948
Structural mean model	**.072**	656.679	464	11.575	6	.945	.949

Participants' Study Backgrounds

The third invariance analysis classifies the participants into two groups according to the participants' study backgrounds (Business-Social and Maths-IT-Engineering groups). The measurement model and mean model results (Table 7) reveal insignificant differences between the Business-Social studies and the Maths-IT-Engineering studies backgrounds. However, structural model results reveal non-invariance (significant) differences between the Business-Social studies and the Maths-IT-Engineering studies groups in determining the relationships between the proposed constructs (Table 8). The relationships between 3D product authenticity→ hedonic, and hedonic → behavioural intention (BI) are the source of this non-invariance. In other words, both groups perceive the importance of the hedonic values differently.

Table 7: Results of factorial, structural and mean invariance analysis for background: assuming model unconstrained to be correct

Model	P	χ^2	df	$\Delta \chi^2$	Δdf	CFI	RAMSE
Measurement model	**.221**	675.953	455	21.115	17	.943	0.040
Structural model	**.010**	696.033	463	20.080	8	.934	.939
Structural mean model	**.664**	681.002	464	4.094	6	.938	.944

Table 8: Results of path coefficient invariance analysis for study background.

Model	P	χ^2	df	$\Delta \chi^2$	Δdf	TLI	CFI	RAMSE
Animation →Authenticity	.221	654.963	439	.125	1	.935	.944	.040
Control→ Authenticity	.589	655.131	439	.292	1	.935	.944	.040
3D Authenticity→ Hedonic	.002**	664.788	439	9.950	1	.932	.941	.041
3D Authenticity →Utilitarian	.128	657.156	439	2.317	1	.935	.943	.040
Utilitarian →BI	.295	655.934	439	1.096	1	.935	.944	.040
Hedonic → BI	.048*	658.745	439	3.906	1	.934	.943	.040
Animation → Control	.326	655.804	439	.966	1	.935	.944	.040
3D Authenticity →BI	.419	655.493	441	.654	1	.935	.944	.040

*$p < 0.05$; **$p < 0.01$.*

Table 9 shows the results of un-standardised indirect, direct and total effects- estimates for the Maths-IT-Engineering studies background group and the Business-Social studies background group.

Table 9: Results of un-standardised indirect, direct and total effects- estimates

Predictor variables	Behavioural intention toward the online retailer		
	Indirect effects	Direct effects	Total effects
Animated colours	.221	------	.221
Control	0.029	------	.029
3D Authenticity	.075	.230	.306
Utilitarian value	------	.169	.169
Hedonic value	------	.029	.029
R^2	.34		

Predictor variables	Behavioural intention toward the online retailer		
	Indirect effects	Direct effects	Total effects
Animated colours	.433	------	.433
Control	0.224	------	.224
3D Authenticity	.156	.419	.574
Utilitarian value	------	.069	.069
Hedonic value	------	.225	.225
R^2	.34		

Un-standardised indirect, direct and total effects- estimates

6 DISCUSSION

This research aims to measure 3D product visualisation virtual experience, to provide a validated conceptual model that integrates different constructs and to clarify the theoretical problems of using different measurement of the 3D virtual experience. Moreover, this research provides invariance analysis to determine the main moderators within our model. Our survey validates the hypothesised model, and the model findings confirm that animated colours and control are the main determinants of 3D authenticity (VE). Moreover, we find that the authenticity of the 3D model, hedonic and utilitarian values are the main determinants of users' behavioural intention. We follow a series of invariance analyses to confirm our results across gender, education levels and study background. Results show that our 3D product authenticity model is invariant in respect of measurement model. Furthermore, we find invariance results regarding the structural model across gender and education level. However, the non-invariance results appear well in the mean model (across gender) and the structural model (across study background). The difference (non-invariance) in the latent mean between males and females groups suggests that females tend to accept the idea of buying from our fictitious e-retailer more than the males group does. This result supports Tversky and Morrison's (2002) findings regarding the ability of the animated graphics to increase females' comprehension and learning. Moreover, the ability of the 3D flashes to enhance users' understanding of the laptops' features especially when using animations makes Females' ability to make purchase decisions (based on non-verbal cues) easier (Dennis et al., 1999) than men.

The non-invariance (significant) differences between Business-Social group and Maths-IT-Engineering groups clearly come in the relationships between the proposed constructs (i.e., the structural model). The 3D authenticity→ hedonic and the hedonic→ behavioural intention relationships are the source of the coefficients non-invariance. In other words, both groups perceive the importance of the hedonic values and the behavioural intention differently. That is, Maths-IT- Engineering group tend to accept that the 3D authenticity and the novelty of the 3D flash increases the level of fun and entertainment. On the other hand, Maths-IT- Engineering group does not accept that the high level of entrainment may end with a positive behavioural intention towards the online retailer. In regards to the un-standardised effects, students with the Maths-IT- Engineering backgrounds perceive the total effects of the 3D authenticity construct on the behavioural intention (.574) more than the Business-Social backgrounds (.306) do. This could be justified due to the Maths-IT- Engineering group ability to understand and criticize the novelty of the 3D more than the Business-Social backgrounds. However, the Business-Social background group perceives the total effects of the utilitarian values (.169) on behavioural intention more than the Maths-IT- Engineering group does. On the other hand, the Maths-IT- Engineering group perceives the total effects of the hedonic values (.225) on behavioural intention more than the human-studies group (.029) does. In contrast to the Maths-IT- Engineering group who perceives the direct effect of the hedonic values (.225) on behavioural intention more than utilitarian values (.069), the Business-Social studies group perceives the direct effect of the utilitarian values on behavioural intention (.169) more than the hedonic values (.029). These results could be explained as follows. First, Raijas (2002) finds that the experienced people know what they are looking for. Moreover, these results support the findings of Dennis and King (2009) and Dholakia and Chiang (2003) regarding shopping styles. In other words, when shopping for technical and expensive products shoppers who are Empathisers turn to become Systemisers and vise verse. Second, in comparison to the Business-Social group, the Maths-IT- Engineering group bought on average more laptops online (M $_{\text{Maths-IT- Engineering}}$ = 1.33, M $_{\text{Business-Social}}$ = 1.3) than the Business-Social group did. The Business-Social group are more interested in a laptop features and characteristics than entertainment features. The animation construct had the strongest indirect effect (.221, 433 respectively) in both groups. However, the indirect effect of the control construct in the Maths-IT- Engineering group (.244) is greater than the indirect effect of control on the Business-Social studies group (.029). Finally, in both groups, the 3D authenticity construct has the strongest direct effect and total effects.

7 CONCLUSION AND CONTRIBUTION

From a theoretical standpoint, our results contribute to the existing literature in several ways. First, previous research on VE has focused on three elements to surpass the offline (direct) experience; interactivity, vividness and 3D telepresence. However, we claimed that the notion of 3D telepresence reflects negative meanings. Instead we propose the notion of 3D authenticity to reflect the 3D virtual experience. Second, to solve the lack of agreement regarding defining and measuring the interactivity and vividness constructs. We narrowed the operationalisations of 3D authenticity antecedents to control and animated colours to reflect a real authentic VE. In line with other online retail researchers who investigated the influence of using 3D product visualisation on VE (Li et al., 2001, 2002, 2003), we find that marketers should focus on specific aspects of interactivity and vividness (rather than on the abstract constructs) when defining 3D virtual experience. For example, when it comes to 3D virtual models, we prefer focusing on the narrowest, most relevant aspects of interactivity (i.e., control). Whereas Heeter (2000, p. 75) describes interactivity as "*an overused and under defined concept*", we posit that control represents a useful construct for 3D models in the online retail context. Moreover, in support of previous research (Ariely, 2000; Coyle & Thorson, 2001) we narrow our conceptualisation of control to consumers' ability to control the content and form of the 3D flashes. In other words, users' ability to zoom in or out, rotate and get more information about the product enhances their perceptions of the authenticity of the 3D products. Furthermore, whereas prior research defines vividness according to sensory breadth and depth, we argue that research might benefit from a tighter focus on specific aspects of vividness through illustration, such as we have applied here. This result is in accordance with Pimentel and Teixeira's (1994, p. 146) study that asserts that visual stimuli are the main sensory cues in producing virtual experiences.

Third, our use of invariance analyses gives this research a plus, since previous research has not examined them in the context of 3D virtual experience. The invariance analyses led to another contribution, which highlights the importance of this research's conceptual framework applicability in the e-retailing area. Following a series of invariance analyses, it could be concluded that our conceptual framework is invariance of the measurement model, structural model and latent mean model across gender, education level, and study background. However, the effect of 3D authenticity on hedonic and the impact of hedonic on behavioural intention are moderated by study background. This result posits that the study background is a significant moderator between the effect of 3D authenticity on hedonic values, and the effect of hedonic value and behavioural intention. Marketers and website developers should focus on this moderator when designing 3D product visualisation for the online retailer. Any 3D flash should reflect more innovation in designing and it should reflect a state of enjoyment for students with Maths-IT- Engineering backgrounds and Business-Social group. This conclusion posits that overall all the subgroups conceptualise the constructs and variables (animated colours, control, 3D authenticity, utilitarian, hedonic, and behavioural intention constructs) similarly. Also, this suggests that our results have no obvious bias of gender, education level, and study background (Lai and Li, 2005).

8 MANAGERIAL IMPLICATIONS

E-retailers should pay more attention to 3D product authenticity antecedents, i.e., control and animated colour when designing their 3D virtual models. Including real colours and flashes that consumers can control easily will lead to more authentic online experiences. The direct and indirect effects of animated colours and control constructs reveal the importance of these constructs within the 3D e-retail context. Any 3D flash should include the essential information that consumers seek rather than just a pretty picture. For example, consumers should be able to click on any part of the 3D flash to get access to information about it. Website developers should take advantage of technological advancements to develop and update online retailers' 3D flashes. Pechtl (2003) asserts a positive relationship between perceived innovation attributes and online adoption behaviour. Algharabat and Dennis (2009a) posit the importance of authentic 3D product to enhance users' hedonic and utilitarian values. Managers and Web sites designers should work together to ensure that the 3D product visualisation provides customers with the complete and accurate information they need. In addition, marketers should decide what information (or knowledge) to focus on before developing 3D flashes. It should be accepted that developing 3D flashes is not a money-free issue. Nevertheless, many companies have already claimed to have improved their sales as a result of designing and using 3D flashes. For example, J.C. Penny, eBags and Wal-Mart claimed that their online sales have increased 10% to 50% after using rich media such as 3D flashes (Demery, 2003). Moreover, Demery (2006) posits that the numbers of companies who are investing in 3D virtual models is increasing steadily because these companies are seeing the potential of the technology for selling more products. Nantel (2004) asserts that consumers shopping online for clothing are 26% more likely to purchase from the sites that have 3D virtual model than from sites that have not. Moreover, Fiore (2008) posits that media richness is an important way to differentiate retailers. Wagner (2000) asserts that online retailers with 3D product visualisations may reap benefits that extend beyond sales. For example, 3D increases site stickiness: users will spend more time on the online retailer, which leads to more opportunities to learn more about the products, interact with them, build trust and confidence. Finally, according to the Social Issues Research Centre (SIRC, as cited in Herrod, 2007) study it is expected that "by 2020 virtual commerce (v-commerce) will replace e-commerce" and the development of 3D virtual models (such as 3D virtual shopping malls) will be leading the whole industry by 2020.

9 LIMITATIONS AND FURTHER STUDIES

Although the generalisability of the results is limited by the student sample, and cannot be generalised to all online consumer groups, we argue that students represent the shoppers of tomorrow (Algharabat and Dennis, 2009b; Balabanis and Reynolds, 2001) and the research thus has prescient value. Second, since this study has focused only on laptops, which we consider to be products that are associated with more search or experience, it is unclear to what extent the results can be generalised and applied to other online products. On the bases of our results, we recommend that website developers should pay more attention to simulating 3D animation colours to reflect the real products more authentically. Moreover, they should work to create an environment in which consumers sense that they can feel the online products when they navigate the site. We recommend research efforts to extend the generalisability of our findings to other contexts (e.g., clothing) and to non-student samples. Further research may add and test other stimuli, for example by simulating real sounds to investigate how auditory vividness may influence 3DPAM.

APPENDIX A

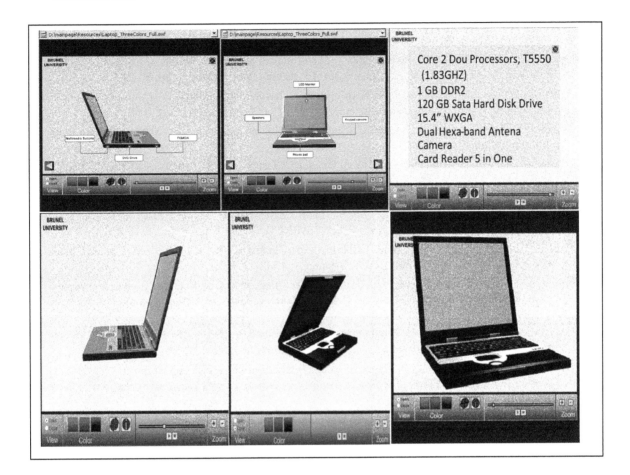

REFERENCES

Algharabat, R. and Dennis, C. (2009a). Using authentic 3D product visualisation for an electrical online retailer. *12th International Conference on Retailing and Commercial Distribution Teaching and Research Issues*, EAERCD, Surrey University, 15-17 July.

Algharabat, R. and Dennis, C. (2009b). Modelling 3D product visualisation on the online retailer. *Academy of Marketing, Annual conference 2009, Putting Marketing in Its Place*, Leeds Metropolitan University, 6-9 July.

Ariely, D. (2000). Controlling the information flow: Effects on consumers' decision making and preferences. *Journal of Consumer Research*, Vol. 26 (September), pp. 233-248.

Babin, Barry J., William R. Darden, and Mitch Griffin. (1994). Work and/or Fun: Measuring Hedonic and Shopping Value, *Journal of Consumer Research*, Vol. 20 (March), pp. 644–56.

Balabanis, G., and Reynolds, N. (2001). Consumer attitudes towards multi-Channel retailers' Web Sites: The role of involvement, brand attitude, internet knowledge and visit duration. *Journal of Business Strategies*, Vol. 18 (Fall), pp. 105-131.

Biocca, F. (1992). Will simulation sickness slow down the diffusion of virtual environment technology?, *Presence*, Vol. **1, No** 3, pp. 334–343.

Biocca, F. (1997). The cyborg's dilemma: progressive embodiment in virtual environments. *Journal of Computer-Mediated Communication*, Vol. 3, No 2. Available at: http://www.ascusc.org/jcmc/vol3/issue2/biocca2.html, [Accessed 14th November 2007]

Biocca, F., and Delaney, B. (1995). Immersive virtual reality technology", In F.Biocca, and M. Levy (Eds.). *Communication in the age of virtual reality* (pp.57-124). Hillsdale, NJ: Erlbaum.

Byrne, B. (2001).*Structural Equation Modeling with AMOS*. Lawrence Erlbaum Associate New Jersey, U.S.A.

Christodoulides, G., Leslie, C., Olivier, F., Eric, S., and Temi, A. (2006). Conceptualising and Measuring the Equity of Online Brands. *Journal of Marketing Management*, Vol. 22, pp. 799-825.

Churchill, G. (1979). A Paradigm for Developing Better Measures of Marketing Constructs. *Journal of Marketing Research,* Vol. XVI, pp. 64-73.

Coyle, James R., and Thorson, Esther. (2001). The effects of progressive levels of interactivity and vividness in web marketing site, *Journal of Advertising*, Vol. 30, No. 3, pp. 65-77.

Demery, P. (2003, October). The latest flash", *Internet Retailer*. Available at http://www.internetretailer.com/article.asp?id=10323 , [Accessed 15th May 2009]

Demery, P. (2006, January). As consumers flock to high bandwidth, e-retailers shake, rattle and roll. *Internet Retailer*, pp. 23-28

Dennis, A., Kinney, S., and Hung, Y. (1999). Gender Differences in the Effects of Richness. *Small Group Research*, Vol. 30, No.4, pp. 405-437.

Dennis, C. and King, T. (2009). Development of a cross-market scale for femininity and masculinity expressed in shopping styles'. *12th International Conference on Retailing and Commercial Distribution Teaching and Research Issues*, EAERCD, Surrey University, 15-17 July.

Dholakia R, R. and Chiang, K-P. (2003). Shoppers in cyberspace: are they from Venus or Mars and does it matter?. *Journal of Consumer Psychology,* 13 (1/2): 171-176.

Fiore, A. M., Kim, J. and Lee, H.H. (2005a). Effects of image interactivity technology on consumer responses toward the online retailing. *Journal of Interactivity Marketing,* Vol. 19, No. 3, pp. 39-53.

Fiore, A., Jin, H. and Kim, J. (2005b). For fun and profit: hedonic value from image interactivity and responses towards an online store. *Psychology & Marketing*, Vol. 22, No. 8, pp. 669-94.

Fiore, A.M., & Jin, H.J. (2003). Influence of Image Interactivity on Approach Responses Towards an Online Retailer. Internet *Research: Electronic Networking Applications and Policy*, Vol. 13, pp.38-48.

Fiore, Ann. (2008). The digital consumer: Valuable partner for product development and production. *Clothing and Textiles Research Journal*, Vol. (26), No. (2), pp. 177-190

Fortin, D., and Dholakia, R. (2005). Interactivity and vividness effects on social presence and involvement with a web-based advertisement. *Journal of Business Research*, Vol. 58, 387-396.

Hair, J., Anderson, R., Tatham, R., and Black, W. (2006). *Multivariate Data Analysis,* Prentice-Hall, Upper Saddle River, NJ.

Heeter, C. (1992). Being there: the subjective experience of presence. *Presence: Teleoperators and Virtual Environments*, Vol. 1, pp. 262-71.

Heeter, C. (2000). Interactivity in the context of designed experiences. *Journal of Interactive Advertising*, Vol. 1, No. 1, pp. 75-89.

Herrod, E. (2007, May). E-commerce to 2020. *Internet Retailing*. Available at http://www.internetretailing.net/news/e-commerce-to 2020/?searchterm=3D [Accessed 15th May 2009]

Hopkins, C. D., Raymond, M, A., and Mitra, A. (2004). Consumer responses to perceived telepresence in the online advertising environment: the moderating role of involvement, *Marketing Theory,* Vol. 4, No. 137, pp. 137-63.

Jahng, J., Jain, H., and Ramamurthy, K. (2000). Effective design of electronic commerce environments: A proposed theory of congruence and an illustration, *IEEE Transactions on Systems, Man, and Cybernetics: Part A*, 30 (July), pp. 456–471.

Kim, J & Forsythe, S. (2007). Hedonic usage of product virtualisation technology in online apparel shopping. *International Journal of Retail and Distribution Management,* Vol. 35, No. 6, pp. 502-514

Kim, J., Fiore, A., and Lee, H. (2007). Influence of online store perception, shopping enjoyment, and shopping involvement on consumer patronage behaviour towards an online retailer. *Journal of Retailing and Consumer Services,* No.14, pp. 95-107.

Klein, L. (2003). Creating virtual product experiences: the role of telepresence. *Journal of Interactive Marketing*, Vol. 17, No. 1, pp. 41-55.

Lai, V., and Li, H. (2005). Technology acceptance model for internet banking: an invariance analysis. *Information & Management*, Vol. 42, pp. 373-386.

Lee, H.H., Fiore, A.M., Kim, J., (2006). The role of the technology acceptance model in explaining effects of image interactivity technology on consumer responses. *International Journal of Retail & Distribution Management*, Vol. 34, No. 8, pp. 621-644.

Li, H., Daugherty, T. and Biocca, F. (2001). Characteristics of virtual experience in electronic commerce: a protocol analysis. *Journal of Interactive Marketing*, Vol. 15, No. 3, pp. 13-30.

Li, H., Daugherty, T. and Biocca, F. (2002). Impact of 3-D advertising on product knowledge, brand attitude and purchase intention: the mediating role of presence. *Journal of Advertising*, Vol. 31, No. 3, pp. 43-57.

Li, H., Daugherty, T. and Biocca, F. (2003). The role of virtual experience in consumer learning. *Journal of Consumer Psychology*, Vol. 13, No. 4, pp. 395-407.

Liu, Y. and Shrum, L.J. (2002). What is interactivity and is it always such a good thing? Implications of definition, person, and situation for the influence of interactivity on advertising effectiveness. *Journal of Advertising*, Vol. 31. No. 4, pp. 53-64.

Lombard, M and Ditton, T. (1997). At the heart of it all: the concept of presence. *Journal of Computer-Mediated Communication*, Vol. 3, No. 2. Available at: http://jcmc.indiana.edu/vol3/issue2/lombard.html.

McGoldrick, P., Keeling, K., and Beatty, S., (2008). A typology of roles for avatars in online retailing. *Journal of Marketing Management*, Vol. 24, No. 3-4, pp. 433-461.

McMillan, S.J. and Hwang, J.-S. (2002). Measures of perceived interactivity: an exploration of the role of direction of communication, user control, and time in shaping perceptions of interactivity. *Journal of Advertising*, Vol. 31, No. 3, pp. 29-42.

Nantel, J. (2004). My virtual model: Virtual reality comes into fashion. *Journal of Interactive Marketing*, Vol. 18, No. 3, 73-86.

Pimentel, K., and Teixeira, K. (1994) *Virtual Reality: Through the New Looking Glass.* 2nd edn. New York: Intel/MacGraw-hill

Pechtl, H. (2003). Adoption of online shopping by German grocery shoppers. *The International Review of Retail, Distribution and Consumer Research,* No. 13, Vol. 2, pp. 145-159.

Pimentel, K., and Teixeira, K. (1994). *Virtual Reality: Through the New Looking Glass* (2nd ed.), Intel/MacGraw-hill, New York.

Rafaeli, S. and Sudweeks, F. (1997). Networked interactivity, *Journal of Computer Mediated Communication*, Vol. 2, No. 4. Available at: http://jcmc.indiana.edu/vol2/issue4/rafaeli.sudweeks.html, [Accessed 10th March 2008]

Raijas, A. (2002). The Consumer Benefits and Problems in the Electronic Grocery Store. *Journal of Retailing and Consumer Services*, Vol. 9, pp. 107-113.

Rowley, J. (2008). Understanding digital content marketing, *Journal of Marketing Management*, Vol. 24, No. 5-6, pp. 517-540.

Schlosser, A. (2003). Experiencing products in the virtual world: the role of goal and imagery in influencing attitudes versus purchase intentions. *Journal of Consumer Research*, Vol. 30, No. 2, pp. 184-198.

Sheridan, T.B. (1992). Musings on telepresence and virtual presence. *Presence, Teleoperators and Virtual Environments*, Vol. 1, No. 1, pp. 120-126.

Shih, C. (1998). Conceptualizing consumer experiences in cyberspace. *European Journal of Marketing*. Vol. 32, No. (7/8), pp. 655-663.

Song, J.H., and Zinkhan, G. M. (2008). Determinants of Perceived Web Site Interactivity. *Journal of Marketing*, Vol. 72(March), pp. 99-113.

Song, K., Fiore, A., and Park, J. (2007). Telepresence in online apparel shopping experience. *Journal of Fashion Marketing and Management*. Vol. 11, No. 4, pp. 553-570.

Steuer, J. (1992). Defining virtual reality: dimensions determining telepresence. *Journal of Communication*, Vol. 42, No. 4, pp. 73-93.

Suh, K., and Chang, S. (2006). User interface and consumer perceptions of online stores: the role of telepresence. *Journal of Behaviour & Information Technology*, Vol. 25, No. 2, pp. 99-113.

Suh, K., and Lee, Y. (2005). The effects of virtual reality on consumer learning: an empirical investigation. *MIS Quarterly*, Vol. 29. No. 4, pp. 673-697.

Tversky, B., and Morrison, J. (2002). Animation: Can it Facilitate?, *International Journal Human-Computer Studies*, 57, pp. 247-262

Wagner, M. (2000). Picture this: E-retailers aims to zoom, spin and model their way to higher sales. *Internet Retailer"*. Available at: http://www.internetretailer.com/internet/marketing-conference/90763-picture-this-e-retailers-aim-zoom-spin-model-their-way-higher-sales.html, [Accessed 15th May 2009]

5

TQM and firms performance: An EFQM excellence model research based survey

Maria Leticia Santos-Vijande
Department of Business Administration, University of Oviedo
Avda. del Cristo, s/n, 33071, Oviedo, Asturias. Spain

Email: lsantos@uniovi.es

Luis I. Alvarez-Gonzalez
Department of Business Administration, University of Oviedo
Avda. del Cristo, s/n, 33071, Oviedo, Asturias. Spain

Email: alvarezg@uniovi.es

Abstract

The purpose of this article is to develop an instrument for measuring TQM implementation following the European Foundation for Quality Management Excellence Model and to provide empirical evidence on the relationship between management practices and measures of business performance in the model. To this end, the study employs survey data collected from Spanish manufacturing and service firms. Confirmatory factor analysis is used to test the psychometric properties of the measurement scales and the hypothesized relationships between total quality management practices and organizational performance are examined using structural equation modeling. The findings of the research indicate that the adoption of the TQM practices suggested in the EFQM Excellence Model allows firms to outperform their competitors in the results criteria included in the Model. Therefore, this paper provides a valuable benchmarking data for firms as it substantiates the EFQM Enabler's contribution to the attainment of competitive advantage.

Keywords: total quality management, business performance, competitive advantage, EFQM excellence model, Spain

1 INTRODUCTION

Since the 1980s, when the total quality management (TQM) concept was firstly defined (Deming, 1986, Crosby, 1979, Juran, 1986), practitioners and researchers alike have broadly defended the positive effects of TQM practices on firms' overall effectiveness and performance. However, although TQM has been clearly conceptualized around basic principles such as consumer focus, continuous improvement and human resource management, there has been a lack of consensus regarding its primary constructs, which prevents comparison across studies and generalizations from the empirical evidence. The 90s mark the starting point of empirical research on critical factors in TQM, although different studies have yielded different sets of TQM factors (Saraph et al., 1989; Flynn et al., 1994; Powell, 1995; Ahire et al., 1996; Black and Porter, 1996; Zhang et al., 2000; Antony et al., 2002). As a result, there is no single measurement instrument to evaluate TQM implementation.

Furthermore, evidence concerning the impact of TQM on business performance is also based on a wide range of indicators that differ across studies and are in some cases contradictory, especially regarding financial performance, which is measured in terms of ROA –return on assets- or ROI –return on investment. Some research has found a positive effect of TQM on the latter (Easton and Jarrell, 1998; Hendricks and Singhal, 2001a,b); whereas other research reports a negative incidence of TQM on these measures (Chapman et al., 1997). In some cases, TQM's repercussion on these financial outcomes is even deemed inexistent (Adam, 1994; Powell, 1995; York and Miree, 2004). The different methodological and conceptual approaches used by researchers may have led to conflicting results but, in response to this controversial evidence, a new body of research is examining a contingent approach to the TQM-performance relationship. This approach assumes that the effects of TQM on business results are mediated by both non-controllable environmental factors, such as market competitiveness, uncertainty or complexity (Fuentes, 2003; Chong and Rundus, 2004), and by internal factors, such as how long TQM has been implemented, or the firms' size, diversification or capital intensity (Terziovski and Samson, 1999; Hendricks and Singhal, 2001a; Brah et al., 2002; Lloréns et al., 2003; Taylor and Wright, 2003).

Obtaining sound evidence of TQM's impact on performance in different contexts should be as much a priority as addressing the potential moderators of this link. TQM is one of the most complex activities that any company can involve itself in; it requires implementing a new way of managing business and a new working culture which not only affect the whole organizational process and all employees but also demand the allocation of significant organizational resources. Firms therefore need to be fully convinced of the trade-offs provided by TQM, particularly if time elapses before the desired results are felt, or if substantial organization stress has to be overcome in the short term to adopt the necessary organizational change (Brah et al., 2002). However, most research undertaken so far relates to companies operating in developed countries, mainly USA, UK and Australia (Sila and Ebramhimpour, 2002), although some researchers have focused on developing economies such as India (Motwani et al., 1997, Rao et al., 1997), Saudi Arabia (Curry and Kadasah, 2002) and Palestine (Baidoun, 2004).

To reinforce the benefits of TQM it is also advisable to facilitate comparison across studies by avoiding differing conceptualizations and TQM-related measures. Accordingly, it has recently become a common practice to link research to the criteria of well-known Quality Award models (Woon, 2000; Rahman, 2001; Prajogo and Sohal, 2004). Quality Awards provide a useful assessment framework against which organisations can evaluate their quality management practices and their end business results, and constitute a common benchmark or standard criteria for firms operating under their area of influence. We advocate the use of these models as a TQM benchmark in their respective geographical area of influence (i.e. countries), as they offer firms several advantages, including the immediate chance to assess their closest competitors' TQM practices and the outcomes that may be expected. Consequently, the aim of this study is to develop an instrument to measure TQM implementation based on Quality Award applicable to the Spanish firms under study, i.e., the European Foundation for Quality Management (EFQM) Excellence Model, as well as to provide empirical evidence on the relationship between management practices and measures of business performance in the model.

The body of literature that analyzes the relationship between quality management and organizational performance resorting to quantitative data analysis, and adopting a comprehensive analysis of the EFQM quality practices and outcomes, is limited. The list becomes even shorter if we seek this analysis based on causal relationships and referred to business organizations (Bou-Llusar et al., 2005; Eskildsen and Dahlgaard, 2000). Given that this model represents the European standard to be achieved by firms involved in the TQM adventure, this study seeks to fill a gap in the literature by employing structural equations modelling (SEM) to test the criteria relationships. Our end purpose is to substantiate TQM's contribution to the attainment of competitive advantage, that is, the outperformance of competition as measured by the results criteria included in the EFQM Excellence Model.

The paper is structured as follows. We firstly review the TQM literature and the EFQM Excellence Model and describe the opportunities derived from the use of this framework as a guide to developing a TQM measurement instrument. The next section covers the methodology followed in the research, including details of how the measure instrument was constructed, the sample obtained and the research method employed. Thirdly, we address the evaluation of the scale's psychometric properties: namely, its reliability, validity of content, convergent validity and discriminant validity. Finally the causal model is tested, providing evidence on TQM outcomes.

2 LITERATURE REVIEW

TQM measurement

The literature's failure to provide a single, systems approach to TQM implementation is illustrated by Sila and Ebramhimpour (2002), who undertake a useful revision of the TQM survey-based research published in English between 1989 and 2000 - a total of 347 articles - and identify up to 25 TQM factors *most commonly* extracted from the 76 empirical studies that adopted an integrated or holistic view of TQM. They also offer a variety of reasons that may justify the appearance of different sets of TQM factors, mainly:

1) Differences in the conceptual approaches taken by researchers.

2) Differences in the empirical methodology followed: some studies use confirmatory factor analysis to verify the underlying factors of TQM (Wilson and Collier, 2000; Kaynak, 2003; Fuentes *et al.*, 2004), although most research basically employs factor analysis (FA).

3) Differences between countries' business, socio-political and socioeconomic environments (i.e. culture, education levels, information technology, government regulations, level of industrialization) that would prevent straightforward transferability and applicability of TQM concepts, principles, and practices (Sila and Ebramhimpour, 2002). This raises the question of the universal applicability of TQM (universalism), which has recently received the attention of several scholars (Newman and Nollen, 1996; Roney, 1997; Rungtusanatham *et al.*, 2005). In short, further research is still needed to determine whether TQM management practices and principles can transcend organizational and national boundaries or whether this concept can be subject to different interpretations in different environments.

In efforts to measure TQM world-wide, several Quality Awards have been used to guide research into TQM. These awards synthesize the common understanding of TQM practices for the firms operating under their area of influence. The most popular of them has been the Malcolm Baldrige National Quality Award (MBNQA) in USA (Black and Porter, 1996; Rao *et al.*, 1999; Samson and Terziovsky, 1999; Wilson and Collier, 2000; Pannirselvam and Ferguson, 2001; Prajogo and Sohal, 2004); although the Australian Business Excellence framework (ABE) (Rahman, 2001) and the Singapore Quality Award (Quazi and Padibjo, 1998; Woon, 2000) have also inspired several studies. This research is based in the EFQM Excellence Model, which is described in the following section together with a justification of its applicability to identifying TQM constructs.

The EFQM Model

The EFQM Excellence Model was introduced at the beginning of 1992 as the framework for assessing organisations for the European Quality Award. It is now the most widely used organisational framework in Europe (Eskildsen and Dahlgaard, 2000) and has become the basis for the majority of national and regional Quality Awards. The EFQM Excellence Model is a non-prescriptive framework based on 9 criteria as shown in Figure 1. Five of these are *"Enablers'* (leadership, people, policy strategy, partnership & resources, and processes) and four are 'Results' (people results, customer results, impact on society results and business results). The 'Enabler' criteria cover what an organisation does. The 'Results' criteria cover what an organisation achieves. 'Results' are brought about by 'Enablers', and 'Enablers' are improved using feedback from 'Results'. The Model, which acknowledges that there are many approaches to achieving sustainable excellence in all aspects of performance, is based on the premise that:

Excellent results with respect to Performance, Customers, People and Society are achieved through Leadership driving Policy and Strategy that is delivered through People, Partnerships and Resources, and Processes (EFQM, 2002).

Figure 1: EFQM Excellence Model

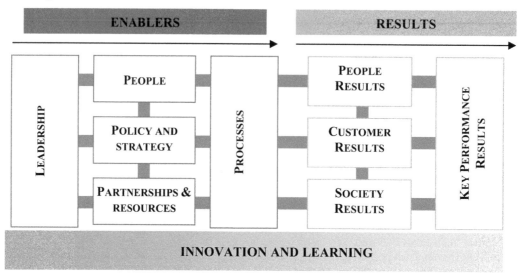

The EFQM Excellence Model is a practical tool that offers several advantages from the empirical research perspective, as do other Quality Awards:

- The model is regularly revised and updated, incorporating the contributions of EFQM consultants. Therefore, the set of constructs underlying the model is not limited to a single researcher's view of TQM, which also guarantees its comprehensiveness, dynamism and tracking of the latest developments in TQM.

- It provides an extensive set of sub-criteria to detail the exact meaning of each criterion. This facilitates the items' identification in the scale development.

- Additionally, award models are intended to be instruments for comparing an organisation with its competitors in order to achieve and/or maintain competitive advantage. When survey data based on these models is provided to the firms, the self-assessment of TQM implementation and the identification of areas for improvement in relation to the firm's closest competitors is substantially facilitated, which increases the practical implications of the research. The EFQM Excellence Model has obvious prestige among European firms as a sound quality standard and there is an ever-increasing number of firms involved in the recognition process to achieve the European Quality Award (EQA) (EFQM, 2006). As this happens, the benchmarking utility of the model increases.

- In the case of the EFQM Excellence Model, the increasing convergence of European markets dissipates any concern regarding the universalism issue. Therefore, empirical evidence relative to the effects on performance of TQM practices according to this model acquires great relevance for all firms competing in the European Union.

Previous research based on the EFQM Excellence Model has been devoted, in many cases, to conceptual developments or reflections on the application of the EFQM model (Cragg, 2005; Martín-Castilla, 2002; Rusjan, 2005; Westlund, 2001; Wongrassamee et al., 2003). Thus, researchers have addressed, for example, the problems associated with the self-assessment methodology used by the EFQM Excellence Model (Samuelson and Nilsson, 2002; Li and Yang, 2003), or the usefulness of the EFQM model to identify organizations' most representative resources and capabilities, that is, their basis for competitive advantage according to the resource-based view of the firm theory (Castresana and Fernandez-Ortiz, 2005). Several papers have also been dedicated to case studies specially within the education (Farrar, 2000; Hides, et al., 2004; Tarí, 2006) and health care sectors (Jackson, 2000; Jackson and Bircher, 2002; Moeller et al., 2000; Stewart, 2003). The literature also provides several research papers on the EFQM Excellence Model (i.e., papers based on quantitative research and that resort to multivariable analysis techniques), although these have not always adopted a holistic view of quality practices (Eskildsen and Dahlgaard, 2000; McCarthy and Greatbanks, 2006; Osseo-Asare et al., 2005). Among the research papers that analyze the full set of relevant dimensions in the EFQM Excellence Model (Bou-Llusar et al., 2005; Calvo-Mora et al., 2005; Eskildsen et al., 2001; Moller and Sonntag, 2001) the employment of methodologies that allow evaluating causal relationships between

Enablers and Results, namely Structural Equations Modeling (SEM), is more scarce (Bou-Llusar *et al.*, 2005).

In this context, our empirical work seeks to validate the nine criteria of the EFQM Excellence Model as constructs. To this end the paper provides an exhaustive analysis of the psychometric properties of the scales employed. The scale validation effort is important to assure the quality of the measure instruments or their ability to provide a sound and accurate measure of the concepts in the research model. The research also aims to determine the impact of the Enabler criteria on the Results predicted in the EFQM Model using SEM, that is, evaluating the notion of causality. Therefore, we give the "Results" constructs a separate status in our study as the dependent variables influenced by the TQM practices followed by organizations. This same approach has been followed by Samson and Terziovski (1999), who relate their investigation to the MBNQA criteria, and by Rahman (2001) who conceptualizes TQM using the Australian Business Excellence (ABE) framework as a guide. Thus, the following hypothesis is formulated:

H1: TQM practices according to the EFQM Excellence Model directly and positively influence organizational performance in the Results criteria shown in the Model.

Among the outcomes of TQM practices, the Key Performance Results category includes a wide variety of different types of performance indicators. In this study, we have selected those most consistently incorporated into previous research (Kaynak, 2003), namely financial performance, supplier support, process efficiency and cost reductions. The model to be tested is shown in Figure 2.

Figure 2: Research Model

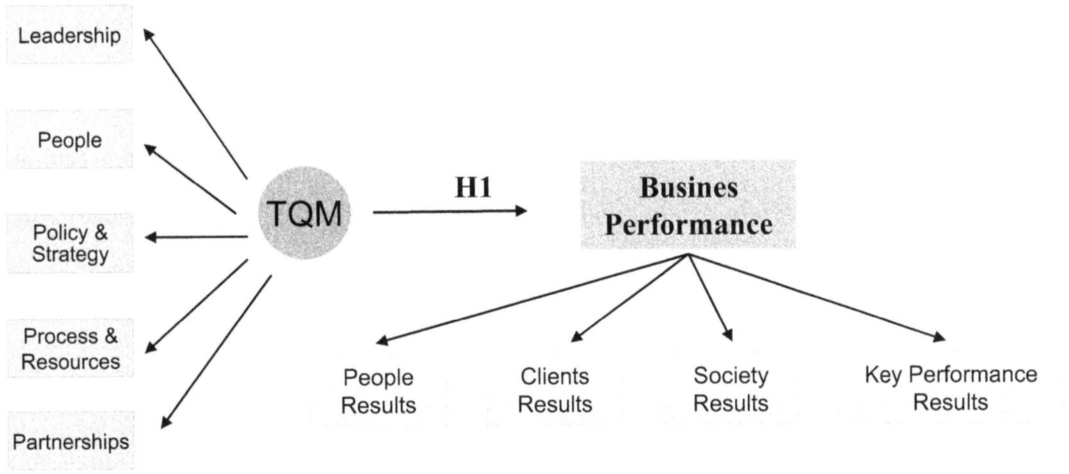

3 RESEARCH METHODOLOGY

Instrument development

There are several sub-criteria under each EFQM criterion that describe aspects of the criterion in more detail. These sub-criteria were used as a guide, as was previous empirical research on factors critical to TQM based on a holistic approach to this concept (Saraph et al., 1989, Flynn et al. (1994), Anderson et al. (1995), Badri et al., (1995), Powell (1995), Ahire et al. (1996), Black and Porter (1996), Ahire and O'Shaughnessy (1998), Grandolz and Gershon (1998), Quazi and Padibjo (1998), Anderson and Sohal (1999), Samson and Terkiovski (1999), Zhang et al. (2000), Antony et al. (2002) and Brah et al. (2002)). Many critical factors obtained in previous research not only show a clear correspondence with the EFQM criteria, but also the items that comprise have come through a validation process, which fully justifies using them in this study. A review of the literature and the EFQM Excellence Model provided over one hundred items from amongst the nine criteria. The different statements were evaluated to avoid duplications and the list was reduced to 81 items. The process entailed careful monitoring to ensure comprehensive coverage of the TQM concept. With statements for all the nine criteria completed, the questionnaire was pilot-tested using six respondents from the regional Quality Club Managerial Board. All the informants were the CEOs of each firm and their corresponding companies were not included in the random sample. The researchers undertook personal interviews of an average length of 90 minutes to carefully review the questionnaire. The interviewees have considerable managerial experience to examine the questions and they provided a valuable opinion about their readability, adequacy to the TQM measurement and correct understanding. As a result, several items were rewritten to facilitate their interpretation, to avoid confusion and thus prevent research bias. The items finally employed are listed and classified according to their main dimensions as shown in Appendix 1. Following Ahire and O'Shaughnessy (1998), a seven-point Likert scale was used for all items to ensure higher statistical variability among survey responses. Thus, for each TQM Enabler criterion, respondents evaluated how well the different statements described their companies practices on a scale from 1 ("strongly disagree") to 7 ("strongly agree"). In order to isolate TQM effects on performance and avoid confusion with other exogenous or endogenous factors, respondents were asked to evaluate the extent to which the sole contribution of these practices had led to the achievement of each of the performance indicators (1="not at all"; 7="a great deal"). That is, respondents are asked to indicate to what extent their firm's quality practices allow to achieve the evaluated variables of performance. This procedure does not "invoke" causality but rather avoids the TQM-performance relationship to be interfered either by uncontrollable variables or other organizational processes that can affect performance. In addition, performance was evaluated against the firms' main competitors to introduce an explicit reference to the attainment of competitive advantages (Weerawardena, 2003a and b; Chong and Rundus 2004; Prajogo and Sohal, 2006). The reference to the major competitor in the industry allows both minimising the industry effect and decreasing the response's subjectivity establishing a point of reference to make the comparison (Kraft, 1990); likewise, this fact allows assessing the achievement of competitive advantages in the matter in the period under consideration (Grant, 1991). The research seeks to establish whether the TQM practices suggested in the EFQM Excellence Model allows firms to outperform their competitors and can be considered a feasible path towards building competitive advantage. Therefore, in most cases performance was evaluated by the firms' CEOs, and the respondents selected their firm's main competitor according to their perceptual judgements. Total quality oriented firms can be presumed to have a strong market orientation which provides them with a reasonable knowledge of their clients and competitors' operations (Yam et al., 2005).

While perceptual judgements have a potential for self-reporting bias, prior research has also shown that perceived performance can be a reasonable substitute for objective measures and that managers prefer to avoid offering precise quantitative data (Taylor and Wright, 2003; Fuentes et al., 2004)

Sample and research method

Data for empirical testing and validating the TQM scale was obtained by means of a mail survey. The research population consisted of all the ISO 9000 registered firms in the Principality of Asturias, a total of 451 organizations according to the data provided by the Regional Quality Club. Certified firms were selected to guarantee a certain interest in quality management practices as well as familiarity with the issues addressed in the questionnaire (Curry and Kadasah, 2002). Similarly, ISO 9000 implementation may be seen as a stepping-stone towards TQM (Antony et al., 2002). The questionnaire was mailed to the General Manager or Managing Director of each organization to ensure a good knowledge of the firms' TQM practices and outcomes in relation to their competence. Thus, it is essential to guarantee that the survey's respondents do possess the knowledge required to answer the questions appropriately (Agus, 2000; Taylor and Wright, 2003; Weerawardena, 2003b). The questionnaire delivery included a cover letter and a pre-paid return envelope. The covering letter outlined the objectives and importance of the study, was signed by the President of the Regional Quality Club and included an assurance of confidentiality. The study was conducted between January and March of 2005. Telephone calls were made three weeks after the start to follow-up the study and another copy of the questionnaire was sent to several organizations when required. A final response rate of 20.6% was obtained, representing 93 firms from a range of manufacturing and service sectors. The proportion of respondents was equally distributed between manufacturing and non-manufacturing sectors (41.8 % and 58.2% respectively). The majority of the respondents (78.5%) were senior managers (General Manager or Managing Director), so they had the knowledge to answer the questions appropriately. Approximately, 8.4% of the firms had less than 10 employees, 44.6% had between 10 and 49 employees, 37% employed between 50 and 249 workers, and 10% had more than 250 employees.

4 PSYCHOMETRIC PROPERTIES OF MEASUREMENT SCALES

The psychometric properties of the measurement scales were assessed in accordance with accepted practices (Gerbing and Anderson, 1988) and included the establishment of content validity, reliability, convergent validity, discriminant validity and criterion-related validity. The scales validation involved both exploratory and confirmatory factor analysis using SPSS12.0 and EQS6.0 software respectively.

Reliability - stage one

The reliability of an instrument assesses its ability to yield the same results on repeated trials. Internal consistency is one of the methods that can be used for assessing reliability (Nunnally, 1978). It indicates how well the different items of a scale measure the same concept and it is generally measured by means of a reliability coefficient such as Cronbach's coefficient alpha. Cronbach's alpha was calculated separately for each of the constructs, with item-to-total scale correlations being plotting. Generally, reliability coefficients of 0.70 or more are considered good and it is advisable to eliminate those items that diminish the coefficient value. The results in Table 1 show that the values of Cronbach's alpha derived for the constructs ranged between 0.773 and 0.951, indicating a high reliability of the scales. Ten items were deleted after the reliability analysis shown in italics in Appendix 1.

At this point in our research we had still not checked for possible item overlap across the dimensions of both TQM practices and results. We therefore undertook a principal components analysis with varimax rotation for each set of Enabler and Result variables. A factor loading of 0.50 was used as the cut-off point. The results show that the statements corresponding to the same dimension load on a single factor, with the only exception of some items relating to resources management from the Partnership and Resources criterion (Part&res5 to Part&res8). These items load on the Processes factor. This fact is not conceptually surprising, given that resources management involves the development of certain organizational processes. For this reason, a new factor, labelled Processes and Resources, is considered in further CFA, while the partnership and resources criterion is subsequently referred to as Partnership. Additionally, it is noteworthy that none of the variables failed to meet the cut-off point considered; nor were there cross loads among factors.

Validity

Validity refers to the degree to which a measure accurately represents what it is intended to measure. Three different types of validity are generally considered: content validity, convergent and discriminant validity, and criterion-related validity (Nunnally, 1978).

Content validity

Content validity represents the extent to which a specific content domain is reflected by an empirical measure. Unlike the other validity analyses, content validity is not evaluated numerically. Researchers must ensure that the survey addresses all issues relevant to the content domain under study in order to guarantee content validity. The scales for measuring TQM practices and outcomes in this research are guided by the EFQM Excellence Model criteria. Quality Award models are viewed as comprehensive by many researchers and practitioners and have been used in previous research to derive empirical constructs (Samson and Terziovski, 1999; Woon, 2000; Rahman, 2001). The development of the items was also reinforced by an extensive review of the literature and detailed evaluations by academics and practitioners alike. It is therefore argued that the TQM constructs can be considered to have content validity.

Convergent validity

Convergent validity refers to the degree to which a measure converges on a same model with the remaining measures forming part of the same concept. Thus, a strong condition of convergent validity is that all scale items load significantly on their hypothesised latent variable and have a loading of 0.6 or better (Anderson and Gerbing, 1988). A single-factor confirmatory factor analysis was carried out when feasible, given that CFA needs at least four items per latent variable to obtain degrees of freedom. When this condition was not achieved, the corresponding construct was allowed to correlate to another construct to obtain the factor loadings. Consequently, a single factor model was performed for Leadership, People, and Policy and Strategy, whereas the Processes and Resources construct correlated to that of Partnership, represented by two items. As three categories of outcomes within Key Performance Results -financial, suppliers and costs- are also estimated by less than four items, we ran a model so that all the Key Performance Constructs could correlate. For the same reason, Results on Society correlate with the results for People and Clients. Table 1 shows the results of these analyses, which prove the convergent validity of each scale. The great majority of the items used proved to achieve convergent validity in their respective scales, although four items were deleted after this analysis (see items in bold type in Appendix 1).

Table 1: Construct validity and reliability

FACTOR Item	Loadings	T-Value	Composite Reliability	AVE	Cronbach's Alpha	Goodness of Fit
LEADERSHIP (LEAD)			0.946	0.716	0.945	$S\text{-}B\ \chi^2$
Leader2	0.86	7.816				$(14)=27.8937$
Leader3	0.87	9.304				P=0.01470
Leader4	0.88	10.931				BBNNFI=0.922
Leader8	0.77	7.713				CFI=0.959
Leader10	0.84	10.156				IFI=0.960
Leader11	0.87	12.065				GFI=0.888
Leader12	0.83	10.458				SRMR=0.034
PEOPLE (PEOP)			0.951	0.611	0.934	$S\text{-}B\ \chi^2$
People1	0.82	13.702				$(35)=42.7784$
People2	0.78	9.788				P=0.17182
People3	0.80	8.675				BBNNFI=0.928
People4	0.76	9.831				CFI=0.986
People5	0.87	10.966				IFI=0.986
People6	0.83	12.829				GFI=0.837
People7	0.72	8.381				SRMR=0.052
People8	0.65	7.104				
People9	0.75	7.877				
People10	0.77	11.058				
POLICY AND STRATEGY (P&S)			0.938	0.685	0.936	$S\text{-}B\ \chi^2$
Polest1	0.85	10.432				$(14)=22.0982$
Polest2	0.88	9.650				P=0.07662
Polest3	0.73	8.008				BBNNFI=0.943
Polest4	0.83	9.972				CFI=0.978
Polest5	0.87	12.289				IFI=0.978
Polest6	0.74	9.638				GFI=0.923
Polest7	0.88	11.163				SRMR=0.030
PROCESSES AND RESOURCES (P&R)			0.971	0.615	0.951	$S\text{-}B\ \chi^2$
Process1	0.70	7.275				$(89)=133.7315$
Process2	0.86	9.132				P=0.00153
Process5	0.74	8.407				BBNNFI=0.909
Process6	0.75	8.500				CFI=0.923
Process7	0.82	8.144				IFI=0.925
Process8	0.71	7.398				GFI=0.813
Process9	0.77	8.137				SRMR=0.050
Process10	0.91	9.191				
Process11	0.83	10.239				
Part&res5	0.72	7.855				
Part&res6	0.75	5.955				
Part&res7	0.78	7.788				
Part&res8	0.75	7.069				
PARTNERSHIPS (PART)			0.807	0.682	0.773	
Part&res1	0.95	8.754				
Part&res2	0.68	7.955				

KEY PERFORMANCE RESULTS (KPERF)						
Financial (FINR)			0.939	0.837	0.939	
Financialr1	0.92	10.672				
Financialr2	0.97	13.851				
Financialr3	0.85	10.100				
Suppliers (SUPPLR)			0.909	0.770	0.905	
Supplr1	0.86	8.332				
Supplr2	0.92	11.325				*S-B χ^2*
Supplr3	0.85	8.910				*(84)=116.4094*
Processes (PROCR)			0.932	0.696	0.930	P=0.01112
Procr1	0.78	8.581				BBNNFI=0.952
Procr2	0.83	8.547				CFI=0.961
Procr3	0.89	10.512				IFI=0.962
Procr4	0.84	8.061				GFI=0.743
Procr5	0.82	8.073				SRMR=0.061
Procr6	0.84	10.409				
Costs (COSTR)			0.839	0.636	0.802	
Costr1	0.81	8.499				
Costr3	0.75	8.557				
Costr4	0.83	10.257				
CUSTOMER RESULTS (CUSTR)			0.917	0.689	0.914	
Custr1	0.89	9.160				
Custr2	0.90	7.150				
Custr3	0.79	8.470				
Custr4	0.76	6.930				
Custr5	0.80	5.628				*S-B χ^2*
SOCIETY RESULTS (SOCR)			0.928	0.865	0.925	*(51)=84.9838*
Socr1	0.91	8.485				P=0.00198
Socr2	0.95	9.287				BBNNFI=0.889
PEOPLE RESULTS (PEOPR)			0.915	0.687	0.905	CFI=0.914
Peopr2	0.78	9.270				IFI=0.917
Peopr4	0.63	7.363				GFI=0.858
Peopr5	0.89	10.369				SRMR=0.053
Peopr6	0.92	9.707				
Peopr7	0.89	8.421				

Reliability - stage two

By using the actual loadings from the confirmatory results, an additional internal consistency measure can be obtained as a test of reliability: composite reliability (Fornell and Larcker, 1981). Composite reliability is a measure of the average variance shared between a construct and its measures; it does not assume, like Cronbach's alpha, that all the loadings are equal to 1; nor is it influenced by the number of attributes associated with each construct. Another measure suggested by Fornell and Larcker (1981) to examine the shared variance among a set of observed variables measuring an underlying construct is the average variance extracted (AVE), which is also calculated when evaluating the reliability of the scales, although, as Fornell and Larcker (1981) note, AVE is an even more conservative measure than composite reliability. In general, composite reliabilities of at least 0.7 and average variances extracted of at least 0.5 are considered desirable (Hair *et al.* , 1999). Therefore, construct reliability was again evaluated using estimated model parameters (e.g., composite reliability, average variance extracted).

As Table 1 shows, each construct manifests a composite reliability greater than the recommended threshold value of 0.7. The AVEs range between 0,611 and 0,837, above the recommended 0.50 level.

Discriminant validity.

Discriminant validity is ensured when the measurement items posited to reflect a construct differ from those that are not believed to make up the construct. This is particularly important when constructs are highly correlated and similar in nature. An alternative test of discriminant validity is to determine whether the correlation between constructs is significantly less than one. In practice, this requires that the 95 percent confidence interval for each pair-wise correlation (i.e., plus or minus two standard errors) does not contain the value 1 (Anderson and Gerbing, 1988). This would prove that the correlation between the dimensions is significantly far from 1, and therefore that the dimensions represent different concepts.

Because we could not include all the criteria in a single model without violating the ratio of sample size to number of parameters (Jöreskog and Sörbom, 1995), we divided the set of scales into various sub-models grouping related constructs to obtain correlations. This approach is well established in the literature (Bentler and Chou 1987; Doney and Cannon 1997; Atuahene-Gima and Li, 2002).

The first set of correlations was obtained from the model run with the four categories of Key Performance Results (see Table 1). Once the discriminant validity of these dimensions had been established, as shown in Table 2, we tested their convergence on a single factor to ensure the unidimensionality of the Key Performance Results (see Table 3). Thus, as the single-factor model has an acceptable fit, the construct is deemed unidimensional (Payan and McFarland, 2005). Accordingly, another CFA was run to obtain the correlations amongst the measures of Results on Clients, Society, People and Key Performance Results (see Table 4).

TABLE 2. Discriminant validity of Key Performance Results

Construct	Covariance	Confidence Intervals of covariance coefficients
FINR-SUPPLR	0.614	(0.488-0.740)
FINR-PROCR	0.671	(0.515-0.827)
FINR-COSTR	0.702	(0.546-0.858)
SUPPLR-PROCR	0.758	(0.650-0.866)
SUPPLR-COSTR	0.727	(0.569-0.885)
PROCR-COSTR	0.750	(0.758-0.842)

Table 3: Unidimensionality of the Key Performance Results

Item	Loadings	T-Value	Composite Reliability	AVE	Cronbach's Alpha	Goodness of Fit
FINR SUPPLR PROCR COSTR	0.73 0.78 0.90 0.82	7.795 8.191 10.793 8.632	0.883	0.656	0.877	*S-B χ^2 (2)=0.0799* P=0.96083 BBNNFI=1.042 CFI=1.000 IFI=1.014 GFI=0.999 SRMR=0.004

Table 4: Discriminant validity of the Results criteria

Construct	Covariance	Confidence Intervals of covariance coefficients		
CUSTR-SOCR	0.575	(0.367-0.783)		
CUSTR-PEOPR	0.826	(0.730-0.922)		
CUSTR-KPERF	0.864	(0.772-0.956)		
SOCR-PEOPR	0.509	(0.257-0.761)		
SOCR-KPERF	0.581	(0.383-0.779)		
PEOPR-KPERF	0.745	(0.613-0.877)		
Goodness-of-fit statistics	*S-B χ^2 (98)=153.8193* P=0.00027	BBNNFI=0.886 CFI=0.907 IFI=0.911	GFI=0.811	SRMR=0.057

A second CFA model included the correlations of each of the TQM Enablers with the Clients, People, Society and Key Performance results. In order to increase sample size relative to the parameter estimates, we used single-scale score indicators to measure the Enablers' latent constructs. Thus, the actual level of the constructs was represented by the median of the measurement items that survived the scales validation process. The measurement error terms for each of these constructs were fixed at (1-composite reliability coefficient) times the variance of each scale score in the final model to determine the extent to which measurement error affected the observed pattern of relationships (MacKenzie *et al.*, 1998).

Table 5: Discriminant validity of research model constructs

Construct	Covariance	Confidence Intervals of covariance coefficients
LEAD-PEOP	0.711	(0.737-0.845)
LEAD-P&S	0.775	(0.649-0.901)
LEAD-P&R	0.715	(0.597-0.833)
LEAD-PART	0.469	(0.297-0.641)
LEAD-CUSTR	0.570	(0.360-0.780)
LEAD-SOCR	0.465	(0.217-0.713)
LEAD-PEOPR	0.610	(0.398-0.822)
LEAD-KPERF	0.582	(0.364-0.800)
PEOP-P&S	0.701	(0.559-0.843)
PEOP-P&R	0.573	(0.415-0.731)
PEOP-PART	0.398	(0.116-0.680)
PEOP-CUSTR	0.468	(0.270-0.666)
PEOP-SOCR	0.429	(0.227-0.631)
PEOP-PEOPR	0.548	(0.358-0.738)
PEOP-KPERF	0.543	(0.351-0.735)
P&S-P&R	0.748	(0.626-0.870)
P&S-PART	0.467	(0.153-0.781)
P&S-CUSTR	0.608	(0.434-0.782)
P&S-SOCR	0.411	(0.139-0.683)
P&S-PEOPR	0.502	(0.248-0.756)
P&S-KPERF	0.530	(0.310-0.750)
P&R-PART	0.580	(0.356-0.804)
P&R-CUSTR	0.750	(0.772-0.828)
P&R-SOCR	0.508	(0.288-0.728)
P&R-PEOPR	0.657	(0.511-0.803)
P&R-KPERF	0.711	(0.585-0.837)
PART-CUSTR	0.422	(0.170-0.674)
PART-SOCR	0.240	(-0.074-0.554)
PART-PEOPR	0.392	(0.152-0.632)
PART-KPERF	0.340	(0.052-0.628)
CUSTR-SOCR	0.557	(0.371-0.743)

CUSTR-PEOPR	0.713	(0.725-0.801)			
CUSTR-KPERF	0.759	(0.769-0.849)			
SOCR-PEOPR	0.474	(0.224-0.724)			
SOCR-KPERF	0.554	(0.360-0.748)			
PEOPR-KPERF	0.727	(0.601-0.853)			
Goodness-of-fit statistics	*S-B χ^2 (163)=253.7822* P=0.00001	BBNNFI=0.971 CFI=0.978 IFI=0.979	GFI=0.769	SRMR=0.116	

The results obtained (see Table 5) show that there is discriminant validity between all the dimensions considered. The highest correlation between dimensions was 0,859 (between the Clients Results and the Key Performance Results scales). The associated confidence interval was 0.77 to 0.95. Hence discriminant validity was supported for all pairs of dimensions. Again, once the discriminant validity of the Enablers' constructs had been proven, their convergence on a single factor was tested to confirm the existence of a single dimension underlying these practices, the actual firms' level of adoption of TQM. The convergence of all the dimensions of business performance considered in the EFQM Model was similarly evaluated. The empirical evidence obtained in both cases is shown in Table 6, this evidence allows considering a single factor to represent the TQM practices and the TQM results in the research model, thus both TQM practices and the TQM results are deemed unidimensional constructs.

Table 6: Unidimensionality of the TQM's Enablers and Results

FACTOR Item	Loadings	T-Value	Composite Reliability	AVE	Cronbach's Alpha
TQM'S ENABLERS Leadership People Policy and Strategy Processes and Resources Partnerships	0.92 0.86 0.87 0.84 0.60	11.295 11.220 10.160 7.554 5.461	**0.912**	**0.678**	**0.900**
Goodness-of-fit statistics	*S-B χ^2 (5)=11.3805* P=0.04434		BBNNFI=0.922 CFI=0.961 IFI=0.962	GFI=0.926	SRMR=0.041
RESULTS Customer Results Society Results People Results Key Performance Results	0.91 0.59 0.81 0.81	7.370 5.012 7.690 9.767	**0.866**	**0.622**	**0.841**
Goodness-of-fit statistics	*S-B χ^2 (2)=0.9739* P=0.61451		BBNNFI=1.037 CFI=1.000 IFI=1.012	GFI=0.993	SRMR=0.017

Criterion-related validity

Criterion-related validity is concerned with the extent to which an instrument is related to an independent measure of the relevant criterion. Thus, a set of quality-management constructs has criterion-relation validity if the collective measure of the constructs is highly and positively correlated with a measure of performance. Although predictive validity can be assessed in this way, it can also be tested in the measurement model if the latter contains the construct of interest and a construct that it should predict (Garver and Mentzer, 1999).

Therefore, criterion-related validity of the five TQM Enablers was initially evaluated by examining the multiple correlation coefficients computed for the five measures and the results of the EFQM programme. The multiple correlation coefficients obtained were in all cases above 0.5 (p < 0.001), providing strong evidence of criterion-related validity. The analysis of the proposed SEM model will provide further evidence on this topic.

6 RESEARCH MODEL TESTING

Our model suggests that there is a latent factor, designed as TQM that represents the quality practices developed by the firms following the EFQM framework. This latent factor achieves higher values if all the Enablers are performed, that is, if a global orientation is adopted in the application of the EFQM Model. Thus, total quality is evaluated by the various Enablers of the EFQM framework and conceived as a primary influence on organizations' performance. Business performance is also represented by a latent construct which embodies the overall performance according to all the Model's results indicators. The SEM results of the relationship between TQM practices and performance show a strong correlation between these variables (ß=0.81; p=0.001) and the structural model explains the 65.0 percent of the variation in business results. The goodness-of-fit statistics used to assess the fit of the data to the hypothesized model are the same as those used to test the measurement models: *(S-B χ^2 (26)=43.6689;* P=0.01640; BBNNFI=0.921; CFI=0.943; IFI=0.945; GFI=0.860; SRMR=0.050). These indices also reveal a good fit of the model to the data. Consequently, the hypothesis formulated (H1) is confirmed. This brings about an important practical implication of the study: the balanced adoption of the TQM practices represented by the Enabler constructs leads to substantially better organizational performance in relation to a firm's main competitors.

7 CONCLUSIONS, LIMITATIONS AND FUTURE RESEARCH

As implementing and developing TQM requires major organisational commitment and effort, there is a need for clear evidence that TQM really has a positive impact on performance. Similarly, results should be susceptible to comparison and useful for firms attempting to achieve total quality. This research uses the EFQM Excellence Model as a guide to measure total quality practices. Its main objectives are to provide empirical evidence on the outcomes that may be expected by firms willing to adopt TQM according to this Model, and to develop and describe a specific measurement instrument to this end. To adequately develop an instrument for measuring the TQM implementation it is devoted a great effort to justify the appropriateness of the scales. This has been made using stringent criteria and combining exploratory and confirmatory analysis. Additionally, the scales are facilitated to allow either undertaking a straightforward replication of the study, or the future development by researchers of comparisons among studies with similar purposes. The excellent works of Eskildsen and Dahlgaard (2000) and Bou-Llusar *et al.* (2005), although resort to SEM to analyze the proposed relationships, do not focus on the former aspects -detailed scales and validity and reliability analysis.

The paper also contributes to TQM literature by proving the positive causal relationship between the EFQM's Enablers and firms' Results. Additionally, the use of a Quality Award as a point of reference to measure TQM practices, and the inclusion of all the EFQM Model's expected outcomes, is a valuable benchmarking data for firms, particularly in the European context. Thus, as the similarities of European regional markets increase, and environmental conditions become smoother, the direct, general applicability of the TQM concept represented by the EFQM Model will grow, obviating any concerns about universalism. Moreover, the EFQM Excellence Model constitutes an unquestionable benchmark in TQM for European firms, and is receiving an ever-growing number of applications for recognition at its different levels (Committed to Excellence, Recognised for Excellence, and the EFQM Excellence Award). We can therefore conclude that: a) adopting the EFQM Excellence Model contributes to firms outperforming competition, i.e., the achievement of competitive advantage; b) there is no concern regarding its universal usability within the European context; and c) it represents the next step to be taken by all European firms committed to quality management in order to surpass the Quality Assurance stage.

The results reported, however, must be treated with caution. The research constitutes a cross-sectional snapshot based on 93 firms operating in the north of Spain. We can neither trace the progress of the companies in our study nor estimate the potential lags between TQM adoption and the outcomes achieved by the firms. A longitudinal study would be necessary to overcome such limitations. Moreover, sample size is far below the number of cases reported in other research, which has led in this case to a more complex data analysis. It would be advisable to replicate the study in broader contexts to confirm the underlying factors identified in this case. The study also suffers from a common limitation in quantitative research: the use of subjective measures for the variables considered. However, it is widely reported in the literature that this procedure increases the response rate as well as that there is a high correlation between subjective and objective data on performance (Venkatraman and Ramanujan, 1986). The use of self-reported data may induce social desirability bias, although the assurance of anonymity can reduce such bias when responses concern sensitive topics (Hair et al., 1999). Finally, although some items have been deleted in the validation process, it must be borne in mind that the different items employed to approximate the underlying constructs "overlap" to some extent to try to capture the underlying constructs measure. Thus, items are expected to be correlated (measures should possess internal consistency reliability) so that dropping some items of the measurement model does not necessarily alter the meaning of the construct (Jarvis *et al.*, 2003). In this respect, four items pertaining to the organization's external orientation (customers, stakeholders and community) are deleted in the Leadership factor. This can be considered a problem since customer satisfaction is basic to TQM. However, several items concerning the anticipation and management of organizational change survive, which involve a careful monitoring of the environment, and a clear intention to meet the market needs.

This research acknowledges the multidimensional nature of TQM. However, future research should consider the interactions not only between specific TQM practices themselves but also between these practices and the different sets of performance variables if we are to obtain a better understanding of quality management. The correlations between the EFQM Excellence Model's constructs indicate that the different activities and outcomes are not independent. Eskildsen and Dahlgaard (2000) illustrate the relationships between the Enabler criteria and People Results within a European service firm. Calvo-Mora *et al.* (2005) replicate this research using a sample of 111 Spanish university centres, assuming the same interactions as the aforementioned study between the Enablers, and including the interactions between the four types of results of the Model (People, Students, Centre and Society). However, in the latter study, Process Management is the only Enabler shown to have a direct impact on performance variables, whereas Eskildsen and Dahlgaard (2000) confirm that it is the People Enabler which directly affects the People Results. In this line, and based on business organizations, the study of Bou-Llusar *et al.* (2005) uses canonical correlations to explore the associations between the EFQM criteria, although indirectly infers the causal relationship between Enablers and Results. In short, this is still a recent line of investigation and more empirical support from different settings is required. This evidence will also enable better understanding of which TQM practices may have a more positive effect on different types of performance. Finally, we believe that the role of firms' competitive environments as an antecedent of the adoption TQM practices, or as a moderator of the TQM-performance relationship, also deserves future research. It is necessary to develop a deeper understanding of the type of environments that favour the TQM adoption, or that could made the TQM a more valuable resource to obtain, if the TQM-performance relationships is positively moderated.

Appendix 1: Research Scales

TOTAL QUALITY MANAGEMENT

LEADERSHIP	
Long-term customer satisfaction is laid down as the organization's mission and basic principle	*Leader1*
Organizational leaders take on the responsibility for developing quality oriented management systems	Leader2
Leaders personally assess the application and progress of total quality principles	Leader3
Leaders allocate resources for continuous improvement of the management system	Leader4
Leaders interact with customers and keep in mind their contributions when designing goods and services	*Leader5*
Leaders always bear in mind stakeholder groups	*Leader6*
Leaders activities seek to provide value for the community and protect the environment.	*Leader7*
Leaders listen and support employees and encourage them to take part in deciding and managing total quality policies and plans.	Leader8
Leaders acknowledge and reward employees' contributions to bettering quality.	Leader9
Leaders pre-empt change needed in the organization and pinpoint the factors that lead to a need for change.	Leader10
Leaders provide a plan detailing the different stages of change, and secure the investment, resources and support needed to achieve change.	Leader11
Leaders measure and review the effectiveness of organizational change and share the knowledge that is obtained.	Leader12
PEOPLE	
In human resource planning, the employee is considered an 'internal customer' who participates in policy, strategies and organizational structure.	People1
Employees know that quality is their responsibility, and they are encouraged to meet customers' and the organization's objectives.	People2
Continuous improvement is consistently fostered and facilitated	People3
Employees are given tailor-made preparation for their jobs and are qualified to solve quality problems.	People4
Staff is continuously trained in the principles of quality, team work and job-specific skills.	People5
Employees are actively involved in quality-related activities and the success of the company, and many of their suggestions are implemented	People6
Employees are responsible for quality and end results of the product/service. They can take decisions independently.	People7
There are quality circles and/or interdepartmental teams to improve quality.	People8
The company has effective two-way communication links with its employees.	People9

The pay and promotion systems acknowledge efforts to improve quality.	People10
Pay and acknowledgement systems are based on quality-related objectives and on company results.	**People11**
Employees receive the right occupational health and safety training at work.	*People12*

POLICY AND STRATEGY

The company draws up strategic action plans (used to regularly review and to establish the organization's short-term and long-term objectives and to pre-empt competitive situations). Their 'gold standard' is a commitment to quality.	Polest1
Strategic plans and related policies always consider customers' needs, suppliers' capacities and the needs of any other stakeholders in the company's activities.	Polest2
Detailed information about such things as competitors' actions, other market agents' behavior, legal and environmental issues, etc is collected to help formulate strategy.	Polest3
Information from all the company's processes is analyzed when strategy is defined.	Polest4
Progress towards achieving strategic objectives is regularly assessed.	Polest5
SWOT analysis is regularly used to review and update business strategy.	Polest6
Resources are allocated to achieve strategic objectives.	Polest7

PROCESSES

Processes are designed ensuring that skills and capacities are right for company needs.	Process1
All processes, procedures and products are assessed regularly in an attempt to bring in change and improvement.	Process2
New products and/or services are designed thoroughly and meticulously before being manufactured and marketed so as to ensure that clients' present and future expectations are met.	**Process3**
Quality-related criteria predominate over speed and cost when developing new products.	*Process4*
The different company departments liaise during the development of new products/services.	Process5
We regularly ask our clients what they want from our products now and in the future.	Process6
Our clients' needs are passed on and are understood at all levels.	Process7
Clients leave is thoroughly analyzed.	Process8
We use clients' complaints and grievances to improve our products.	Process9
Present relationships with clients are analyzed and regular attempts are made to improve them.	Process10
We strive to increase our level of commitment towards our client via policies designed to encourage customer loyalty, guarantees, etc.	Process11

PARTNERSHIPS AND RESOURCES

We have close, long-term relationships with our supplies designed to resolve quality-related problems.	Part&res1
Our suppliers help to improve our products and/or services and also provide technical assistance.	Part&res2
The company is prepared to form alliances with partners and collaborator in the market in an attempt to achieve competitive advantage.	*Part&res3*
Work is organized around reducing and optimizing physical, economic and financial resources.	*Part&res4*
Our company makes ongoing efforts to keep their facilities clean and in order.	Part&res5
The company coordinates its strategies and it technological equipment, machinery and know-how.	Part&res6
Our company strives to improve operational efficiency by efficient use of technology.	Part&res7
Our company creates databases and files with the information it has in order to analyze and learn.	Part&res8
There is updated quality-related data available to all members of the company.	*Part&res9*

CLIENTS' RESULTS

Improved satisfaction of our clients.	Custr1
Improved communication with our clients.	Custr2
A reduction in the number of customer complaints and grievances.	Custr3
Client consolidation, returning clients and loyal clients	Custr4
Improved client perception of the company.	Custr5

PEOPLE RESULTS

Enhanced communication between employees	**Peoprs1**
Improved satisfaction of the employees	Peoprs2
Improved Absenteeism	*Peoprs3*
Less staff turnover	Peoprs4
Improved ability of staff to react to changing customer requirements.	Peoprs5
Improved ability of staff to inform and advise clients about products and services.	Peoprs6
Improved skills of employees.	Peoprs7

SOCIETY RESULTS

Improved social image.	Socr1
Improved view of the company as a responsible member of the community that, when possible, creates employment, implements equal rights policies, concerns itself with accident and environmental damage protection, and encourages and sponsors activities that are beneficial to society as a whole.	Socr2

KEY PERFORMANCE RESULTS

Increased sales	Financialr1
Increased market share	Financialr2
Increased profit	Financialr3
Improved quality of suppliers' goods.	Supplr1
Better relationships with suppliers.	Supplr2
Improved delivery deadlines from suppliers.	Supplr3
Improved process efficiency (faulty parts per total production).	Procr1
Enhanced knowledge of the best way to handle processes.	Procr2
Improved manufacturing time and customer delivery times.	Procr3
More process flexibility.	Procr4

More process productivity.	Procr5
Improved delivery times of customer orders.	Procr6
Lower percentage of faulty products and/or sub-standard service provision.	Costr1
Quality of products/ services compared to competitors.	**Costr2**
Less waste products	Costr3
Lower costs of quality management	Costr4

References

Adam Jr., E.E. (1994), "Alternative quality improvement practices and organizational performance". Journal of Operations Management, Vol. 12 No.1, pp. 27-44.

Agus, A.; Krishnan, S.K.; Latifah, S. and Kadir, S.A. (2000), "The structural impact of total quality management on financial performance relative to competitors through customer satisfaction: a study of Malaysian manufacturing companies". Total Quality Management, Vol. 11 No. 4/5/6, pp. 814-819.

Ahire, S.L. and O'Shaughnessy, K.C. (1998), "The role of top management commitment in quality management: an empirical analysis of the auto parts industry", International Journal of Quality Science, Vol. 3 No. 1, pp. 5-37.

Ahire, S.L., Golhar, D.Y. and Waller, M.M.A. (1996), "Development and validation of TQM implementation constructs", Decision Sciences, Vol. 27 No. 1, pp. 23-56.

Anderson, J.C. and Gerbing, D.W. (1988), "Structural equation modeling in practice: A review and recommended two-step approach", Psychological Bulletin, Vol. 103 No. 3, pp. 411-423.

Anderson, J.C.; Rungtusanatham, M.; Schroeder, R.C. and Devaraja, S. (1995), "A path analytic model of a theory of quality management underlying the Deming management method: preliminary empirical findings", Decision Sciences, Vol. 26 No. 5, pp. 637-658.

Anderson, M. and Sohal, A.S. (1999), "A study of the relationship between quality management practices and performance in small business", International Journal of Quality and Reliability Management, Vol. 16 No. 9, pp. 859-877.

Antony, J.; Leung, K., Knowles, G. and Gosh, S. (2002), "Critical success factors of TQM implementation in Hong Kong industries", International Journal of Quality and Reliability Management, Vol. 19 No. 5, pp. 551-556.

Atuahene-Gima, K. and Li, H. (2002), "When Does Trust Matter? Antecedents and Contingent Effects of Supervisee Trust on Performance in Selling New Products in China and the United States". Journal of Marketing, Vol. 66 No. 3, pp. 61-81.

Badri, M.A.; Davis, D. and Davis, D. (1995), "A study of measuring the critical factors of quality management", International Journal of Quality and Reliability Management, Vol. 12 No. 2, pp. 36-53.

Baidoun, S. (2004), "The implementation of TQM philosophy in Palestinian organization: a proposed non-prescriptive generic framework ", The TQM Magazine, Vol. 16 No. 3, pp. 174-185.

Bentler, P.M. and Chou, C-P. (1987), "Practical Issues in Structural Modeling," Sociological Methods and Research, Vol. 16 (August), pp. 78-117.

Black, S.A. and Porter, L.J. (1996), "Identification of the critical factors of TQM", Decision Sciences, Vol. 27 No. 1, pp. 1-21.

Bou-Llusar, J.C.; Escrig-Tena A.B., Roca-Puig, V. and Beltrán-Martín, I. (2005), "To what extent do enablers explain results in the EFQM excellence model?: An empirical study. International Journal of Quality & Reliability Management, Vol. 22 No. 4; pp. 337-353.

Brah, S.A.; Tee, S.S.L. and Rao, B. M. (2002), "Relationship between TQM and performance of Singapore companies", International Journal of Quality and Reliability Management, Vol. 19 No. 4, pp. 356-379.

Calvo-Mora, A., Leal, A.G. and Roldán, J.L. (2005), "Relationships Between the EFQM Model Criteria: a Study in Spanish Universities, Total Quality Management & Business Excellence, Vol. 16 No. 6, pp. 741-770.

Calvo-Mora, A.; Leal, A. and Roldán, J.L. (2006), "Using enablers of the EFQM model to manage institutions of higher education", Quality Assurance in Education, Vol. 14 No. 2, pp. 90-122.

Castresana Ruiz-Carrillo, J.I. and Fernández Ortiz, R. (2005), "Theoretical Foundation of the EFQM Model: The Resource-based View", Total Quality Management, Vol. 16 No. 1, pp. 31–55.

Chapman, R.L, Murray, P.C and Mellor, R (1997), "Strategic quality management and financial performance indicators", International Journal of Quality & Reliability Management, Vol. 14 No. 4, pp. 432-448.

Chong, V.K. and Rundus, M.J. (2004), Total quality management, market competition and organizational performance. . British Accounting Review, Vol. 36 No. 2, pp. 155-172.

Cragg, P.B. (2005), "The information systems content of the Baldrige and EFQM Models", Total Quality Management & Business Excellence, Vol. 16, No. 8/9, pp. 1001-1008.

Crosby, P.B. (1979), Quality is free: The Art Of Making Quality Certain. New American Library, New York.

Curry A. and Kadasah N. (2002), "Focusing on key elements of TQM – evaluation for sustainability", The TQM Magazine, Vol. 14 No. 4, pp. 207-216.

Deming, W.E. (1986), Out of the Crisis. MIT Center for Advanced Engineering. Cambridge University Press.

Doney, P.M. and Cannon, J.P. (1997), "An Examination of the Nature of Trust in Buyer-Seller relationships", Journal of Marketing, Vol. 61 (April), pp. 35-51.

Easton, G.S. and Jarrell, S.L. (1998), "The effects of total quality management on corporate performance: an empirical investigation", Journal of Business, Vol. 71 No. 2, pp. 253-307.

Eskildsen, J.K. and Dahlgaard, J.J. (2000), "A causal model for employee satisfaction", The TQM Magazine, Vol. 11 No. 8, pp. 1081-1094.

Eskildsen, J.K. Kristensen, K.i and Juhl H.J. (2001), "The criterion weights of the EFQM Excellence Model". International Journal of Quality & Reliability Management, Vol. 18, No. 8, pp. 783-795.

Eskildsen, J.K.; Kristensen, K. and Juhl, H.J. (2001), "The criterion weights of the EFQM excellence model", International Journal of Quality and Reliability Management, Vol. 18 No. 8, pp. 783-795.

European Foundation for Quality Management (2002), Modelo EFQM de Excelencia. European Foundation for Quality Management and Club Gestión de Calidad, Madrid.

European Foundation for Quality Management (2006), Homepage of EFQM, Online: http://www.efqm.org/ (01/06/2006)

Farrar, M. (2000), "Structuring success: a case study in the use of the EFQM Excellence Model in school improvement", Total Quality Management, Vol. 11, No. 4/5/6, pp .691-676.

Flynn, B.B., Schroeder, R.C. and Sakakibara, S. (1994), "A framework for quality management research and an associated measurement instrument", Journal of Operations Management, Vol. 11, pp. 339-366.

Fornell, C. and Larcker, D. F. (1981), "Evaluating Structural Equation Models with Unobservable Variables and Measurement Error," Journal of Marketing Research, Vol. 18 (February), pp. 39-50.

Fuentes-Fuentes, M.A. (2003), "La incertidumbre percibida del entorno como moderadora de la relación entre la gestión de la Calidad Total y el desempeño", Cuadernos de Economía y Dirección de la Empresa, No. 14, enero-abril, pp. 139-160.

Fuentes-Fuentes, M.M., Albacete-Sáez, C. A. and Lloréns-Montes, F.J. (2004), "The impact of environmental characteristics on TQM principles and organizational performance", Omega, Vol. 32 No. 6, pp. 425-442.

Garver, M.S. and Mentzer, J.T. (1999), "Logistics research methods: employing structural equation modeling to test for construct validity ", Journal of Business Logistics, Vol. 20 No. 1, pp. 33-57.

Gerbing, D.W. and Anderson, J.C. (1988), "An updated paradigm for scale development incorporating unidimensionality and its assessment", Journal of Marketing Research, Vol. 25 No. 2, pp. 186-192.

Grandzol, J.R. and Gershon, M. (1998), "A survey instrument for standardizing TQM modeling research", International Journal of Quality Science, Vol. 3 No. 1, pp. 80-105.

Grant, R. (1991), "A Resource-Based Theory of Competitive Advantage: Implications for Strategy Formulation". California Management Journal, Vol. 33 No. 3, pp. 114-135.

Hair, J.F.; Anderson, R.E; Tatham, R.L. and Black, W.C. (1999), Análisis multivariante. Prentice Hall, 5ª ed., Madrid.

Hendricks, K.B. and Singhal, V.R. (2001a), "Firm characteristics, total quality management, and financial performance", Journal of Operations Management , Vol. 19 No. 3, pp. 269–285.

Hendricks, K.B. and Singhal, V.R. (2001b), "The long-run stock price performance of firms with effective TQM programs", Management Science, Vol. 47 No. 3, pp. 359–368.

Hides, M.T.; Davies J. and Jackson, S. (2004), "Implementation of EFQM Excellence Model self-assessment in the UK higher education sector – lessons learned from other sectors", The TQM Magazine, Vol. 16, No. 3, pp. 194-201.

Jackson, S. (2000), "Achieving clinical governance in women's services through the use of the EFQM Excellence Model", International Journal of Health Care Quality Assurance, Vol. 13, No. 4, pp. 182-190.

Jackson, S. and Bircher, R. (2002), "Transforming a run down general practice into a leading edge primary care organisation with the help of the EFQM Excellence Model", International Journal of Health Care Quality Assurance, Vol. 15, No. 6, pp. 255-267.

Jarvis C., MacKenzie S. and Podsakoff P. (2003), "A Critical Review of Construct Indicators and Measurement Model Misspecification in Marketing and Consumer Research", Journal of Consumer Research, Vol. 30, September, pp. 199-218.

Jöreskog, K.G. and Sörbom, D., 1995. LISREL 8. Scientific Software International, Inc., Chicago

Juran, J. (1986), "The quality trilogy'', Quality Progress, No. 9, pp. 19-24.

Kaynak, H. (2003), "The relationship between total quality management practices and their effects on firm performance", Journal of Operations Management, Vol. 21, pp. 405–435.

Kraft, K. (1990), "Are Product and Process Innovations Independent of each other?". Applied Economics, Vol. 22 No. 8, pp. 1029-1038.

Li, M. and Yang, J.B. (2003), "A decision model for self-assessment of business process based on the EFQM excellence model", International Journal of Quality & Reliability Management; Vol. 20 No. 2, pp. 164-188.

Lloréns Montes, F.J.; Verdú Jover, A. and Molina Fernández, L.M. (2003), "Factors affecting the relationship between total quality management and organizational performance", International Journal of Quality and Reliability Management, Vol. 20 No. 2, pp. 189-209.

MacKenzie, S.B.; Podsakoff, P.M. and Ahearne, M. (1998), "Some Possible Antecedents and Consequences of In-Role and Extra-Role Salesperson Performance", Journal of Marketing, Vol. 62 No. 3, pp. 87-98.

Martín-Castilla, J.I.. (2002), "Possible Ethical Implications in the Deployment of the EFQM Excellence Model", Journal of Business Ethics, Vol. 39, No. 1/2, pp. 125-134.

McCarthy, G. and Greatbanks, R. (2006), "Impact of EFQM Excellence Model on leadership in German and UK organisations", International Journal of Quality & Reliability Management, Vol. 23 No. 9, pp. 1068-1091.

Merino-Díaz de Cerio, J. (2003), "Factors relating to the adoption of quality management practices: an análisis for Spanish manufacturing firms", Total Quality Management, Vol. 14 No. 1, pp. 25-44.

Moeller J.; Breinlinger-O'Reilly, J. and Elser J. (2000), "Quality management in German health care – the EFQM Excellence Model", International Journal of Health Care Quality Assurance, Vol. 13, No. 6, pp. 254-258.

Moeller, J. and Sonntag, A.K. (2001), "Evaluation of health services organisations – German experiences with the EFQM excellence approach in healthcare", The TQM Magazine, Vol. 13, No. 5, pp. 361-367.

Motwani, J., Ashok K., Mohamed, A.Y. and Essam M. (1997), "Forecasting quality of Indian manufacturing organizations: An exploratory analysis", Total Quality Management, Vol. 8 No. 6, pp. 361-374.

Newman, K.L. and Nollen, S.D. (1996), "Culture and congruence: the fit between management practices and national culture", Journal of International Business Studies Vol. 27 No. 4, pp. 753–779.

Nunnally, J.C. (1978), Psychometric Theory. McGraw-Hill, 2ª ed., New York.

Osseo-Asare A.E.; Longbottom, D. and Murphy, W.D. (2005), "Leadership best practices for sustaining quality in UK higher education from the perspective of the EFQM Excellence Model", Quality Assurance in Education, Vol. 13 No. 2, pp. 148-170.

Osseo-Asare, A.E. and Longbottom, D. (2002), "The need for education and training in the use of the EFQM model for quality management in UK higher education institutions", Quality Assurance in Education, Vol. 10, No. 1, pp. 26-36.

Pannirselvam, G.P. & Ferguson, L.A. (2001), "A study of the relationship between the Baldrige categories", International Journal of Quality & Reliability Management, Vol. 18 No. 1, pp. 14–34.

Payan, J.M. and McFarland, R.G. (2005), "Decomposing Influence Strategies Argument Structure and Dependence as Determinants of the Effectiveness of Influence Strategies in Gaining Channel Member Compliance", Journal of Marketing, Vol. 69 No. 3, pp. 66-79.

Powell, T.C. (1995), "Total quality management as competitive advantage: a review and empirical study", Strategic Management Journal, Vol. 16, pp. 15-37.

Prajogo, D.I. and Sohal, A.S. (2004), "The multidimensionality of TQM practices in determining quality and innovation performance — an empirical examination", Technovation, Vol. 24 No. 6, pp. 443-454.

Prajogo, D.I. and Sohal, A.S. (2006), "The integration of TQM and technology/R&D management in determining quality and innovation performance", Omega Vol. 34 No. 3, pp. 296-312.

Quazi, H.A. and Padibjo, S.R. (1998), "A journey toward total quality management through ISO certification – a study on small- and medium-sized enterprises in Singapore", International Journal of Quality and Reliability Management, Vol. 15 No. 5, pp. 489-508.

Rahman, S-U. (2001), "A comparative study of TQM practice and organisational performance of SMEs with and without ISO 9000 certification", International Journal of Quality & Reliability Management, Vol. 18 No. 1, pp. 35-49.

Rao, S.S., Raghu-Nathan, T.S. and Solis, L.E. (1997), "A comparative study of quality practices and results in India, China and Mexico", Journal of Quality Management, Vol. 2, pp. 235-250.

Rao, S.S., Solis, L.E. and Raghunathan, T.S. (1999), "A framework for international quality management research: development and validation of a measurement instrument", Total Quality Management, Vol. 10 No. 7, pp. 1047-1075.

Roney, J. (1997), "Cultural implications of implementing TQM in Poland", Journal of World Business, Vol. 32 No. 2, pp. 152-168.

Rungtusanatham, M., Forza, C., Koka, B.R., Salvador, F. and Nie, W. (2005), "TQM across multiple countries: Convergence Hypothesis versus National Specificity arguments", Journal of Operations Management, Vol. 23 No. 1, pp. 43-63.

Rusjan, B. (2005), "Usefulness of the EFQM Excellence Model: Theoretical explanation of some conceptual and methodological issues", Total Quality Management & Business Excellence, Vol. 16, No. 3, pp. 363-380.

Samson, D. and Terziovski, M. (1999), "The relationship between total quality management practices and operational performance", Journal of Operations Management, Vol. 17, pp. 393-409.

Samuelsson, P. and Nilsson L.-E. (2002), "Self-assessment practices in large organisations: Experiences from using the EFQM excellence model", International Journal of Quality & Reliability Management; Vol. 19 No. 1, pp. 10-23.

Saraph, J.V.; Benson, P.G. and Schroeder, R.C. (1989), "An instrument for measuring the critical factors of quality management", Decision Sciences, Vol. 20, pp. 810-829.

Sila, I. and Ebrahimpour, M. (2002), "An investigation of the total quality management survey based research published between 1989 and 2000: A literature review", International Journal of Quality & Reliability Management, Vol. 19 No. 7, pp. 902-970.

Stewart, A. (2003), "An investigation of the suitability of the EFQM Excellence Model for a pharmacy department within an NHS Trust", International Journal of Health Care Quality Assurance, Vol. 16 No. 2, pp. 65-76.

Tarí, J.J. (2006), "An EFQM model self-assessment exercise at a Spanish university", Journal of Educational Administration, Vol. 44 No. 2, pp. 170-188.

Taylor, W.A. and Wright, G.H. (2003), "A longitudinal study of TQM implementation: factors influencing success and failure", Omega, Vol. 31, pp. 97-111.

Terziovski, M. and Samson, D. (1999), "The link between total quality management practice and organizational performance", International Journal of Quality & Reliability Management, Vol. 1 No. 3, pp. 226-237.

Venkatraman, N. and Ramanujam, V. (1986), "Measurement of Business Performance in Strategy Research: A Comparison of Approaches", Academy of Management Review, Vol. 11 No. 4, pp. 801-815.

Weerawardena, J. (2003a), "Exploring the role of market learning capability in competitive strategy", European Journal of Marketing, Vol. 37 No. 3/4, pp. 407-429.

Weerawardena, J. (2003b), "The role of marketing capability in innovation-based competitive strategy", Journal of Strategic Marketing, Vol. 11 No. 1, pp. 15-36.

Westlund, A.H. (2001), "Measuring environmental impact on society in the EFQM system", Total Quality Management, Vol. 12, No. 1, pp. 125-135.

Wilson, D.D. and Collier, D.A. (2000) An empirical investigation of the Malcolm Baldrige National Quality Award causal model, Decision Sciences, 31(2), pp. 361–390.

Wongrassamee, S.; Simmons J.E.L. and Gardiner P.D. (2003), "Performance measurement tools: the Balanced Scorecard and the EFQM Excellence Model", Measuring Business Excellence, Vol. 7 No. 1, pp. 14-29.

Woon, K.C. (2000), "TQM implementation: comparing Singapore's service and manufacturing leaders", Managing Service Quality, Vol. 10 No. 5, pp. 318–331.

Yam, R.C.M., Tam, A.Y.K., Tang, E.P.Y. and Mok, C.K. (2005). "TQM: a change management model for market orientation", Total Quality Management & Business Excellence, Vol. 16, No. 4, pp. 439-461.

York, K.M. and Miree, C.E. (2004), "Causation or covariation: an empirical re-examination of the link between TQM and financial performance", Journal of Operations Management, Vol. 22, pp. 291-311.

Zhang, Z.; Waszink, A. and Winjgaard, J. (2000), "An instrument for measuring TQM implementation for Chinese manufacturing companies", International Journal of Quality and Reliability Management, Vol. 17 No. 7, pp. 730–755.

6

New Frontiers in e-Business and e-Government: Emerging opportunities and Challenges

Alexis Barlow
Caledonian Business School, Glasgow Caledonian University
Cowcaddens Road, Glasgow, Scotland, G4 0BA United Kingdom
Tel: +44 (0) 141 331 8816
Fax: +44 (0) 141 331 3193
Email: a.barlow@gcal.ac.uk

Peter Duncan
Caledonian Business School, Glasgow Caledonian University
Cowcaddens Road, Glasgow, Scotland, G4 0BA United Kingdom
Tel: +44 (0) 141 331 3723
Fax: +44 (0) 141 331 3193
Email: p.b.duncan@gcal.ac.uk

Feng Li
Business School, Newcastle University
Newcastle upon Tyne, NE1 7RU, UK,
Tel: +44 (0) 191 222 7976
Fax: +44 (0) 191 222 8131
Email: feng.li@ncl.ac.uk

Savvas Papagiannidis
Business School, Newcastle University
Newcastle upon Tyne, NE1 7RU, UK,
Tel: +44 (0) 191 222 5724
Fax: +44 (0) 191 222 8131
Email: savvas.papagiannidis@ncl.ac.uk

Abstract

This paper is intended to provide an overview of the key issues that emerged from the presentations and discussion of a successful workshop organised by the British Academy of Management (BAM) e-Business & e-Government Special Interest Group at Newcastle University Business School on 9-10 November 2006. In addition to introducing the three main papers and the research note, which are based on the keynote presentations but have been revised in light of the discussions and questions as well as reviewers' comments on early drafts of the papers, we also highlight some of the key questions the participants raised and debated as well as issues that emerged from the open discussions.

Keywords: e-business, e-government, e-public services, new technologies

INTRODUCTION

Professor Feng Li, Convener of the e-Business and e-Government Special Interest Group, opened the workshop by outlining the key aims, which were primarily to identify the main issues at the forefront of this exciting and dynamic area of research. Many people are currently researching the e-business and e-government phenomenon from a range of different fields, such as strategy, information systems and marketing, but often e-Business and e-Government are on the fringe of their research. In order to gain a more coherent understanding of e-Business in general, it is important that the field is examined in a more systematic and all-embracing manner. Key issues surrounding e-Business that require further investigation include the most significant technical and non-technical developments, current and future applications, emerging opportunities and potential implications. Many developments and opportunities are arising which are turning industries upside down and enabling them to be transformed e.g. newspapers, music. Moreover, it is essential that once the most important issues are identified, existing frameworks are examined to determine their appropriateness for analysing the resulting business, political, social and economic issues.

Throughout the workshop, participants presented, discussed and debated a wide range of emerging issues in the broad area of e-Business and e-Government, ranging from the uncharted territories of MMORPGs and their profound business, social and policy implications, to the very sophisticated conceptual, methodological, theoretical and practical issues in the e-Government and e-Public services.

The keynote presentations and subsequently the three main papers and the research note were delivered by:-

- o Professor Tony Manninen, University of Oulu, Finland – "MMORPG: Is it a product or is it a service - challenges and implications of online games"
- o James Cornford, AIM Public Services Fellow – "Focusing on Customer Focus in E-government"
- o Professor Mike Martin, Newcastle University – "Identity and Relationship Management: The new challenges in public and commercial services"
- o Professor Paul Beynon-Davis, University of Cardiff – "e-Business maturity and regional development"

Further discussions took place on 'New Media Industries' and 'Emerging Technologies and Applications'.

"MMORPG: Is it a product or is it a service - challenges and implications of online games"

The first keynote presentation, by Professor Tony Manninen, focused on perhaps one of the most profound technological developments – Massively multiplayer online role play games (MMORPGS). MMORPGS emerged in the 1990s and are virtual games involving virtual characters, levels, tools (e.g. weapons, islands), buying and selling resources and gaining social status. Drivers such as rewards and puzzles motivate and challenge people.

Recent MMORPGS have become far more than just computer games and indeed many of them have developed into goldmines for economic activities and social interactions. Millions of players are spending as much as 40 hours per week playing them, interacting with virtual characters of other players and building up networks of relationships and bonds. There are business opportunities for product and service based models. Current business models are evident in a variety of forms: subscription-based; one time fee; free basic services and charges for additional services; free games and advertisement revenue. Future Business Models could potentially place more focus on the secondary markets emerging and may involve trading virtual assets outside the MMORPG e.g. e-Bay. This will of course have a range of political and legal implications. Business models also need to focus on the significance of the total business value that may be attained through product and service- based models and the potential level of sustainable competitiveness advantage.

Opportunities also abound for developing business applications e.g. moving away from mainstream entertainment to using game-like features in business applications e.g. teaching, marketing, training, process modelling. In process modelling the game could be used to get people interacting, for gathering process data and analysing data. For example, it could be used for process modelling an area such as hospital management. However, the question needs to be raised as to whether or not it is rationally viable to connect the virtual fantasy worlds of MMORPGs to real world business applications and would practitioners be able to connect, synthesise and draw meaningful business value from both worlds? This is an area of research that requires future investigation.

Focusing on Customer Focus in E-government

The second keynote presentation, by James Cornford, examined the online interaction between government and citizens (customers) within the UK. Most of this level of interaction takes place with local government e.g. local authorities, schools, local health services.

The presenter argues that despite customers being supposedly placed at the centre of e-government within the UK, it has probably been one of the most underperforming aspects of e-government in the UK. This had led to the rising phenomenon of 'customer focus without customers'. A number of potential reasons are offered for this, including customers being resistant to change, poor online design and a lack of marketing.

However, the presenter offered a more fundamental reason for the lack of customer participation, which relates to the way in which customers have been represented within e-government CRM systems. Customers have been represented as one set of individuals that are rational, coherent, self knowing, self-interested, time pressured, demanding and as having rising expectations of the standards of public sector services. Moreover, the CRM systems are programmed to respond to these particular types of individuals and in certain types of ways. The CRM systems are expecting customers to act in certain ways and say certain things and are unable to handle a deviation away from this. Therefore, unfortunately, for a large proportion of customers who have been misrepresented within the systems, this creates an 'I'm not listening effect'!

Rather than involving customers in the way in which they are represented within e-government CRM systems, customers have been represented in a way which is meaningless to the majority of customers. Representation within CRM systems is not necessarily a bad thing but only if customers are engaged and take a role in deciding how they are represented. Consideration needs to be given to whether or not it would be useful for a coherent framework to be developed that provided guidance on representing customers more accurately in CRM systems. Furthermore, is it just down to one fundamental issue or a range of issues and do these vary in different environments and sectors?

Identity and Relationship Management: The new challenges in public and commercial service

The third keynote presentation, by Professor Mike Martin, concerned the nature of identity and relationship management in the public and private sector, and the related challenges. In particular, he suggested that despite the, stereotypically, outdated nature of systems in the public sector - the private sector could learn from the public sector on how it deals with identity and relationships. Professor Martin's presentation dovetailed very well with James Cornford's talk the previous afternoon regarding 'customer focus' in e-Government.

The first part of Professor Martin's presentation gave a detailed description of the case of 'Mary' and her relationships with the national charity Barnardo's through SureStart (a drop-in family support Centre) and MOSAIC (a counselling service). The father of her child was also attending MOSAIC (in a relatively close but different geographical area) creating further issues relating to the need to keep Mary's data/identity separate and secure within different parts of the system. The complexity of Mary's case set the scene for discussion of identity and relationships, particularly within an information system (IS). Professor Martin noted that the typical private sector model, focusing on accountability and integration of the data, may not be helpful where separation of the various interactions Mary had with Barnardo's was paramount - a system is not the real world.

Drawing on the work of Charles Sanders Pierce, Professor Martin argued that relationship and identity management is frequently seen as a dyadic relationship between an individual and the system where data about the individual is stored (an 'object' and its 'attributes'). In this situation, the relationship and the access/control mechanisms are separate, and issues regarding identity/relationship are frequently resolved, simply, by putting in place more access and control mechanisms. He argues, however, that this dyadic model has limited value and that a more interesting, important and significant way of looking at relationships is to view them as *triadic*: with interactions between the individual, the system and, importantly, the owner of the system who determines the purpose of the system and its use.

Explicit governance and governance structures were seen as the key to these triadic relationships – not technology. Identity and relationship were seen as separate responsibilities and services, but in terms of operation were inextricably linked. Information systems are inherently reductionist in an attempt to 'keep it simple'. However, real life is more complex and individuals may have multiple identities and relationships, with information flowing from one encounter to another. In Professor Martin's view any system must be, at least, expressive enough to capture and keep separate (as appropriate) the complexity of Mary's relationships (for example) with the drop-in centre, her counsellor, and her appearance in the records of the father of her child. Professor Martin concluded that the bottom line was to devise and enhance systems which "improve the quality of the mistakes we are making". Although perfection is unlikely, avoiding making the same mistakes was vital.

e-Business maturity and regional development

The fourth and final keynote presentation was given by Professor Paul Benyon-Davis based around the work of the E-Commerce Innovation Centre (eCIC) (Cardiff Business School, Cardiff University), where he is currently Director. His talk reflected on what he has learned about the nature of e-commerce/e-business as it affects the 99.5% of United Kingdom (UK) businesses who are small and medium-sized enterprises (SMEs).

E-business was seen as a socio-technical discipline spanning both technology and organisations, with the broad aim of improving the performance of organisations. Hence e-business is a practical and applied discipline. Professor Benyon-Davis noted that although, currently, Third Mission work (innovation, engagement with industry and knowledge transfer activities) is perhaps perceived by Universities as less of a priority than teaching and research - this is changing. The balance between the rigour and relevance of research may also be changing: rigorous research takes time, and in an evolving and dynamic field such as e-business greater time taken may erode the relevance. As the balance shifts towards relevance, the concept of what constitutes rigour may have to adapt.

According to Professor Benyon-Davis, the conventional wisdom is that greater adoption of information and communications technologies (ICTs) and electronic business (EB) yields increased business benefits in terms of, for example, competitiveness and the ability to be 'locationally independent' and compete in a global marketplace. However, he argued, the aggregate regional benefits of adopting ICTs/EB are hard to measure, as most businesses (SMEs and larger organisations) tend not to evaluate their ICT/EB investments.

The work of the eCIC could be characterised as relating to the information society, with the 'e' of e-business referring to technology's embeddedness in everyday life. In counterpoint to this, Professor Benyon-Davis reminded the audience of the Digital Divide, whereby not everyone has access to online technologies, or the skills to use them. This impacts business strategy as e-business may not be appropriate for a particular demographic, if access and skills are limited.

A significant part of Professor Benyon-Davis' presentation focused on the work of eCIC, which has provided e-business related support to SMEs in Wales. Results of the eCIC 'State of the Nation' annual survey(s) were presented, based on an e-commerce adoption ladder which SMEs 'climb' as their engagement with e-business and related technologies increases. Strengths and weaknesses of such 'stages of growth' models were identified, and the speaker gave the audience an insight into his current thinking on how theories of e-business, and the work of eCIC, could be enhanced in the future. Key themes included: the use of value networks for understanding, explaining and engaging with SMEs; conceptualising e-business as having both an internal and external focus, with the technology providing not only a vehicle for competition, but also cooperation and collaboration (Partner-to-Partner networks); and replacing the adoption ladder with a maturity assessment form/index. Professor Benyon-Davis concluded his presentation by describing a number of the issues facing the SME e-business area. For example, the tension between the need to support businesses at the *lower end* of the e-business adoption ladder, and funding bodies focusing their support on activity engaging with *advanced uses* of e-business technologies. Encouragement of strategic thinking and the related managerial skills could be crucial, and there is the ongoing challenge of encouraging organisations of all sizes to justify and evaluate more clearly their investments in ICTs/e-business.

This presentation raised a number of issues that need to be challenged e.g. is more mature adoption and investment in ICTs and E-Business always more beneficial to SMEs. If not, how should SMEs strategically evaluate which advances, technologies and applications would be most beneficial for them to embrace and which stage of the maturity assessment index they should strive to achieve.

The New Media Industries

Joanna Berry led an interesting and wide ranging discussion based around the question: What are 'new media industries'? The response to this question depended on how you framed the question itself. Social networking phenomena such as YouTube and MySpace could be considered 'new media' industries ie new media providing a break from the traditional industries of, for example, print and television. On the other hand, perhaps they are 'new' media industries, in other words simply the latest incarnation of existing media industries. Joanna guided the audience through the discussion, bringing to bear both her academic expertise, and a wealth of industry experience from her work as Communications Director for a London based record label.

A wide range of examples was discussed: the well known and popular YouTube and MySpace; Yahoo Answers, where questions posed can be answered by interested, and sometimes highly knowledgeable, members of the public; to less well known websites such as iStockPhoto (where the public can buy or sell their photographs online for a modest flat fee). Key examples were social networking/bookmarking sites such as digg and del.icio.us, where users can tag/vote on the material they find interesting.

A particular strand of the discussion was that it is no longer enough for content to be provided to consumers as passive recipients of 'the message'. Consumers are becoming more demanding and want to be involved in the co-creation of consumer content, where the act of creation is linked to the act of consumption, for example: viewing material on digg (consumption) and voting on what you have seen, thereby informing others who may hold similar interests (co-creation of 'best' content). To what extent, then, are these new media messages more, or less, or equal, in value to traditional media messages? And what are the implications for businesses - empowered consumers are happy consumers; happy consumers spend money. Do we require new theories to support our investigations and understanding of these phenomena? A range of views was expressed, and it is clear that there are significant, and exciting, research and business opportunities available through this blurring of boundaries between old and new media.

Emerging Technologies and Applications

The theme of this discussion session was 'Emerging Technologies and Applications'. More generally, it provided the audience with a final chance for discussion, reflection and comment on the presentations and discussions across the two days of the event. To set the scene and prompt discussion the facilitator, Peter Duncan, asked the audience to consider three questions:

Firstly, what are the currently emerging technologies and applications (ie those currently 'arriving' or at least 'on the horizon')? Secondly, a more speculative view about what will be the emerging technologies and applications (ie those which are beyond/over the horizon at the moment)? Finally, the audience was asked to challenge any pro e-business or e-government bias they might have - are there any areas where e-business or e-government will not be relevant, or at best be a 'slow burner' in terms of development?

The example was given of the Funeral Services Sector in the United Kingdom, where some small scale research had found that for, in particular, sociological reasons - e-business may not, currently at least, be appropriate. This prompted some lively discussion relating to funeral planning, cardboard coffins, procurement within the industry as well as consumers, and the global sourcing of stone for monuments. More generally, points were made regarding cultural presuppositions assuming 'one size fits all' regarding e-business. For example 'Linn', who make top of the range sound systems, rely on potential customers hearing the actual system itself, rather than having the sound adulterated through, for example, a computer's soundcard. The pervasiveness of information and communications technologies in everyday business and life may be such that 'opting out' may be extremely difficult even if we were to try to.

A number of emerging technologies and applications were identified. Nano technology may lead to scanners and data being embedded in our bodies. Location was a theme. However, the transparency of Who does what where potentially brought about by technologies such as Radio Frequency Identification (RFID) or Global Positioning Systems (GPS) was seen to be a double-edged sword raising threats of 'big brother', and intrusion into our private lives. Tom Tom uses GPS as a navigation aid, whereas TravelEyes2 is designed to, potentially, be concealed to monitor the travel patterns of others, such as a "teenager's late night activity". Another example related to Smart Cards at one University Library, where the card could be used to plot your location within the library – bringing to mind the Marauder's Map in the Harry Potter books where Harry could 'see' Professor Dumbledore pacing in his study. In the non-magical 'Muggle' world, RFID could provide the backbone of a system whereby as a student left the library, any books taken out would (via an RFID tag/scanner) be logged against the student's account (determined via the Smart Card).

It may be that the 'E' in e-business and e-government could be electronic, but also stand for embedded, entrepreneur or even expectations (as in raising the expectations of consumers or citizens).

Summary & Conclusions

Professor Li closed by highlighting how the workshop had clearly demonstrated that e-Business and e-Government is an exciting and rapidly evolving area. The field of e-business and e-government provides researchers and practitioners with many opportunities relating to both theory and practice. However, such a rapidly evolving field also presents serious challenges, relating to conducting research which is both rigorous and relevant and also in understanding what is actually going on in the world.

The workshop covered considerable ground, from the unchartered, emerging territories of MMORPGs and the potential business opportunities and social and ethical problems, to the extremely sophisticated conceptual, methodological and practical challenges in e-Govenrment. The rapid development and proliferation of the Internet and related technologies in our society and economy has brought about radical changes in the way we work, play, communicate and learn, but we have probably barely scratched the surface of the phenomenon and more radical changes are yet to come.

Fundamental challenges remain and it is more relevant than ever to ask: what is e-Business or e-Government? More importantly, what can we do about it to ensure the benefits accrue to the generic public in a fair, transparent, and equal fashion between individuals, different segments of our society, as well as between cities, regions and nations; and emerging problems from privacy to online risks are adequately addressed. It is the mission of this SIG to promote focused research in this area and contribute to the development of theory, practice and policy in the increasingly networked, knowledge based economy.

Some video clips of the event are available at http://www.ebusiness-newcastle.com/news/events/06_11_ebusiness.php.

7

Customer protest: Exit, voice or negative word of mouth

Bernt Krohn Solvang
Department of Work Life and Innovation, University of Agder
Service box 509, 4898 Grimstad, Norway

Email: Bernt.K.Solvang@uia.no

Abstract

Of the three forms of protest the propensity of word of mouth (WOM) seems to be the most common, and the most exclusive form of protest seems to be exit. The propensity for voice lies in between. The costs linked to voice influence the propensity for WOM. The customers seem to do an evaluation between the three forms of protest, yet the rational picture of the customers should be moderated.

Leaders should improve their treatment of the customers making complaints. The more they can treat customer complaints in an orderly and nice way the less informal negative word of mouth activity they will experience and they will reduce the exit propensity and lead the customers to the complain organisation. They should also ensure that their customers feel they get equal treatment by the staff.

Keywords: voice, word of mouth, WOM, exit, satisfaction, loyalty

1 INTRODUCTION

The customer's potential to complain or make positive comments is hidden from the shop prior to the purchase being made (Brief, 1998). This potential is of considerable significance for shops in a market where there is competition and where keeping customers is of the greatest importance (Aaker, 1991; Fornell, 1992). Hirschman (1970) presents two main forms of protest: protest to the shop or to a public complaints body (voice) or changing shop (exit). To complete the analysis of protest behaviour we include the third form of protest, Word of Mouth (WOM), a complaint to friends and acquaintances.

Figure 1: Customer loyalty and freedom of choice. Developed based on the work of Hirschman (1970).

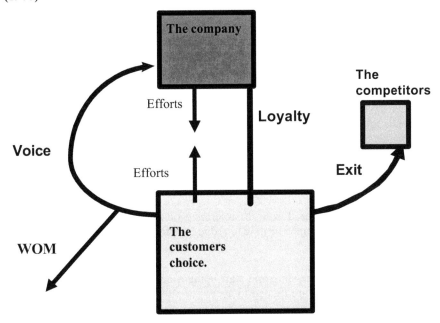

The customers can choose among these forms of complaint, and according to Hirschman's theory (1970) it is the costs and potential gains of the two alternatives that decide which is chosen. The costs of exit are connected to access to alternatives and to the degree of loyalty (Hirschman, 1970; Singh, 1991). Even though Hirschman's theory looks at the relationship between the two forms of protest, an empirical study of the three main forms is lacking. However, studies have been done on the relation between voice and WOM (Bearden and Oliver, 1985; Richins, 1983; Singh, 1990b; Ping, 1997; Naylor and Klaiser. 2000). Ping (1997) has considered the relation between satisfaction, exit costs and complaint behaviour. We want to consider the relation between these three types of complaint:

- protest to the shop (voice) or a complaint to friends and acquaintances (WOM) or exit.
- What is the relation between these three types of protest?
- What influence the customer's choice of protest method?

2 THE THEORETICAL PERSPECTIVE

Hirschman (1970) is focusing on the situation of choice when a customer is dissatisfied. A dissatisfied customer could choose between various forms of protest methods as voice (complain to the supplier, exit (leave the supplier for another one) or WOM (talk negatively to friends an acquaintance). Hirschman (1970) did not treat WOM, but we include that form of protest here in order to obtain a complete picture. This illustration of Hirschman's (1970) theory shows three forms of protest. Exit, voice and WOM are customer protests if they become dissatisfied with the delivery from the company in relation to their own efforts to achieve what they want. According to Hirschman's theory the loyalty is a key variable. High degree of loyalty will increase the costs linked to exit. An alternative form of protest (voice) is thus more likely. Accordingly the voice protesters are expected to be more loyal than the average in the customer, as "the like hood of voice increases with the degree of loyalty" (Hirschman, 1970: 77). Hirschman (1970: 35) sees the protest form of voice as a complement to exit and not as a substitute for it. According to this theory exit is associated with costs and gains as the form of voice is. The costs linked to exit might be of emotional character and travel distance and price and quality variation. The voice costs are linked to bargaining power and by that to education.

We are focusing on the connection between these forms of protest since, to our knowledge these connections have not been treated empirically in a study.

The form of protests

Dissatisfied customers may react in various ways that often manifest itself through frustration and anger: for instance to go to the representative of the shop, respond in private by means of negative comments to friends and acquaintances, or go to a formal complaints body (Richins 1983; Singh, 1990b; Singh, 1990; Singh, 1991; Strauss, Schmidt and Schoeler 2005). Singh (1990) divides customers into four groups according to their pattern of response. The passive ones have a low score for all types of reaction.

Only a few of those who are dissatisfied, make themselves heard, (Teknologisk Institutt 1993; Grønhaug 1977). Andreasen and Best (1977) reported that more than half of those who were dissatisfied did not complain at all, while according to Brief (1998) only 20% of Americans complained in response to unsatisfactory service. The tendency to complain is, then, a function of insufficient satisfaction and of frustration behaviour (Strauss, Schmidt and Schoeler 2005). Many of the customers who are dissatisfied do not complain directly to the shop. Several authors, (Andreasen and Best, 1977; Tarp, 1986; Grønhaug and Gilly, 1991; Hernandez et al., 1991; Bearden and Oliver, 1985; Richins, 1983) see this in connection with the possibility of winning one's case against the costs of complaining in the best Hirschman tradition (1970). Berry and Parasuraman, (1991) state that customers have a zone of tolerance where a performance that lies within the zone will be accepted. Performances exceeding the zone create delight and loyalty, while performances falling short of the zone create dissatisfaction.

Will loyalty be able to create an increased zone of tolerance or is the degree of loyalty not significant for the zone? Will the zone of tolerance be able to reduce the tendency to protest?

Exit

The main behaviour in exit is to leave the shop and start being a customer in another shop. This behaviour has costs and gains. The exit costs are related to access to alternatives and to the degree of loyalty. Hirschman (1970) argues that the exit costs are higher in those cases where there is no alternative shop. If the customer is convinced that complaining will be effective that could delay exit (Hirschman, 1970: 37). Customer loyalty will work as a barrier against exit. The barrier may be compared to a cost ('protective tariffs') (Hirschman, 1970:79). Exit propensity means the probability of a customer choosing the exit option.

How is the exit propensity affected by the degree of loyalty? When loyalty increases, we expect that the exit propensity will decrease since the costs of exit increase with increasing loyalty. How does exit stay as a protest form in relation to voice and WOM? Do the customers have equal access to each form of protest?

Voice

Voice works as a supplement to exit and not as a replacement for it (Hirschman, 1970: 35). A decreasing degree of satisfaction and increasing exit costs may seem to play an equal role in encouraging complaint behaviour (Ping, 1997). Those who are loyal are over-represented among the complainers if Hirschman's theory (1970) holds. The complainers score high on complaining and low on the other forms of reaction. Those who are angry score high on comments to friends and acquaintances (WOM), while the activists score high on complaining and high on third-party action (consumer bodies) (Singh, 1990). Other factors which should be considered in an analysis of complaint behaviour are understood risk, confidence in the success of the complaint as well as the advantages and costs of complaining (Bearden and Teel, 1983; Tarp, 1986; Richins, 1985; Andreasen, 1997).

Grønhaug and Gilly (1991) suppose that the greater tendency to complain about the service industries may be linked to the fact that the services are difficult to standardise. Grønhaug (1972) finds that consumers with a high risk evaluation have a greater tendency to make use of consumer-related sources of information, while those with a lower risk evaluation make greater use of market-dominated sources.

When focusing on technology based service encounters Snellman and Vihtkari (2003) find that customers who actually consider themselves guilty for the outcome were the most frequent complainers, while the ones attributing the outcome to technology failures or service process failures complain less often. Online customers are less likely to complain than offline customers and online customers are more sensitive to benefits/costs of complaining. The difference could be explained by a difference in personal competence expressed where the offline customers have highest score (Cho, Hiltz and Fjermestad 2002).

Complain, protest and avoidance have also been seen as negative effects of loyalty programs (Strauss, Schmidt and Schoeler 2005).

Each fourth of the potential complainers do not complain. The main reasons for this are linked to perceived costs of complaining as time and efforts (Voorhees, Brandy and Horowitz 2006). According to Grønhaug and Zaltman (1981), making a complaint is positively linked to experience, education and income, but negatively linked to age.

Voice handling

Poor handling of a complainer who chooses to complain instead of changing shop because he has a certain loyalty will weaken the complainer's faith in the supplier. This results in fewer satisfied customers and reduced loyalty. The risk of exit and a reduction in repeat purchase increase, together with the increased probability of negative private comments (WOM) (Bearden and Oliver, 1985; Grønhaug, 1987; Richins, 1983). Griffin (1995: 191) points out those complainers who have obtained a quick solution have a repeat-purchase tendency of 82%, in contrast to those who have experienced a major problem without complaining and whose repeat-purchase tendency is 9%. Those who complain, irrespective of the result, have a repeat purchase figure of 19%. Gilly and Hansen (1985) point out that effective complaint handling results in customer satisfaction and loyalty.

We must suppose that many of the complainers are loyal customers. They choose to complain instead of changing shop because their loyalty has increased the costs perceived in changing shop. On the other hand a greater zone of tolerance among the loyal customers may keep them from complaining. Good handling of this type of complainer will strengthen the complainer's faith in the supplier: 'only moderate degrees of satisfaction with service recovery are needed to restore future repurchase intention' (Andreassen, 1997: 195; Singh, 1990b; Gilly and Hansen, 1985).

Good complaint handling results in satisfaction and increased loyalty, and reduces the probability of negative private comments (WOM) (Bearden and Oliver, 1985; Grønhaug, 1987; Richins, 1983). This in turn reduces the risk of exit and increases the probability of repeat purchase. Increased probability of repeat purchase means a better financial result for the supplier. Calculations show that an increase of 5% in the repeat purchase share from 60% to 65% increases receipts by 15%. 'On the other hand a fall in customer loyalty from, for example, 90 to 80 will result in future sales being halved.' (Andreassen, 1997: 4) This is also shown by Oliver (1997, pp. 368-369). A better financial situation helps the supplier to satisfy complainers. A weaker situation makes it more difficult for the supplier to offer good complaint handling.

Negative WOM

Bearden and Oliver (1985) found that a higher potential loss stimulates various forms of complaint, and that the extent of private complaint behaviour is inversely linked to satisfaction with the response from the firm. They point out that if the organisation makes a mistake in its complaint handling, this may lead to loss of goodwill and negative WOM. Grønhaug (1977) pointed out that the complaints seem to build up round complex products which involve a high risk.

Richins (1983) found a connection between the consumers' evaluation of the complaint handling and comments about the shop. The more negative the complaint handling expected by the complainer, the greater the probability of negative private comments (WOM). In another work Singh (1990b) points out that exit and negative WOM are linked to an evaluation of the probability of the complaint being successful. But Naylor and Kleiser (2000) do not find any effect of earlier complaint handling on negative WOM. No complainers are less likely to engage in negative word of mouth than the dissatisfied and recovery groups (Voorhees, Brandy and Horowitz 2006).

Some of the protest forms turn out the public against a firm that has wronged them. Protests published at the Internet are rooted in injustice, identity and turn out as a personal grievance into a "cause" worthy of public attention and support (Ward and Ostrom 2006).

Customer satisfaction

Customer satisfaction and dissatisfaction are associated with the expectations of the customer. If high expectations are met, the customer will be satisfied, but if low expectations are not exceeded by the delivery the customer will be dissatisfied (Oliver, 1997). The customer's experiences could be linked to various sources as service performance, product quality, transactions, product delivery and other factors (Zeithaml, Parasuraman, Berry, 1990).

Churchill, Gilbert and Surprenant (1982) found possible effects of satisfaction dependent on product characteristics (durable and non-durable). Whilst Snellman and Vihtkari (2003) do not find any difference in complaining rate between customers in retail banking and traditional technology based service encounter, while Oliver (1997) finds a greater tendency to complain about durables than about non-durables, but the largest group is those who do not want to complain. This can also be linked to the significance of design, which plays a central role for durables.

Grønhaug and Gilly (1991) point out that customer dissatisfaction can be connected with lack of confidence concerning the transaction, and that much of the dissatisfaction could be linked to market-institutional circumstances beyond the seller's responsibility, such as no product delivered or a long delivery time. Grønhaug and Zaltman (1981) find that it was the transaction frequency, and not the qualities of the good, which best explains the variation in customer dissatisfaction. Ping (1997) maintains that the tendency to complain is related to satisfaction and involvement in the relationship, in the case of firms. Richins (1985) shows a positive connection between potential financial loss and the tendency to complain.

However, there is no simple connection between satisfaction and loyalty. Even satisfied customers can switch to another store because there is no one-to-one connection between satisfaction and loyalty. The relation between satisfaction and loyalty is influenced by characteristics of the consumer such as age and income (Homburg and Giering 2001). Bloemer and Kasper (1995) and Bloemer and de Ruyter (1998), differentiate between two types of satisfaction. Manifest satisfaction conveys a customer who has made a deliberate choice and has reached the conclusion that he/she is satisfied with the offer. Latent satisfaction expresses an unconscious customer who has not compared the offer with other suppliers. They find that an increase in the manifest satisfaction has a greater impact on customer loyalty than an increase in the latent satisfaction.

Customer loyalty

In literature concerning consumer behaviour there are different approaches to view/define customer loyalty. It is differentiated between consumer loyalty in the consumer goods market, customer loyalty in the business-to-business market and the synthesis between consumer and customer loyalty (Kotler 1987; Oliver, Rust and Varki 1997).

The loyalty phenomenon is characterized by diffuse and vaguely delimited contents of meaning (Jacoby and Chestnut, 1978; Peter and Olson, 1993; Dekimpe and Steenkamp 1997). Hirschman's loyalty concept is equated with "non-exit" and hence it is too simple (Huefner and Hunt 1994). In addition to being an unclear concept, several researchers have equated loyalty with repurchase (Carman 1970; Wind, 1978; Grønhaug and Gilly 1991). It is indicated that customer loyalty and repurchase can be increased through establishing barriers that make it more difficult for the customer to go to another store, and consequently repurchase increases (Aaker, 1991; Selnes and Reve 1994; Andreassen and Bredal 1996).

Loyalty as a development pattern in phases: This concept in particular has given inspiration to our approach. Oliver (1997) presents customer loyalty in the form of four Loyalty Phases, viewed as steps of a loyalty ladder:

- Step 1 Cognitive loyalty – The customer has favourable knowledge of the supplier, but a better offer will result in exit to the competitor. The loyalty is only based on cognition.
- Step 2 Affective loyalty – is an emotional attitude based on cognitive loyalty.
- Step 3 Conative loyalty – is intentional loyalty that includes a deeply felt obligation to buy.
- Step 4 Action loyalty – a determination to defy any obstacles in order to buy (Oliver, 1997: 392-393).

This seems to be a fruitful approach to this diffusing concept.

Research questions
1. How are the various forms of protest distributed?
2. How is the variation in satisfaction and loyalty distributed in each form of protest?
3. How could the variation in the propensity for each of the protest forms best is explained by customer related variables?
4. How do external factors as competition and type of shop branch influence the factors associated with each form of protest?

3 METHODOLOGY

Sample of shops
We choose a quantitative design in order to be better able to answer our research questions. The framework for the sample consists of four shops in the southern region of Norway, two in the grocery trade and two in the furniture trade. For each shop 100 customers were selected, a sample of 400 customers altogether. In the case of the grocery shops the interviews were carried out outside the shops on a Saturday and a Tuesday in October 1998. The sample of grocery customers was thus selected out of convenience (those who came out of the shop).

In the case of the furniture shops the plan was to carry out the interviews in the shop. However, because of a shortage of customers, a random sample of customers was selected from the shops' customers list. The interviews were conducted by telephone. The Saturday customers were collected in one group since customers on this specific day of the week can have a different shopping pattern with several family members taking part.

The four shops differed on two criteria: type of trade to get variation in risks for the customers (grocery and furniture) and competition situation and by that getting higher variation in the exit costs. Consequently we included two grocery shops, one in a highly competitive area (low exit costs) and one in a less competitive area (higher exit costs), and two furniture shops, one in a highly competitive area and one in a less competitive area. All four shops are members of retail chains.

Definition of and Measurement of central variables

Loyalty
First we tried to establish an index variable based on loyalty as an attitude and a repurchase indicator: the percentage share of the respondent's own trade in that type of shop for the shop in question. This index variable was not reliable since Cronbach Alfa came out under 0.7 (Hair, Anderson, Latham and Black, 1998).

Then we established an index variable based on loyalty as an attitude and an indicator of an emotional variable: To what extent the respondents would recommend the shop to others if they were asked for advice. This indicator of affective loyalty come out with a significant Cronbach Alfa 0.70 (N=396). Consequently our indicator of Affective Loyalty is measured like this:

Measurement of loyalty
a) Self-evaluation of loyalty to the shop in question on a scale from 0 (extremely low) to 10 (extremely high).
b) Self-evaluation of to what extent the respondents would recommend the shop to others if they were asked for advice on a scale from 0 to 10.

A reflective index (Troye, 1994) was worked out on the basis of these two indicators by the sum (a+b). In a reliability analysis Cronbach Alfa came out with 0.70 (Hair, Anderson, Latham and Black, 1998). This indicates satisfactory reliability. The customer loyalty variable is then measures in values from 0 to 20.

Satisfaction
Customer satisfaction comprises the opinion about the positive response in the exchange and the degree of satisfied expectations (Andreassen, 1997).

Satisfaction was measured as follows:
a) Self-evaluation of satisfaction with the shop in question measured on a scale from 0 to 10.
b) Self-evaluation of the perceived balance between the costs related to being a customer in the shop in connection with costs involving money and time, and the feeling of what one is left with in return for these costs, measured on a balance scale from 0 to 10.

The sum of a) and b) make up our index variable for satisfaction, a reflective index measurement (Troye, 1994). Coronach Alfa between these two indicators is 0.861, which indicates high reliability. The satisfaction index is measured in values from 0 to 20.

Interaction between loyalty and satisfaction
By multiplying the two variables satisfaction and loyalty we got a new variable representing the interaction between them.

Service quality

Zeithaml, Parasuraman, Berry (1990) presented five dimensions in their Service Quality Concept. We have indicators to include three of these dimensions in our study. These are the following dimensions:

a) Reliability (ability to perform the promised service)
b) Responsiveness (Willingness to help customers and provide prompt service)
c) Assurance (Knowledge and courtesy of employees and their ability to convey trust and confidence)

As an indicator on Reliability we used respondent evaluation of the shop on how polite they found the employees in the shop on a scale from 0 to 10. As an indicator on Responsiveness we used respondent evaluation of the shop on willingness to serve you, they assessed the employees in the shop on a scale from 0 to 10. As an indicator on Assurance we used respondent evaluation of the shop on the level of relevant knowledge they assessed the employees in the shop on a scale from 0 to 10. We made our index variable, service quality, by first running a factor analysis of theses three indicators (Principle Component Analyses).

The component Matrix comes up with one component.

Table 1: Factor analysis of service indicators. Component Matrix

Polite staff (reliability)	0.900
Willingness to serve (Responsiveness)	0.901
Knowledge (Assurance)	0.800
N	396

The three indicators are all in compliance with a common factor we will call *service quality*. We then performed a reliability analysis to see if these three variables could be joined together in an index variable. Conbach's ALPA=0.84. This indicates high reliability if we make an index variable consisting of the sum of these three variable. Consequently this index variable is our service quality variable with values from 0 to 30.

Exit costs: Self-evaluation of perceived costs in changing shop measured on a scale from 0 to 10.

Propensity to exit: Propensity to exit is a self-evaluation of the probability of the customer continuing to use the shop in question. Those answering *very likely* or *likely* were given the value 0 for the variable tendency to exit, while those answering *fairly unlikely* or *unlikely* and *do not know* were given the value 1 for the variable propensity to exit. The group average is between 1 and 0 and is interpreted as the propensity to exit for the group.

Voice costs: Self-evaluation of the costs related to complaining on a scale from 0 to 10.

Propensity to voice: Self-evaluation of the propensity to complain measured on a scale from 0 (have never complained to the shop) and 1 (have complained once or several times to the shop). The group average lies between 1 and 0 and is interpreted as the propensity to complain for the group.

Negative Word of Mouth (WOM): Self-evaluation of to what extent one complains to friends and acquaintances rather than to the shop measured on a scale from 0 to 10.

Propensity to WOM: Self-evaluation of the propensity to WOM measures on a scale from 0 to 1. Those who found WOM actual or very actual we defined as high propensity (1) and those who found WOM little or not actual as low propensity (0).

Experience with complaining: The method chosen was self-evaluation of how the complaint was received and handled. 23% of the respondents had experience with complaints to the shop. They answered according to these categories: bad (1), less good (2), satisfactory (3), good (4) and extremely good (5).

Discriminated treatment: Self-evaluation of perceived discriminated treatment measured on a scale from 0 to 1. "Some times we may feel that other customers are getting better treatment than ourselves. To what extent is such discriminated treatment happing here?" Those who answered "it happens often" and those who answered "now and then" and those who answered "seldom" were all given value 1 and those who answered "never "were given value 0.

Perceived risk linked to the shop: Self-evaluation of risk linked to the customers' shop. To what extent do you feel a risk by doing your shopping at this outlet? Scale from 0 to 10 where 10 are measured as extremely high risk. This question was only presented to customers from the furniture shops since the risk linked to grocery shopping is considered low.

Shopping frequency: How many times have you done your shopping in this outlet the last 4 weeks?

Age: The age of the respondents in years.

Education: The number of years of education after primary school.

4 ANALYSIS OF THE RESEARCH QUESTIONS

How is the various form of protest spread among the customers?
What are the portions of the various forms of protest? Our data from this research might give an idea.

Table 2: the distribution of propensity and costs for each form of protest.

	Exit	Voice	WOM
The propensity for	0.1	0.3	0.4
Costs linked to each protest form, scale from 0-10.	2.3	3.0	42% answered actual and very actual
N	380	396	396

According to these data, the propensity of Exit is lowest, of WOM protest highest and Voice in between. Dissatisfied customers would choose to complain to friends and family four times more often than make an exit and three times more often than to make "voice" to the shop. More than each three of the customers in this sample have not been engaged in any form of protest. On the other hand only 2% of the respondents have been engaged in all three forms. Of those with two protest forms, the ones with Voice and WOM constitute the largest group (13%).

We do not have WOM costs measured in the same way as Exit and Voice, but the costs of WOM seem to be low. The subjective costs linked to the other two forms are small and comparable.

How are the customers distributed on various combinations of protest forms?

Table 3: the distribution of combinations of the protest forms.

Protest form	%	N
No protest form	36	380
Exit	10	380
Voice	31	396
WOM	42	396
All three forms	2	380
Voice and WOM	13	396
Voice and exit	5	380
Exit and WOM	5	380

More than each three of the customers in this sample have not been engaged in any form of protest. On the other hand only 2% of the respondents have been engaged in all three forms. Of those with two protest forms, the ones with Voice and WOM constitute the largest group (13%). More than each three of the sample does not make any protest at all.

Is there any association between the various forms of protest?

Are the resources favourable for each protest form accumulative or following a Matthew effect so that those who have, shall have more and those who have less shall loose what they have (Merton, 1968)?

Table 4: Correlations between the propensities for protest forms

Propensities	WOM	Exit	Voice
WOM	-	0.04	0.00
Exit	0.3	-	0.12*
Voice	0.00	0.12*	-
N	396	394	396

Significant at 0.05

The only significant association between the propensities for protest is the association between voice and exit. WOM has no significant correlation with the other two forms of protest.

WOM do not fit in with the pattern linked to voice and exit. Voice and Exit, however, are fitting in well in the same dimension as we may call "formal active protest", while the informal form of protest of WOM do belong in another dimension which we may call "informal active protest".

We do a small sociological analysis of each protest form in order to look for possible explanations of the difference between the formal and informal form of protest.

Is there variation in sociological characteristics between these three forms of protest?

The similarities between the protest groups are more striking than the differences. The WOM group and none protest have got the lowest degree of education, but the difference is not significant. These results indicate that the active forms of exit and voice are linked with educational level.

Table 5: Age, education and sex within each form of protest.

Protest form	Age	Education after primary school	Sex	Sex	Sample size
	Mean years	Mean years	% Men	% Women	N
WOM	39	4.5	40	60	165
Voice	42	4.9	42	58	122
Exit	38	4.8	26	74	51
Non- protest	43	4.4	40	60	144

Table 5 shows no significant differences between the various forms of protest. The voice form of protest has highest age, education and highest portion of men, but the differences are not significant.

How is the satisfaction and loyalty distributed in each form of protest?

Behind any form of protest there is some sort of dissatisfaction. The dissatisfaction and what creates it could be linked to a lot of factors and unfulfilled expectations (Oliver, 1977).

Table 6: Satisfaction and loyalty in each protest propensity group.

Protest propensity	Mean satis- faction	F value on the difference between (1) and (0)	Sig.	Mean loyalty	F value on the difference between (1) and (0)	Sig.	N
Exit (1)	10.3	63.6	**	6.1	39.4	**	50
Exit (0)	13.8			11.3			326
Voice (1)	12.0	31.9	**	9.4	10.2	*	116
Voice (0)	14.0			11.2			254
WOM (1)	12.6	12.8	**	10.1	2.6	-	159
WOM (0)	13.9			11.0			211
None protest (1)	14.7	38.0	**	12.0	16.1	**	132
None protest (0)	12.5			9.8			224

** $S <= 0.01$
* $S <= 0.05$

Table 6 shows for all protest propensity groups, the customers without experience with the protest form (with values 0) have highest score on satisfaction and loyalty. The differences are most profound in the exit group. The differences in value on satisfaction and loyalty are all significant except for degree of loyalty in the WOM group.

Exit seems to be the most potent form of protest with marked differences between those with exit experience and those without. WOM experiences do not influence the degree of loyalty in any significant way. The none protesters (with value 1) have both higher degree of satisfaction and loyalty than the protesters (with value 0) on the none- protest variable.

What is the association between protest propensity and loyalty? According to Hirschman's theory (1970) voice propensity could be associated with high degree of loyalty and exit propensity would be associated with low degree of loyalty since a high degree of loyalty would tend to prevent the customer from exit. Table 6 seems to fit nicely to Hirschman's theory (1970). The lowest degree of loyalty in the group of high propensity for exit and the degree of loyalty in the two other groups are marked higher.

How could the variation in the propensity for each of the protest form best be explained?

We will perform a series of logistic regression with each protest form as dependent variable and the theoretical based variables as independent. The results are listed up in Tables 7-12. We include an interaction variable between loyalty and satisfaction with a view to survey interaction effects. We use an exploratory approach since there are a lot of studies linked to each of the forms of protest.

Table 7: theoretical factors that might influence each form of protest

Theoretical factors	Exit	Voice	WOM
Affective loyalty	X	X	X
Satisfaction	X	X	X
The interaction between satisfaction and loyalty	X	X	X
Costs linked to the protest form	X	X	[3]
Service quality	X	X	X
Transaction frequency	X	X	X
Perceived risk linked to the shop[1]	X	X	X
Voice experience in separate analysis since only 93 respondents had experience[2]	X	X	X
Discriminated treatment	X	X	X
Age	X	X	X
Education	X	X	X
Sex	X	X	X

[1] *This question was only asked to Furniture respondents and the variable is used in a special analysis.*
[2] *Only a ¼ of the respondents had any complaining experience with the shop they left when interviewed so this variable is studied in special analysis.*
[3] *We have no variable describing how difficult the customers felt it was to talk to friends and acquaintances.*

We will sum up the factors that could influence the forms of protest. Subsequently we will run logistic regression and sum up with the significant variables for each form of protest.

The exit form of protest

We have seen the exit form of protest as the most exclusive one. How could we best explain the variation in the propensity for exit? Our start model is based on variables in Table 7. The significant model is presented in Table 8.

Table 8: Logistic regression with propensity to exit as dependent variable

Propensity to:	Exit	Significant test: Wald statistics
	ß	
Satisfaction	-.31**	12.7
Affective loyalty	-.16**	7.6
Shopping frequency	-.16**	7.1
Initial – 2 LOG likelihood	220.6	
Model – 2 LOG likelihood	144.8	
Difference	75.8	
Significance for model	P<.001	
Nagelkerke R^2	.42	
Prediction ability	91%	
N	396	

** S<= 0.01

Exit propensity could partly be explained by dissatisfaction, low degree of loyalty and low frequency visit in the shop. Table 8 shows the association when satisfaction, loyalty and shopping frequency increase the propensity for exit decrease. High shopping frequency seems to have a preventive effect on exit propensity. This finding fits nicely to Hirschman's (1970) theory. Loyalty and satisfaction creates costs for the customers preventing them from making exit from the shop. The model is significant and explains 42% of the variance leaving 58% for other factors and explanations.

In a special analysis of the customers with voice experience, we find a tendency showing "the better the treatment of complaining customers, the fewer propensities for exit".

The difference in evaluation the complain treatment between those without exit propensity (0) and those with exit propensity (1) is 4.0 and 3.1 (N=92, F=7.0, Sig.=0.009).

In another special analysis of respondents linked to furniture shops, we could estimate the possible effects of risk linked to shopping in the shop were the customers were interviewed. The risk evaluation was done on a scale from 0 to 10. Average evaluation of risk was 2.1 (N=199). Those with low exit propensity (0) had an evaluation score on 1.9, and those with high exit propensity (1) had an evaluation on 2.8, N=190, F=4.0, Sig.=0.005. There seems to be a tendency that increasing risk evaluation is linked to increasing exit propensity.

How does external variables as competition and type of shop branch (external variables) influence the factors associated with each form of protest?

Exit propensity influenced by external variables

We will trace possible effects of environment factors such as competition and of branch on the factors explaining the variation in each form of protest.

Table 9: Effects of degree of competition and of branch on propensity to exit. Four analytical models

	Degree of competition		Branch	
	Low	High	Grocery	Furniture
Exit propensity	0.14	0.12	0.10	0.16
Factors explaining variation in exit propensity	ß	ß	ß	ß
Affective loyalty	-.31**	-.49**	-.33**	-.43**
Shopping frequency		-.47**	-.16**	-.24**
Age		-.10**		
Initial -2 log likelihood	125.3	97.9	118.7	108.8
Model -2 log likelihood	93.0	52.1	94.4	54.1
Difference	32.3	45.8	24.3	54.7
Nagelkerke R^2	0.33	0.54	0.26	0.59
Percentage correct predicted	88	94	90	94
N	179	200	197	199

*** S<= 0.01*

The effects of competition

When the competition increases the exit costs are reduced. Moreover, the quality of the offer from the shops could be increased by the competition. When we compare the factors in Table 8, we find a "better" model for explaining exit propensity when competition is high with some negative effect of age reducing the propensity for exit. Shopping frequency seems to be more important in a competitive environment and loyalty and satisfaction seem to reduce the propensity for exit both when the competition is high and when it is low. When the competition is low there is an effect of loyalty, in high competition the effect is linked to satisfaction. Does low degree of competition promote positive attitudes towards the shops?

The effects of branch

Exit propensity seems to be higher in furniture shops then in grocery shops. The customers' dependence of the shops might be higher for the grocery shops since they are more frequently visited than furniture shops. The difference between grocery shops and furniture shops is linked to shopping frequency which is a more important variable for grocery shops reducing propensity to exit. We tried to include the risky variable in the furniture shop model, but it turned out to be not significant. The satisfaction variable is a potent variable in both types of shops. In the furniture shops positive loyalty attitudes seems to reduce the propensity for exit.

When competition is low, and for shops with lower visit frequency (furniture shops), the loyalty seem to play an important role in preventing exit.

The four models in Table 9 are all significant. Models for furniture shops and shops in a competitive environment have the strongest explanatory power.

Voice propensity

We start the study of variance in voice propensity with all the theoretical variables listed in Table 7. The final significant model for voice propensity is shown in Table 10. We do a separate analysis of the customers with experience from previous complains.

Table 10: Logistic Regression with the propensity for voice as dependent variable

Propensity for voice	Voice ß	Significant test: Waldstatistics
Satisfaction	-.19**	28.3
Age	.02*	4.9
Initial – 2 LOG Likelihood	464.7	
Model-2 LOG Likelihood	431.8	
Difference	32.9	
Model significance	P<.001	
Nagelkerke R²	.12	
Prediction ability	71%	
N	396	

** S<= 0.01
* S<=0.05

The propensity for voice is influenced by the satisfaction variable. The negative influence of the satisfaction variable fits with Hirschman's theory (1970), but the relatively weak effects could reflect the effect of the theory of Zone of Tolerance (Berry and Parasuraman, 1991). Customers with high loyalty refrain from making voice more often than customers with a lower degree of loyalty. An increase in age increases the propensity for voice. Age is a resource for voice. The Logistic model is significant and it exp lains only 12% of the variation in the dependent variable.

In a special analysis of the respondents with voice experience, we find the same tendency as we found concerning exit propensity, but with opposite direction. The better the treatment of a complaining customer, the more increased propensity for voice we have. Those who had not complained to the shop had an average on treatment of 3.0, whilst those who had complained to the shop had an average on 3.9 (N=93, F=2.2, Sig.=0.15). However, the difference is not significant.

In another special analysis of the respondents in the furniture shops, we studied the possible effect of risk linked to do shopping in the actual shop on voice propensity. Those with low voice propensity (0) had a risk evaluation on 1.8, whilst those with high voice propensity (1) had a risk evaluation on 2.7, (N=192, F=8.8, Sig.=0.003). The propensity for voice seems to proportional related to risk evaluation, the higher risk evaluation the higher voice propensity.

Possible effects of external factors on voice propensity

We will see how these internal customer related factors are influenced when we differentiate between high and low degree of competing environment for the shops and between grocery (with low risk) and furniture (with higher risk) shops.

Table 11: Effects of branches and competition on the propensity to voice.

	Degree of competition		Branch	
	Low	High	Grocery	Furniture
Voice propensity	0.30	0.34	0.34	0.29
Factors explaining variation in voice propensity:				
Satisfaction	-.18**	-.21**	-.20**	-.19**
Age	.03*		,03*	
Initial – 2 LOG Likelihood	222.4	247.4	236.5	229.2
Model -2 Likelihood	204.9	228.3	217.6	215.1
Difference	17.5	19.1	18.9	14.1
Model significance	P<0.001	P<0.001	P<0.001	P<0.001
Nagelkerke R²	0.13	0.13	0.14	0.10
Percentage correct predicted	73	73	67	74
N	179	194	184	186

** S<= 0.01
* S<=0.05

Possible effects of competition on voice propensity

The effects of competition on voice propensity seem to be linked to one factor; satisfaction. Table 11 indicates that the higher the satisfaction the lesser the propensity for voice. When competition is low, age could be a resource for voice propensity. The two models linked to competition are very week and unable to explain much of the variation in voice propensity.

Possible effects of branch on propensity to voice

The level of voice propensity seems to be somewhat higher in grocery shops than what is the case in a competitive environment.

Possible effects of branch on voice propensity are linked to age in the grocery shops. Age seems to promote voice behaviour to a certain extent in the grocery shops. We tried to include the risk variable in the model for Furniture shops, but it turned out as not significant.

The four models are all significant.

The voice propensity seems to be reduced by satisfaction in all the four models. Age seems to promote voice to a certain extent when competition is low and in grocery shops.

WOM propensity

We noted that the propensity for WOM is the most common form of protest among the customer.

Again we start the study of variation in the WOM propensity with all the theoretical variables in Table 7. In Table 12 we show the significant result. In addition we tried a model with those who had complaint experience, but did not succeed in reaching a significant solution.

Table 12: Logistic Regression with the propensity to WOM as dependent variable

Propensity for WOM	WOM ß	Significant test : Wald statistics
Satisfaction	-.12*	9.7
Voice costs	.17**	14.9
Discriminated treatment	.79*	8.7
Initial-2 LOG Likelihood	390.5	
Model -2 LOG Likelihood	352.1	
Difference	38.4	
Significance for model	P<.001	
Nagelkerke R^2	.17	
Prediction ability	68%	
N	288	

** S<= 0.01

* S<=0.05

Factors influencing the WOM propensity are the satisfaction variable, voice costs, and discriminating treatment. Increased satisfaction reduces the propensity for WOM. As voice costs increase the propensity for WOM increase as well. This fit nicely in a rational model for customer's decisions. When the customers feel dissatisfied he/she normally evaluate either to voice or to WOM. With high costs linked to voice the customer turn to negative WOM. Increased feeing of discriminating treatment seems to increase the WOM propensity. The Logistic model is significant and it explains 17% of the variation in the dependent variable leaving room for other explaining factors.

A special analysis shows no significant difference in propensity for WOM between those who have tried WOM and those who have not tried WOM with respect to treatment of complain.

In another special analysis of the furniture respondents we tried to trace effects of risk evaluation to the actual shop. The risk evaluation was 1, 8 for those with low WOM propensity (0) and 2.6 for those with high WOM propensity (1). N=192, F=6.2, Sig.=0.014. The difference in evaluation score is significant. The higher the risk evaluation linked to a shop the higher the propensity for WOM.

We aim to investigate how these internal customers' related variables are influenced by the external variables as competition and shopping branch.

Table 13: Effects of branches and competition on the propensity to WOM

	Degree of competition		Branch	
	Low	High	Grocery	Furniture
Voice propensity	0.50	0.39	0.45	0.39
	ß	ß	ß	ß
Satisfaction	-.12*		-.15*	
Voice costs	.13*	.23**	.19**	.20**
Age	-.03*			
Discriminated treatment		1.0*	1,0*	0.8*
Initial – 2 LOG Likelihood	241.0	188.8	202.6	193.3
Model – 2 LOG Likelihood	224.8	166,2	178,7	177,4
Difference	16.2	22.6	23.9	15.9
Model significance	P<0.001	P<0.001	P<0.001	P<0.001
Nagelkerke R^2	0.12	0.20	0.20	0.14
Percentage correct predicted	60	74	64	68
N	174	151	147	147

** $S <= 0.01$
* $S <= 0.05$

Effects of competition on WOM propensity

When competition increases the voice costs hold its important position, yet show an increase. The discriminated treatment variable has a role in high competition, but is not present in low competition. Experiencing discriminating treatment is probably a subject in WOM conversations!

The models are having poor explanatory power leaving most of the variance in WOM propensity unexplained.

Effects of branch on WOM propensity

There is no clear difference between the two branches concerning factors for WOM propensity. The voice costs are important in both branches and so is the equity treatment.

The level of WOM propensity seems to be high when competition is low and for customers in grocery shops. The high level of WOM when competition is low could be explained by increasing costs linked to an alternative form of protest, exit. WOM flourish more when alternative forms of protest are more difficult.

Increased voice costs seem to increase the propensity for WOM. Feeling unequal treatment will increase WOM propensity when there are low degree of competition and for customers lnked to furniture ships. The models are all significant, but their explanatory power is low.

5 CONCLUSION

Of the three forms of protest the propensity for WOM seems to be the most common with a propensity factor of 0.4. The most exclusive form of protest seems to be exit with a factor score of 0.1. The propensity for voice has a factor of 0.3.

Of the three forms of protest, we have the best model to explain the voice propensity. Nagelkerke R^2 is 0.79. The model for exit propensity is second best having a Nagelkerke R^2 of 0.42. The model for WOM propensity is not powerful, but we have identified some factors of importance to explain variance in the WOM propensity. Nagelkerke R^2 is 0.14.

How do customers decide how to make a protest? A theoretical reflection

The effect of satisfaction on the propensity to perform a protest is strongest on the exit propensity and weakest on the WOM propensity. The exit propensity seems to be the most serious form of protest. An increase in the evaluation of risk linked to the shopping has positive influence on the propensity to protest. An increase in the risk makes the deal more important for the customer.

The basis for any form of customer protest is low score on satisfaction. There are linkages between the various forms of protest, exit and voice are positively correlated. The costs linked to voice influence the propensity for WOM. The customers seem to do an evaluation between the three forms of protest. If the customers feel high voice costs, the WOM propensity increase. Voice is a more often a chosen form of protest than exit, which seems to be more drastic and rare.

Customer protest seems to be a calculated behaviour governed by degree of loyalty, satisfaction and of possible gains. If the costs linked to voice are high some customers prefer to go to friends and acquaintances with negative WOM. The feeling of not being treated equally compared to other customers is a strong motive for negative WOM. This fits into a calculated behaviour. The calculated behaviour is seen as a sort of rational behaviour summing up feelings and factors linked to satisfaction and calculating possible gains and losses, costs linked to exit and voice or WOM before the form of protest is decided.

However, the calculated pattern is influenced and disturbed by a zone of tolerance created by loyalty and by shopping frequency. The rational picture of the customers should also be moderated since 1/3 of the customers (linked to grocery and furniture shops) do not use any form of protest. And only a small number (2%) has experience in using all three forms of protest.

Treatment of customers complains is an important variable. A good treatment increase the propensity for voice (instead of exit), while a good treatment reduce the propensity for WOM. A bad treatment will increase the propensity for WOM, but reduce the propensity for voice.

Exit propensity

Exit propensity is influenced by satisfaction, loyalty, shopping frequency, risk evaluation and treatment of complaints. Satisfaction, shopping frequency and treatment quality of complaining behaviour will all reduce the propensity for exit if increased, and function as barriers for exit.

When the competition increases the exit costs are reduced. But the quality of the offer from the shops could be increased by the competition. Shopping frequency seems to be more important in a competitive environment and loyalty and satisfaction reducing the propensity for exit both when the competition is high and when it is low. When the competition is low there is an effect of loyalty, in high competition the effect is linked to satisfaction. Does low degree of competition promote positive attitudes towards the shops?

Moreover, exit propensity seems to be higher in furniture shops than in grocery shops. The customers' dependence of the shops might be higher for the Grocery shops being more frequently visited than a Furniture shop.

Voice propensity

Voice propensity is influenced by satisfaction and age, and a good complain treatment will increase the propensity for voice (instead for exit). The negative influence of satisfaction on voice propensity could have been weakened by a zone of tolerance since the effect variable is small, but significant. An increase in risk evaluation does have the same effect. There are small effects if any of external factors as competition and branch on the propensity to exit. Competition seems to make the effects of satisfaction on voice propensity somewhat stronger

WOM propensity

Word of Mouth (WOM) is influenced by satisfaction/loyalty as the other two forms of protest. If voice costs increases, the propensity for WOM also increases. A good treatment of complain behaviour will reduce the propensity for WOM. Shopping frequency is also linked to WOM propensity, the higher the risk evaluation, the higher the WOM propensity. The effects of competition seem to increase the importance of voice costs and complain treatment. Complain treatment have a stronger effect in Furniture shops than in Grocery shops.

For leaders

What measures should be made by leaders in shops in order to reduce formal and informal protest? Firstly, they should make it more easy and comfortable for customers to make a complaint. The more they can treat customer complaints in an orderly and nice way the less informal negative word of mouth activity they will experience and they will reduce the exit propensity and lead the customers to the complain organisation. Secondly, they should ensure that their customers feel they get equal treatment.

REFERENCES

Aaker D. A. (1991) .Managing Brand Equity. New York: Free Press.

Andreassen T. W. and Bredal Dag. (1996). Kundepleie i praksis. Oslo: Ad Notam, Gyldendal.

Andreasen A.R. and A. Best 1977. Consumer complaint: Does business respond? Harvard Business Review, July-August, 55-101

Andreassen T. W. (1997). Dissatisfaction with Services. Dissertation. Stockholm: Företaksøkonomiska institusjonen, Stockholm University

Bearden W.O. and R.L. Oliver (1985). The Role of Public and Private Complaining in Satisfaction with Problem Resolution. The Journal of Consumer Affairs. 19, 2, 222-240.

Bearden W.O. and J.E. Teel (1983). Selected Determinants of Customer Satisfaction and Complaint Reports. Journal of Marketing Research, 20, 21-28.

Berry, L.L. and A. Parasuraman (1991). Marketing Service: Competing through Quality. New York: The Free Press.

Bloemer, J.M., Kasper, H.D. (1995). The complex relationships between consumer satisfaction and brand loyalty. Journal of Economic Psychology, 16,311-329.

Bloemer J.M., de Ruyter K. (1998). On the relationship between perceived service quality, service loyalty and switching costs.- In: International journal of service industry management, 9p. 436-454.

Brief P. A. (1998). Attitudes In and Around Organizations. Sage Publications Inc.

Cho Y, Im I, Hiltz R, Fjermestad J. (2002). The effects of post-purchase evaluation factors on online vs. off line customer complaining behaviour: Implication for customer loyalty. Advances in consumer research, Volume XXIX (29): 318-326.

Carman, J.M. 1970. Correlates of Brand Loyality: Some Positive Results. Journal of Marketing Research nr.7: 67-76.

Churchill Jr., Gilbert A., Surprenant. (1982). An investigation into the determinants of customer satisfaction. Journal of Marketing Research, Vol.19 Issue 4, pp 491- 504.

Dekimpe M.G., Steenkamp J.B. (1997). The Increasing Power of Store Brands: Building Loyalty and Market Share. Long range planning.Vol.30.mr.6:917-930.

Griffin Jill. (1995). Customer Loyalty. How to Earn It. How to Keep It. New York: Lexington Books

Gilly M.C. and R.W. Hansen (1985). Consumer complaint handling as a strategic marketing tool. The Journal of Consumer Marketing, 2, 5-16.

Grønhaug Kjell (1987). Exploring the Problem-Prone Consumers: Hypotheses and Empirical Findings. European Journal of Marketing 21.1, 74-82.

Grønhaug Kjell. (1972). Risk indicators, Perceived risk and consumer's choice of information sources. The Swedish Journal of Economics. 7, 2, 246-262.

Grønhaug Kjell (1977). Kjøpers klageadferd: Noen undersøkelsesresultater (The Customer's Complaint Behaviour: Some Survey Results). Tidsskrift for Samfunnsforskning, 6, 6, 240-250.

Grønhaug Kjell and Mary C. Gilly. (1991). A transaction cost approach to consumer dissatisfaction and complaint actions. Journal of Economic Psychology 12; 165-183.

Grønhaug K. and G. Zaltman (1981). Complainers and no complainers revisited: Another look at the data. Journal of Economic Psychology 1, 121—195.

Hair.J.F. R.E. Anderson, R.L. Tatham and W.C. Black. (1998). Multivariate Data Analysis. New Jersey: Prentice Hall.

Hernandez S.A., W. Strahle, H.L. Garcia and R.C. Sorensen. (1991). A Cross-cultural Study of Consumer Complaining Behavior: VCR owners in U.S. and Puerto Rico. Journal of Consumer Policy 14, 35-62.

Hirschman, A. O. (1970). Exit, Voice and Loyalty. Harvard University Press, Cambridge Ma.

Homburg, C., Giering, A. (2001). Personal Characteristics as Moderators of the Relationship between Customer Satisfaction and Loyalty. Psychology & Marketing. Vol. 18: 43-66.

Huefner, J.C., Hunt, K.H. (1994). Extending the Hirschman Model: When voice and exit don't tell the whole story. Journal of consumer satisfaction, dissatisfaction, and complaining Behavior. Vol 7. P.267-270

Jacoby J., Chestnut, R. (1978). Brand Loyalty Measurement and Management Ronald Press Publication, New York

Kotler Philip (1987). Marketing management New Jersey: Prentice-Hall.

Merton R.K. (1968). The Matthew Effect in Science. Science, 159 (3810): 56-63

Nayor G. and S.B. Kleiser. (2000). Negative versus Positive Word-of-Mouth. Journal of Consumer Satisfaction, Dissatisfaction and Complaining Behavior. 13, 26-36.

Oliver R.L. (1997). Satisfaction. A Behavioural Perspective on the Consumer. New York: McGraw-Hill Company.

Oliver R.L., Rust R.T. Varki S. (1997) Customer Delight: Foundations, Findings, and Managerial Insight. Journal of Retailing. 73. NO.3:311-336.

Peter J.P. & Olson J.C. (1993) Consumer Behavior and Marketing Strategy Homewood Illinois 3rd ed.: Irwin.

Ping R.A. (1997). Voice in Business-to-Business Relationships: Cost-of-Exit and Demographic Antecedents. Journal of Retailing 73, 261-281.

Richins M.L. (1983). Negative Word-of-Mouth By Dissatisfied Consumers: A Pilot Study.

Journal of Marketing 47, 68-78.

Richins M.L. (1985). The role of product importance in complaining behavior. In HK. Hunt and R.L.Day (eds) Consumer Satisfaction, Dissatisfaction and Complaining Behavior. Bloomington, Ind.: Department of Marketing, Indiana University. 50-53.

Selnes Fred and Reve Torgeir (1994) Relasjonsmarkedsføring-keiserens nye klær? Praktisk økonomi og ledelse.2:61-70.

Singh J. 1990, B. Voice, Exit, and Negative Word-of-Mouth Behavior: An Investigation Across Three Service Categories. Journal of the Academy of Marketing Sience.18,1, 1-15.

Singh J. (1990). A Typology of Consumer Dissatisfaction Response Styles. Journal of Retailing, 66, 57-99.

Singh J. (1991). Industry characteristics and consumer dissatisfaction. Journal of Consumers Affairs. 25, 19-57.

Snellman,K.,Vihtkari,T. (2003). Customer complaining behaviour in technology-based service encounters. International journal of service industry Management,14 (2): 217-231)

Strauss B, Schmidt M,Schoeler A. (2005). Customer fustration in loyalty programs.

International Journal of Service Industry Management 16 (3-4): 229-252

Tarp (1986). Consumer complaint handling in America: An update study. Technical Assistance research programs, Washington DC.

Teknologisk Institutt (1993). Kunden i fokus. Los-serien Consumer complaint handling in America: Summary of findings and recommendations. Technical Assistance Research programs, Washington. DC.

Troye S. V., (1994) Teori- og forskningsevaluering (Theory and Research Evaluation). Tano.

Voorhees, C.M., Brandy, M.K., Horowitz,D.M. (2006). A Voice From the Silent Masses: An Exploratory and Comparative Analysis of Noncomplainers. Journal of the Academy of Marketing Science.Volum 34,No. 4. pp 514- 527

Ward, J.C., Ostrom,A.L. (2006). Complaining to the Masses: The Role of Protest Framinig in Customer- Created Complaint Web Sites. Journal of Consumer Research.Vol. 33 pp. 220-230.

Wind,Y. (1978) Issues and Advances in Segmentation Research. Journal of Marketing research 15,317-337. John Wiley & Sons.

Zeithaml,V.A.,Parasuraman,A.,Berry,L.L. (1990). Delivering quality service. Balancing Customer Perceptions and Expectations. New York: The Free Press.

Mobile technology and the value chain: Participants, activities and value creation

Constantinos Coursaris
Department of Telecommunication, Information Studies, and Media
Michigan State University, East Lansing, Michigan, U.S.A., 48824

E-mail: coursari@msu.edu

Khaled Hassanein
DeGroote School of Business
McMaster University, 1280 Main Street West, Hamilton, Ontario, Canada, L8S 4M4

E-mail: hassank@mcmaster.ca

Milena Head
DeGroote School of Business
McMaster University, 1280 Main Street West, Hamilton, Ontario, Canada, L8S 4M4

E-mail: headm@mcmaster.ca

Abstract

Technology has evolved significantly and it is increasingly being used by businesses and consumers alike. Technologies such as those supporting electronic business (e-Business) and mobile business (m-Business) are being used across organizations extensively in an attempt to improve operations and subsequently translate in either financial gains or strategic advantages. Opportunities for realizing either of the two types of benefits can be identified through an examination of a business' value chain.

This conceptual study begins by proposing a business-centric interaction model that helps explain the interactions among all participants involved in an organization's possible activities. The paper then explores the potential fit of wireless and mobile technologies across a company's value chain through the citation of potential mobile and wireless business applications currently available. Finally, a discussion on the expected benefits and relevant concerns of mobile technology, as well as considerations for future research are provided.

Keywords: mobile technology, value chain, mobile applications, m-Business, concerns

Acknowledgements: The authors thank the journal's reviewers for their comments. An earlier version of this paper was presented in the 2006 International Conference on Mobile Business (ICMB), Copenhagen, Denmark, June 26-27, 2006.

1 INTRODUCTION

Technology has evolved significantly and it is increasingly being used by businesses and consumers alike. For businesses, the last two decades have been marked by the transition of large and cumbersome mainframe computing systems, to personal computers offering increased capabilities and occupying only a small area of personal and work space. The latest innovation is found in mobile devices that introduce higher levels of flexibility and personalization. Technologies such as those supporting electronic business (e-Business) and mobile business (m-Business) are being used across organizations extensively in an attempt to improve operations and subsequently translate in either financial gains or strategic advantages. Opportunities for realizing either of the two types of benefits can be identified through an examination of a business' value chain.

The paper begins by defining m-Business and presenting a business-centric interaction model that helps explain the interactions among all participants involved in an organization's possible activities. Then, an overview of the value chain and the impact of m-Business on it are provided through the citation of potential mobile and wireless business applications currently available. Finally, a discussion on the expected benefits and relevant concerns of mobile technology, as well as considerations for future research are provided.

2 M-BUSINESS

Mobile business (m-Business) can be defined as electronic business interactions/transactions enabled at least in part by mobile technology that may target businesses and consumers alike (Coursaris and Hassanein, 2002). For the purpose of this paper the term m-Business incorporates m-Commerce activities which represent the transactions enabled by mobile technology.

There are several mobile technologies that support m-Business. These are typically grouped as devices and networks (White, 2005). Mobile devices range from small radio frequency identification (RFID) and global positioning system (GPS) chips to barcode scanners and wirelessly-enabled handheld personal computers. Mobile networks range from Bluetooth and RFID readers to mobile telecommunications networks and GPS. These mobile technologies are being used by organizations to help address their needs while offering opportunities for flexibility and customization.

Unlike e-Business, which leverages wired and consequently immobile access points (e.g. PCs), m-Business offers value by enabling users to be mobile and reachable anytime and anywhere. Therefore, value creation can occur by supporting either mobile users (e.g. employees) or mobile activities (e.g. tracking raw materials and supplies). A growing industry trend is found in Fixed-Mobile Convergence (FMC), in which centralized management and infrastructure support a mobile workforce, providing "full access to business applications from any location or network connection" (Winther, 2007). Thus, the greater the size of the mobile workforce and/or the higher the ratio of mobile activities within an organization, the greater the value proposition of m-Business for a firm. It is therefore important to explore the types of wireless interactions relevant to businesses.

3 A BUSINESS-CENTRIC MODEL OF MOBILE INTERACTIONS

In crafting the value proposition of m-Business for a business, three components are of interest: relevant actors, unique attributes of mobile technology, and the types of activities supported. We begin by identifying the relevant actors. These are described below and included in Figure 1, where interactions occurring among them within a wireless environment (i.e. at least one actor is using the wireless channel) are mapped:

Employees (E) – These are individuals that are part of an organization (in Figure 1 the association is identified by the matching subscripts, e.g. Business 1 has two employees E_{1A} and E_{1B}). Employees may need or want to interact with other colleagues or employees of other businesses. In addition, employees may be at the receiving end of an interaction initiated by both internal and external information systems. One example of a business application in this area is wireless notification by a *System* via SMS for a critical update. To this end, the possible wireless interactions are Employee-to-Employee (E2E), Employee-to-Consumer (E2C), and Employee-to-System (E2S). It is important to note that most such interactions could naturally involve activities in the reverse direction, e.g. a wireless System-to-Employee (S2E) interaction mode as well.

Systems (S) – These are machines that are run by businesses and could either be front-end (e.g. web interface) or back-end systems (e.g. corporate database). An example of this type of interaction is an employee engaged in wireless (and possibly remote) access of the business' Enterprise Resource Planning (ERP) system. To this end, the potential wireless interactions are System-to-Consumer (S2C), System-to-Employee (S2E), and System-to-System (S2S). Again, the activity could occur in the reverse direction as well.

Consumers (C) – These are individuals that a business may interact with wirelessly. One example is an interaction between an employee and the consumer by means of SMS or e-mail. To this end, the potential wireless interactions are Consumer-to-System (C2S), Consumer-to-Employee (C2E), and Consumer-to-Consumer (C2C) to the extent it relates to the business activities (e.g. community-based interactions).

Figure 1: A Business-Centric Model of Mobile Interactions

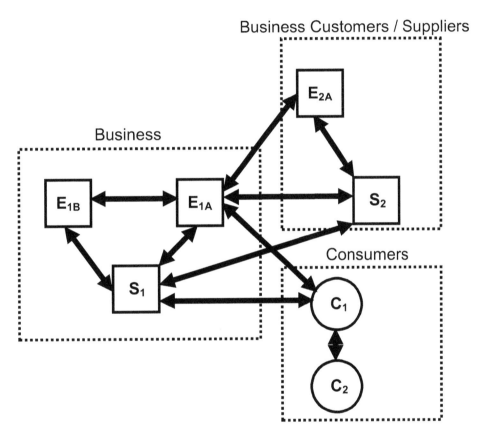

Key:
  The Business entity shows two potential employees (E_{1A} and E_{1B}), and a potential internal I.T. system (S_1)
  The Business Customers and/or Suppliers entity shows a potential employee (E_{2A}), and an I.T. system (S_s)
  The Consumers entity shows two potential consumers (C_1 and C_2)

Having identified the mobile interactions, the next relevant component in formulating a value proposition for mobile technology to organizations is to understand its unique or enhanced attributes, which include connectivity, personalization, and localization (Turban, 2002).

Connectivity - A wireless infrastructure enables mobile workers with 24/7 connectivity supporting "anytime, anywhere" communication and information exchange.

Personalization - Mobile devices are typically assigned to single users, who are then able to personalize interface and application settings that may not only increase their satisfaction with using the device but may also improve the efficiency and effectiveness of the system.

Localization - Localization is particularly important as it adds a new dimension to reachability extending from the Internet's ability to reach a location (i.e. IP address) to reaching a user (i.e. a mobile worker) or an item (e.g. tracking a shipment).

The context of value creation for mobile technology becomes complete by the types of organizational activities supported. These activities are explored next in more detail within the framework of Porter's (1985) value chain.

4 THE VALUE CHAIN

Michael Porter (1985) coined the term "value chain" as the set of linked activities performed by an organization that impact its competitiveness. As seen in Figure 2, the value chain consists of five primary and four support activities. Primary activities are directly concerned with the creation or delivery of a product or service. These include inbound logistics (e.g. receiving and storing raw materials), operations (e.g. converting raw materials through manufacturing into finished goods or service creation process), outbound logistics (e.g. delivering of goods or services to customer), marketing and sales (e.g. identifying opportunities and processing customer orders) and service (e.g. providing after-sales support to customers). These primary activities are facilitated by support activities, which include infrastructure (e.g. organization-wide administrative and managerial systems), human resource management (e.g. managing personnel), technology development (e.g. R&D and continuous enhancements of technology-related activities), and procurement (e.g. purchasing materials and equipment). Support activities span the entire organization, as shown in Figure 2. For example, technology development initiatives could attempt to optimize business activities such as fleet management (inbound/outbound logistics), assembly line operation (operations), sales processing (marketing and sales), and help desk (service). In addition, technology optimization may be used in streamlining operations and freeing up resources "for the strategic initiatives that drive growth and competitive advantage, and accelerate time to business outcomes" (HP, 2007). "Margin" refers to the potential profit margin that an organization could realize through the sale of its product or service, provided the customer is willing to pay more than the cost of the good sold (i.e. cost of all value chain activities involved, from start to finish, in selling a good).

Figure 2: Porter's Value Chain (Source: Porter, 1985)

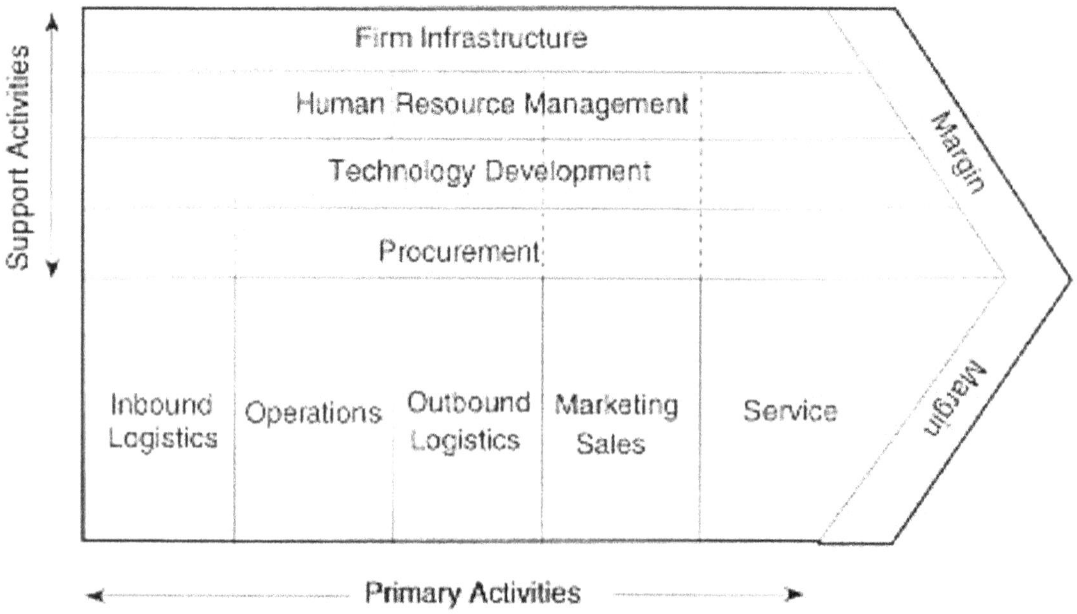

Organizations search constantly for technological opportunities that could yield a lower cost of the goods sold, increased revenue, or improved customer satisfaction, all of which would translate into strengthening a firm's viability. The next section examines how mobile technology can impact an organization's value chain in these areas.

5 MOBILE TECHNOLOGY AND THE VALUE CHAIN

In a landmark paper, Porter examines the impact of the Internet on the competitive positioning of a firm (Porter, 2001). In this work he argues that the basic tool for understanding the impact of information technologies, such as the Internet, on companies is the value chain. According to this approach, the impact of information technologies on a company can be assessed by examining the influence of such technologies on the primary and support activities in the value chain. Here, we employ this approach to gain an understanding into the impact of mobile technologies on companies.

Primary activities

Inbound / Outbound logistics

During these activities a company manages the process of receiving, storing raw materials (i.e. supplies), and distributing finished goods to customers. Supply chain integration and demand chain management are recent extensions in enterprise modeling that require a novel enablement of on-demand information exchanges (Hsu et al., 2007). These information exchanges typically involve a large number of enterprise databases that belong to multiple business partners, and consequently visibility of materials and resources facilitates operational readiness in receiving and delivery timeliness. A current trend highlights the implementation of RFID-augmented systems to integrate enterprise information along the life cycle of a product (Hsu et al., 2007).

RFID tags can be used to track products throughout the entire shipment process (AT&T, 2007c), improving the efficiency of placing new items on the sales floor. For example, after the deployment of their new RFID tagging system, Wal-Mart realized a 19% increase in their use of (RFID tagged) promotional display items. This improvement was attributed to the displays being put up on time and in a correct manner because of the information carried on the RFID tagging system (Hoffman, 2006). In the absence of such visibility, errors can be costly for both inbound logistics, where wrong shipments translate to problems down the supply chain (e.g. meeting outbound deadlines), as well as for outbound logistics where unfeasible order confirmations would otherwise be rejected or rescheduled had real-time inventory data been available at the time the order was being made (Ericson, 2003). Logistics activities can yield strategic business value for a company by lowering distribution costs, reducing inventory, improving customer service, and increasing working capital (Roberts, 2002). Typically neglected, effective inbound logistics can also create value through shorter production and time-to-market cycles of goods produced by the company.

E-Business has been instrumental in generating significant savings during these activities by optimizing processes that previously had been predominantly handled manually. With extensive e-Business applications available in this area, the main driver for using mobile technology is the inherent nature of mobile activities occurring in this segment of a firm's value chain. Receiving raw materials may require the use of a vehicle fleet (e.g. trucks) operated by the company. In this case, wireless fleet management enables real-time visibility of shipment status and performance reporting by providing the location of the shipment's delivery vehicle. For highly valuable products, web-based wireless item-tracking is also possible. Wireless modules are integrated in barcode scanners that allow for automatic registration of shipped products at designated transfer points. This information is then sent wirelessly to a central server for storage. Wireless item-tracking is one of many applications of RFID technology (AT&T, 2007c), making it even more valuable at locations where barcodes cannot be read by fixed devices.

In addition, two-way connectivity between mobile workers (e.g. drivers) and dispatch allows for real-time driving directions, route changes, and delivery schedule updates. General Motors and Siemens are just two of many vendors offering wireless fleet management solutions. These solutions typically make use of the Java2ME platform combined with GPS and GSM/GPRS and other digital networks to enable real-time connectivity between the vehicle, the mobile worker, and dispatch. Solutions are web-based and do not require additional software beyond a web browser (Siemens, 2004).

In addition to the above benefits, fleet management is optimized with integrated wireless solutions. By monitoring a vehicle's status wirelessly, companies are able to improve their "situational awareness, security and decision making in tracking and managing shipments… as they move through global supply chains" (Biesecker, 2006). This area presents significant opportunity for mobile solution providers, since one-third of U.S. transportation companies have been using mobile technology since 2003 (Collett, 2003). Enabling their entire fleet with wireless tracking and messaging can result in these companies eliminating loading errors, improving productivity, and customer service. In a related example, FedEx adopted handhelds that allowed for data exchange directly with the company's back-end system and its Web-based item-tracking application (Collett, 2006). In another case, Lockheed

Martin teamed up with Savi technology to track all of its shipments using RFID-integrated packaging. Not only can customers track the location of their orders, "the tags can also be equipped with sensors that measure humidity, temperature, light, and vibration, which let the shippers know the condition of their goods and whether security may have been breached" (Biesecker, 2006).

20th Century Fox Home Entertainment International was successful in implementing a mobile strategy that involved the use of wireless devices by sales advisors in the UK market. These mobile professionals switched from the traditional pen-and-paper system to wireless PDAs and Bluetooth-enabled mobile phones for collecting necessary information (e.g. retail store DVD stock levels). An integrated SCM solution that exploited the capability for data synchronization via the wireless Web resulted in improved logistics: the stock replenishment cycle shrunk from three days to one day, while product returns diminished from six-seven weeks to one day. A number of additional benefits apply throughout the value chain, including a five percent increase for on-shelf product availability, a ten percent increase in sales, and a 150-labour-hours-per-month reduction in capturing data (Extended Systems, 2004).

Operations

Operations reflect value-creating activities that transform inputs into final products or services. With emphasis on manufacturing and warehouse activities, mobile technology presents organizations with an opportunity to introduce new or enhanced business processes that would result in greater productivity, efficiency, and effectiveness. It could also result in increased employee satisfaction and lower voluntary turnover (AT&T, 2007c).

The use of mobile technology in manufacturing is particularly evident in the automotive and aerospace industries, where approximately two-thirds of all U.S. based companies are actively using it. For example, General Motors installs wireless computers on forklifts so that drivers can send and receive data, such as work instructions and updates, directly from the factory or warehouse floor. This ability is expected to yield savings in excess of one million dollars at a single GM facility by decreasing use of the forklifts by 400 miles per day, and also in productivity increases as the number of deliveries doubled since implementing the wireless solution (Collett, 2003).

Another opportunity for wireless operations is found in quality control (AT&T, 2007c). MicroElectroMechanical Sensors (MEMS) are being developed that will allow for wireless detection of defects. These sensors will identify out-of-range vibrations in industrial equipment and send, and receive data wirelessly with a range of one thousand feet (Collett, 2003). Their small size, approximately the size of a grain of sand, makes them particularly suited for installation on cumbersome machinery, for which quality inspections would otherwise be lengthy and consequently costly. Predictions of wireless operations in the future show a trend toward machine-to-machine (M2M) communications – or S2S according to Figure 1 - for tracking maintenance, service, and status issues (Morley, 2007). By utilizing databases and wireless networking technologies, machines within an operations facility can be monitored automatically, reducing the amount of human labour hours needed to maintain manufacturing equipment.

Real-time wireless asset tracking and inventory visibility is also employed in Operations. Through the use of location-based technologies, e.g. radio frequency identification (RFID) tags and wireless access points (Bryant, 2007), items moved around in a particular facility can be tracked continuously. This allows for faster retrieval of needed items, thus lowering labour costs, increasing productivity and expediting delivery to customers, and subsequently improving customer satisfaction (Collett, 2003). Until recently, the adoption of such technology has been scattered and limited. However decreases in costs and improvement in sensitivity, range and durability have enabled more widespread use of RFID in logistics and operations (Williams, 2004). Powerful players, such as Wal-Mart, have encouraged adoption by requiring their top 100 supplies to place RFID tags on shipping crates and pallets as of January 2005. By the end of 2007, Wal-Mart had over 600 suppliers on board. After two years of RFID implementation, Wal-Mart is starting to reap the benefits, including a 26% reduction in stock-outs along with a plethora of available logistics and sales data (Hoffman, 2006).

BMW is another company that has benefited from RFID implementation by utilizing this technology in its Assembly Finish System to locate any vehicle coming off the assembly line and being parked in any one of 3000 spaces available on site. Similar benefits to those described above are realized through a web-based solution that graphically displays the location of each car on site (WhereNet, 2004).

Inventory visibility is also critical in parts replenishment. Several automakers have implemented wireless solutions that support "just-in-time" manufacturing processes. Typically, the solution continuously monitors and updates inventory levels as stock is being used, and automatically sends a wireless request specifying the type, volume, and delivery location of a material when needed in real-time. This is an innovative alternative to the traditional "paper-based Kanban parts replenishment systems or hardwired electronic call systems, and it offers the twin advantages of low installation costs and unparalleled flexibility in industrial manufacturing environments" (WhereNet, 2004). Benefits include lower inventory levels, decreased operating costs, and improved productivity, all of which contributed in a significant "Return On Investment" (ROI) of less than one year in the case of the Hummer vehicles. Similar benefits were gained by Monroe Truck Equipment by replacing a broad supplier base with a single provider of raw materials (steel), all enabled through the implementation of a novel wirelessly-enabled just-in-time ordering system (Anonymous, 2007).

Moving away from plant operations and manufacturing, mobile technology can offer significant benefits in the service industry as well. YouthPlaces, a non-profit organization offering youth-related after-school programs, was able to leverage scannable I.D. cards and wireless devices in tracking youth participation in real-time as opposed to experiencing a 30-day lag. This information was then used for activities such as staff scheduling and training (Extended Systems, 2004).

Marketing and Sales

M-Business has been argued by many to be a new channel for commerce. While the objective here is not to support or reject this view, mobile technology certainly enables uniquely two elements of the marketing mix, namely promotion and place (or distribution). Promotion takes the form of wireless advertising and, although it is still at its infancy, it presents significant potential as wireless devices increasingly penetrate the consumer market. Coupled with location-based technology and future built-in sensors and personalization capabilities, wireless promotions can be targeted and more effective. Extending from the promotional opportunities presented, distribution of goods and services to a wireless device is a novel capability, allowing for immediate access/delivery of pertinent data, such as business-related information. By improving the availability of information, mobile workers are more knowledgeable and consequently more productive and effective in satisfying customer needs. Through mobile technology, customer concerns can be addressed immediately by accessing needed resources (e.g. questions on product specifications), without mobile workers having to prepare and carry excessive amount of paper documentation. Finally, in terms of sales, wireless point-of-sale devices enable immediate order fulfillment, reduce the incidence of incomplete transactions (e.g. abandoned shopping carts on the wired Internet), reduce paperwork and waste, improve accuracy of orders, and enhance customer service.

To illustrate these three wirelessly-enabled areas, namely promotion, distribution, and sales, the following examples are cited. Wireless Point-of-Sale (POS) devices are being utilized in retail settings to help employees assist customers on the sales floor without requiring them to wait in long lines for price queries and item availability. On-demand service helps reduce customer turnover, especially during the holidays when large crowds and long lines deter customers (AT&T, 2007a). As an example of promotional activities enabled by mobile technology, SkyGo has been delivering advertisements on wireless devices. Initial consumer feedback has been positive, in particular for time-sensitive coupons from restaurants and media related-promotions such as audio clips for upcoming concerts and movie trailers that further allow users to buy tickets from their wireless Web-enabled phones (News.Com, 2001). While potential benefits of wireless promotions are extensive (e.g. high recall and response rates, reaching clients in a high-growth market sector) (Bergells, 2004), businesses need to place the consumer at the centre of such campaigns and effectively address their concerns. The consumer's ability to personalize the type, volume, and delivery time of advertisements are key success factors in obtaining customer acceptance of this service. In addition to wireless advertising, other forms of wireless promotions include mobile research surveys, e-news sponsorships, and banner ads displayed on wireless Websites.

In terms of distribution, mobile technology provides a new channel for the delivery of simple information such as static web pages, dynamic real-time updates such as location-based traffic information, and rich media such as video streaming of news and movies. Users of web services over mobile phones benefit from "anytime connections," enabling activities that required time-sensitive data. Services such as driving directions and weather updates are frequently needed in a mobile setting where a wired connection is not feasible (e.g. while traveling). Mobile e-mail access also helps users increase productivity and respond to important information in a timely manner. These services are being utilized by employers desiring a centrally managed mobile workforce.

For example, MyPrimeTime utilizes wireless distribution of its articles in real-time to members' mobile devices. These life management related articles can be viewed directly on Web-enabled mobile phones or downloaded for future access on a PC via synchronization. To achieve this, MyPrimeTime has partnered with AvantGo to make use of the latter's mobile Internet service (Petersen, 2000).

Drawing from sales applications, Nappi sales force uses wireless devices to send in orders directly to the corporate back-end system, allowing for timely load and schedule updates, which are then automatically forwarded to the plant. Mobile workers are able to save time from placing phone calls to complete an order and the company realizes savings in terms of communication costs. A barcode scanning feature of some mobile devices further reduces the time to complete a sales transaction and eliminates errors as sales people are not required to key in the order (Collett, 2003).

A similar solution implemented by M.R. Williams, a wholesale distributor of various products, involves the use of PDAs for the collection and wireless transmission of critical data (e.g. inventory levels) from retail stores to corporate back-end systems. This integrated approach resulted in sales increases of 34 percent in the first year of the system's use, as well as in freeing up 60 percent of field sales consultants' time by automating product returns and credits. Additional benefits include improved customer satisfaction and inventory control, as well as increased efficiencies and profits (Extended Systems, 2004).

Service

Corporate responsibility does not end with the sale of a product or service. It continues with ongoing support through after-sales activities that aim to maintain or enhance product value. Most often access to information in a timely manner is a critical component in this endeavor. The flexibility of mobile technology is ideal for supporting mobile workers in unplanned situations that call for information with high variability. Equipping mobile workers with knowledge enhances their ability to solve even the most challenging business problems in less time while improving productivity and customer service (IBM, 2004).

The ability to provide time-sensitive information to mobile workers is a growing competitive necessity. Mobile technology can support collaboration through anytime anywhere access to important information including discussions, documents, workflows, notifications, and e-mail, and provides mobile workers with abilities of synchronization, working offline, and flexibility in the device type used. SiteScape addresses this need for information availability through its wireless collaboration solution. Mobile workers have access to corporate information and key business applications such as Customer Relationship Management (CRM), Sales Force Automation (SFA), Supply Chain Management (SCM), and others that improve productivity, reduce cost of communication, and convert captured data into knowledge thus providing a competitive advantage. Similar benefits can be found through push applications such as emails and system updates (e.g. security updates) sent to wireless devices without requiring mobile workers to log in (Ewalt, 2003). As illustrated through the previous examples, most of these benefits can be realized during other activities as well and not only for Service.

Mobile technology can benefit not only businesses and mobile workers, but also customers. Service technicians are equipped with wireless laptops that contain a library of product repair information (e.g. schematics). When a part is required service technicians can immediately place the order wirelessly directly with the supplier (Collett, 2003). This results in a faster repair and consequently improved customer satisfaction. A similar situation is encountered in the health care industry: integrated mobile devices assist health care professionals with checking-up on patients, keeping track of patient status and medications. Mobile integration offers further benefits by helping workers locate necessary equipment and other workers in emergencies, when time is critical (AT&T, 2007a).

In the service industry, caregivers for in-home patient care employed by STBNO were equipped with wireless PDAs that provide them with current information and real-time updates in terms of patient schedules and care data. With just one fourth of the work force enabled with the new system, the company has achieved a five percent increase in field service productivity. Additional benefits include fewer errors, shorter billing cycles, lower administrative costs, and an improved level of patient care and satisfaction (Extended Systems, 2004).

Support Activities

Firm Infrastructure

A competitive business environment calls for a firm's ongoing effort to develop competitive advantage. This may be found in any of the following gains: operational efficiency (e.g. reducing costs, improving communication); innovation (e.g. implementing new business processes); revenue generation (e.g. increased productivity, introduction of new revenue streams); and customer satisfaction (e.g. improved service). Mobility support is a factor that can positively influence any of the above areas. While employee reachability via mobile phones may be a good start, a truly mobile-enabled enterprise emerges only when employees, applications, and infrastructure are fully integrated. A firm's infrastructure supports the entire organization and its value chain through systems and mechanisms for planning and control, such as accounting, legal, and financial services (IDA, 2000). Thus, value creation is optimal when a mobile worker is not only able to receive phone calls, but rather able to communicate with business partners, retrieve data, and analyze it by means of applications made available through a mobile device of any type.

Monitoring and supporting a mobile workforce presents a business challenge that goes beyond traditional management requirements. In a pilot study, AT&T devised a new management strategy for over 5,000 employees, whose mobile communications were carried on a variety of networks with an array of calling plans and pricing schemes. By analyzing the multi-carrier system, it was determined that 23% of mobile employees had calling plans that did not fit their usage. By measuring employee usage against hundreds of calling plans in their Multi-Carrier Solutions platform, AT&T was able to streamline their mobile strategy and reduce average monthly cost for mobile systems by 21% (AT&T, 2007b).

While e-Business technologies were responsible for integrating an organization across its value chain, mobile technology will extend this integration across time and place as well. Two areas that benefit from such wireless platforms are communication and information. Wireless devices enable two-way communication through voice, text messaging (and its variants), e-mail, and video-conferencing. Information availability is supported through the integration of mobile technology on existing Enterprise Resource Planning (ERP) systems and all associated modules, such as accounting (e.g. filing expense claims), manufacturing (e.g. monitoring production levels), and quality (e.g. remote management of information technology) among others. Integration across time and place enables synchronization. Synchronous communication, for example, can be realized more often as the time an employee is not reachable is minimized. Synchronous communication will also translate into faster processing of orders, requests, etc. Finally, integrated systems can increase productivity and subsequent profit. Research in Motion's (RIM) Blackberry provides one such solution for mobile workers requiring access to information and communications. This platform integrates voice, email, SMS, wireless Web, organizer and other productivity applications. The proprietary Enterprise Server seamlessly connects multiple enterprise systems (RIM, 2005).

Another platform offering integrated communications and extensive functionality is IT Solution's "m-Power". By utilizing Bluetooth-enabled mobile phones, wireless PDAs and laptops distributed to the company's field service engineers, information technology initiatives including notifications to mobile workers, confirmations of orders, and time sheet management were implemented. This resulted in the following benefits: 50 percent reduction in HelpDesk personnel, 60 percent and 15 percent savings in communication costs to and from field service engineers respectively. Additional benefits include shorter billing cycles and more accurate and reliable expense claim submissions (Extended Systems, 2004).

Human Resource Management

An organization is responsible for employee recruitment, selection, training, development, motivation, and rewards. As employees are an expensive and vital resource to an organization, effective and efficient human resource management (HRM) can add significant value to a firm. Striving for this goal, Motorola decided to redesign its HRM system in an attempt to address present inefficiencies; it was estimated that some employees spent up to 75 percent of their time on administration rather than activities that could be of more value. The solution came in the form of Enet, an HRM system based on Internet technology. This Web-based system, also accessible through wireless devices, allows employees to access critical HR-related information and services anytime anywhere, such as "initiating, approving and tracking administrative change requests such as merit increases, leaves of absence and department job changes" (Accenture, 2005). Thus, clerical work for HR employees is reduced, subsequently reducing paperwork, and allowing them to concentrate on higher value-adding activities, such as relationship management. Benefits of Enet for employees span the entire organization. For example, mobile workers have a direct line of communication with human resources. As a result, there is improved employee satisfaction and greater credibility for the HRM system given a higher level of consistency than previously achieved through paper-based processes. Savings will be realized in the form of "more consistent and efficient processes, cost avoidance, improvements in data integrity and reduced process cycle time, which has dropped from two weeks to two days or less. As a result, the system is expected to pay for itself in just one year. The company also expects Enet to increase employee satisfaction and retention by improving communication and making human resources services more accessible and useful for employees" (Accenture, 2005).

Furthermore, in recent years there is a trend towards satisfying the need for a balanced lifestyle or that of increased work-related mobility through telecommuting and flexible work practices. These policies can be achieved by adopting mobile technology. While mobile technology is popular among mobile workers in sales, support and field service, only a few companies have implemented wireless services in HR. However, an organization's workforce is becoming increasingly mobile. For example, the U.S. led the world in 2006 with 68% of its workforce being mobile and it is estimated to reach 75% by 2011 (IDC, 2008). At a global level, the mobile workforce is expected to grow by more than 20 percent, with 878 million people working remotely by 2009 (Gosling, 2007) and 1 billion doing so by 2011 (IDC, 2008).

Consequently, wireless HR solutions will become a critical component in successful HRM strategies (Roberts 2001). For example, Wireless-i offers complete solutions for expense and time sheet management that allow employees to enter work-related claims and up-to-date time sheet information easily anytime anywhere (Wireless-I, 2005). By monitoring time utilization and expenses, these solutions allow organizations to reduce HR-related costs, empower employees, improve employee satisfaction, and improve productivity (AT&T, 2007d).

Similar control over field service representatives (FSRs) was desired by Valspar, a leader in the paint and coatings industry. By using their wireless PDAs to scan retail store inventory and update back-end systems, FSRs were tracked in terms of their location and time spent for each job. This feature resulted in better time management by FSRs and in a decrease from three weeks to two days for generating results on ad-hoc requests (Extended Systems, 2004).

Technology Development

Activities focusing on technology development add value to an organization by introducing innovative technology that improves services, products, and business processes. Hence, technology development is an important catalyst for competitive advantage. The latest trend in technology development involves m-Business, where the utilization of mobile technology can potentially reap the above benefits thereby strengthening a firm's value chain. Whether in-house or outsourced, development of wireless solutions can target any of the primary activities and/or their linkages. At the same time, mobile technology can enhance the research process with real-time access to pertinent information regardless of time and/or geographic location, such as real-time consumer feedback transmitted from the user's device (e.g. wireless survey) and wireless access to the organization's knowledge base and knowledge directory. Communication may be initiated by the user or it may be set up to occur automatically between a mobile device and the network at specified times. In addition, mobile technology can foster product development by providing a flexible yet powerful platform for collaboration across locations. Furthermore, the use of the Internet has been shown to have a significant positive impact on Research and Development (R&D) (Linder and Banerjee, 2005). Since m-Business delivers the Internet wirelessly, the benefits gained from e-Business are transferable, thus creating additional value for the organization (caution is needed given the novel usability issues associated with mobile technology). Expected benefits of mobile technology, both current and emerging as in the case of WiMax (AT&T, 2006). in Technology Development include improved productivity through greater accuracy (as calibration can be constantly corrected), improved production times due to reduced downtime, greater flexibility in production times and volumes (DTI, 2005).

One company that has utilized mobile technology in this context is 3Com. The company was able to leverage these wireless networks to strengthen the relationships among team members by improving the communication amongst them and the availability of information to them (3Com, 2005).

Improved communication may also be realized through "On Demand Mobile Conferencing" (ODMC), a solution offered by Zeosoft, a provider for mobile infrastructure software and application development technologies. ODMC enables real-time exchange of information through text messages, file sharing, and live group discussions with white boarding capabilities on a virtual work space accessed by wireless devices. The solution improves "existing business processes, increases employee productivity, and reduces the cost of conducting meetings" (ZeoSoft, 2005).

The ability to gain access to Personal Information Management (PIM) (e.g. e-mail, contact lists) and groupware data was also enabled by First Command's wireless solution. First Command, an international financial management company, implemented a system that allowed for real-time synchronization of sales associates' mobile devices, which not only enabled anytime, anywhere collaboration via the corporate Microsoft Exchange system, but also resulted in savings for each associate of up to three hours per day (Extended Systems, 2004).

Procurement

This support activity encompasses all purchasing transactions for goods and services. Optimal conditions include the lowest price and highest quality for what is being purchased. Mobile technology can add value by enhancing current electronic procurement practices, such as web-based order fulfillment. Transactional cost savings, increased flexibility, and customer satisfaction are a few of the expected benefits realized when enabling an organization with wireless procurement. Corrigo, a service management solutions provider, offers an application to property managers that enables field technicians to order repair parts through a WAP-enabled mobile device. Eliminating the burden of searching through catalogs for part numbers, followed by phone calls to place an order, apartment maintenance and repair workers can directly access supplier data and order needed parts. In addition, this IT solution brings property managers closer to customers (i.e. residents) by allowing them to enter a service call either by phone or online instead of having them visit the property management's office, and relaying that information immediately to the mobile repair worker. The application also allows residents to track the work order status, while property managers are given visibility to maintenance personnel activities (Moozakis, 2000).

Elcom International, on the other hand, has extended their Internet Procurement Manager to wireless devices. Initially capable only for routing and approvals, eMobileLink enables e-mail notifications of requests for quotes (RFQs), downloading and viewing RFQs, and approving/rejecting them from a wireless device, while integrating settlement capabilities (Ferguson 2001).

A new trend in mobile workforce management is Fixed-Mobile Convergence (FMC), which utilizes a centralized management structure which oversees mobile employees. By using equipment that operates over a variety of networks including cellular, Wi-Fi, and possibly WiMAX in the near future, employees can access and transmit data. When associated with an office private branch exchange (PBX), FMC-enabled devices offer all the functionality of an office phone and laptop computer while allowing the freedom of wireless networks and cellular coverage (Winther, 2007).

In terms of order entry, Zync Solutions, a provider of web-hosted software solutions, equipped field representatives with mobile devices for scanning bar codes instead of placing orders manually, as well as recording any additional information that may be obtained during the store visit. With time savings of 30 percent (i.e. 150 labour hours per month), the information is sent up the value chain wirelessly via the corporate back-end system. Additional benefits include improved information flow, efficiency, productivity, reporting accuracy, response time to retailers' needs, which subsequently improve sales and a faster return on investment (ROI) (Extended Systems, 2004).

Figure 3: Prominent m-Business applications in the Value Chain

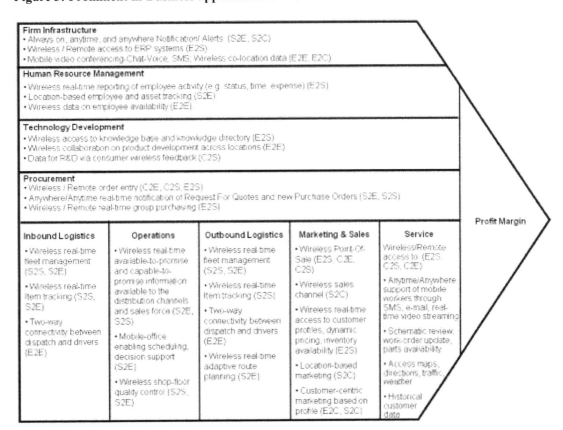

6 DISCUSSION

The foregoing discussion found in the previous section was summarized in Figure 3. Figure 3 describes an organization's primary and support activities in terms of both representative applications currently found in industry, as well as the interaction types (included between brackets) that convey which interactions, from those depicted in Figure 1, are being enhanced by the listed application. Cognizant of these value-adding mobile technologies, managers can then better leverage m-Business to support and enhance both the primary and support activities of an organization's value chain contributing to a firm's overall competitiveness.

By exploring the impact of mobile technologies on the various components of the value chain and through citing extensive industry examples, this paper has demonstrated the potential of such technologies. The applications outlined in the previous section can be generalized and grouped according to the following classification:

Asset tracking – Referring to either physical objects (e.g. merchandise) or human resources (e.g. employees), these applications allow organizations to access tracking information. The organization then leverages the assets' visibility for optimizing processes (e.g. timeliness of deliveries). The function of tracking employees could also be combined with the capability for continuous communication thereby increasing the value of these applications (e.g. a mobile worker equipped with a GPS enabled mobile phone).

Data access – Access to time-sensitive information could enhance an organization's efficiency and effectiveness resulting in competitive advantages. Information could either be pushed to the employees, business partners, and/or consumers (e.g. through SMS), or pulled by employees from remote locations (e.g. field technicians requiring specifications for various jobs). Data access may also optimize an organization's data management, with collaboration applications that support knowledge sharing and increase knowledge flow.

Automation – Mobile technology can be used to automate some tasks previously performed by employees. Benefits for an organization may include lower workforce requirements, improved employee time allocation, and improved quality by automating processes and reducing employee errors. One company that implemented such mobile workforce automation processes is Intermountain Gas Company (IGC). IGC serves more than 275,000 "natural gas customers across Southern Idaho and employs 350 people in seven district offices" (IGC, 2008; Itron, 2005). Unlike many utilities, IGC did not have an integrated dispatch system for work orders rather routed orders either by paper or radio. By enabling dispatch and field service workers to communicate and share data in real time through a wireless, web-based mobile communications and automated solution, IGC "improved emergency response by quickly identifying the nearest field representative with appropriate skills; decreased fleet mileage through tighter, more efficient routing and streamlined order processing by eliminating reams of paper orders and reducing data entry errors. Employee productivity and customer satisfaction increased while the costly paperwork and time associated with traditional manual work order processing was eliminated" (Itron, 2005).

Despite the above applications and associated benefits of mobile technology, it is still in its infancy and companies are faced with the dilemma of why, and if so, when they should invest in it. The decision will depend on many factors, one of which is whether the organization's workforce needs to be or is already mobile. In this case, opportunities arise according to the environment in which it operates. Within a B2B and B2E environment, the value propositions are similar in that mobile technology and the corresponding applications aim to improve the productivity of the parties involved, while the focus varies between the two settings. In B2B it is the efficiency and effectiveness of the interactions between organizations that is of interest. In B2E the efficiency and effectiveness of a single worker and/or a team can be enhanced by wireless solutions that help increase productivity, streamline administrative processes, and build competitive advantage by simplifying and improving the effectiveness of collaboration.

In addition to the above considerations, there are several concerns that arise with using mobile technology in a business setting. Such concerns exist at the level of employees, organizations, and even society at large, and include the following:

Employees - Poor ease of use and low perceived usefulness may be deterrents in workers' adoption of a newly implemented technology (Davis et al., 1989). This usability concern is related to the concern for compatibility between current mobile technology capabilities and employee expectations, values and experiences. Also, privacy concerns may arise, as the content of an employee's communication, but also his/her whereabouts may be perceived as intrusive and as a threat to their individual privacy.

Organization – Given the unique nature of mobile technology and its vulnerability (Coursaris et al., 2003), concern regarding the safety of information exchanged over a wireless network increases with the degree of interaction and the sensitivity of the information exchanged (Rogers, 1995). In addition to security, there is concern over the reliability of the technology. Connection quality should be maintained for the specified network coverage. The inherent concern here is that loss of the connection can result in loss of data (Nielsen, 2000). Lastly, organizations are faced with the concern over the cost of implementing mobile technology and the expected return on that investment. As some benefits may be intangible and difficult to quantify (e.g. improved communication, timely decision making, improved customer satisfaction through increased responsiveness, etc.), it may be challenging for a business to have sufficient evidence in support of adopting mobile technology.

Society – Social skepticism around the growing use of mobile technology is in part due to the confusion over its effects on people's health. Studies have been inconclusive on whether this technology can be potentially harmful in the long-term, but in the absence of a clear answer there is apprehension towards use of such systems. Concerns over an individual's privacy and security may also deter them from using mobile solutions put forth by businesses. For example, location tracking may be perceived as threatening, both in the context of unsolicited messages/advertising and physical safety, as this information could be dangerous if intercepted. Furthermore, anytime and anywhere access offered through mobile technology provides employees with valued flexibility, but further blurs the line between work and home. Since mobility may provide 24/7 access to employees, expectations of 24/7 availability and responsiveness may also surface. This may have detrimental effects on the quality (and quantity) of leisure time and home life.

7 CONCLUSION

This paper examines the potential for mobile technologies to provide value to various business activities. Resulting benefits of mobile technology implementations may include improved productivity through enhanced process efficiency and effectiveness, as well as improved customer service. Organizations, however, need to be cognizant of potential concerns among employees and society at large in their assessment and implementation of such technologies. This paper can serve managers as a go-to resource during their initial consideration of mobile technology. Rather than making multiple choices and adopting various technological standards, a comprehensive consideration of the organization's value chain can provide a holistic representation of the company's needs. Having identified such an aggregate set of needs, information technology (I.T.) managers can proceed with the adoption of integrated systems that either include or entirely consist of mobile technologies and span multiple areas of the organization supporting a subset of services presented in this paper and delivering maximum value. In addition, I.T. managers were provided in this paper with a different lens that could be used during their assessment of I.T. resource needs. Moving beyond the individual user's needs and considering each individual's potential interactions with other employees and systems, an enhanced set of user requirements is produced from which, again, I.T. choices pertaining to mobile technology adoption are likely to become less risky and may have a higher return on investment.

While the value-chain framework provided in this paper can help managers employ new mobile technologies or assess the value and appropriateness of existing mobile applications, there are several fruitful areas for further investigation. Future research could delve more deeply into each primary or support activity to explore specific advantages and obstacles across various industries. Detailed case studies can be examined to provide managers with concrete best practices in their industry or comparable industries. Additionally, the value chain framework could be used as a lens to understand the current mobile technology platforms and how they support specific needs and expectations of employees, trading partners and customers. Lastly, empirical data could be gathered to provide further evidence of mobile technology usefulness for various value chain activities. Such data could focus on the perceived value of such technologies from various stakeholder perspectives.

REFERENCES

3Com (2005). 3Com Goes Wireless To Improve Employee Productivity. Retrieved February 5, 2008, from http://www.3com.com/solutions/en_US/casestudy.jsp?caseid=137286

Accenture (2005). Internet-Based Human Resource Solution Empowers Motorola Employees. Retrieved on January 28, 2005, from http://www.accenture.com/xd/xd.asp?it=enweb&xd=industries%5Ccommunications%5Chigh-tech%5Ccase%5Chigh_motorola.xml

Anonymous (2007). Just-in-time model eliminates Posat Monroe Truck Equipment. *Purchasing*, 136, 11, 32-37.

AT&T. (2007a). Vertical Applications for Wireless LANs. *AT&T Knowledge Ventures*. Retrieved October 25, 2007, fromhttp://www.business.att.com/resource.jsp?repoid=ProductCategory&repoitem=eb_mobility&rtype=Whitepaper&rvalue=vertical_applications_for_wireless_lans&download=yes&segment=whole

AT&T. (2007b). Making the Case for Enterprise Mobility. *AT&T Knowledge Ventures*. Retrieved October 25, 2007, from http://www.business.att.com/content/whitepaper/POV-TCO-mob_11495_V03_11-07.pdf

AT&T (2007c). Radio Frequency Identification. *AT&T Knowledge Ventures*. Retrieved October 25, 2007, from http://www.business.att.com/content/whitepaper/radioidentification.pdf

AT&T (2007d). Market brief: The Age of the Wireless LAN. *AT&T Knowledge Ventures*. Retrieved October 25, 2007, from http://www.att.com/Common/merger/files/pdf/wireless_LAN.pdf

AT&T (2006). Laying the Groundwork for WiMAX. AT&T Knowledge Ventures. Retrieved October 25, 2007, from http://www.business.att.com/content/article/wimax_gndwk_pov.pdf

Bergells, L. (2004). Wireless Advertising Plan in Six Steps. *Maniactive*. Retrieved October 25, 2007, from http://www.maniactive.com/wireless.htm.

Biesecker, C. (2006). Lockheed Martin Forms Savi Group to Zero In On Supply Chain Solutions. *C4I News*. November 23, 2006. 1. Retrieved November 15, 2007.

Bryant, J. (2007). WiFi on the plant floor. *Control Engineering*. 54, 8, 8.

Collett, S. (2003). Wireless Gets Down to Business. *Computer World*, May 23, 2003. Retrieved on January 28, 2005, from http://www.computerworld.com/mobiletopics/mobile/story/0,10801,80864,00.html

Coursaris, C., and Hassanein H. (2002). Understanding m-Commerce: A Consumer-Centric Model. *Quarterly Journal of Electronic Commerce*, 3, 3, 247-272.

Coursaris, C., Hassanein, K., & Head, M. (2003). M-Commerce in Canada: An Interaction Framework for Wireless Privacy. *Canadian Journal of Administrative Sciences*, 20, 1, 54-73.

Davis, F. D., R. P. Bagozzi, and P. R. Warshaw (1989). User acceptance of computer technology: A comparison of two theoretical models. *Management Science*, 35, 8, 982-1003.

DTI (2005). Wireless & Mobile. *Department of Trade and Industry*. Retrieved on October 25 from http://www.dti.gov.uk/bestpractice/technology/wireless-mobile.htm

Ericson, J. (2003). Considering Inbound Logistics. *Line 56*, August 23, 2003. Retrieved on July 30, 2004, at http://www.line56.com/articles/default.asp?ArticleID=4936&ml=2.

Ewalt, D. (2003). OneBridge Mobile Groupware lets companies support remote workers across multiple networks, hardware, and platforms. *InformationWeek*, August 4, 2003. Retrieved on January 28, 2005, from

http://www.informationweek.com/story/showArticle.jhtml?articleID=12808297

Extended Systems (2004). Success Stories. Retrieved on January 28, 2005, from

http://resolution.extendedsystems.com/esi/products/mobile+data+management+products/shared/success+stories/_success+stories.htm.

Ferguson, B. (2001). E-Procurement Goes Wireless. *eWeek*, February 7, 2001. Retrieved on January 28, 2005, from http://www.zdnet.com.au/news/communications/0,2000061791,20156914,00.htm.

Gosling, A. (2007). Lumension Integration For Enterprise Security. *Mobilise*, December 14, 2007. Retrieved on March 4, 2008, from http://www.mobilised.com.au/content/view/1205/96/.

Hoffman, W. (2006). Wal-Mart Tags Up. *Traffic World*. August 16, 2006, 1.

Hsu, C., Levermore, D., Carothers, C., Babin, G. (2007). Enterprise Collaboration: on-demand information exchange using enterprise databases, wireless sensor networks, and RFID systems. *IEEE Transactions on Systems, Man, and Cybernetics—Part A: Systems and Humans*, 37, 4, 519-532.

HP (2007). HP BTO software: Accelerate time to business outcomes – White Paper. Revised June 1, 2007. Retrieved on March 3, 2008, from https://h10078.www1.hp.com/cda/hpms/display/main/hpms_content.jsp?zn=bto&cp=1-11%5E4864_4000_100__

IBM (2004). RFID solution for supply chain management and in-store operations. Retrieved from http://www-1.ibm.com/industries/wireless/doc/content/solution/1025230104.html

Introducing a truly Mobile Server (2005). Retrieved on January 28, 2005, from

http://www.zeosoft.com/htmlsite/downloads/Product_Overview.pdf.

IDA (2000). Infocomm21: Leadership Dialogue. *IDA Singapore 2000*, August 2000. Retrieved on January 28, 2005, from

http://unpan1.un.org/intradoc/groups/public/documents/APCITY/UNPAN011538.pdf.

IDC (2008). IDC Predicts the Number of Worldwide Mobile Workers to Reach 1 Billion by 2011. Press Release, January 15, 2008. Retrieved on March 3, 2008, from

http://www.idc.com/getdoc.jsp?pid=23571113&containerId=prUS21037208.

IGC (2005). About IGC. Retrieved on March 3, 2008, from

http://www.intgas.com/aboutigc/aboutigc.html.

Itron (2008). Itron to Provide Service-Link® Mobile Workforce Automation Technology to Intermountain Gas Company. Press Release, June 27, 2005. Retrieved on March 3, 2008, from http://www.itron.com/pages/news_press_individual.asp?id=itr_000131.xml.

Linder, J. and Banerjee, P. (2005). Research and Development in the 21st Century: Web-Enabled Innovation Comes of Age. *Accenture*. Retrieved on October 25, 2007, from

http://www.accenture.com/xd/xd.asp?it=enweb&xd=ideas%5Coutlook%5Cpov%5Cpov_randd.xml.

Moozakis, C. (2000). Procurement App Will Go Wireless. *InternetWeek*, December 11, 2000.
Retrieved on January 28, 2005, from http://www.internetweek.com/ebizapps/ebiz121100-2.htm.

Morley, D. (2007). M2M—The New Robotics. *Manufacturing Engineering*, 138, 4, 144.

News.com (2001). Cell phones: The next great ad conduits? Retrieved from
http://news.com.com/Cell+phones+The+next+great+ad+conduits/2009-1033_3-254140.html

Nielsen, J. (2000). Designing Web Usability: The Practice of Simplicity. Indianapolis, Indiana, New
Riders Publishing.

Petersen, L. (2000). MyPrimeTime, Inc. Gains Wireless Distribution Through AvantGo.
MyPrimeTime, November 2000. Retrieved on January 28, 2005, from
http://www.myprimetime.com/misc/press/Avant_Go.shtml.

Porter, M. (1985). The value chain and competitive advantage, Chapter 2 in Competitive Advantage:
Creating and Sustaining Superior Performance. *Free Press*, New York, 33-61.

Porter, M. (2001). Strategy and the Internet. *Harvard Business Review*, 79, 3, March 2001, 21pgs.

RIM (2005). Products. Retrieved on October 25, 2007, from http://www.rim.com/products/index.shtml

Roberts, B. (2001). HR Unplugged: Wireless technology could help practitioners better serve an
increasingly mobile work force - HR Technology: Systems & Solutions - Human Resources -
Statistical Data Included. *HR Magazine*, December 2001. Retrieved on January 28, 2005, from
http://www.findarticles.com/p/articles/mi_m3495/is_12_46/ai_81393642/pg_2.

Roberts, M. (2002). Inbound Logistics Recognizes Schneider Logistics as Top Logistics IT Provider.
Schneider Logistics, May 20, 2002. Retrieved on January 28, 2005, at
http://www.schneiderlogistics.com/company_info/news_releases/ibltop100_0502.html.

Rogers, Everett M. (1995). Diffusion of Innovations. New York: The Free Press.

Siemens (2004). GSM/GPRS Modules keep a Constant Watch on Goods and Products. Retrieved on
October 25, 2007, from
http://communications.siemens.com/cds/frontdoor/0,2241,hq_en_0_2245_rArNrNrNrN,00.html.

Turban, E., Lee, J., Warketin, M., and Chung, M. (2002). Electronic Commerce: A Managerial
Perspective, Prentice Hall, page 867.

WhereNet (2004). Hummer Factory Implements WhereNet's Wireless Solutions to Enhance Assembly
Line Operations and Expedite Production. *WhereNet*, March 9, 2004. Retrieved on January 28,
2005, from http://www.wherenet.com/pressreleases/pr_03_09_2004.html.

White, A. and, Breu, K. (2005). Mobile Technologies in the Supply Chain: Emerging Empirical
Evidence of Applications and Benefits. *Proceedings of the 26th World Congress on the
Management of E-Business*, Hamilton, Ontario, Canada, January 19-21, 2005.

Williams, D. (2004). The Strategic Implictions of Wal-Mart's RFID Mandate. Retrieved from
http://www.directionsmag.com/article.php?article_id=629&trv=1&PHPSESSID=8beb74b1215e23
26d82ac11e775091c5

Winther, M. (2007). Fixed-Mobile Convergence: Lowering Costs and Complexity of Business
Communications.

Wireless-i (2005). Products. Retrieved from http://www.wireless-i.com/ourProducts.asp.

ZeoSoft (2005). A New Approach To Enterprise Wireless Strategies. Retrieved on October 25, 2007, from http://www.zeosoft.com/htmlsite/downloads/Product_Overview.pdf.

9

Teleworking in United Arab Emirates (UAE): An empirical study of influencing factors, facilitators, and inhibitors

Mohamed G. Aboelmaged
Ajman University of Science and Technology
Po Box 346, Ajman, UAE

Email: gaboelmaged@yahoo.com

Abdallah M. Elamin
King Fahd University of Petroleum and Mineral (KFUPM)
Po Box 488, Dhahran 31261, Saudi Arabia

Email: elnagar@kfupm.edu.sa

Abstract

This research constitutes an empirical study of influencing factors, facilitators, and inhibitors to the choice of teleworking mode in the UAE context. The research reveals that gender, marital status, nationality, residence location, and work profession are relevant, whereas educational level, Internet use, number of children, age, and years of experience are irrelevant influencing factors for the choice of teleworking mode. Furthermore, the research identifies six distinct facilitators and seven distinct inhibitors. The perceived importance of most identified facilitators and inhibitors to the choice of teleworking mode in the UAE context are found almost similar among the respondents. An exception, however, is made to the association between choice of teleworking mode and individual freedom, travel overload, cost reduction, and union resistance. The study outlines the limitations of the present research and suggests some practical implications and recommendations for managers.

Keywords: teleworking, information technology, facilitators, inhibitors, UAE

1 INTRODUCTION

Teleworking has recently received a considerable amount of attention both at the academia and professional world, as one of the remarkable changes in business practices (Morgan, 2004). The last few years have witnessed an increasing interest in the concept of teleworking, particularly in Europe and USA. Current predictions suggest that teleworking may become a common mode of working in future, as Knight (2004) points out that 20 million people in Europe will be teleworking by 2007, taking the enterprise boundary with them.

The concept of using information technology to work at a distance from the regular work site, referred to initially as *telecommuting* working and later as *teleworking*. The term first came to wider public attention in the USA in the early 1970s, when it was initially coined by Nilles in 1973 (Nilles, 1994), and it has been described as a growing trend and the future way of organizing work. In some publications, telecommuting and teleworking are often used interchangeably, but telework is generally used in a broader sense, covering a wider array of distributed work. In general, the motives of telecommuting are mainly aimed at achieving travel-time savings, while teleworkers (which may include telecommuters) attempt to work in alternative workplaces.

2 LITERATURE REVIEW

Various authors (e.g. Mann, 2000) have pointed out the diverse meanings assigned to the term "teleworking". Accordingly, several researchers have tried to establish their own definition. For example Nilles (1994) states that teleworking is "...the partial or total substitution of telecommunications technologies, possibly with the aid of computers, for the commute to work". In the same vein, Mokhtarian (1991) contends that the term refers to "...working at home or at an alternate location and communicating with the usual place of work using electronic or other means, instead of physically traveling to a more distant work site". Due to such an inconsistency shaping the definition of the term, one could argue that the definitions applied to telework can be grouped in two main blocks; on the one hand those that emphasize the location of the teleworker and on the other hand, those that stress the use of information communication technologies (ICT).

The empirical literature on teleworking has grown significantly over the last decade and most studies are western-based. Researching teleworking in developing world is unsurprisingly new, an Arab world being no exception. According to Cooper and Schindler (2003), literature can be descriptive, conceptual, empirical, or case study in nature. This section reviews the mainstream empirical teleworking literature.

On empirical side of teleworking research, researchers present results from surveying and analyzing large number of teleworkers, prospected teleworkers, or companies. Golden (2006), for example, use a sample of 393 professional-level teleworkers in one organization to investigate the intervening role of work exhaustion in determining commitment and turnover intentions. Similarly, Neufeld and Fang (2005) conduct two-phased research study to point out that teleworker beliefs and attitudes, and the quality of their social interactions with managers and family members, were strongly associated with productivity. In the similar thought, Thériault *et al.*, (2005) assess differences between home-based working and teleworking behavior among genders and professions considering age groups, household status, car access location within the city and travel distances. They conclude that gender, professional status, and age are influencing factors to the choice to teleworking. For example, older workers are more likely to telework than younger ones, with the exception of lone parents which are seeking for more flexibility. Furthermore, Carnicer *et al.* (2003) analyze the results of a survey about labor mobility of a sample of 1,182 Spanish employees. Their study indicates that women have lower mobility than men, and that the mobility of men and women is explained by different factors such as employee's perceptions about job satisfaction, pay fairness, and employment stability. In a study of emotional impact of teleworking, Mann (2000) found that respondents of two service industries in the UK perceive teleworking advantages as follows: less travel (57%); more freedom/flexibility (57%); better working environment (50%); fewer distractions (43%); cheaper (29%); freedom to choose comfortable clothes (14%); freedom from office politics (7%); and easier to complete domestic chores (7%). On the other hand, Mann (2000) found the perceived disadvantages of teleworking include isolation (57%); longer hours (50%); lack of support (28%); less sick leave (21%); career progression (14%); and cost (7%). Similarly, Mannering and Mokhtarian (1995) explored the individual's choice of teleworking frequency as a function of demographic, travel, work, and attitudinal factors. They show that the most important variables in explaining the choice of frequency of teleworking from home were the presence of small children in the household, the number of people in the household, gender of respondent, number of vehicles in the household, whether respondent recently changed departure time for personal reasons, degree of control over scheduling of different job tasks, supervisory status of respondent, the ability to borrow a computer from work if necessary, and a family orientation. In addition, Yap and Tng (1990) conducted a survey of the attitudes of female computer professionals in Singapore towards teleworking. The study reveals that 73% of the 459 respondents were in favor of teleworking. Most would prefer to work at home 1 to 3 days a week and at the office on the other days, rather than working at home full time. They would telework only in times of need (e.g. when they have young children) and were concerned with work and interaction-related problems which might arise from teleworking. Furthermore, Yap and Tng (1990) suggest that teleworking will be of particular interest to employees who are married, those with a high proportion of work that can be done at home, those who find their journey to work frustrating, and those with supervisors and coworkers who are supportive of teleworking.

3 RESEARCH OBJECTIVES

The objective of this research is twofold:
1. To examine the influence of specific demographic and individual variables on the choice for teleworking mode.
2. To examine the differences in employees' perception of importance of the facilitators and inhibitors based on their choice of the teleworking mode.

4 RESEARCH RATIONALE

The rationale behind the study was driven by the fact that most of the teleworking literature has generally taken their roots in the developed countries, most notably North America and Western Europe (Kowalski and Swanson (2005). This point indicates that there is a gap worth filling in the literature resulting from the lack of studies in developing contexts. Considering the uniqueness of the UAE economical, political and socio-cultural contexts, this study would contribute to filling that identified gap.

Though the benefits of teleworking are widely accepted within the literature, there is very scarce empirical research about how demographic and individual variables influence teleworking choice (full-time, part-time, not to telework) in non-western contexts. Examining such relationships between teleworking choice for both actual and prospective teleworker and various demographic and individual variables as well as facilitators and inhibitors in an Arab context, namely UAE will add to the body of knowledge in this regard.

Finally, the outcome of the present study will provide employees, managers and practitioners with important insights that help them make better decisions concerning teleworking programs aiming at improving organizational processes and fostering strategic goals.

5 DEVELOPMENT OF RESEARCH HYPOTHESES

5.1 The role of demographic and individual variables

The extant literature has shown that there are numerous demographic and individual variables influence the choice of teleworking mode, including gender, age, martial status, profession, educational level, internet use, nationality, residence, number of children, and years of experience. The subsequent paragraphs review some of the relevant literature on this regards.

Peters *et al.* (2004) indicate that socio-demographic variables, such as gender and age, are found to influence teleworking adoption and its preference. Similarly, Thériault *et al.*, (2005) suggest that gender and professional status influence teleworking choice, and older workers are more likely to telework than younger ones. Moreover, Yeraguntla and Bhat (2005) show that women households with children are likely to be part-time teleworkers, reinforcing the notion that women are the primary caregivers of children. All in all, they consider age as one of the important individual socio-demographic variable that turned out to be significant predictor of teleworking. The age effect indicates that young adults (less than 25 years) are more likely to prefer part-time employment than older adults. These results are also consistent with the findings of Bagley and Mokhtarian (1997). Moreover, they reveal that race, job type, and length of service are also important influential factors for the choice of teleworking mode. Caucasians and Hispanics, For instance, are more likely to telework than other races (African-Americans, Asians and other). As for job type, their study indicates that employees working for an educational institution are more likely to be part-time teleworkers than employees in other kinds of organizations. For the length of service, Yeraguntla and Bhat's (2005) study reveals that employees who have worked less than a year in the firm are more likely to be part-time teleworkers than those who have been working for longer periods of time.

A survey conducted by Mokhtarian and Salomon (1996) for the employees of the city of San Diego about teleworking, revealed that only 3% of the sample report that they face no constraints to telework but do not have a preference for it and do not currently do it. Based on such a survey they conclude that people who have longer commutes are more likely to report that they want to telework, especially if they are women and younger people. Having children, however, seems to have no effect on the desire to telework.

In the same vein, Mannering and Mokhtarian (1995) use survey data collected from employees of three government agencies in California to model the frequency of teleworking. The results show that being a mother of small children had a positive influence on teleworking, as did the number of vehicles per capita in the household.

Similarly, Wells *et al.* (2001) conduct surveys of employees at a public agency and a private firm in Minnesota. They find that 43% of the surveyed employees engaged in teleworking. Furthermore, they report that Public agency workers teleworked, on an average, three days a week, while private firm workers teleworked, on an average, 1.92 days a week. The authors find that teleworkers are more likely to be women, married, and have children.

It is worth noting that, Popuri and Bhat (2003) use data from a national survey of 14,441 households conducted by the New York Metropolitan Transportation Council to show factors that increase the likelihood that an individual telework. Such factors include women with children, college education, a driver's license, being married, working part-time, household income, working for a private company (rather than government), and having to pay parking fees at work. Also, it has been found that the longer an individual has worked at her current place of employment, the greater the probability she teleworks.

In their analysis of the telework Survey conducted by the Southern California Association of Governments (SCAG), Safirova and Walls (2004) confirm that having high educational level, more professional experience in general, and a longer tenure with one's current company and one's current supervisor will boost the probability of teleworking. Such a study has also revealed a very surprising finding that teleworkers are more likely to be male and have smaller households than non-teleworkers, which is inconsistent with other studies' findings that have shown women, and especially women with children, to be likely teleworkers.

In the view of the aforementioned discussion, the following hypothesis seems to be relevant for studying the teleworking in the UAE.

Hypothesis 1: There is no difference among employees in their choice for teleworking based on their:

H1a: Gender
H1b: Marital status
H1c: Educational level
H1d: Internet use
H1e: Nationality
H1f: Residence
H1g: No of children
H1h: Age
H1i: Years of experience
H1j: Profession

5.2 Facilitators of Teleworking

Teleworking was originally seen as part of a solution to an energy crisis involving the reduction of commuting (Gray et. al., 1993). In this regard, Kurland and Cooper (2002) show that employees choose teleworking to reduce lengthy commutes, to decrease work-related stress, to balance work and family responsibilities, to work longer hours but in more comfortable environments, and to provide uninterrupted time to focus on their work. Organization-wise, teleworking improve employee morale and productivity (Kurland and Bailey, 1999). Interestingly, Gray et al. (1993) find that teleworkers are more productive than office-bound staffs that have to travel to work and tend to suffer a higher level of stress. In addition, Productivity will increase through teleworking if employees are well motivated and satisfied when they are able to manage their own time and assume greater responsibility for their own work. And also because teleworking contributes to the reduction of costs of absenteeism, stress related to traffic congestions, train delays and continuous office interruptions (Lim et al., 2003).

Lupton and Haynes (2000) identify four significant driving forces for teleworking: (1) a change in management attitudes; (2) savings in office costs; (3) demand from staff; and (4) improvements in technology. Other facilitators include improved productivity, improved staff retention, improved morale/motivation, and improved staff recruitment opportunities. These forces are confirmed by Mann (2000) who also points to less travel, more freedom/flexibility, better working environment, fewer distractions, freedom to choose comfortable clothes, freedom from office politics, and easiness to complete domestic chores.

Another classification of teleworking facilitators can be found in the literature is adopted by Mills *et al* (2001) and Tung and Turban (1996) who distinguish among three categories of facilitators include organizational, individual, and societal facilitators.

According to Mills *et al* (2001) and Tung and Turban (1996) organizational facilitators for teleworking adoption may include securing skilled employees, saving office space, reducing turnover and absenteeism, computer literacy and usage, productivity gains, overcoming limitations of distance and time, providing service from home terminals, and reducing operating cost. Individual facilitators for teleworking, on the other hand, include initiating personal freedom, autonomy, and flexibility (Feldman and Gainey (1997), support no conflicting working environment (Pulido and Lopez, 2005), increasing personal productivity, avoiding a commute, working with fewer interruptions, working in more pleasant surroundings, wearing informal casual clothes, saving the costs of meals, clothes, and commuting, greater time flexibility, greater job satisfaction, and bridging the career gap by avoiding a long career break staying at home (Mills *et al.*, 2001; Tung and Turban, 1996).Community or societal related teleworking facilitators may include reduction of air pollution and dependence on fuel, enable disabled people to work from home, conserve energy and reduce traffic during rush hours and demand on transportation, and solving the problem of rural depopulation (Mills *et al.*, 2001; Tung and Turban, 1996).

Although all these facilitators can support the trend of teleworking implementation, there is still a literature gap about the role of teleworking choice (full-time, part-time, not to telework) in influencing perceived importance of teleworking facilitators. In conjunction with this line of reasoning, the following hypothesis is developed:

Hypothesis 2: There is no difference among employees in the perceived importance of teleworking facilitators based on their choice for teleworking.

5.3 Inhibitors of teleworking

Despite the potential facilitators, teleworking raises two important inhibitors: supervisors' resistance to manage employees that they cannot physically observe (managerial control), and employees' concerns about professional and social isolation (Kurland and Cooper, 2002). Studies, which have addressed these issues, are largely surveys (e.g., Mokhtarian *et al.*, 1995). One exceptional is made to the study conducted by Baruch and Nicholson (1997). They gathered interview data from 62 teleworkers representing five different companies. However, they only noted that isolation and managerial reluctance were factors that could hinder teleworking. In line with this, Reid (1993) cites loss of status and professional isolation as potential dangers for workers moving into teleworking. The likely outcome of isolation is the lack of interaction with colleagues, which stands as a serious inhibitor.

As far as management control is concerned, Kurland and Cooper (2002) has demonstrated that managers may lose control over employees' behavior as employees gain autonomy by teleworking. Teleworking can diminish a manager's perceived control as it physically removes the employee from the conventional work environment. At the same time the employees believe that the isolation may result in lack of promotional opportunities.

Other inhibitors may include cost of implementation and resistance of management to change, longer hours, lack of support, less sick leave, career progression (Lupton and Haynes, 2000; Mann, 2000).

Another classification of teleworking inhibitors is adopted by Mills *et al* (2001) and Tung and Turban (1996) who distinguish among three categories of inhibitors include organizational, individual, and societal inhibitors. According to Mills *et al* (2001) and Tung and Turban (1996) organizational inhibitors of teleworking adoption may include technology cost inefficiencies, managing out-of-sight employees, need for collaboration with other employees, security risks, problems of supervision, performance control difficulty, work coordination difficulty, legal liability, maintenance of equipment. From the individual point of view, inhibitors may include isolation, doubts and lack of knowledge of the state of a task, unavailability of necessary supplies or equipment, family interruptions and household distractions, no separation of work and home life, lack of interactions with co-workers, and potential lack of loyalty to company, not having a regular routine, workaholics, impedes career opportunities, and missing "what's going on", problem of 'guilt', and increase in cost of equipment and utilities at home (Mills *et al.*, 2001; Tung and Turban, 1996; Pulido and Lopez, 2005). From the community perspective, teleworking may be inhibited as a result of promoting dispersion of housing, increasing commuting distances, slowing down of real estate market, and declining clothing industry (Mills *et al.*, 2001; Tung and Turban, 1996).

Although all these inhibitors can hinder teleworking implementation, there is a notoriously unfilled literature gap about the role of teleworking choice (full-time, part-time, not to telework) in influencing perceived importance of teleworking inhibitors. Based on the above discussion, the following hypothesis is suggested:

Hypothesis 3: There is no difference among employees in the perceived importance of teleworking inhibitors based on their choice for teleworking.

6 RESEARCH METHODOLOGY

This research follows the underlying principles of quantitative research methodology. It entails the collection of numerical data as exhibiting a few of the relationships between theory and research as deductive, and as having an objectivist conception of social reality (Bryman, 2008). A survey research method was applied to obtain insight about the issues explored in the study. Primary research data are collected through structured questionnaire on a voluntary basis. To ensure the right level of teleworking awareness, several studies recommend sampling employees from organizations involved in information technology profession, when studying teleworking (Teo and Lim, 1998; Tung and Turban 1996). The researchers, therefore, consider an employee in an organization within information technology sphere as the unit of analysis in this research. Organizations in Dubai Media City (DMC) and Dubai Internet City (DIC) are selected as target. Both cities include more than 500 organizations in the field of networking, software development, programming, consultancy, broadcasting, publishing, advertising, public relations, research and development, music and creative services. A total of 350 questionnaires are distributed; of these, 148 were returned. 12 questionnaires are ignored due to ignoring complete section(s) or missing data in certain sections, leaving a balance of 136 useful questionnaires for this study, with a valid response rate of 39%. Respondents represent eleven ICT and media organizations specialized in media organization and dissemination, software development, wireless technology, communication tools and equipment, media production, and consultancy services. All organizations are small to medium in size varying from 20 to 300 employees. Questionnaire data were aggregated, and no analysis was conducted linking individual responses to a specific organization.

6.1 Measurement development, reliability, and validity

The survey instrument included several statements designed to measure the research constructs. First, choice for teleworking is presented in a nominal scale with three options: (1) not to telework; (2) part-time teleworking; and (3) full-time teleworking. Second, the perceived importance of each of teleworking facilitators and inhibitors is measured based on a four-point Likert scale from "strongly disagree" to "strongly agree". The survey also gathers demographic information on the respondents' gender, marital status, educational level, internet use, nationality, residence location, number of children, age, years of experience, and work profession. A nominal scale is developed for each of these constructs.

Content validity is assessed by examining the process that is used in generating scale items, and its translation into other languages (i.e., Arabic in this study). The determination of content validity is judgmental and can be approached through careful definition of the topic of the concern, the scaled items, and used scales (Cooper and Schindler, 2003). Teleworking facilitators and inhibitors are developed based on extensive review of teleworking literature, and then reduced using a varimax rotated principal component factor analysis. Furthermore, Cooper and Schindler (2003) suggest another way to determine content validity through panel of persons to judge how well the instrument meets the standards. Thus, the researchers conducted independent interviews with two professors of human resources and one professor of information technology applications to evaluate whether research covers relevant constructs. They suggested that the procedure and Arabic translation of the questionnaire were generally appropriate, with some modifications in the translated version of the questionnaire.

6.2 Data Presentation and Analysis

Responses from the surveys were coded and entered into SPSS spreadsheets for data analysis. For a descriptive analysis, means, SD, cross tabulation, factor analysis, and Kruskal-Walllis test were applied to the sample.

6.3 Profile of research demographics

The survey's demographic descriptive statistics are presented in Table 1. Of the 136 respondents, 54.4% select part-time teleworking option, 33.1% decide not to telework, and 12.5% choose full-time teleworking option. 50.7 % of the respondents are male and 49.3 % are female. 67.6% are single and 32.4% are married. 31.7% of married respondents have one child, 26.8% have two children, 22.0% have three children, and 19.5% have four or more children. The research respondents are relatively young; the majority of survey respondents age is between 20 and 29 years (44.9 %), while 25.7% are between 30 – 39 years, 18.4% are less than 20, and only11% are above 40 years old. The education level reported by respondents showed that 75.7% had university degree or equivalent. Respondents were mainly non-UAE national (66.2%), national Respondents are only represent 33.8%. 40.4% of research respondents live in the emirate of Sharajah 40.4%, Ajman 25.7%, Dubai 22.1%, Abu Dhabi 6.6%, and UmQuin 5.1%. The description shows that 39% of the respondents are internet users for 1-3 times a week, 34.6% use the internet 7 or more times a week, 19.8% use the internet 4-6 times a week, and 6.6% are not using the Internet. According to years of experience, most of the respondents (72.8%) had less than 7 years, and approximately 27.2% had more than 7 years of experience. Respondents in ICT professions are 18.4%, while 27.2% of respondents are in media professions, 27.2% are in management and marketing professions, and 27.2% are in accounting professions.

In conclusion, majority of respondents in this study prefer part-time teleworking, graduate male, single, between 20 – 29 years of age, care for one child if married, with non UAE nationality, live in Sharjah, use the internet 1-3 times a week, working in different ICT and media professions, with less than 7 years of experience.

Table 1: Profile of research respondents (N=136)

%	N		%	N	
		Marital status			**Teleworking choice**
67.6	92	Single	12.5	17	Full-time
32.4	44	Married	54.4	74	Part-time
			33.1	45	No choice
		Nationality			**Gender**
33.8	46	UAE	49.3	67	Female
66.2	90	Non UAE	50.7	69	Male
		Freq. of internet use			**Educational level**
34.6	47	7 or more times /week	7.4	10	Postgraduate
19.8	27	4-6 times /week	75.7	103	Graduate
39.0	53	1-3 times /week	16.9	23	Undergraduate
6.6	9	No use /week			
					Children
		Residence	31.7	13	1
6.6	9	Abu Dhabi	26.8	11	2
22.1	30	Dubai	22.0	9	3
40.4	55	Sharjah	19.5	8	4 or more
25.7	35	Ajman			
5.1	7	UMQ			**Years of experience**
			36.8	50	0-3
		Age	36	49	4-6
18.4	25	Less than 20	17.6	24	7-9
44.9	61	20 – 29	9.6	13	9 or more
25.7	35	30 – 39			
11	15	40 or more			**Profession**
			18.4	25	IT
			27.2	37	Media
			27.2	37	Mgt. & Marketing
			27.2	37	Account. & Finance

6.4 Testing the first hypothesis

A cross tabulation analysis is conducted to assess whether there is no difference among employees in their choice for teleworking based on specific demographic variables. Tables 2 presents frequencies, percentages, and associations of teleworking choice (i.e., full-time, part-time, and not to telework) with a number of selected demographic and individual variables including gender, marital status, educational level, internet use, nationality, residence, number of children, years of experience, and occupation.

Table 2 indicates that there is a significant difference among employees in their teleworking choice based on their gender ($\chi^2 = 12.06$, $p < 0.01$). It is clear from the cross tabulation presented in Table 2 that females constitute the majority of employees who select full-time teleworking option (88.2%), while males are the majority who select part-time teleworking (58.1%) as well as not to telework (53.3%). It also shows the association between marital status and teleworking. In that sense, employees' marital status does significantly influence teleworking choice ($\chi^2 = 6.69$, $p < 0.05$). The table demonstrates that single employees are over represented among non teleworkers (80%). On the other side, married employees are over represented among full-time teleworkers (52.9%). Educational levels and their distribution cross teleworking choices are illustrated in also reflected in the Table. The analysis suggests no significant difference among employees in their teleworking choice based on their educational level ($\chi^2 = 1.451$, n.s.). The analysis shows that graduate employees with a university degree or equivalent are over represented in each of teleworking groups; full-time (76.5%), part-time (75.7%), and no teleworking group (75.6%). Similarly, the table suggests no significant difference among employees in their teleworking choice based on their level of Internet use ($\chi^2 = 11.19$, n.s.). Employees who use the internet 1-3 times weekly form the majority of two contradictory teleworking groups; full-time teleworking (70.6%) and no teleworking (42.2%). While the majority of employees who prefer part-time teleworking are using the Internet for 7 or more times per week (39.2%). Further, the table indicates that there is a significant difference among employees in their teleworking choice based on their nationality ($\chi^2 = 6.33$, $p < 0.05$). It is clear from the cross tabulation presented in Table 2 that employees with UAE nationality are over represented among full-time teleworkers (58.8%), while employees with non UAE nationality (e.g., Egyptians, Indians, etc.) are over represented among part-time teleworkers (73.0%) as well as non teleworkers (64.4%). Surprisingly, difference among employees in their teleworking choice based on their city of residence is significant ($\chi^2 = 33.99$, $p > 0.001$). Moreover, the table illustrates that part-time teleworking is the main choice of employees living in emirates of Dubai, Sharjah, and Ajman, while the main teleworking choice of employees living in UmQuin emirate is full time. However, employees who are living in Abu Dhabi tend to prefer not to telework. Distribution of number of children cross teleworking choices is also illustrated in the table suggesting that there is no significant difference among employees in their teleworking choice based on their number of children ($\chi^2 = 5.65$, n.s.). Employees who select full-time teleworking are equally distributed among those who have two (28.6%), three (28.6%), and four or more (28.6%) children, while part-time teleworking choice is dominated by employees who have one child only (38.5%). Similarly, the table suggests no significant difference among employees in their teleworking choice based on their age ($\chi^2 = 3.78$, n.s.). Employees between 20-29 years dominate the majority in every teleworking group; full-time teleworking (47.1%), part-time teleworking (43.2%), and not to telework (46.7%). Moreover, the relationship between employees' teleworking choice and their years of experience is not significant ($\chi^2 = 11.11$, n.s.) as demonstrated by the table which indicates that employees who have 4-6 years of experience represent the majority of employees who choose two contradictory options; to telework full-time (56.8%) and not to telework (44.4%), while part-time teleworking choice is dominated by employees who have less than four years of working experience (45.9%). Finally the table illustrates the relationship between teleworking choice and profession. It shows that employees' profession does significantly influence teleworking choice ($\chi^2 = 21.95$, $p < 0.01$). The table demonstrates that 46.7% of employees who prefer not to telework are in accounting and finance profession, 28.4% of employees who prefer part-time teleworking are in management and marketing profession, while employees in media profession are over represented among full-time teleworkers (52.9%).

Table 2: Cross tabulation results

	Teleworking Choice			Total	χ^2	p value
	Full-time	**Part-time**	**No**			
Gender					12.06**	0.002
Male	2 (11.8)	43 (58.1)	24 (53.3)	69 (50.7)		
Female	15 (88.2)	31 (41.9)	21 (46.7)	67 (49.3)		
Marital status					6.69*	0.03
Single	8 (47.1)	48 (64.9)	36 (80)	92 (67.6)		
Married	9 (52.9)	26 (35.1)	9 (20)	44 (32.4)		
Educational level					1.45	0.83
Undergrad.	3 (17.6)	11 (14.9)	9 (20)	23 (16.9)		
Graduate	13 (76.5)	56 (75.7)	34 (75.6)	103 (75.7)		
Postgrad.	1 (5.9)	7 (9.5)	2 (4.4)	10 (7.4)		
Internet Use					11.19	0.08
No use	0 (0)	5 (6.8)	4 (8.9)	9 (6.6)		
1-3 times	12 (70.6)	22 (29.7)	19 (42.2)	53 (39)		
4-6 times	2 (11.8)	18 (24.3)	7 (15.6)	27 (19.9)		
7 or more	3 (17.6)	29 (39.2)	15 (33.3)	47 (34.6)		
Nationality					6.33*	0.04
UAE	10 (58.8)	20 (27)	16 (35.6)	46 (33.8)		
Non UAE	7 (41.2)	54 (73)	29 (64.4)	90 (66.2)		
Residence location					33.99**	0.00
Abu Dhabi	0 (0)	2 (2.7)	7 (15.6)	9 (6.6)		
Dubai	2 (11.8)	16 (21.6)	12 (26.7)	30 (22.1)		
Sharjah	5 (29.4)	34 (45.9)	16 (35.6)	55 (40.4)		
Ajman	5 (29.4)	21 (28.4)	9 (20)	35 (25.7)		
UMQ	5 (29.4)	1 (1.4)	1 (2.2)	7 (5.1)		
No. of Children					4.65	0.58
One	1 (14.2)	10 (38.5)	2 (25)	13 (31.7)		
Two	2 (28.6)	8 (30.8)	1 (12.5)	11 (26.8)		
Three	2 (28.6)	5 (19.2)	2 (25)	9 (22)		
Four or more	2 (28.6)	3 (11.15)	3 (37.5)	8 (19.5)		
Age					3.78	0.706
> 20	1 (5.9)	15 (20.3)	9 (20)	25 (18.4)		
20 - 29	8 (47.1)	32 (43.2)	21 (46.7)	61 (44.9)		
30 - 39	6 (35.3)	17 (23)	12 (26.7)	35 (25.7)		
40 ≤	2 (11.8)	10 (13.5)	3 (6.7)	15 (11)		
Years of experience					11.11	0.085
0-3	2 (11.8)	34 (45.9)	14 (31.1)	50 (36.8)		
4-6	10 (56.8)	19 (25.7)	20 (44.4)	49 (36)		
7-9	3 (17.6)	13 (17.6)	8 (17.8)	24 (17.6)		
9 or more	2 (11.8)	8 (10.8)	3 (6.7)	13 (9.6)		
Profession					21.95**	0.001
IT	4 (23.5)	18 (24.3)	3 (6.7)	25 (18.4)		
Media	9 (52.9)	19 (25.7)	9 (20)	37 (27.2)		
Mgt. & Market.	4 (23.5)	21 (28.4)	12 (26.7)	37 (27.2)		
Account. & Finance	0 (0)	16 (21.6)	21 (46.7)	37 (27.2)		
Total	17 (100.0%)	74 (100.0%)	45 (100.0%)	136 (100.0%)		

In conclusion, results from ensuing presentation show significant association between teleworking choice and gender, marital status, nationality, residence, and profession. On the other hand, there is no significant association between teleworking choice and educational level, Internet use, number of children, age, and years of experience. Accordingly, hypothesis H1 is partially supported.

6.5 Testing the Second and Third hypotheses
The data collected concerning employees' perception of teleworking facilitators and inhibitors are reduced using a varimax rotated principal component factor analysis. Tables 3 and 4 display the various facilitators and inhibitors used in this study and show the factor loadings for each of the items. The loadings indicate a significant relationship between items in each of the factors since all but three are greater than .50, the critical value for significant loadings (Hair *et al.*, 1992).

Table 3: Factors analysis of teleworking facilitators *

7	6	5	4	3	2	1		
Community concerns						**(α = 0.85)**		
0.093	-0.046	0.202	0.046	0.122	0.097	0.753	Environmental pollution	F20
-0.125	0.235	0.087	-0.055	0.193	0.257	0.749	Working opport. for disabled	F21
0.005	0.169	0.094	0.220	0.008	0.174	0.724	Traffic Jams	F22
0.038	0.088	0.232	0.305	0.141	0.238	0.676	Increasing oil prices	F19
0.169	0.067	-0.059	0.379	-0.020	-0.072	0.647	Severe weather conditions	F24
0.281	-0.082	0.069	0.103	0.320	0.072	0.629	Family care	F23
Individual freedom					**(α = 0.78)**			
-0.076	-0.066	0.125	0.089	0.143	0.782	0.122	Flexible working time and location	F11
0.246	0.214	0.109	0.075	0.190	0.749	0.120	Personal freedom	F9
0.255	-0.041	0.064	0.036	0.146	0.745	0.178	Avoid work stress	F10
0.178	0.108	-0.039	0.368	0.267	0.427	0.152	No absenteeism	F14
Productivity improvement				**(α = 0.78)**				
-0.107	0.167	0.073	0.046	0.785	0.158	0.130	Developing ICT usage	F17
0.109	-0.165	0.221	0.077	0.727	0.007	0.056	Better utilization of working time	F8
-0.018	0.093	0.174	-0.024	0.603	0.439	0.203	Improving output quality and quantity	F13
-0.170	0.284	-0.034	-0.081	0.593	0.419	0.152	Increasing employees loyalty	F16
0.417	0.180	0.176	0.015	0.481	0.237	0.101	Paperless work	F18
Travel load			**(α = 0.71)**					
0.076	0.180	-0.047	0.797	-0.035	-0.126	0.146	Travel preparation	F6
0.036	-0.178	0.132	0.724	0.153	0.247	0.219	Travel time	F5
-0.087	0.049	0.368	0.624	0.007	0.298	0.298	Travel effort and cost	F3
Cost reduction		**(α = 0.66)**						
-0.025	0.017	0.821	0.022	0.180	0.193	0.137	Saving org. space and equipments	F2
0.279	-0.100	0.671	0.136	0.134	-0.003	0.365	Increasing cost of real states	F1
-0.158	0.469	0.518	0.460	0.017	0.102	0.121	Increasing cost of clothes and accessories	F4
Empowering people	**(α = 0.51)**							
0.226	0.801	0.033	0.0091	0.103	0.096	0.102	Minimizing supervisory functions	F15
0.012	0.471	-0.282	0.313	0.355	-0.158	0.217	Task focus	F7
0.831	0.158	0.023	0.042	-0.076	0.209	0.161	Doing other more things	F12
1.382	1.529	1.893	2.346	2.743	2.826	3.512	*Eigenvalue*	
5.76	6.37	7.89	9.77	11.43	11.78	14.63	*Percentage of variance explained*	
67.63	61.87	55.50	47.61	37.84	26.41	14.63	*Cumulative percentage of total var. explained*	
0.993	0.710	0.716	0.743	0.589	0.665	0.645	*Standard deviation*	

Correlation Matrix Determinant = 0.0000179

Kaiser-Meyer-Olkin Measure of Sampling Adequacy = 0.814

Bartlett's Test of Sphericity ($\chi2 = 1378.98$, $df = 276$, $p < 0.001$)

* *Principal components analysis; varimax rotation with Kaiser Normalization*

Table 4: Factors analysis of teleworking inhibitors *

7	6	5	4	3	2	1		
Management concerns (α = 0.77)								
-0.132	0.164	0.055	0.013	-0.201	0.161	0.727	Org. vision and mission are misplaced	B15
0.102	0.060	0.199	0.029	0.224	0.028	0.714	Safety criteria are not guaranteed	B16
0.156	0.147	0.012	0.228	0.045	0.192	0.683	Inapplicable work rules and regulations	B13
0.039	0.261	0.032	0.447	0.088	0.098	0.569	Access difficulty to decision info.	B17
0.265	- 0.029	- 0.056	0.154	-0.054	0.392	0.559	Hard to control and evaluate performance	B14
Isolation (α = 0.79)								
0.169	-0.015	- 0.020	0.124	0.111	0.766	0.089	Misguidance regarding use of org. resources	B11
0.077	0.009	0.257	0.295	0.330	0.672	0.149	Need to interact with work colleagues	B8
-0.167	0.433	0.063	0.199	0.014	0.596	0.265	Lack of teleworking experience	B10
0.205	0.135	0.120	0.062	0.187	0.528	0.385	Feeling guilty toward the organization	B7
0.048	0.293	- 0.037	0.480	0.124	0.509	0.194	Missing promotional opportunities at work	B9
Union resistance (α = 0.77)								
-0.207	-0.097	0.139	-0.016	0.800	0.115	-0.045	Union resistance	B23
0.148	0.017	0.027	0.073	0.793	0.104	0.026	Clothing and makeup industry loss	B22
-0.008	0.194	0.036	0.170	0.705	0.196	-0.066	Negative impact on real state sector	B21
-0.010	0.144	-0.020	0.218	0.672	- 0.157	0.227	Unclear insurance	B24
Home inadequacy (α = 0.71)								
0.017	0.112	0.192	0.664	0.266	0.053	-0.068	Increased home noise	B20
0.017	-0.091	0.142	0.631	0.150	0.261	0.213	Data insecurity	B19
0.236	-0.148	0.106	0.568	-0.021	0.336	0.438	Coordination difficulty	B12
0.276	0.318	-0.150	0.531	0.020	0.239	0.317	Inapplicable team working	B18
ICT cost (α = 0.86)								
0.134	0.073	0.900	0.017	0.017	0.117	0.130	ICT acquisition cost	B1
0.036	0.145	0.871	0.219	0.125	0.074	0.062	ICT maintenance and upgrading cost	B2
Time mismanagement (α = 0.51)								
0.208	.802	0.068	-0.046	0.021	0.199	0.169	Home time mismanaged	B6
0.094	.594	0.323	0.152	0.289	-0.109	0.091	Org. time expansion	B3
Family intervention (α = 0.62)								
0.835	0.106	0.105	0.217	-0.087	0.111	0.046	Family rights	B4
0.612	0.303	0.187	-0.117	0.095	0.266	0.350	Family – work intervention	B5
1.570	1.747	1.969	2.307	2.595	2.639	3.010	*Eigenvalue*	
6.54	7.28	8.20	9.61	10.81	10.99	12.54	*Percentage of variance explained*	
65.97	59.43	52.15	43.95	34.34	23.53	12.54	*Cumulative percentage of total var. explained*	
0.710	0.694	0.745	0.661	0.688	0.611	0.579	*Standard deviation*	
Correlation Matrix Determinant = 0.00002334								
Kaiser-Meyer-Olkin Measure of Sampling Adequacy = 0.794								
Bartlett's Test of Sphericity ($\chi 2 = 1345.59$, df = 276, p < 0.001)								

* Principal components analysis; varimax rotation with Kaiser Normalization

Cumulative percentage of total variance explained for factor analysis of perceived teleworking facilitators is 67.63% with Kaiser-Meyer-Olkin measure of sampling adequacy = 0.814, while cumulative percentage of total variance explained for factor analysis of perceived teleworking inhibitors is 65.97% with Kaiser-Meyer-Olkin measure of sampling adequacy = 0.794. The Cronbach alpha coefficient is used to assess reliability of the generated facilitators and inhibitors. As shown in Tables 3 and 4, the alpha reliabilities range from a low of 0.51 to a high of 0.86. All the reliability figures, except two variables, were higher than 0.6, the lowest acceptable limit for Cronbach's alpha suggested by Hair *et al.* (1992), variables with reliabilities lower than 0.6 deserve a further refinement in future research.

6.6 Study-based generated facilitators

The ensuing factor analysis generates six distinct perceived facilitators for teleworking, including community concerns, individual freedom, productivity improvement, travel load, cost reduction, and empowering people (see Table 3).

(1) Community concerns: this factor includes a number of community concerns such as reducing environmental pollution; provision of working opportunities for disabled; reducing traffic jams; continuous increasing of oil prices; severe weather conditions all over the year; and family care issues. No doubt, these concerns make adoption and implementation of teleworking programs in UAE is an appealing option, particularly in case when distance from home to the workplace is far or when traffic congestion is a problem.

(2) Individual freedom: Items in this factor reflect the notion that teleworking is forced by the need to reduce stress level and increase job commitment and quality of work life. One likely reason is that the flexibility in working schedule of teleworkers offers opportunities for them to engage in non-work activities to a much larger extent than otherwise possible. Such scheduling freedom may allow time for personal interests.

(3) Productivity improvement: Items in this factor suggest that improving productivity is perceived as a driving force for teleworking adoption since individuals can avoid interruptions at the office and get work done in an effective and efficient manner. In addition, teleworking also allows the individual's autonomy by enabling individuals to work during hours where they are most productive (Teo and Lim, 1998).

(4) Travel load: Items in this factor suggest that the adoption of teleworking will reduce travel burden, including travel preparation time and effort, time of travel, effort consumed in the travel, and cost of travel preparation and expenses.

(5) Cost reduction: Items in this factor reflect the notion that teleworking is a cheap work mode, since it contributes to saving office space and equipments, cost of real states, and cost of clothing and accessories (Mills *et al.*, 2001; Tung and Turban, 1996).

(6) Empowering people: Items in this factor show that teleworking is perceived as a method to empower employees through minimizing supervisory functions and giving the employee opportunity to focus on task at hand.

6.7 Study-based generated inhibitors

The ensuing factor analysis generates seven distinct perceived inhibitors for teleworking, including management concerns, isolation, union resistance, home inadequacy, ICT cost, time mismanagement, and family intervention (see Table 4).

(1) Management concerns: Items in this factor propose that managers may find placing organizational vision and mission, control, supervision, and designing an equitable compensation scheme for teleworker and appraising their performance are difficult (Teo and Lim, 1998).

(2) Isolation: Items in this factor illustrate the concept of professional and physical isolation which is reflected in misguidance regarding use of organizational resources, need to interact with work colleagues, lack of teleworking experience, feeling guilty toward the organization, and missing promotional opportunities at work. This isolation is found to be one of the key inhibitors of teleworking implementation (Kurland and Cooper, 2002; Rognes, 2002).

(3) Union resistance: This factor reflects the power of union resistance supported by clothing and makeup industry loss, negative impact on real state sector, and unclear insurance. This inhibitor may hinder the implementation of teleworking.

(4) Home inadequacy: Items of this factor shows that home is inadequate place to telework, when teleworkers face increasing home noise, data insecurity at home, work coordination difficulty, and missing the chance of team working.

(5) ICT cost: Items in this factor suggest that accountability for repairs / maintenance of equipment placed at employees' homes may be a problem. Furthermore, the initial investment in equipment to enable employees to telework may be substantial.

(6) Time mismanagement: Items in this factor suggest teleworking time is mismanaged and expanded since it intervenes with organization's working time and follows flexible working mode.

(7) Family intervention: This factor proposes that teleworking may be hindered by the introduction of family rights and family – work intervention process.

Kruskal-Wallis nonparametric test is applied to assess the relationship between employees' perceived teleworking facilitators and inhibitors as ordinal variables and teleworking mode choices as a nominal variable. Results are illustrated in Tables 5 and 6. Table 5 shows Kruskal-Wallis test result of the relationship between perceived teleworking facilitators and teleworking choice. With regard to teleworking facilitators, the analysis demonstrates that there is significant difference among employees in their perceived importance of individual freedom ($\chi 2 = 17.11$, p < 0.01), travel load ($\chi 2 = 6.76$, p < 0.05), and cost reduction ($\chi 2 = 10.67$, p < 0.01) based on their teleworking choice.

On the other hand, there is no significant difference among employees in their perceived importance of community concerns ($\chi 2 = 5.62$, n.s.), productivity improvement ($\chi 2 = 4.98$, n.s.), and empowering people ($\chi 2 = 4.13$, n.s.) based on their teleworking choice. Consequently, hypothesis H2 is partially supported for teleworking facilitators related to individual freedom, travel load, and cost reduction.

Kruskal-Wallis test result of the relationship between perceived teleworking inhibitors and teleworking choice is presented in Table 6 The analysis shows that there is significant difference among employees in their perceived importance of teleworking inhibitors related to union resistance ($\chi 2 = 6.65$, p < 0.01). However, there is no significant difference among employees in their perceived importance of teleworking inhibitors related to all other categories. Accordingly, hypothesis H2 is only supported for teleworking inhibitors related to union resistance.

Table 5: Kruskal-Wallis test result of the relationship between perceived teleworking facilitators and teleworking choice

χ^2	Perceived teleworking facilitators	
5.62	**Community concerns**	
5.54	Environmental pollution	**F20**
0.52	Working opportunity for disabled	**F21**
13.28**	Traffic Jams	**F22**
9.87**	Increasing oil prices	**F19**
3.45	Severe weather conditions	**F24**
0.63	Family care	**F23**
17.11**	**Individual freedom**	
10.77**	Flexible working time and location	**F11**
9.63**	Personal freedom	**F9**
13.17**	Avoid work stress	**F10**
6.34*	No absenteeism	**F14**
4.98	**Productivity improvement**	
1.41	Developing ICT usage	**F17**
0.87	Better utilization of working time	**F8**
10.15**	Improving output quality and quantity	**F13**
0.81	Increasing employees loyalty	**F16**
9.36**	Paperless work	**F18**
6.76*	**Travel load**	
2.54	Travel preparation	**F6**
10.33**	Travel time	**F5**
5.88	Travel effort and cost	**F3**
10.67**	**Cost reduction**	
15.65**	Saving org. space and equipments	**F2**
2.85	Increasing cost of real states	**F1**
3.21	Increasing cost of clothes and accessories	**F4**
4.13	**Empowering people**	
5.26	Minimizing supervisory functions	**F15**
0.34	Task focus	**F7**

*p < 0.05, **p <0.01

Table 6: Kruskal-Wallis test result of the relationship between perceived teleworking facilitators and teleworking choice

χ^2	Perceived teleworking inhibitors	
0.84	*Management concerns*	
1.40	Org. vision and mission are misplaced	**B15**
0.67	Safety criteria are not guaranteed	**B16**
2.13	Inapplicable work rules and regulations	**B13**
1.25	Access difficulty to decision info.	**B17**
2.55	Hard to control and evaluate performance	**B14**
2.93	*Isolation*	
3.91	Misguidance regarding use of org. resources	**B11**
1.76	Need to interact with work colleagues	**B8**
4.28	Lack of teleworking experience	**B10**
1.27	Feeling guilty toward the organization	**B7**
0.31	Missing promotional opportunities at work	**B9**
6.65*	*Union resistance*	
6.78*	Union resistance	**B23**
1.78	Clothing and makeup industry loss	**B22**
0.99	Negative impact on real state sector	**B21**
9.38**	Unclear insurance	**B24**
0.40	*Home inadequacy*	
2.82	Increased home noise	**B20**
1.80	Data insecurity	**B19**
1.73	Coordination difficulty	**B12**
3.79	Inapplicable team working	**B18**
0.74	*ICT cost*	
2.57	ICT acquisition cost	**B1**
1.16	ICT maintenance and upgrading cost	**B2**
0.67	*Time mismanagement*	
1.83	Home time mismanaged	**B6**
0.71	Org. time expansion	**B3**
1.17	*Family intervention*	
0.11	Family rights	**B4**
4.16	Family – work intervention	**B5**

* p < 0.05, ** p <0.01

7 DISCUSSION AND REFLECTION

7.1 Demographic variables

The results have manifested the important role of selected demographic variables in influencing teleworking choice, namely, the role of gender. Accordingly, results of the test have shown that females in the UAE tend to prefer full-time teleworking. Women are found to be motivated by some considerations such as work flexibility, convenience and increased personal freedom (O'Connor, 2001). UAE females have perceived telework as promising avenue to change their traditional work orientation and prove their personal freedom in handling work responsibilities. This is in harmony with Popuri and Bhat (2003), Yap and Tng (1990), and Wells *et al.* (2001) who suggest that teleworking will be of particular interest to women employees. However, in contradiction to the result generated by this research, some studies show that women employees are not interested in teleworking because they perceived work, not home, as the less stressful and more emotionally rich environment (Hochschild, 1983). In the same thought, Teo and Lim's (1998) study shows that males tend to perceive teleworking as enabling improvement in the quality of life and improvement in productivity/reduction of overheads to a greater extent than females. In line with this argument, Peters *et al.* (2004) suggest that three out of four teleworkers were male in EU member states, and that this stands in sharp contrast to the widespread opinion that telework was predominantly female. Moreover, research confirms the association between marital status and teleworking choice found in previous research. This is in harmony with Popuri and Bhat (2003), Yap and Tng (1990), and Wells *et al.* (2001) who suggest that teleworking will be of particular interest to employees who are married. Furthermore, with regard to the educational level, the study indicates no association between educational level and teleworking choice. This result challenges Peters *et al.*, (2004) when mention that well-educated employees were found to be more likely to practice teleworking. Consequently, this research finding is inconsistent with the notion that well-educated individuals are able to telework as they exercise more control over their work schedule than are their co-workers (Yeraguntla and Bhat, 2005).

The present research proves that there is an insignificant association between frequency of Internet use and teleworking choice. Such a finding falsifies the widely held claim that employees master certain level of IT skills including Internet skills are typically suited for teleworking. This research results are inconsistent with the result obtained from the Euro survey 2000, which alleged that telework was most widespread among employees, who used IT frequently in their job (Peters *et al.*, 2004).

Nationality is also found to be significantly associated with teleworking choice. Non-UAE national employees prefer part time and no teleworking compared to UAE national employees who prefer fulltime teleworking. Such findings could be attributed to the fact that Non-UAE national employees attempt to be present at the traditional workplace and establish good work records in order to renew their working contracts, rather than asking for teleworking scheme, though they may prefer. UAE national, on the other hand, are not subject to the stress of being present at the traditional workplace as non UAE employees. This result is in agreement with Yeraguntla and Bhat (2005) who indicate that resident Hispanics are more likely to telework than other races such as immigrants African and Asian who need to demonstrate their working skills, and support their legibility to work and follow work regulations. Similarly, the study shows that residence is associated with teleworking choice. Employees living in Sharjah, Ajman and Umquin are over presented among part-time and full-time teleworkers. This may be interpreted as employees living in these northern emirates always face severe traffic jams in their way to work in Dubai, so that teleworking is perceived as the magic solution for them. This result is consistent with Yen and Mahmassani (1997) when they suggest that the greater the distance from home to workplace, the more likely the employee is to prefer teleworking. Also, Mokhtarian and Salomon (1996) show that people who have longer commutes are more likely to report that they want to telework. This contrasts with Drucker and Khattak (2000) who find that distance to work is negatively correlated with working at home—that is, the farther the individual lives from his job, the less likely he/she to work from home.

Number of children is found to be not associated with teleworking choice. This result confirms Mokhtarian and Salomon (1996) when propose no effect of having children on the desire to telework. Nevertheless, this is in disagreement with Popuri and Bhat (2003), Yap and Tng (1990), Wells *et al.* (2001) who suggest that teleworking will be of particular interest to employees who have children. Although, working parents may highly value the time-savings of teleworking due to the elimination of commuting time and allow a parent to stay at home with a sick child (Peters *et al.*, 2004), albeit, this is not the case of UAE. In UAE culture, parents (working and not working) depend entirely on foreign maids to take care of their children regardless how many children they may have. Similarly, age is found to be not associated with teleworking choice. In consistent with that, Belanger (1999) does not reveal significant age differences between those practicing telework and those not doing so in her study of a high technology organization in USA. Nevertheless, many studies have revealed contradictory results with regard to the relationship between age and teleworking. Mokhtarian and Salomon (1996), and Bagley and Mokhtarian (1997) show that younger people are more likely to report that they want to telework. Yeraguntla and Bhat (2005) indicate that young adults (less than 25 years) are more likely to be in part-time employment than older adults. This is perhaps a reflection of the fact that many young adults are studying and working part-time at the same time. Inconsistently, the EU member states survey data indicated that the age group 30–49 was over represented among teleworkers (Peters *et al.*, 2004).

Research result related to years of experience tends to be not in agreement with Yeraguntla and Bhat (2005) who suggest that employees who have worked less than a year in the firm are more likely to be part-time teleworkers than those who have been working for longer periods of time. In UAE context, the situation may be different since employees with less working experience try to prove their skills, establish good impression, and get supervisor's support through being presenting at the traditional workplace. After long years of experience, employees may consider teleworking as an alternative work scheme that facilitate managing other concerns such as managing own small business.

The results of the present research prove the existence of an association between employees' profession and teleworking choice. While employees with accounting and finance professions tend to avoid telework, employees with IT, media and management profession tend to telework either on part-time or full-time basis. This result is consistent with Gray *et al.* (1993) who suggest that computer programmers, systems analysts, catalogue shopping telephone order agents, and data entry clerks fit full-time telework category.

7.2 Facilitator and inhibitors

This research confirms the importance of individual freedom, community concerns, and productivity as key teleworking facilitators perceived by employees. This is in agreement with the mainstream literature that support the perceived importance of personal freedom and autonomy as an immediate symbolic result of employees' interaction with teleworking adoption (Feldman and Gainey (1997; Pulido and Lopez, 2005). In addition, teleworking impact on the society as expressed by employees is clear and tangible on the short run. Mills *et al.* (2001) and Tung and Turban (1996) consider community and societal related teleworking facilitators such as reduction of air pollution and dependence on fuel, conserve energy housebound and disabled people can work from home, and reduced traffic during rush hours and transportation demand as important determinants of teleworking success in the short run. Moreover, increasing productivity gains is also considered as key derivers for organizations to adopt teleworking (Kurland and Bailey, 1999; Lim *et al.*, 2003; Mills *et al.*, 2001; Tung and Turban, 1996). However, a recent study analyzed the findings of over 80 previous studies, indicating that "little clear evidence exists that telework increases job satisfaction and productivity, as it is often asserted to do" (Bailey and Kurland, 2002: p. 383).

As far as teleworking inhibitors are concerned, the present research confirms the importance of isolation as a key inhibitor of teleworking. Recent research indicates that isolation is perceived as one of the key factors that may hinder the implementation of teleworking (Kurland and Cooper, 2002; Rognes, 2002). Isolation is a factor that may result in lack of interaction with colleagues and lack of commitment (Hobbs and Armstrong, 1998). Besides isolation, this research also points to the perceived importance of home inadequacy as a place of working. Although teleworking is treated as working from home, home is perceived by employees as inadequate place for work. Many reasons contribute to this claim involve lack of needed collaboration with other employees, security risks, difficulty of performance control and work coordination (Mills *et al.*, 2001; Tung and Turban, 1996).

Based on the analysis of test results related to hypotheses two and three, most of teleworking facilitators and inhibitors are not associated with teleworking choice. This means that employees with different teleworking modes (i.e., full-time, part-time, not to telework) do not differently perceive the importance of teleworking facilitators and inhibitors. In other words, teleworking facilitators and inhibitors are visible for all employees regardless of their teleworking preference mode. However, teleworking choice is found to be associated with the perception of specific teleworking facilitators and inhibitors. This implies that employees who prefer not to telework tend to perceive less importance for such teleworking facilitator or inhibitor, while employees who prefer to telework part-time or full-time tend to perceive higher importance. Such teleworking facilitators which are associated with teleworking choice include individual freedom, travel overload, and cost reduction. . Union resistance is the only teleworking inhibitor that is associated with teleworking choice. This is consistent with other teleworking studies such as Feldman and Gainey (1997) and Pulido and Lopez (2005) who suggest that individual freedom is highly perceived among part-time teleworkers. In addition, teleworkers are more likely to report longer commutes to workplace (Yen and Mahmassani, 1997; Mokhtarian and Salomon, 1996). Finally, perception of cost saving is also over presented among part-time and full time teleworkers in other context (Kurland and Bailey, 1999; Reid, 1993)

8 RESEARCH LIMITATIONS

There are several limitations of the present study that may restrict its generalizability. First, sample size is relatively small compared to other studies that have nation-wide samples. Second, the descriptive and exploratory nature of the topic does not allow the researchers to go into the depth of predicting the discovered relationships. Despite that, this study is the first of its kinds to examine teleworking choice and related facilitators and inhibitors in UAE, and in the Arab context. Third, eight out of eleven organizations do not allow the researchers to collect organization's related data such as income of employees, managerial level, degree of computer use in the organization, level of autonomy, decentralization, etc. Consequently, such organization's related variables are eliminated from the original questionnaire in order to maintain access to the respondents. Fourth, as the study focuses on prospective teleworkers in ICT context, results cannot be generalized to other non-ICT contexts.

9 PRACTICAL IMPLICATIONS AND RECOMMENDATIONS

The following are some practical implications and recommendations that have emerged from the study of teleworking choice in the UAE:

- Firms employ relatively large percentages of married, female, IT profession, individuals living in remote areas are recommended to adopt flexible work practices such as teleworking.

- Managers are advised to adopt part-time or full-time teleworking scheme in order to integrate and maintain two contradictory strategies; individual freedom and productivity improvement.

- Successful implementation of teleworking requires managers to effectively manage professional and physical isolation of teleworkers through regular office visits and meetings with colleagues. Other practical strategies could include regular e-mail intranet systems, news bulletins and social events. They should also take measures to allow social comparisons to be made, perhaps through use of newsletters, as well as helping teleworkers maintain visibility (perhaps with on-line discussions). Given that these measures are implemented the part-time teleworking is highly recommended compared with full-time teleworking.

- If home is inadequate place for teleworking, managers can rely on telecenters as a substitute. In telecenters, collaboration with other employees can be conducted, and performance control can be facilitated.

- Managers should ensure that any teleworking initiatives are backed up with the appropriate technical support in such way that technicians are available and able to respond quickly to technical problems and equipment failure.

- When initiating teleworking schemes, managers should devise a teleworking policy document that would cover issues such as expectations regarding working when sick, hours to be worked, salary, meetings and visits, deadlines, continuing training, opportunities for career development, management by distance, responsibility for hidden costs (such as electricity) and no hidden costs (such as postage), etc. The aim of such a document is to let workers feel that they have "permission" to call when they are sick or to switch off the computer at the end of the working day, as well as helping managers manage by outlining to distant workers what is expected of them.

- The importance of data security, privacy, and confidentiality cannot be overlooked when work is performed at home. An organization should invest in the appropriate security measures needed to ensure the confidentiality of data.

- It is necessary to provide training both to the teleworkers and their managers or supervisors. Training areas may include information technologies and networking procedures as well as psychological preparation to work in a new environment.

10 CONCLUSION

This study examines the concept of teleworking choice as it applies to UAE context. The relationship between demographic and individual variables, and teleworking choice is investigated. The research reveals that there is no difference among employees in their teleworking choice based on their educational level, Internet use, number of children, age, and years of experience. On the other hand, there is a difference among employees in their teleworking choice based on their gender, marital status, nationality, residence location, and work profession. In addition, the research identifies six distinct teleworking facilitators and seven distinct teleworking inhibitors in the UAE context. Generated facilitators are community concerns, individual freedom, productivity improvement, travel load, cost reduction, and empowering people, while generated inhibitors are management concerns, isolation, union resistance, home inadequacy, information and communication technology (ICT) cost, time mismanagement, and family intervention. Perceived mean importance of these facilitators and inhibitors is computed and ordered. Individual freedom, community concerns, and productivity are perceived by employees as the most important facilitators, while isolation and home inadequacy are perceived as the most important inhibitors. A further statistical test has revealed that there is no difference among employees in the perceived importance of most teleworking facilitators and inhibitors based on their teleworking choice. An exception is the association between teleworking choice and individual freedom, travel overload, cost reduction, and union resistance. The study points out the limitations of the present research and suggests some practical implications and recommendations for managers.

REFERENCES

Bagley, M.N., and P.L. Mokhtarian (1997), "Analyzing the preference for non-exclusive forms of telecommuting: modeling and policy implications," *Transportation*, Vol. 24, pp. 203-226

Bailey, D.E. and Kurland, N.B. (2002), "A review of telework research: Findings, new directions, and lessons for the study of modern work." *J. Organizational Behavior*, Vol. 23 No. 4, pp. 383–400

Baruch, Y. and Nicholson, N. (1997), "Home, sweet work: requirements for effective home working," *Journal of General Management*, Vol. 23 No. 2, pp. 15–30.

Belanger, F. (1999), "Workers' propensity to telecommute: an empirical study," *Information & Management*, Vol. 35, pp. 139-153.

Bryman, A. (2008), *Social Research Methods*, Oxford University Press Inc., New York

Carnicer, M., A. Sanchez, M. Perez, and M. Jimenez (2003), "Gender differences of mobility: analysis of job and work-family factors," *Women in Management Review*, Vol. 18 No. 4, pp. 199-219

Cooper, D and Schindler, A. (2003), *Business Research Methods*. Irwin, MA

Drucker, J., and A.J. Khattak (2000), "Propensity to work from home – modeling results from the 1995 nationwide personal transportation survey," *Transportation Research Record*, Vol. 1706, pp. 108-117

Feldman, D. and Gainey, T. (1997), "Patterns of telecommuting and their consequences: framing the research agenda", *Human Resource Management Review*, Vol. 7 No. 4, pp. 369-88.

Gray, M., Hodson, N. and Gordon, G. (1993), *Teleworking Explained*, John Wiley & Sons, New York, NY.

Golden, T. (2006), "Avoiding depletion in virtual work: Telework and the intervening impact of work exhaustion on commitment and turnover intentions," *Journal of Vocational Behavior*, Vol. 69, pp. 176–187

Hair, Joseph, Ralph E. Anderson, and Ronald L. Tatham (1992), *Multivariate Data Analysis with Readings*, 3rd edition, Macmillan Publishing Company, New York

Hobbs, D. and Armstrong, J. (1998), "An experimental study of social and psychological aspects of teleworking", *Industrial Management & Data Systems*, Vol. 98 No. 5, pp. 214-8.

Hochschild, A. (1983), *The Managed Heart: Commercialization of Human Feeling*, University of California Press, Berkeley, CA

Knight, William (2004), "Working drives switch to federated access rights, *Info Security Today*, September/October, p. 22-25

Kowalski, K. and J. Swanson (2005), "Critical success factors in developing teleworking programs," *Benchmarking: An International Journal*, Vol. 12 No. 3, pp. 236-249.

Kurland, N. and Bailey, D. (1999). When workers are here, there, and everywhere: a discussion of the advantages and challenges of telework. *Organizational Dynamics*, pp. 53–68.

Kurland, N. and Cooper, C. (2002), "Manager control and employee isolation in telecommuting environments," *Journal of High Technology Management Research*, Vol.13, pp. 107–126

Lim, H., A. van der Hoorn, V. Marchau, (2003), "the effects of telework on organization and business travel," Paper submitted for "Symposium on Teleworking", *4th Interbalkan Forum International IT conference*, Sofia, Bulgaria, 6-7 October 2003

Lupton, P. and Haynes, B. (2000), "Teleworking – the perception-reality gap", *Facilities*, Vol. 18. No. 7/8, pp. 323-8.

Mann, Sandi (2000), "An exploration of the emotional impact of tele-working via computer mediated communication," *Journal of Managerial Psychology*, Vol. 15 No. 7, pp. 668-690.

Mannering J. and P. Mokhtarian (1995), "Modeling the choice of telecommuting frequency in California: An exploratory analysis," *Technological Forecasting and Social Change*, Vol. 49, pp. 49-73

Mills, J., Wong-Ellison, C., Werner, W., and Clay, J. (2001), "Employer liability for telecommuting employees," *Cornell Hotel and Restaurant Administration Quarterly*, Vol. Oct-Nov., pp. 48 – 59

Mokhtarian, P. L. (1991), "Definig Telecommuting", *Transportation Research Record*, Vol. 1305, pp. 273-281.

Mokhtarian, P. L., Handy, S. L. & Salomon, I. (1995), "Methodological issues in the estimation of the travel, energy, and air quality impacts of telecommuting," *Transportation Research*, Vol. 29, pp. 283–302.

Mokhtarian, P. L., and I. Salomon (1996) Modeling the choice of telecommuting: the importance of attitudinal factors in behavioral models. *Environment and Planning*, Vol. 28, pp. 1877-1894.

Morgan, Robert (2004), "Teleworking: an assessment of the benefits and challenges," *European Business Review*, Vol. 16 No. 4, pp. 344-357

Neufeld, D. and Fang, Y. (2005), Individual, social and situational determinants of telecommuter productivity, *Information & Management*, Vol. 42, pp. 1037–1049

Nilles, J. M. (1994), *Making Telecommuting Happen: A Guide for Telemanagers and Telecommuters*. Van Nostrand Reinhold, New York

O'Connor, V. (2001), "Women and men in senior management", *Women in Management Review*, Vol. 16 No. 8, pp. 400-4.

Peters, P., Tijdens, K. and Wetzels, C. (2004), "Employees' opportunities, preferences, and practices in telecommuting adoption", *Information & Management*, Vol. 41 No. 4, pp. 469-82.

Popuri, Yasasvi, and Chandra R. Bhat. 2003. "On modeling choice and frequency of home-based telecommuting," *Transportation Research Record*, Vol.1858, pp. 55–60

Pulido, J., and Lopez, F. (2005) "Teleworking in the information sector in Spain," *International Journal of Information Management*, Vol. 25, pp. 229–239

Reid, A. (1993), *Teleworking as a Guide to Good Practice*, NCC Blackwell.

Rognes, J (2002), "Telecommuting resistance, soft but strong: Development of telecommuting over time, and related rhetoric, in three organizations," *SSE/EFI Working Paper Series in Business Administration, No 2002:1*, Stockholm School of Economics, Sweden

Safirova, Elena and M. Walls, 2004. "What have we learned from a recent survey of teleworkers? Evaluating the 2002 SCAG Survey." *Discussion Paper 04–43*. NW: Resources for the Future, Washington, D.C

Teo, T. and Lim, V. (1998), "Factorial dimensions and differential effects of gender on perceptions of Teleworking," *Women in Management Review*, Vol. 13 No.7, pp. 253–263

Thériault, M., P. Villeneuve, M. Vandersmissen, and F. Des Rosiers (2005), Home-working, telecommuting and journey to workplaces: are differences among genders and professions varying in space?," *the 45th. Congress of the European Regional Science Association*, 23-27 August 2005, Vrije Universiteit Amsterdam

Tung, L-L. and Turban, E. (1996), "Information technology as an enabler of telecommuting", *International Journal of Information Management*, Vol. 16 No. 2, pp. 103-18.

Wells, Kimberly, F. Douma, H. Loimer, L. Olson, and C. Pansing. (2001), "Telecommuting implications for travel behavior: case studies from Minnesota." *Transportation Research Record*, Vol. 1752, pp. 148–5

Yap, C. S. and Tng, H. (1990), 'Factors associated with attitudes towards telecommuting', Information & Management, Vol. 19, pp. 227–235

Yen, Jin-Ru, and Hani S. Mahmassani. (1997), "Telecommuting adoption: conceptual framework and model estimation." *Transportation Research Record*, Vol. 1606, pp. 95–102

Yeraguntla, A. and C. Bhat (2005), "A Classification Taxonomy and Empirical Analysis of Work Arrangements," *Working Paper # 05-1522*, The University of Texas, Austin

10

Customer Focus in UK e-Government: Or, Putting the Politics back into e-Government

James Cornford
Centre for Social and Business Informatics, Newcastle University
Newcastle upon Tyne, NE1 7RU, UK,

Email: james.cornford@ncl.ac.uk

Paul Richter
Centre for Social and Business Informatics, Newcastle University
Newcastle upon Tyne, NE1 7RU, UK,

Email: p.a.d.richter@ncl.ac.uk

Abstract

The techniques and technologies of customer service, as introduced under the guise of e-government, have brought certain aspects of public service users into sharp focus, but at the expense of other aspects. It is hypothesised that this effect may lie behind the failure of half a decade of IT-enabled change in public services to improve 'customer satisfaction'. Remedying this situation, it is suggested, will require a re-examination of the model of the customer which underpins customer service as it has been adopted by public service organisations.

Keywords: e-government; public services; customer service; representation; CRM

Acknowledgements: A much earlier version of this paper was presented at the British Academy of Management e-Business & e-Government Special Interest Group meeting "New Frontiers in e-Business, e-Government and e-Learning" at Newcastle University November 9-10, 2006. We would also like to acknowledge the useful comments of two anonymous referees.

1 INTRODUCTION: THE PROBLEMATIC

Achieving widespread citizen acceptance and take-up of services via new channels presents an urgent and important challenge if we are to realise the benefits from these new and innovative ways of working. In order to do this, we need to improve our understanding of customer preferences, as well as their needs (Cabinet Office, 2006: 52).

In this paper we address an apparent anomaly in UK e-government. Bluntly put, the problem that we want to start with is this: the IT-enabled reform process that goes by the name of e-government has had the idea of customer focus at its very centre, yet there is remarkably little evidence that the actual customers are responding to being focused on in this way. International comparisons have begun to draw a picture of UK e-government matching international standards in terms of the "supply side" but with disappointing take up by the intended users: in short customer focus without (many) customers.

How can we explain this phenomenon of e-government without e-citizens? A range of explanations have been put forward to account for this denouement. Is this just a matter of low awareness, remediable by another advertising campaign and the passage of time? Or are our supposedly world class e-government systems in fact poorly designed and plagued by what Richard Heeks (2006) calls 'design-reality gaps'. Or is it a matter of relative performance in which, however much public services have improved, they have failed to keep pace with improvements in the private sector?

Our contention in this paper is that there is something more fundamentally wrong here. Specifically, we argue, the problem concerns the representation of the customer underpinning the technologies and techniques of customer focus as they have been adopted by government. We start by pointing out that organisations don't actually focus on customers; rather they focus on a representation of the customer. These representations shape – perhaps better focus – the attention and the capacity of the organisation to respond to their customers. Issues and areas which fall outside of this focus become invisible, inaudible or incomprehensible to the organisation. It is, we argue, at least partially this problem that generates the 'they're not listening' effect associated with a broad sense of public disaffection with public services.

We complete the paper by arguing that what is required is a democratisation of e-government which is focused on a process of rethinking the representations that underpin the technologies, systems and processes constituting e-government. To recycle a well known slogan from a rather different context, we conclude that there should be "no taxation without representation!"

2 CUSTOMER FOCUS.... WITHOUT CUSTOMER SATISFACTION?

Governments have been putting the customer at the centre of e-government in the UK since the late 90s. The *Modernising Government* 1999 White Paper makes clear the close links between the customer, or user, focus and the joining up of services. The emphasis on public service users builds on a long established critique of the public services as being particularly liable to 'producer capture' – that is, services which come to be designed and managed for the benefit of the professionals producing those services rather than their 'users.' The adoption of the business concept of 'customer focus' was, at first, tentative. The White Paper is clearly informed by the notion of customer focus, albeit couched in the more acceptable terms of a focus on 'public service users'. According to the White Paper the overarching goals of the modernising process are:

Ensuring that policy making is more joined up and strategic.
Making sure that public service users, not providers, are the focus, by
matching services more closely to people's lives.
Delivering public services that are high quality and efficient.
(Cabinet Office, 1999: 6, emphasis in original).

While UK national Government was, at first, somewhat reluctant to use the "customer" label, the suppliers of hardware, software and consultancy who have sought to supply the increased demand which e-government represents have been less coy. A good example comes from the consultants Deloitte Touche, who have produced an influential set of 'Global public sector studies' (2000; 2001; 2003a; 2003b) on e-government. As early as 2000, the company's e-government report, *At the Dawn of E-government* was subtitled 'The citizen as customer,' while the 2001 report, *e-Government's Next Generation* was subtitled, 'transforming the government enterprise through customer service.' By

2003, however, (Deloitte Touche 2003a; 2003b) the theme (and language) of the reports had shifted to highlight the cost saving potential of e-government. Those earlier reports had, however, done their job and had placed the notions of customer service, customer focus and customer satisfaction at the centre of the e-government agenda.

Subsequent central government policy documents have been far more upfront about using the notion of customer focus. Almost any UK policy document relating to e-government in the period since 2000 would suffice to make the point. Here we use the example of a 2002 ODPM Guidance to local authorities on the principles that should guide their e-government efforts.

Joined up in ways that make sense to the *customer·*

Accessible at times and places most convenient to the *customer.*
Customers will have more choice over the way in which they contact and receive public services.

Delivered or supported electronically, facilitating faster, more reliable and better value services.

Delivered jointly, where appropriate, by local and regional partnerships, and connected to a national infrastructure.

Delivered seamlessly, so that *customers* are not asked to provide the same information more than once and service providers are better able to identify, reach and meet the needs of service users.

Open and accountable so that information about the objectives, standards and performance of local service providers and their elected representatives will be freely and easily available.

Used by *e-citizens* through effective promotion of available and accessible new technologies and helping local people to gain the necessary skills to take advantage of the Internet. (ODPM, 2002b: 4 – italics added)

Customer service is, it seems, widely accepted as the core goal of e-government. In spite of this consistent emphasis on the need for customer service, it is precisely this aspect of the e-government programme above all others that is widely seen as underperforming.

First, there are concerns about the poor level of service users' actual take up of the new, customer-focused channels and media which have been built in the name of e-government. For example, in her recent review of UK E-government, Helen Margetts has characterised the situation as follows:

From the demand side, in the United Kingdom at least, the rhetoric is still
running ahead of the results. The evidence … suggests that some of the
potential for e-government remains unused. For most citizens, the Internet
has brought far more change to their relationship with their bank or
various commercial outlets and to their social life than to their relationship
with government. Although the United Kingdom scores highly in some of
the international rankings of e-government when it comes to actual usage
it lags behind other European countries, North America and Australia
(Margetts, 2006: 262; See also Jones and Williams, 2005).

European comparisons carried out by Eurostat (2005) indicated that the UK was below the European average for citizen take up of internet-based e-government channels and that it was at the bottom of the 25 Member of States of the EU for business take up of new channels.

It is not only the poor citizen take-up of the new channels offered by e-government that has caused concern. We should not fall into the trap of thinking of e-government as simply 'government on the web'. The technologies and techniques of customer focus are not reliant on any particular channel – modern CRM (Customer Relationship Management) systems support telephony and face-to-face contacts as well as web-based interaction. There appears to be strong evidence of an entrenched preference among UK citizens for face-to-face and, above all, the telephone channel (see DCLG, 2006 and Dawn Hands/BMG, 2001). E-government technologies should be having effects in these, more traditional, channels too. But there is, at best, limited evidence that they have had this effect. For example, recent Ipsos MORI research on public attitudes (Page, 2007) suggests that overall satisfaction with public services has actually declined between 1998 and 2004 (see figure 1.). The picture which the research paints is, of course, more subtle than that bald assertion: there is a group for whom public services have improved significantly, even if this group is outnumbered by those whose expectations have not been met. A similar mixed picture emerged from the Cabinet Office's (2004) attempt to review user satisfaction across a range of public services. However, this research did note that in respect of local government, which both delivers a lot of citizen interaction and has seen substantial investment in Customer Service technologies, 'overall satisfaction … has dropped notably over the past three years' (2004: 6).

Figure 1: Satisfaction with Public Services (Source: Page, 2007)

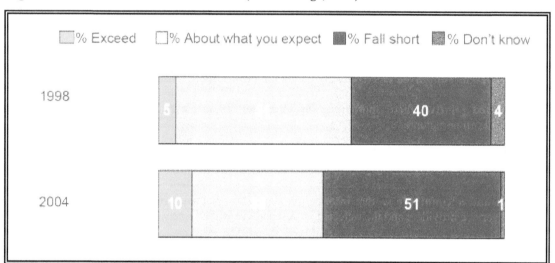

Responses to the Question 'Thinking generally about what you expect of public services like local councils, schools, would you say they greatly exceed or slightly exceed your expectations, are about what you expect, fall slightly short or fall a long way short of your expectations?' Base: 2004 - all respondents (1,502); 1998 (5,064).

What is clear is that the investments that have been made in the technologies of 'customer focus' and the techniques of Customer Relationship Management have not (yet) led to the expected improvements in measured levels of customer satisfaction. The British government seems puzzled by the apparent contradiction. Its most recent initiative in this area is the formation of Citizen Panels which directly confront the relationship between the individual and the state in terms of three core questions. First among these is the question of customer care:

1. How can public services make a step change on customer care?
   …

2. What can the state and individuals do to change culture, expectations and aspirations? How far can the state go in tackling damaging behaviour, and promoting positive, and what should be left to individuals and communities?
   ….

3. How should we update the relationship between citizens and the state, focusing on rights and responsibilities?

   …

   (Page, 2007)

This initiative follows on from the local government 'e-citizen' project (http://www.e-citizen.gov.uk/ [Accessed 17 January 2007]) which bills itself as 'raising awareness and driving take-up of Local Authority e-channels'. The 'E-citizen' project includes a 'take-up campaign' advertising the existence of e-channels through which individuals can interact with local government services, a set of 'e-citizen' 'proof of concept' research studies and a set of 'e-Citizen Live' dissemination events.

There are even some signs that the current government love affair with the customer label might be waning. The 2006 review for HM Treasury by Sir David Varney is suggestive of a new caution about the use of the customer label. Varney argues that the customer identity is, for public services a 'partial' identity and that an exclusive focus on the individual customer can obscure the wider needs of 'citizens and businesses.' Varney is clear that 'there is a lot public services can learn from the best parts of the private sector on how to engage and deliver services for the customer.' Nevertheless, he continues:

> Many of those in public services also focus on the customer. However, within the public service this is often taken to mean the individual who receives a particular benefit or entitlement, rather than considering the needs of the individual as a whole. People rarely identify themselves as being customers of a particular government service. Often they are trying to deal with a task or an event that does not fall neatly and obviously on any one part of government, such as becoming unemployed, getting married, starting a business or dealing with bereavement. As these events will often cut across departmental responsibilities, the focus has to be on understanding what the individual needs. If the government continues to interpret the term 'customer' as being limited to those who transact with government at single points then government will continue to serve citizens and businesses without fully addressing their needs (Varney, 2006: 23).

For Varney then, the 'customer' works against a fully 'rounded' view of the citizen by focusing only on that aspect of the individual which a particular department or agency interacts with: not so much a customer focus as customer blinkers. Yet Varney's perspective does not challenge the notion of Customer Focus (or in Varney's preferred terms , Customer Insight) – rather it argues for a more 'joined-up' approach to implementing customer focus based on 'setting some common standards to ensure that public sector organisations can deliver genuinely joined-up services' (2006: 31).

To what extent there is widespread public acceptance of the customer label is also not clear. The Ipsos MORI research (Page, 2007) suggests that, when confronted with statements such as 'Britain's public services need to start treating users and the public as customers' some 81% of those surveyed (adults 16+) agreed. (On the conceptualisation and measurement of customer satisfaction in the public sector in the UK see Donovan, Brown and Bellulo, 2001; MORI, 2002; Van Ryzin, 2006). However, more in depth research has shown that at least some individuals, in at least some specific public service contexts, are wary of the customer label. John Clarke and Janet Newman (2005), for example, found that health service users are far more inclined to think of themselves as 'patients' or 'service users' than 'consumers' or 'customers'. Neither 'citizens' nor 'consumers' are "the primary categories through which [people] live, and think about, their connections to public services". Clarke and Newman conclude that the resilience of people's conceptions of 'publicness', 'membership', and 'collaboration' are both a resource and a problem for New Labour's approach – "the assertiveness of health users (their willingness to 'stand up') is constantly glossed by New Labour as 'consumerist', but the desires and anxieties about both the present state of the NHS and its imagined futures suggest a failure to install a consumerist subjectivity" (2005: 13).

To summarise the situation crudely, over half a decade of attempts to bring about technology-enabled re-orientation of public services around the needs of the customer not only has failed to see customer satisfaction in public services rise significantly, but has actually seen it decrease. In homage to Robert Solow's famous encapsulation of the productivity paradox, we might say 'we can see the technologies and techniques of customer focus everywhere in public services, except in the customer satisfaction numbers.' Why? This question is taken up in the next section.

3 COMPETING EXPLANATIONS FOR A LACK OF SATISFACTION

A range of explanations for this paradox have been suggested, each identifying a different culprit. One answer is simply to deny that the very visible investment in contact centres, CRM software, customer service training, and so on has brought about any discernable change in the individual customer's experience of local government. A variant of this perspective would hold that it is too early to be looking for decisive evidence of changes in customer satisfaction. The key point for this school is that the apparent rapid pace of change in terms of structures and technologies within the public services masks a much slower process of cultural change. Such a cultural change has to overcome a deep rooted resistance to change within the public services. In some versions of this story, such resistance may be conscious and explicitly or implicitly organised (the bureaucrats are hanging on to their privileges for grim death) or unconscious and disorganised, but nevertheless powerful. The implicit solution set for this school includes: maintaining the pressure for customer service; further structural change to 'unfreeze' deeply held habits within the public services (e.g., through the introduction of greater choice); and further promotion of the disciplines of customer service among front line staffs (e.g., through customer training). In short a cultural strategy focused on changing the culture of public service workers.

An alternative solution shifts the focus from the 'customer-facing' workers to the technologies themselves and their suppliers, both within and outside the public services. The most eloquent exponent here is Richard Heeks (2006). Heeks begins his recent book on implementing e-government with the bald assertion that 'most e-government projects fail' (2006: 3). The dominant reason for these failures, according to Heeks, is what he describes as 'design-reality gaps' – in short the failure to adequately capture the organisational and individual 'requirements' at the design stage leading to technologies which are not 'fit for purpose' when it comes to implementation. Other explanations which focus on the technology either concentrate on the quality of design (e.g., web site usability[1], etc.) or, more typically, on the capacity of public servants to manage large and complex IT projects. In some variants of this perspective, a portion of blame is placed on the IT and systems supplier community (providers of hardware, software and, most importantly, consultancy) who are accused, at best, of overselling the capabilities of their products and services.

If the management of the design and implementation of the technologies and techniques of e-government is to blame, the solution is focused on improving the design and implementation capacity of public services and their ability to manage IT systems and services contractors.

Each of these explanations focuses on processes and forces within the public services and their supplier community. A final set of explanations focuses on relations outside the public services themselves. A first version of this outward perspective examines communication between public services and the public. In this explanation, the public are unaware of the benefits of new customer-focused technologies because they have not experienced them. The solution, then, is clear: advertising and other marketing activities such as the 'connect to your council' campaign, (part of the E-Citizen project mentioned above). A second externally focused explanation looks even further. This final perspective is framed in terms of the 'relative' performance of public services when set against (the best of) private services. This argument does not deny that the investments in customer service have produced improvements in the customer experience of public services over time (i.e., when compared with the customer experience of the same services years earlier) but argues that this is irrelevant. For this school of thought, customer satisfaction (CS) is determined by the simple equation

CS = expectation – experience

It is, then, customer service performance relative to expectations, that is important, and if expectations rise faster than the quality of our experiences of customer service, then customer satisfaction will decrease, even with improvements in customer experiences. The final point in this perspective is to argue that our expectations of customer service are set, not by out past experience of public service interactions, but by (the very best of) our interactions with the private sector. In short: why can't public services be as good as amazon.co.uk or as personalised as myspace.com?

Each of these explanations – whether focused on customer facing staff, the design and implementation of IT or the communications or the marketing functions of public services and customer expectations and comparisons – retains the basic framework of the customer service model. What if it is this model itself, rather than the ways in which it is implemented, that is at the heart of the problem of low take-up of, and poor satisfaction with, the outcomes of e-government enabled customer service?

4 A THEORY OF REPRESENTATION

There is, of course, nothing new about questioning the adoption of the customer model in public services (see, for example, Aberbach and Christensen, 2005; Alford, 2002; Fountain, 2001, du Gay 2000 for some flavour of the various critiques). The general tenor of these critiques has been to highlight the collective, that is public, nature of public services on the one hand, and the significance of egalitarianism in the distribution of public services (contrasted with strategies of 'customer segmentation' in private services) on the other.

In this paper we want to take a different tack. We want to focus on what, in practice, adopting a technology-supported customer service strategy actually means. What, exactly, is the focus of customer focus technologies? The obvious reply is that customer focus implies focusing on the customer. This is, however, too simple an answer. To begin to develop a more sophisticated response we will make a

---

[1] A major UK government website cull announced in January 2007 entails a reduction from 951 to 26

websites and the streamlining of information through two 'supersites'.

short detour via Gregory Bateson's 1972 essay, pathologies of epistemology (in his *Steps to an Ecology of Mind*, 2000[1972].

Bateson begins his essay thus:

> First I would like you to join me in a little experiment. Let me ask you for a show of hands. How many of you will agree that *you see me*? I see a number of hands – so I guess that insanity loves company. Of course, you don't "really" see *me*. What you "see" is a bunch of pieces of information about me, which you synthesise into a picture of me. You make that image. It's that simple (Bateson, 2000[1972]: 456).

What Bateson is so elegantly alluding to is the motivated aspect of vision or seeing. What we see is, to some extent, the product of our own activity of organising sense data into something meaningful for us. From this point of view, while the environment is certainly 'out there' (it is, fundamentally, a realist ontology), our perception of it is always the work of choosing and ordering which elements to bring into focus and which to ignore or leave as a blur, of making decisions about where to draw the boundaries between objects and between figure and ground. We make those choices and impose meaning on the constant stream of sense data that bombard us. We make the image. It is that simple.

We make that image. But we do not, of course, make that image alone or without help. The most basic categories and frameworks which we use to make sense of sense data are, to a very large extent, inherited from the wider culture. In the context of the organisation, this general cultural framework, or common sense, is supplemented (and sometimes contradicted) by more specialist, domain specific organisational or professional frameworks and taxonomies. Thus, what is true of individuals is, in this case, also true of organisations. Organisations don't react to "the environment" – they react to a representation of the environment (see e.g., Manturana and Varela, 1998 for one interesting take on this phenomenon). This representation is not a mere refection of the environment but rather a carefully constructed image of the environment built on often painstaking collection of data and its subsequent organisation into charts and tables, facts and narratives. What we must always remember, however, is that it is within the organisation that the choices about which facts and which narratives to select are made.

In so far as 'the customer' is seen as a part of the organisational environment, it too is a representation, constructed using a *selection* of 'customer' data drawn from a variety of mechanisms, but selected and ordered according to a representation that is built and maintained within the organisation. Thus, while the concept of customer focus is intended to orient the organisation externally, to do this it must first orient the organisation internally, towards its own processes and techniques and the categories and narratives which underlie them. Before the organisation can turn outwards, it must turn inwards. Strictly speaking, then, public services thus cannot be built "around the customer" – they must be built around a *representation of the customer*.

The need for such a representation predates the introduction of e-government. However, prior to the adoption of computer-based CRM Systems and the like, the representations of public service users remained diffuse, localised and shared through a mixture of bureaucratic process (forms and filing) and the shared norms introduced by professional training and supported by professional practice. The technologies of e-government have imposed a new requirement for a much more explicit and shared representation of the customer. As Paul Dourish has argued,

> …there is simply no questioning the central role of representation in developing computer systems. Software is a representational medium, from the interface on the screen to the bits on the disk. What is called for then is a more nuanced understanding of the role that those representations play, how they are subject to a variety of interpretations, and how they figure as part of a larger body of practice (Dourish, 2004: 208).

The adequacy of the representations which are embodied in information systems is a well established academic concern. Academic computer scientists explicitly worry about 'ontologies' (although there is less evidence of these concerns feeding through into much of the software that is deployed in typical e-government implementations).

If the organisational routines of customer service and, the information systems on which they are built, rely on representations, then our concern here is with three important questions. Who gets to build these representations? What tools and materials are used to build these representations and what constraints do these impose? What are the consequences when these individuals and groups build these representations with these tools and materials and they are employed in practice?

5 "CUSTOMER INTIMACY": KNOWING THE CUSTOMER AND SEEING LIKE A STATE

Customer Relationship Management is based on the goal or target of knowing your customer, of establishing what Varney (2006: 24) calls customer insight, or in Laudon and Laudon's unfortunate phrase, 'customer intimacy' (2007: 260). We cannot, post-Foucault, see such knowledge, let alone such *intimate* knowledge, as a purely innocent appropriation of facts from a stable, objectively knowable world. Foucault's coupling of knowledge with power should orient us to the extent to which knowledge constitutes its object. Indeed it is possible to make a coherent argument that contemporary Customer Relationship Management technologies do not record information about the customer but rather call that identity into being, shaping a new customer subjectivity (Zwick and Dholakia, 2004).

Our argument here is less radical. Let us start by drawing attention to the visual metaphor behind the notion of 'customer focus'. Knowledge about the customer is to be gained by looking. But as we have argued, seeing is an active process: in an important sense we see what we are looking for. In figure 2, for example, those who are told to look for a man playing a saxophone (perhaps even implicitly, for example by viewing the picture in the context of other pictures of musicians) will tend to see a man playing a saxophone. By contrast, those told or led to expect a picture of a woman's head are more likely to see that image. You can only *re*cognise what you have already 'cognised' (i.e., that of which you have established a mental model). The paradox is that, in order to make sense of the external world we must first look inward to our taxonomies, models and schemas.

Figure 2: Is it Bill (playing the sax) ... or Hilary?

Customer service technologies embody just such taxonomies and models. Customer Relationship Management systems which are precisely designed to focus the organisation's attention on the (external) customer, similarly require the organisation to first focus on the (internal) model of the customer. And this model is, to a very large extent, one that is built into the systems which support Customer Focus. These technologies increasingly form the 'lens' through which public services focus on their users.

There is, of course, a substantial literature on how the state envisages its populations, in James Scott's (1998) memorable phrase 'seeing like a state'. As Scott has argued

> certain forms of knowledge require a narrowing of vision. The great advantage of such tunnel vision is that it brings into sharp focus certain limited aspects of an otherwise far more complex and unwieldy reality.' (Scott, 1998, 11)

However this literature has focused on the state's vision of aggregates of individuals – populations, groups, classes – and the (statistical) technologies and techniques used to order and represent them *en mass* (see e.g., Porter, 1995; Bowker and Star, 2002). The technologies and techniques of Customer Focus and Customer Relationship Management take Scott's notion of focus to a new and much more individualised level.

Which aspects of the public service user are brought into sharp focus by these technologies and which aspects are softened or rendered less visible? The customer that is brought into being is, of course, the classical *homo economicus* of positive economics. This public service user is envisaged as individual, characterised by means-ends rationality, coherence, self-knowledge and self-interest. Additionally the model of the customer that emerges from the rhetoric of customer service in public services is time pressured, demanding and constantly susceptible to rising expectations. This is the model that CRM systems and their associated technologies are built on and this is what they are looking for, what they are ready to re-cognise.

6 COMPUTER SAYS "NO"

If the techniques and technologies of customer service enable public services to see certain aspects of their users, they also obscure other aspects. Behaviours that are not comprehensible in terms of the self interested, self-knowing individual become meaningless or their meaning is blurred. To shift the metaphor from vision to hearing, we can point to the increasingly noted opinion of public service users that 'they're not listening,' that the management of public services are unable to process and comprehend certain aspects of what their users are trying to tell them (see e.g., McHugh, 2006). To mix the two metaphors then – 'they're not listening because they can't see us'.

This effect is not restricted to public services. The disempowered worker, portrayed in the television comedy programme Little Britain, whose catch phrase is 'computer says "no",' is as likely to work in the private as the public sector. Linda Penny (2005) has beautifully captured the mock sincerity – in her phrase, the 'corporate bullshit' – of private sector customer service with its refrain of "your call is important to us." As Harry Frankfurt (2005) has pointed out, what makes this kind of statement into Bullshit is not that it isn't true. After all, your call really is, in the end, important to the organisation. What makes it bullshit is the lack of sincerity behind it. Your call is important to us, not because you are important, but because your business is important to us. All that changes with the transfer to the public sector or the monopoly infrastructure provider is that what is important about your call is reflected not in the 'bottom line' but in the performance management statistics or the volume of complaints to the regulator.

What is to be done? First it is clear that representation *as such* is not the problem. Organisations can only interact with their environments through the mediation of a representation of that environment. The vision of a more direct and "authentic" interaction with the users of public services is another kind of Bullshit (Frankfurt, 2005). Rather than try to avoid the problems of representation by going around it, we propose to tackle representation head on.

One approach here would be to join those who extol 'the active citizen' and the much more direct participation of individuals in the governance and management of public services, through mechanisms such as the membership of boards and citizen juries. In this sense, then, users might seek to increase their 'representation' within public services. This approach has it limits. As Declan McHugh has recently argued, the desire to be heard does not imply that people are keen to participate more directly in the governance and management of public services:

> While the call for more participatory democracy has a visceral emotional appeal, in practice it may only succeed in engaging those already over-represented amongst voters and party members—that is, the educated, affluent and middle-aged. Mechanisms designed to provide greater opportunities for citizens to participate more directly in decision making as a means of increasing legitimacy and reducing the perceived democratic deficit may therefore have the opposite effect (McHugh, 2006: 551).

Such approaches also underestimate the extent to which experiences are shaped by operational decisions taken by professionals, rather than policy decisions taken by governing bodies. Even if we were to endorse widespread acceptance of the 'active citizen' role, we would emphasise the importance of first examining how this role relates to the models which underpin the techniques and technologies that mediate service users' interaction with state bodies.

The problem then, for us, is much more one of opening up representation at the level of the models – representations that are embedded in the standard operating procedures of customer service and its associated technologies. Perhaps the most important component of this is to reverse the desire for 'intimate' or 'personal' knowledge that is deeply embedded in the theory and practice of customer service. Richard Sennett (2004) has, as usual, got to the heart of the matter. For Sennett the problem with such knowledge is that it shows a lack of respect for the autonomy of the other, the public service user. It doesn't give space to the other to present themselves as an autonomous being because the public service organisation already 'knows', or thinks that it knows, what the user is like. Sennet puts it as follows:

> Autonomy, as we have seen is not simply an action; it requires also a relationship in which one party accepts that he or she cannot understand something about the other. The acceptance that one cannot understand things about another gives both standing and equity in the relationship. Autonomy presupposes at once connections and strangeness. (2004: 177)

What is necessary is not that the public services gain intimate knowledge, constructed through the categories and classifications of customer service with their ready-made understandings of the needs of the user, but rather that the user is given some space to define themselves and their priorities. This requires, ironically, that public services show more humility about their levels of understanding of the priorities and needs of users – in Sennett's phrase 'the acceptance that they cannot understand things about the other'. The danger is that throwing more 'understanding the customer' technology at customer service will actually undermine the capacity of public services to listen to their users and register their needs and concerns.

7 CONCLUSION: LEARNING TO 'REALLY' LISTEN?

Let us briefly rehearse the argument. Customer service in public services is only working in so far as the model – the representation of the customer – of the customer on which it is based is meaningful to that customer. When the model is not meaningful it creates dissonance – the public service provider can only see and register their effect on the customer in the terms provided by their model of the customer. Public service user responses that fall outside the parameters of the representation or model become meaningless or have their meaning blurred. This generates the 'they're-not-listening' effect that surveys of public service users have noted.

This kind of effect cannot be reduced by "better marketing" but only by rethinking the model of the customer in a more complex way. That rethinking will involve actually engaging with "customers" and letting them take a role in building the way they are represented. This is, of course, a political process. But it need not imply the dreadful vision of more 'participation' in focus groups and meetings as much as the recognition that each service encounter needs a little space for the negotiation of the representation of the user – which might go well beyond the bounds of the customer stereotype.

There are some signs that, in parts of the public sector reform movement, this kind of realisation is being taken seriously. Some of the conclusions to a recent study for local government (Back/RBA, 2006) chime well with this view. For example, the research showed that young people 'want to set the agenda not just respond to yours' [that is, the council's]. Even more tellingly, e-democracy national project leader is quoted as saying: 'Rather than concentrating on mechanisms to help them speak, authorities should focus on improving their ability to listen, understand and engage...' (Back/RBA Research, 2006: 7-8)

Yes, of course, most people will respond to the 'customer' label to some extent, if it implies an improved choice of access channels; more efficient delivery and other benefits that are relevant to them as individuals. Some data do suggest that some users of public services do want to be treated more as they are by private sector service providers some of the time. But when they are engaged with on a deeper level it seems that they do not relate so easily to the idea of being a 'customer' (Clarke & Newman, 2005). They see their relationship with the state differently. So even if uptake of e-channels begins to improve over coming years, feelings of satisfaction towards the public's relationship with public services may not necessarily follow without a re-thinking of the basis of that relationship.

How can public service organisations solve this satisfaction gap? This paper is not the place to prescribe detailed solutions – a task, no doubt, for a major socio-technical research programme. What we would suggest here, however, is that by approaching e-government by way of the 'customer' model that infuses the concept of customer service (and its associated techniques and technologies) at the core of the programme, we start to appreciate how the service user is being represented – and hence understood – by public service organisations. And this is a good place, we argue, from which to begin to understand why service users may not be fully satisfied with their relationships with those organisations. It leads us to question whether a set of customer-focused practices that have emerged in a commercial setting and which rest on a particular notion of the relationship between server and served can be expected to reliably deliver satisfaction in a public services setting. Further, it suggests that any attempt by government policymakers and practitioners in public services to re-think how the complexity of the service user's role(s) may be more adequately accommodated, needs to be sensitive to the ways in which those roles are re-presented within the technologies and techniques of e-government. Finally, we would suggest that those technologies and techniques should be based on listening to, understanding, and engaging with those users – enabling the user to represent themselves and not to always have the work of representation done for them.

REFERENCES

Aberbach, J. D. & Christensen, T. (2005). Citizens and Consumers: An NPM Dilemma. *Public Management Review,* 7(2), 225-245

Alford, J. (2002). Defining the client in the Public Sector: a social-exchange perspective, *Public Administration Review.* 62(3), 337-346.

Back, P./RBA Research (2006). Understanding the customer: Increasing take-up from harder to reach groups. Presentation to at the SOCITM South Regional Event, 16 June [Available at https://www.socitm.gov.uk/socitm/Library/Understanding+the+customer.htm; Accessed 08, February 2007]

Bateson, G. (2000[1972]). *Steps to an Ecology of Mind.* (Chicago: University of Chicago Press).

Bowker, G. & Star, S.L. (2002). *Sorting things out: Classification and Its Consequences.* (Cambridge, MA: MIT Press).

Brown, J. S. & Duguid, P. (2000). *The Social Life of Information.* (Boston: HBR Press).

Cabinet Office (1999). *Modernising Government.* (London: HMSO)

Cabinet Office (2004). *Customer Satisfaction with Key Public Services,* November 2004. (London: Cabinet Office)

Cabinet Office (2006). *Transformational Government: Enabled by Technology, Annual Report 2006* (cm 6970). (London: HMSO. [Available at http://www.cio.gov.uk/documents/annual_report2006/trans_gov2006.doc; Accessed 24 January 2007])

Cabinet Office (2007). *HM Government: Policy Review.* (Available at http://www.cabinetoffice.gov.uk/policy_review/index.asp [Accessed 17 January 2007])

Clarke, J. & Newman, J. (2005). What's in a name? New Labour's citizen-consumers and the remaking of public services. Paper for the CRESC conference: *Culture and Social Change: Disciplinary Exchanges*, Manchester, 11-13 July 2005

Coleman, S. & Goetze, J (2001). *Bowling Together: Online Public Engagement in Policy Deliberation.* [available at http://www.bowlingtogether.net/; Accessed 18 January 2007]

Hands, D./BMG (2001). Local Government on-line Pathfinder Dissemination: Baseline Survey Results, BMG/Local Government On-Line, November.

DCLG (2006). *A Review of the Department for Communities and Local Government Take up Campaign (Burst 1 May-July 06).* (London: DCLG [Available at http://www.communities.gov.uk/index.asp?id=1503744; Accessed 24 January 2007])

Deloitte Touche (2000). *At the Dawn of E-Government: The Citizen as Customer.* [Available at http://www.egov.vic.gov.au/pdfs/e-government.pdf; Accessed 23 January 2007]

Deloitte Touche (2001). e-Government's Next Generation: Transforming the government enterprise through customer service. [Available at

http://www.deloitte.com/dtt/research/0,2310,sid%253D1037%2526cid%253D19329,00.html; Accessed 23 January 2007].

Deloitte Touche (2003a). *Citizen Advantage: Enhancing economic competitiveness through e-government.* [Available at

http://www.deloitte.com/dtt/newsletter/0,1012,sid%253D15288%2526cid%253D26079,00.html; Accessed 23 January 2007]

Deloitte Touche (2003b). *Cutting Fat, Adding Muscle: The Power of Information Technology in Addressing Budget Shortfalls.* [Available at

http://www.deloitte.com/dtt/research/0,2310,sid%253D1037%2526cid%253D20683,00.html; Accessed 23 January 2007]

Donovan, N., Brown, J. & Bellulo, L. (2001). *Satisfaction with Public Services: A Discussion Paper.* (London: Cabinet Office. [Available at

http://www.cabinetoffice.gov.uk/strategy/downloads/files/satisfaction.pdf; accessed 18 January 2007])

Dourish, P. (2004). *Where the Action Is: Foundations of Embodied Interaction.* (Cambridge Mass: MIT Press).

du Gay, P. (2000). *In Praise of Bureaucracy: Weber, Organisation, Ethics.* (London: Sage)

Eurostat (2005). Internet usage by individuals and enterprises 2004, Statistics in Focus Series 18/2005. [Available at http://www.egovmonitor.com/reports/rep11401.pdf; Accessed 24 January 2007]

Fountain, J.E. (2001). Paradoxes of Public Sector Customer Service. *Governance: An International Journal of Policy and Administration*, 14 (1), 55-73.

Frankfurt, H. (2005). *On Bullshit.* (Princeton, N.J.: Princeton University Press.)

Heeks, R. (2006). *Implementing and Managing e-Government: An International Text.* (London, Sage).

Herdan, B. (2006). *The Customer Voice in Transforming Public Services*, Report for the Chancellor of the Duchy of Lancaster.

Hood, C., Peters, G. & Wollman, H. (1996). 'Sixteen ways to consumerize public services: pick 'n' mix or painful trade offs', *Public Money and Management*, October-December, 43-50.

House of Commons Public Administration Select Committee (2004-5). *Choice, Voice and Public Service:* [Available at

http://www.parliament.uk/parliamentary_committees/public_administration_select_committee/pasc_choice.cfm; Accessed 18 January 2007]

Jones, A. & Williams, L. (2005). *What ICT? Providing More Citizen Focused Services.* (London: The Work Foundation). [Available at

http://www.theworkfoundation.com/products/publications/azpublications/whatictprovidingmorecitizenfocusedservices.aspx; Accessed 23 January 2007]

Laudon, K. C. and Laudon, J. P. (2007). *Essentials of Business Information Systems* (Seventh Edition). (Upper Saddle River NJ: Pearson Education).

McHugh, D. (2006). 'Wanting to be Heard But Not Wanting to Act'? Addressing Political Disengagement. *Parliamentary Affairs,* 59(3), 546-552.

Manturana, H & Varela, F. (1998). *The Tree of Knowledge: The Biological Roots of Human Understanding* (revised edition). (Boston MA: Shambhala Publications)

Margetts H. (2006). E-Government in Britain—A Decade On, *Parliamentary Affairs*, 59(2), 250–265.

Miller, D. (1998). Conclusion: A theory of virtualism, pp. 187-216 in Carrier, J. and Miller, D. (eds) *Virtualism: A New Political Economy*. (Oxford: Berg).

MORI (2002). *Measuring and Understanding Customer Satisfaction: A Review for the Office of Public Services Reform*. (London: Prime Minister's Office for Public Services Reform). [Available at http://www.number-10.gov.uk/files/pdf/MeasuringCustomerSatisfaction.PDF; Accessed 18 January 2007]

ODPM (2002). *Implementing Electronic Government Guidance*, August2002. (London: ODPM). [http://www.localegov.gov.uk/images/Implementing%20Electronic%20Government%20Guidance%20August%202002_200.pdf]

Page, B. (2007). Questions raised by MORI for the citizen forums. Presentation on the Cabinet Office web site at http://www.cabinetoffice.gov.uk/policy_review/pr_presentation.pdf [Accessed 16 January 2007]

Penny, L. (2005). *Your Call Is Important to Us: The Truth About Bullshit*. (New York: Crown).

Porter, T. (1995). *Trust In Numbers: The Pursuit of Objectivity in Science and Public Life*. (Princeton, NJ: Princeton University Press).

Putnam, Robert D. (2000). *Bowling Alone: The Collapse and Revival of American Community*. (New York: Simon & Schuster).

Scott, J. C. (1998). *Seeing Like a State: How Certain Schemes to Improve the Human Condition have Failed*. (New Haven and London: Yale University Press.)

Sennett, R (2004) *Respect: The Formation of Character in an Age of Inequality*. (Harmondsworth: Penguin).

Van Ryzin, G. G. (2006). Testing the Expectancy Disconfirmation Model of Citizen Satisfaction with Local Government. *Journal of Public Administration Research and Theory*, 16, 599–611.

Varney, D (2006). *Service transformation: A better service for citizens and businesses, a better deal for the taxpayer*. (London: HM Treasury). [Available at http://www.hm-treasury.gov.uk/media/53D/F2/pbr06_varney_review.pdf].

Zwick, D & Dholakia, N. (2004). Consumer subjectivity in the Age of Internet: the radical concept of marketing control through customer relationship management. *Information and Organisation*, 14, 211–236.

11

Broadening the focus of evaluation: An experiment

Subrata Chakraborty
Jaipuria Institute of Management
Vineet Khand, Gomti Nagar, Lucknow - 226010, India

Email: sc@jiml.ac.in

Shailja Agarwal
Jaipuria Institute of Management,
Vineet Khand, Gomti Nagar, Lucknow - 226010, India

Email: shailja@jiml.ac.in

Abstract

Evaluation of student performance in any course, especially those delivered in a management programme, poses a serious challenge; more so, in a course like 'Business Communication', where oral communication ought to form an integral part of evaluation. This paper presents various details of an experiment, conducted with a view to introduce this much needed component in the evaluation process. Essential purpose of the exercise was to try and broaden the focus of evaluation, simultaneously enlarging its scope. The need to maintain certain amount of objectivity and transparency was taken as critical. Group Discussion was used as a tool. A process was developed with the objective of getting every student evaluated on both written as well as non-written skills. A two-sided evaluation mechanism was put in place to achieve the dual purpose of leaning and evaluation. Statistical analysis of the results suggests that the experiment was a useful one. The student feedback, too, was favourable.

Keywords: business communication, non-written skills, written skills, group discussion, evaluation

1 INTRODUCTION

Education in business management has gained considerable popularity over the last couple of decades. Several business schools have sprung up in different parts of the world to cater to this seemingly growing demand. Despite this significant quantitative growth in numbers of schools, quality of education provided in business schools often comes under a question mark. Even while there is a recognition that management is more experiential than experimental, and more a state of the art than being formulaic, classroom activities largely remain confined to mere theoretical discourses.

Among the various courses taught in a management program, those dealing with promotion of communication skills assume particular importance. This is so because, in the discharge of one's day-to-day functions, effective communication – oral as well as written – plays a critically important role. How to build the needed skills remains a key challenge before many business schools. This is so because not only are there issues relating to language of communication, there are also other aspects like mannerism, body language, etc. Schools frequently, struggle to address this challenge effectively. Sometimes a bigger challenge is faced in coming up with fair and objective evaluation of students while the course is in progress, including at the stage of its completion. Problems arise because of certain stated and implied needs. These are: reliability, validity, objectivity and verifiability. A proper solution often remains elusive.

This paper constitutes a step towards addressing the above four needs. An experimental approach was undertaken. Outcome of the experiment, developed and used recently, on a batch of first trimester students pursuing a one credit compulsory course on Business Communication, in a-two-year graduate management program is shared in this context. Group Discussion is the tool used for the purpose. The focus was on the assessment of Listening, Speaking, Reading and Writing skills, technically coined as LSRW skills. Two questions are addressed: (i) how can oral as well as written skills be simultaneously incorporated in an assessment tool? and (ii) how effective can peer assessment be?. The paper reports the details of what was done to reconfigure assessment processes dovetailing traditional paper-and-pencil assessment by the instructor with those of the peers. Analysis of the results seems to suggest that not only can oral and written skills be assessed simultaneously; the technique used can also prove to be useful in catering to the four needs (reliability, validity, objectivity and verifiability) outlined above.

2 LITERATURE SURVEY

2.1 Evaluation Challenges in Business Schools

In most educational programs, a substantial proportion of teacher and student time is devoted to activities which involve (or lead directly to) evaluation by the teacher (Crooks, 1988). The same is true of a program in business management. Though the idea of evaluation 'generally evokes groans' (Feinberg, 1979) from the instructors as well as the students, it has powerful impacts- direct and indirect, positive or negative, deserving considerations towards a very careful planning and implementation.

Evaluation also serves as a communicative device between the world of education and that of the wider society. Since the results of any particular assessment device must be accorded 'trust' by the stake holders if the consequences are to be acceptable, different parts of the world continue to be grappling with assessment challenges (Broadfoot and Black, 2004). New tools of evaluation like use of reflection in evaluation (Thorpe, 2007), in-basket writing exercise (Feinberg, 1979), business games (McKenney, 1962) etc. are constantly being experimented upon and developed. Such experimentation helps in enriching our understanding of the complexity of the many links that may exist between assessment and learning and their various interplays. Further these provide certain advances to assess the link between teachers' practices in formative and in summative assessment, and to construct some alternatives towards strengthening the quality and status of teachers' summative assessments.

In a business education program, development of a student's ability to apply skills and knowledge in a variety of contexts is a critical need (Broadfoot and Black, 2004). Therefore, assessment of student progress in acquiring this ability becomes imperative. However business education in India, and also in many parts of the world, seems to depend primarily, if not exclusively, upon the traditional examination system for achieving this. One apparent reason for doing so is that the method is transparent and verifiable. Another reason could be that many Business Schools, inadvertently or otherwise, tend to focus more upon content knowledge and hence end up using examinations to test such content knowledge in students (Ogunleye, 2006). Students are assessed during two years of their study using an array of examinations. However, to be fair to these schools, it must be said that the tools available to make assessments are also limited.   The need, therefore, is to design a systematic evaluation design mechanism which, on one hand, should be transparent and objective and, on the other hand, should achieve the intended purpose. As is the case in many other courses, evaluation remains a sensitive as well as a contentious aspect of the business communication course too. Needless to say, it elicits the same groans from students and instructors. Before proceeding further, it may be beneficial to remind ourselves of the primary objective of a business communication course, which is to improve communication skills of students. These skills are to be improved and assessed as a whole rather than limiting only to some components, predominantly the written skills alone.

2.2 Dissatisfaction with Evaluation in Business Communication

Dissatisfaction with tests currently used to assess communication ability is neither new nor uncommon. Homer L Cox, in his study, as far as 1970, observed: "Overall, educators agreed that they were most dissatisfied with, and students were weakest in, ability to communicate in writing; however, dissatisfaction with tests and weakness observed varied in other areas of communication. It is probably safe to assume that other areas of communication ability are not being tested as frequently as ability to write, and weakness in these other areas may not be accurately assessed. The fact that other areas are undoubtedly less frequently measured may indicate that weakness in these areas is less easily assessed. Most effort seems to be made in improving writing ability, but writing ability remains the greatest weakness. Of course, we do not know how much worse the situation might be if efforts to improve this area were not made; but, on the other hand, we do not know how effective present efforts are. Writing may lend itself to testing; whether it should get the greatest amount of attention has not been clearly established."

Arguably, while the "English further education sector can be described as a hotbed of qualifications" (see Cantor, Roberts and Pratley 1995); it is only the written communication skills that are generally evaluated. It must be remembered that good communication skills comprise the four major aspects of communication- LSRW. Of course, ability to distinguish between fact and assumption is also a vital part of communication skills as are a number of other abilities, but a test feasible in a limited span of time can include only the items which are basic to all others, namely: LSRW. Ironically, even all these skills do not get evaluated in the traditional system of examination that is followed in communication skills evaluation in Indian Business Schools and across. Generally it is an assessment of writing skills through writing while research has established the importance of oral skills as well with the corporate (Mainkar and Avinash, 2008; Maes, Weldy and Icenogle, 1997; Cox, 1970). As mentioned earlier, research (Cox, 1970) establishes that assessment in areas other than written skills is less frequently measured whereby indicating that weakness in these areas is less easily assessed; hence there appears to be an acute need to develop such tools as may be helpful to assess these other areas, i.e. non-written skills.

2.3 Peer Assessment and Group Tasks

Studies in the past have shown firm evidence that innovation in fine-tuning the evaluation process yields substantial learning gains (e.g. Crooks, 1988; McKenney, 1962). Peer learning has been identified as a valuable strategy for teaching and learning (Broadfoot and Black, 2004). But, peer assessment, which could be an equally important strategy, has not been sufficiently explored.

The benefits of peer learning were established long before the 1970s, when education research began to focus on such approaches (for an overview, see Jacobs and Hannah, 2004). But, little work has been done on the benefits of peer assessment and on making students play a vital role in awarding marks to their fellow compatriots. It is widely accepted that 'alternative methods of assessing student knowledge' (Desrochers, Pusateri and Fink, 2007) are useful since assessment, largely, is a pointer towards the received curriculum. Research (Krashen, 1981) has focused on the importance of a rich and varied input as a prerequisite for learning to take place. In this light, the output, and evaluation of this output, becomes equally significant. As was mentioned earlier, typically the method used for evaluation is written examination, ending up assessing how well the inputs provided in the class have been received in a theoretical sense as opposed to a task oriented assessment. This method, if used with some thought, can probably end up assessing all the four LSRW skills of a student. In case there are time constraints, and one wants to use the latter method, a group task can be considered to attain the objectives, but group work per se does not create opportunities for learning. Important conditions in group tasks are that group members must be encouraged to (i) share; (ii) jointly analyze and evaluate the ideas; (iii) come to a joint solution of the problem; and (iv) share the ownership of a product (Mercer, 1995; Storch, 2002). Group assessment tasks are now being designed by large-scale assessment programs (Fall and Webb, 2000), however, whether or not these tasks serve as a tool of evaluation of the LSRW skills, is yet to be known.

An important objective of evaluation is to be able to provide students with an immediate and constructive feedback. Psychologists have observed that feedback on the effectiveness of a person's performance enhances learning and influences future performance (Feinberg, 1979). While "talk" as an aid to learning is an accepted way to provide classroom input, it is not extremely clear whether such "talks" are indeed useful in bringing a range of effects in specific interactions. So much so, it needs to be studied whether "talks" can be used for evaluation purposes. It comes to be seen that participants in group discussions naturally tend to limit effective participation of certain other participants (Miragua, 1964). Equal participation among group members is uncommon, as almost about 40 percent of total talk time in discussion in groups with sizes as small as three and as large as eight is taken by the most active participant (Bales, 1970). According to Koschmann, Kelson, Feltovich, and Barrows (1996), meaningful group discussions can lead to effective learning by way of students engaging in deep reflections on their ideas. By self-reflection and by adding others' perspectives to their own reflections, learners learn to integrate new ideas into their existing knowledge. Also, the processes involved in asking questions, responding to questions, and elaborating upon these responses, all contribute to learning (Cohen, 1994; Slavin, 1996). Research also supports the hypothesis that group discussions can contribute to increased self-efficacy.

Mainkar and Avinash (2008) in their study observe that although practiced widely, grading of student participation in class discussions has been often criticized by researchers. They further observe that, in such discussions, the instructor simultaneously adopts two incompatible tasks- of facilitating class discussion and of evaluating student participation. Students' focus, in such situations is on earning points instead of on drawing learning. Instructor-based grading schemes do not motivate all students equally. In summary, evaluation poses both a challenge as well as an opportunity. It is a challenge because the process has to be fair and objective and yet deliver achievement of the intended purpose. It is an opportunity because evaluation can be innovatively designed to cope with these challenges and also use it to impart learning. The present study constitutes a humble attempt in this direction.

2.4 Research Proposition
Evaluation of student performance in any course, especially those delivered in a management programme, poses a serious challenge, more so, in a course like 'Business Communication' where oral communication ought to form an integral part of evaluation. It also needs to be remembered that effective evaluation, based on all the components of any course, lends appropriate seriousness to the course and its modules. Research establishes that classroom evaluation has powerful impacts- direct and indirect; positive or negative, and thus deserves very careful planning and implementation. (Crooks, 1988)

The present study, keeping these concerns in mind, proposes to explore the following propositions:
1. Whether the method adopted does any better?
2. Is the method effective?
3. Is the method setting independent?
4. How replicable is the method?

3 THE STUDY

3.1 The Problem
This paper presents various details of an experiment, conducted with a view to introduce this much needed component in the evaluation process. Essential purpose of the exercise was to try and broaden the focus of evaluation and simultaneously enlarging its scope. The need to maintain certain amount of objectivity and transparency was taken of getting every student evaluated on both written as well as non-written skills, and keeping as critical. Group Discussion was used as a tool. A process was developed with the objective of getting every student engaged as an active participant in the process. A two-sided evaluation mechanism was put in place to achieve the dual purpose of learning and evaluation. This was done not only to ensure objectivity and participation but also to provide the entire class a feel of how individuals behave when involved discussions take place. Statistical analysis of the results suggests that the experiment was a useful one. The student feedback was favourable too.

One might ask: Why seek experimental evidence of the impact of one assessment tool when few other standard evaluation methods have been accepted and established? One reason is to add to and gain acceptance within the accepted evaluation tools that have been experimented upon and developed gradually and that have proved themselves by their quality. Perhaps of greater importance is to develop a design enabling business communication instructors to evaluate students on something more than written skills. Time and again various stakeholders have emphasized on the possession of both verbal and non-verbal communication skills with the business management students (Gray, Ottesen, Chapman and Whiten, 2007) and while business communication syllabus across Indian business schools is a balanced mix of both written and non-written skills, the evaluation pattern, across the globe, is such that there is little provision of assessment on non-written skills. Hence, though the non-written modules of the business communication course do get taken up, there is little evaluation upon them, thus leaving a sense of incompleteness not only in terms of instructor and the course delivery but also in terms of students having a feeling of acquiring the said skills. The reasons behind this dichotomy could be:

1. Evaluation of non-writing skills could be too time consuming with an average batch of sixty students.
2. Lot of subjectivity might creep in or could be suspected leading to loss of 'trust' in the evaluation process, which, according to research is crucial to the acceptance of the evaluation result. (Broadfoot and Black, 2004)
3. Evaluation of non-writing skills might not be accorded proper seriousness amongst students.

Despite the limitations observed above, the community of business communication faculty has very often felt the need of evaluating the non-written skills of students as well but only after overcoming these constraints. (Badenhausen; Eileen; Lesley and Robert, 2000)

3.2 The Objective

Keeping in focus the above constraints and the stakeholders' concern, an experiment was designed and implemented with the following objectives:

1. To evaluate students both on written and non-written skills simultaneously.
2. To create learning opportunities for students.
3. To enable students to receive an immediate instructor and peer feedback.
4. To conduct the evaluation in a manner that there would be little scope of any element of subjectivity in the process.
5. To present a challenge to the students so that there is no lack of seriousness amongst them.

3.3 Demography

The study was conducted at an AICTE (All India Council for Technical Education) accredited institution offering a two-year graduate management program. The experiment, as a part of end-term evaluation, was developed and used on a batch of fifty-seven students, pursuing a one credit compulsory course on business communication as a part of the program. All the participants were non-native speakers of English, 8 students were females and 49 were males. Female participants were comparatively few in number as the batch itself had very few female students which did not seem to have rippled any effect on the experiment given its objective nature. 31 participants had taken their schooling from English medium instruction, 23 from Hindi medium instruction and 3 from Vernacular medium. All participants were between the age group of 20 to 30 years with an average age of 23 and with 10 students having prior work experience.

3.4 Tool Development

Group Discussion was taken as the tool of assessment as research indicates that group discussion is suitable for assessment process. (Glauco Devita, 2000; Joan Swann, 2007) The process was designed in a manner that a student would be tested on both written and non-written skills simultaneously through participating in the entire process. A two-way evaluation criterion was designed to ensure objectivity. That is both –peer and faculty would conduct the evaluation by awarding marks to the students participating in the group discussion. Thus, while each student was himself/ herself getting evaluated, he/ she was also evaluating a set of pre-allotted students of the batch. This was done in order to meet all the objectives explained earlier. Another objective behind involving students in the evaluation process was to educate them on handling responsibility with accountability, one of the key skills expected of a manager.

The class was divided into groups of eight members each, thus forming seven groups. This led to a total of fifty-six students. As the batch was of fifty-seven students, one group had nine members so as to accommodate the extra student.

While one group would participate in the group discussion, the members of the other six groups were required to evaluate one different member per group on pre-set parameters. Thus, each student would be evaluated by six students (one student per group) and would also evaluate the group discussion performance of six students i.e. one student/ group. This means that at all times, students would either evaluate a peer or be evaluated themselves by peers. Apart from this, work constituting the written evaluation of peer evaluators would proceed simultaneously.

The entire procedure was video taped in order to further assess the receptivity and involvement of the students to the new mode.

The procedure had two parts, each of 10 marks, running concurrently:
- Non-written Evaluation
- Written Evaluation

3.5 Non-Written Evaluation

Major aspects of non-written skills were considered and an Assessment Sheet was designed, to be used both by the students and the faculty member. (Figure 1, Appendix 1)

A cumulative weight age of 50% was given to student evaluation and 50% to faculty evaluation

Since there were seven groups comprising eight members each, each student had the opportunity of participating in one group discussion and evaluating one student each from the other groups when they had the group discussion, thus giving each student a chance to be responsible and accountable for the evaluation of six students.

Hence, at any point of the procedure, the students were either participating in the group discussion or evaluating one of their batch mates. Thus, each student, undertaking the group discussion, was assessed on pre-determined parameters, making a total of 120 marks. These marks were later scaled down to 5 marks (50% of 10 marks) and added to the 5 marks by the faculty member (scaled down to 5 from 20), who also assessed the students on the same parameters.

N=57
No. of groups= 7
No. of members per group= 8 (except for one group which had nine members)
Each respondent evaluated by= six respondents (one member per group, excluding his own group) + one instructor
MM= 20 (per student) + 20 (instructor)
Therefore, 120 marks (scaled down to MM=5) + 20 marks (scaled down to MM=5)
Thus, 5 marks (peer evaluation) + 5marks (instructor evaluation) = 10 marks.

To ensure maximum objectivity amongst the students, groups were formed ensuring that there was no overlapping, i.e. no two students evaluated each other. Attendance Sheet was used to divide the students into groups. Hence, there was no selection of students in any manner for group formation. Sets of eight students, in order of their enrolment numbers were formed, making one group (G-1, G-2 and so on). Thus eight heterogeneous groups were formulated. This sheet (Appendix 5) was displayed to the respondents towards the beginning of the evaluation process. The respondents were not aware of the process prior to the process.

3.6 Written Evaluation

While the students were assessing the group discussion performance of the students allotted to them, simultaneously, they were to justify in writing, in about seventy-five words per evaluation, why they thought the student deserved particular marks. Thus, they needed to critically comment on the performance of six students each. While this ensured their accountability towards the awarding of marks, it also comprised their own written evaluation of ten marks to be awarded by the faculty member. This meant that their awarding marks to a particular student contributed to his evaluation but their written comment on his performance led to their own written evaluation. It is assumed here that the test was not on classroom instruction but on language proficiency- a component of LSRW, their listening skills, their receptivity to what was discussed, judgment of its relevance and consequently of communication skills.

4 METHODOLOGY

Topics were allotted one week prior to the group discussion as evaluation component was attached. On the day of the experiment, the detailed procedure was explained to the batch. The list of group division and who would evaluate whom was displayed on a LCD screen. (Appendix 5)

Assessment Sheets (Appendix 1, Figure 1) and writing sheets were circulated. The assessment parameters were explained thoroughly. The Assessment Sheets carried the names of all the students with the instruction that they would only evaluate the students according to the list on display. The entire procedure, which took approximately three hours, was video taped.

To further analyze the objectivity of evaluation and validity of results, statistical tests were conducted on the marks awarded by peer evaluators and instructor. To test the receptivity of the technique among students, a questionnaire was administered on the participants after the process was completed.

5 RESULTS/ DISCUSSION

Since it was the first time such intensive two-way evaluation procedure was experimented upon, some trepidation regarding the effectiveness was natural. The major concerns were:
1. Its receptivity and acceptance among the students.
2. Would peer assessment be as objective as intended?
3. Would a simultaneous assessment of written and non-written skills be effective?

Students preferred the group discussion assessment condition more and also perceived it as a more accurate measure of their communication skills. Some research suggests that group discussion (Myers, 2007) did not emerge as a very effective technique in promoting learning but the present study suggests that if exercised with complete clarity, it could be a useful technique for learning and evaluation.

Cox (1970), in his study indicated that a test brief enough should approximately be of 90 minutes. The current process took approximately 180 minutes, but considering the fact that the test successfully faced a major challenge of evaluating students on more than written skills alone, the time duration appears to be suitable.

A very significant finding of the technique was that, in the non-written evaluation, when the marks awarded by the faculty (M=3.49. Std. = .71) and students (M=3.63. Std. = .55) were scaled down to 5 marks each, in 63.15% cases, the marks awarded were the same. This is validated by the mean values and standard deviation values of the peer assessment (M= 12.67, Std. = 2.06) and faculty assessment (M= 12.29, Std. = 2.51) on 20 marks each. It is important to note here that this observation was only a bi-product of the technique and it served the purpose of substantiating the fact that that an objective assessment can be made possible, even through peer assessment. (Appendix 2, Table 1)

Appendix 3, Table 2, shows that the mean value of the students' evaluation of group discussion performance of the students was 3.63 with a standard deviation of .56, whereas the mean value of the faculty evaluation of group discussion performance of the same students was 3.49 with a standard deviation of .71. It can be said that in general, the peer assessment of the group discussion performance was slightly higher as compared to that of faculty evaluation which is acceptable as student benchmarks would any time be a bit lower than the faculty benchmark. The fact that the student peer assessment was slightly higher than the faculty assessment does not lead us to conclude that there was a play for marks as has been suggested by Mainkar (2008). The reasons behind this conclusion could be that variation was not very high and secondly, since no student was evaluating one another, no apparent benefit seemed to have been achieved by marking somebody on the higher side.

A high variation (Std. = .71) was observed in case of faculty assessment of students' performance. It indicates the objectivity of faculty evaluation of the group discussion indicated by high differences in faculty assessment scores. Higher coefficient of variation in case of faculty assessment (coefficient of variation = 21%> 16%) supports higher relative variation in case of faculty assessment. The testing of hypothesis between the means of peer assessment and faculty assessment (1.63< 1.84 at .01 level of confidence) also validates the above conclusion.

A correlation analysis of the same further verifies this. Appendix 4, Table 3, shows that students' evaluation and faculty evaluation are found to be moderately correlated. (Correlation = .56) at .01 level of significance. It can be said that in 99% cases there would exist a significant positive correlation between peer and faculty evaluation barring the 1% chance factors. Therefore, the results suggest that faculty and peer both follow the same pattern to a moderate extent.

This revelation leads to certain very interesting conclusions. It perhaps is reflection on the clarity of the assessment parameters to the students. Also, the batch should be given credit for being actually objective in their approach towards evaluating their peers. It also points out that students are well aware of the right skills to be used in group discussion but their performance suffers due to certain other external factors. What these external factors are needs to be further researched.

It was also observed that since evaluation was involved and topics were pre-determined, students' performance was better. Significantly, the usual errors that students make in regular group discussions like grammatical errors, poor structuring of thoughts, improper non-verbal signals etc were far less in number. It needs to be studied if preparation of the topic helps in reducing behavioural, para-language and body language errors. Further, research needs to assess what factors lead to making same errors when the students are required to express themselves extempore.

However, grammatical and other language errors in the writing part appeared to be almost similar as that of in a standard examination, though a standard examination is on a pre-decided curriculum and practice is possible, while in this case, the fact that written assessment would also be a part of the technique was revealed to the students when the process started and there was no pre-determined syllabus. This perhaps leads us to conclude that grammatical correctness comes from correctness of thought rather than practicing for a short period of time. This leaves a major scope for further research.

A post questionnaire based feedback of the technique revealed that an overwhelming number of students appeared be satisfied with the experiment. In particular, 75% students (M=3.98), (on a five-point Likert scale, where 1= Strongly Disagree, 5= Strongly Agree), felt such techniques be made an integral part of the curriculum as they help in putting to test the real objective of a communication class- confident expression. Performance was found to be better and stress level far lower than that of in a standard examination, as indicated by a mean of 3.57, perhaps because this technique appeared less formidable. That this process also gave students an opportunity to learn and to practice better structuring and expression of thoughts was substantiated by a mean score of 4.07 and 4.12 respectively.

6 LIMITATIONS

The primary constraint in implementing the test effectively across business schools would be the batch size. If the same exercise were to be carried out in more than one section, lack of a carefully planned strategy, in the sense of clever division of groups and students so that there is no overlapping of student evaluators, may affect the impact of the tool. It is highly important for the instructor to explain the parameters clearly to the students; else, peer assessment could be effected. It is also felt that the test would be even more effective if the batch size is of around thirty students but this would also mean less number of student evaluators. Whether or not this reduced number of peer evaluators lead to play for marks, has yet to be determined. However, further experimentation and subsequent research is in the process and the outcome of these observations, when tested, would be reported.

7 IMPLICATIONS

One objective of this experiment was that apart from evaluation, the exercise should also enhance the learning of students. A post-discussion revealed that the objective was largely achieved by way of students sharing, discussing and listening to various view points on diversified topics. Therefore, the authors believe that, the experiment, if replicated, should provide reliable results as it seems to be a win-win situation for both- the evaluator and the participants. The experiment, if replicated successfully, would help instructors achieve, to a large extent, multi-fold objectives of a class on communication- improvement of written and non-written skills, evaluation of written and non-written skills, training students on group discussion, and above all, training them on confident expression.

8 CONCLUSION

The experiment, still in its nascent stage, appears to have the potential of being further modified and developed into a useful tool of assessment. The correlation between faculty and student scores and the post feedback of the approach validates not only the above stated fact but also that peer assessment, if implemented properly, can be a useful tool for student evaluation.

REFERENCES

Badenhausen, Kurt; Henderson, Eileen; Kump, Lesley and Stanfl, Robert. (2000) Forbes,Volume.165 Issue 3, pp.100-104.

Bales, R.F. (1970). Personality and Interpersonal Behavior. New York: Holt, Rinehart and Winston.

Broadfoot, Patricia and Black, Paul. (March 2004). Redefining assessment? The first ten years of assessment in education. Assessment in Education: Principles, Policy & Practice, pp. 7 – 26.

Cameron, D. (2000) Good to Talk?: Living and Working in a Communication Culture. London: Sage.

Cantor, L.; Roberts, L. and Pratley, B. (1995) A guide to further education in England and Wales (London, Cassell Education).

Cohen, E. G. (1994). Restructuring the classroom: Conditions for productive small groups. Review of Educational Research, Volume 64, No. 1, pp. 1–35.

Cox, Homer L. (1970). Communication testing practices: A survey of selected universities. Journal of Business Communication, Volume8, No.1, pp.13-23.

Crooks, Terence J. (1988). Impact of classroom evaluation practices on students. Review of Educational Research, Volume 58, No. 4, pp. 438-481.

Desrochers Marcie N.; Pusateri Jr, Michael J. and Fink, Herbert C. (October 2007). Game assessment: Fun as well as effective. Assessment & Evaluation in Higher Education, Volume 32, Issue 5 , pp. 527 – 539.

Devita, Glauco. (2000). Inclusive approaches to effective communication and active participation in the multicultural classroom -An international business management context. Active Learning in Higher Education, Volume 1, No. 2, pp. 168-180.

Fall, Randy and Webb, Noreen M. (2000). Group discussion and large-scale language arts assessment: effects on students' comprehension. American Educational Research Journal, Volume 37, No. 4, pp. 911-941.

Feinberg, Susan. (1979). Evaluation of business communication techniques. Journal of Business Communication, Volume 16, No. 3, pp. 15-30.

Gray, Brendan J., Ottesen, Geir Grundvag; Bell, Jim; Chapman, Cassandra and Whiten, Jemma. (2007) Marketing Intelligence & Planning, Volume. 25, No. 3, pp. 271-295.

Haigh, Martin. (August 2007). Sustaining learning through assessment: An evaluation of the value of a weekly class quiz. Assessment & Evaluation in Higher Education, Volume 32, Issue 4, pp. 457 – 474.

Hancock, Dawson R. (2007). Effects of performance assessment on the achievement and motivation of graduate students. Active Learning in Higher Education, Volume 8, No. 3, pp. 219-231.

Holmes, J. (1992) Women's voices in public contexts. Discourse and Society. Volume3, No.2, pp. 131-150.

Jacobs, G. and Hannah, D. (2004) Combining cooperative learning with reading aloud by teachers. International Journal of English Studies, Volume 4, pp. 7–118.

Koschmann, T., Kelson, A. C., Feltovich, P. J., and Barrows, H. S. (1996). Computer-supported problem-based learning: A principled approach to the use of computers in collaborative learning. In T. Koschmann (Ed.), Computer-supported collaborative learning: Theory and practice of an emerging paradigm (pp. 83–124). Mahwah, New Jersey: Lawrence Erlbaum.

Krashen, S. (1981) Second Language Acquisition and Second Language Learning. Oxford: Pergamon.

Lee, Yekyung in full collaboration with Ertner, Peggy A. (2006). Examining the effect of small group discussions and question prompts on vicarious learning outcomes. Journal of Research on Technology in Education, Volume39, No.1, pp.66-80.

Maes, Jeanne D; Weldy, Teresa G. and Icenogle, Marjorie L. (1997). A managerial perspective: oral communication competency is most important for business students in the workplace. The Journal of Business Communication, Volume 34.

Mainkar, Avinash V. (Feb2008). A student-empowered system for measuring and weighing participation in class discussion.Journal of Management Education, Volume 32 Issue 1, pp. 23-37.

Malmqvist, Anita. (2005). How does group discussion in reconstruction tasks affect written language output. Language Awareness, Volume14, No. 2&3.

McKenney, James L. (July 1962). An Evaluation of Business Game in an MBA Curriculum. JSTOR: The Journal of Business, Volume 35, No.3, pp. 278-286.

Mercer, N. (1995) The Guided Construction of Knowledge. Talk amongst Teachers and Learners. Clevedon: Multilingual Matters.

Miragua, Joseph F. (1964). Communication network research and group discussion. Today's Speech, Volume12, No.4.

Myers, Greg. (2007). Enabling talk: How the facilitator shapes a focus group Text & Talk; Volume 27 Issue 1, pp. 79-105.

Ogunleye, James. (February 2006). A review and analysis of assessment objectives of academic and vocational qualifications in English further education, with particular reference to creativity. Journal of Education & Work, Volume19, No.1, pp. 91-204.

Reese, Curt and Wells,Terri. (December 2007). Teaching academic discussion skills with a card game. Simulation & Gaming, Volume 38, No. 4, pp. 546-555.

Slavin, R. E. (1996). Research on cooperative learning and achievement: What we know, what we need to know. Contemporary Educational Psychology, Volume 21, pp.43–69.

Storch, N. (2002) Patterns of interaction in ESL pair work. Language Learning, Volume 52 No.1, pp.119–55.

Swain, M. (1985) Communicative competence: Some roles of comprehensible input and comprehensible output in its development. In S.M. Gass and C.G. Madden (eds) Input in Second Language Acquisition (pp. 235–53). Rowley, MA: Newbury House.

Swann, Joan. (2007). Designing 'Educationally Effective' discussion. Language & Education, Volume 21, No.4.

Thorpe, Mary. (2000). Encouraging students to reflect as part of the assignment process: Student responses and tutor feedback. Active Learning in Higher Education, Volume 1, No. 1, pp. 79-92.

APPENDICES

Appendix 1
Figure 1: Assessment Sheet

Name of Student	Participation (3 marks)	Listening (3marks)	Speaking (3marks)	Body Language/ Voice Modulation (3 marks)	Content organization, Flow (3 marks)	Emotional Projection, Sincerity, Respect, Confidence, Timing (3 marks)	Overall Impact (2 marks)	Total (20 marks)
Name of Peer Assessor: _____. Date: _____.								

Appendix 2
Table 1: Descriptives

		Peer Assessment	Faculty Assessment
N	Valid	57	57
	Missing	0	0
Mean		3.63	3.49
Std. Deviation		.56	.71
Coefficient of variation		16%	21%

Appendix 3
Table 2: Significance of difference between means of Peer and Faculty Assessment

		Paired Differences					t	df
		Mean	Std. Deviation	Std. Error Mean	95% Confidence Interval of the Difference		Mean	Std. Deviation
		Lower	Upper	Lower	Upper	Lower	Upper	Lower
Pair 1	Peer assessment Faculty Assessment	.37719	1.74561	.23121	-.08598	.84037	1.631	56

Appendix 4
Table 3: Correlations

		Peer Assessment	Faculty Assessment
Peer Assessment	Pearson Correlation	1	.56 (**)
	Sig. (2-tailed)		.000
	N	57	57
Faculty Assessment	Pearson Correlation	.56 (**)	1
	Sig. (2-tailed)	.000	
	N	57	57

** *Correlation is significant at the 0.00 level (2-tailed).*

Appendix 5

The seven groups (1st column from the left) were- G-1, G-2, G-3, G-4, G-5, G-6 and G-7. While one group would participate in the group discussion, all the other members of the other six groups were required to evaluate one member per group on pre-set parameters (as shown in peer evaluation column below). For e.g. member 1 from G-1 would be evaluated by member 9 from G-2, member 17 from G-3, member 25 from G-4, member 33 from G-5, member 41 from G-6 and member 49 from G-7.

Groups	PEER EVALUATION					
	1	**2**	**3**	**4**	**5**	**6**
G-1						
1	9	17	25	33	41	49
2	10	18	26	34	42	50
3	11	19	27	35	43	51
4	12	20	28	36	44	52
5	13	21	29	37	45	53
6	14	22	30	38	46	54
7	15	23	31	39	47	55
8	16	24	32	40	48	56
G-2						
9	8	24	25	33	41	49
10	7	23	26	34	42	50
11	6	22	27	35	43	51
12	5	21	28	36	44	52
13	4	20	29	37	45	53
14	3	19	30	38	46	54
15	2	18	31	39	47	55
16	1	17	32	40	48	56
57	8	17	31	36	30	23
G-3						
17	5	9	32	33	41	49
18	4	10	31	34	42	50
19	3	11	30	35	43	51
20	1	12	29	36	44	52
21	2	13	28	37	45	53
22	6	14	27	38	46	54
23	7	15	26	39	47	55
24	8	16	25	40	48	56
G-4						
25	8	14	17	33	41	49
26	6	15	18	34	42	50
27	7	16	19	35	43	51
28	5	11	20	36	44	52
29	3	12	21	37	45	53
30	4	13	22	38	46	54
31	2	9	23	39	47	55
32	1	10	24	40	48	56
G-5						
33	4	16	20	28	48	50
34	3	9	22	29	47	52
35	5	15	24	32	46	51
36	1	10	18	31	45	56
37	2	14	21	27	44	54
38	6	11	19	25	43	55
39	7	13	17	26	42	53
40	3	12	23	30	41	49
G-6						
41	2	10	21	26	33	49
42	5	12	24	28	34	50
43	7	14	19	30	35	51
44	6	16	17	32	36	52
45	4	9	18	25	37	53
46	3	11	20	27	38	54

47	8	13	23	29	39	55
48	1	15	22	31	40	56
G-7						
49	7	13	20	29	33	42
50	1	16	24	28	34	44
51	8	14	19	32	35	46
52	2	12	21	31	36	48
53	6	9	17	25	37	41
54	3	11	23	26	38	43
55	5	10	18	30	39	45
56	4	15	22	27	40	47

12

Transnational corporations from Asian developing countries: The internationalisation characteristics and business strategies of Sime Darby Berhad

Syed Zamberi Ahmad
Policy and Business Strategy Department, University of Malaya
50360 Kuala Lumpur, Malaysia

Email: szamberi@um.edu.my

Philip J. Kitchen
The Business School, Hull University,
Hull, HU6 7RX, United Kingdom

Email: p.j.kitchen@hull.ac.uk

Abstract

There is limited empirical research on the internationalisation processes, strategies and operations of Asian multinational corporations (MNCs), particularly MNC's based in Malaysia. The emergence and development of an MNC from this developing country represents a significant addition to the literature on this topic which augments and supplements the information already available with regard to nascent MNCs from Asian Newly Industrialised Countries (NIC's). Drawing on primary data from in-depth interviews with 12 key executives from Sime Darby Berhad (SDB), a developing Malaysian-based MNC, this paper will examine and investigate the firm's internationalisation process, its characteristics and strategies, including motivations, patterns, and sources of competitive advantage. The empirical findings, limitations and areas for further research are discussed.

Keywords: internationalisation, Malaysia multinational corporations, business strategies, Sime Darby Berhad

Acknowledgements: We gratefully acknowledge the generous participation of senior executives from Sime Darby Berhad (SDB) which allowed this case to be developed and cited here.

1 INTRODUCTION

Theories and research on the internationalisation of firms (or their expansion across national borders) have received significant attention from many scholars and researchers within the areas of international business, international marketing, and business strategy (Anderson, 1993; Calof and Beamish, 1994; Blomstermo and Sharma, 2003a and 2003b; Ramamurti, 2004, Sim, 2005, and UNCTAD, 2005). To some key authors, internationalisation is the process by which firms gradually increase their involvement in international business activities, and establish and conduct transactions in other countries beyond their national jurisdiction (Welch and Luostarinen, 1988; Beamish, 1990; Pananond and Zeithaml, 1998; Luo, 1999; Sim and Pandian, 2003, Kitchen and Ahmad, 2007). In spite of the importance of understanding the dynamism of the internationalisation process however, most studies have been confined to firms operating in well-established developed countries namely, North America, the European Union, and Japan. Therefore, these early studies exhibit – perhaps of necessity - a distinct Western perspective on the process of international expansion of firms to create competitive advantage, and advance a view that takes into account the development of MNC's from the most advanced and successful economies in the world (Erramilli et al., 1999). However, few studies have investigated the internationalisation process of developing country MNCs and specifically those based in Malaysian.

This paper will analyse and describe the internationalisation process of a leading Malaysian-based MNC, namely Sime Darby Berhad (SDB), through an historical approach. The paper will identify the form and behaviour of this corporation in streamlining its expansion processes including the motivations for international investment, competitive strategies, and selection for foreign entry modes. Although results from a single case study of a Malaysia multinational corporation cannot be generalised as representative of all developing-country multinationals, the case does offer interesting insights which can contribute to the literature of developing-country MNCs.

2 THEORETICAL PERSPECTIVES ON DEVELOPING COUNTRY MNCS

Theories on the internationalisation of firms are largely based on Western multinational corporations. Starting from Vernon's product life cycle theory (1966, 1971) through the Uppsala international expansion stage model (Johanson and Weidersheim-Paul, 1975; Johanson and Vahlne, 1977) and the more recent works of Dunning on his eclectic paradigm theory (Dunning, 1993, 1995) and Investment Development Path (Dunning, 1981, 1986) - predominantly concerned multinational firms from industrialised developed countries. Dunning's work on electic paradigm sometimes referred to as 'OLI theory' links coherently ownership, location, and internationalisation advantages all of which are pertinent in the following case study. However, while the model does appear to be relevant in the early stages of internationalisation, the model is purely static, and unreflective on issues concerning strategic elements, situational contingency, and competitive forces. Moreover, as the trend of outward investments from developing countries began to accelerate in the 1990s (United Nation, 1988, 1993) the body of literature concerning these latter investments and entry modes has been augmented and developed significantly. Recent studies of these emergent or nascent MNC's include papers by Cantwell (1997), van Hoesel (1997a, 1997b, 1999), Dunning et al., (1997), Yeung (1997, 1998a, 1998b, 1998c), Mirza (2000), Mathews (2000), Tolentino (1999, 2000), Adrian (2002), Sim and Pandian (2003), Ibeh et al., (2004), Sim (2005) and Kitchen and Ahmad (2007). Most of these studies focus upon the challenges faced by developing country corporations in becoming respected international players in the global market.

According to the scholars on developing country MNCs, ownership advantages of these corporations differ, and there are two separate "waves" of development: differing as regards historical background, nature of business, extent of the role of government in operations and transactions, geographical direction, and mode of internationalisation activity. Scholars characterised developing country MNCs in the 1980s as those more concerned with cost competitiveness vis-à-vis their competitors (van Hoesel, 1999). Developing country MNCs in the 1990s, on the other hand, placed greater emphasis on the development and/or redirection of business strategies in response to the changing patterns of world business structure brought about by trade liberalisation and economic globalisation (Dunning et al., 1997). In addition, they placed more emphasis on technological competence as the source of competitive advantage (Pananond and Zeithmal, 1998). The sources of ownership advantages for developing-country MNCs have grown through a gradual accumulation of skills, information and technological effort.

Such views are consistent with the internationalisation process literature (Johanson and Wiedersheim-Paul, 1975). Known now as the 'Uppsala Internationalisation Model', this literature stresses the importance of internationalisation knowledge and experience accumulation process throughout a firm's internationalisation expansion. The model states that lack of knowledge of foreign markets and operations creates an obstacle to internationalisation, and that this knowledge can only be acquired by operating in, and experience of international markets. Admittedly, firms may lack knowledge of the internationalisation process, institutional knowledge or business knowledge (Eriksson et al., 1997). The Uppsala school extended the idea of incremental international development to the entire process of a firm's internationalisation from exporting to foreign direct investment (FDI). Given the fact that Malaysian MNCs are new and nascent to the international arena, particularly in terms of outward investment, internationalisation theory is of value in explaining the emergence of these corporations.

3 METHODOLOGY

Given the evident gap or paucity of studies on the area of an internationalisation process undergone by Malaysian-based multinational corporations, this study employs a case study research method to examine a single firm's learning and internationalisation process. The research design requires an exploratory case study drawing upon multiple units of analysis (Yin, 1994). The main data collection method was a series of in-depth interviews with 12 key senior executives in Sime Darby to develop the case study as relying on a single source of information would be inappropriate. Thus, semi-structured open-ended interviews were conducted. All executives including the following titles: Directors, Executives, Senior Managers, and Managers), interviewed claimed to have an in-depth knowledge of their firm's international operation and investment and there seemed no reason to doubt their veracity. Each interview took between one to one and a half hours, and were digitally recorded, carefully listened to, and transcribed verbatim. A second listening accompanied by the typed transcription was performed to ensure full correspondence between the recorded and transcribed data. Complete case reports were sent back to interviewees to ensure validity and authenticity of the collected data. In addition, telephone and email interviews were used to collect further information from the interviewees. In order to give a clearer description of a case study, multiple sources of evidence, including both primary and secondary data, including internal unpublished documentation, internal brochures, archival records, internet web sites, company annual reports, company newsletters, newspaper clippings, magazines and other sources (published and unpublished materials) (Punch, 1998; Yin, 1994) were also collected in order to construct the case and to increase validity.

4 CASE COMPANY: SIME DARBY BERHAD (SDB)

Sime Darby was chosen as a case sample, based for the following main reasons:
a) it was the first Malaysian multinational conglomerate and is one of Southeast Asia's leading and largest corporations;
b) it is among the most internationally-oriented corporations with a long history of international business and trading activities;
c) the company has been a Malaysian multinational from its inception as it became a Malaysian entity through acquisition by the Malaysian Government in 1977, which has focused attention on how the management acquired internationalisation knowledge and experience when operating the organisation; and finally
d) the group is aggressively and widely diversified with interests in almost all economic sectors including plantations, energy, heavy equipment, motor vehicle distribution, travel and tourism, healthcare, and property development, both domestically and internationally.

SDB thus represented the country's dominant business organisation as a diversified conglomerate.

5 BUSINESS DEVELOPMENT OF THE COMPANY

The group structure[1], product and geographical diversification is a complex and overlapping process, but it falls into four chronological periods: its early development: from a plantation-based to a trading-based business (1910-1929), followed by domestic expansion (1929-1950s), conglomerate diversification (1950s-present), and international expansion (1970s-present). It is important to understand the group's history, as this offers knowledge about organisational progression and is expected to provide insights that might act as a basis for decisions about the future (Eisenhardt, 1989; Gummesson, 1991).

Early Development: from Plantation-based to Trading-based business (1910 - 1929)

Sime Darby was founded in 1910, when two British planters, William Middleton Sime, a Scottish gentleman, and Henry Darby, teamed up to form a company to manage 500 acres of Radell Rubber estates in the state of Malacca with a capital of US$20,000. The company was known as Messrs Sime Darby & Co Limited (Malaysian Business, 1 September 2003). Acting as managing agent for a number of plantation companies, it then moved into general trading as demand for goods and services from the rubber estates grew. In 1915, a branch office was set up in Singapore. With increasing volume of trade, it became an agency house which undertook many general trading activities including acting as selling agents for various firms and manufacturers, import and export businesses, in supplying a wide range of consumer and other products domestically and internationally. A London office was set up as a network branch to market the company's rubber. Profits from the rubber were literally ploughed back to buying more plantation land. In 1926, it bought a British competitor, R.G. Shaw & Co and ventured into discounting, money brokering and insurance brokering (Utrecht, 1981).

Domestic Expansion (1929 - 1950s)

The group's first wave of expansion was concentrated in the plantation-based business, particularly in rubber, palm oil and cocoa plantations. An important milestone in the company's growth was in 1929, when it acquired the Sarawak Trading Company which held a franchise of Caterpillar equipment (now known as Tractors Malaysia) (Cheong, 1989). As SD invested in more land, acquisitions were needed for heavy earth-moving equipment for developing these. After the Second World War, in 1952, SD started to enter other lucrative business areas, such as engineering, electronics and management services (Allen and Donnithorne, 1957). Over the years, its activities grew to include supply, finance, sales and shipping of products for many plantations, and by 1954 it was managing some 80,000 acres of rubber land with a total of 18 branch offices in Malaysia, Singapore, Brunei, and British North Borneo (ibid). The development continued when the company acquired Ewart & Co. in 1946, which was later, renamed Sime Singapore.

Conglomerate Diversification (1950s - present)

By the late 1950s, the company had grown large enough to establish a holding company, Sime Darby Holding Limited, in London. The company then naturally extended its activities from trading and management to manufacture in the late 1960s. In 1971, Sime Darby established itself as a major force in the plantation industry through the acquisition of Seafield Amalgamated Co. and the establishment of Consolidated Plantations. The rapid growth and extensive diversification of Sime Darby gave the company multinational status even prior to Malaysian independence (Ragayah, 1999). Because of this strategic importance as an MNC, and to protect the national interest whereby many critics viewed the largely British management of the company as a sore reminder of colonial exploitation, the Malaysian Government through its trust agency Pernas or National Corporation acquired the company in the mid-1970s. According to Utrecht (1981):

> "The SD take-over is a clear sign that the Malaysian government wants a greater say in producing and marketing its resources"

---

[1] Some of the literature refers to multinationals from third-world countries (see Wells, 1983; Tolentino, 1993; Dunning, van Hoesel and Narula, 1997; Sim and Pandian 2003; Ramamurti, 2004). It refers to domestic firms with head-quarters in developing nations, which control assets and/or exert influence in the decision-making process of one or more cross-border subsidiaries and/or affiliates in another country (Yeung, 1994).

Through this process, SD became among the first Malaysian multinationals in the country.

SD initially expanded within plantations. The group's desire to grow further into non-core activities led to major diversifications in many industries, starting in the early 1980s. To name a few, these included motor vehicles, paint and tyre manufacturing in 1981, oil and gas in 1983, property and insurance in 1984, health and hospitality in 1990, travel and tourism in 1991, power generation in 1994, finance in 1996, hypermarkets in 2000, and retail petroleum in 2001. Through its own subsidiaries, Sime Darby diversified into a variety of projects including hospitals, housing development, manufacturing, gasoline and motor fuel distribution, shipping operations, shop lots, golf courses and many others.

In brief, Sime Darby's domestic growth was made up of three major waves. The first wave of expansion was focused in the plantations sector. The second wave was based on geographical expansion of its trading business, and finally, the third wave covered a range of diversified business strategies both upstream and downstream, such as oil and gas, financial services, property development, energy, and motor vehicle distribution. It can be seen that the group's diversification strategies were incremental, rather than revolutionary within each specific industry. The group has used a market segment strategy to expand its business operations both domestically and internationally.

Following this account of the domestic development of the group, the international activities are discussed in the next part of this paper.

International Expansion (1970s - present)

Sime Darby's international exposure began through international trading activities particularly exports of commodity products, as Malaya during that period was the biggest rubber and cocoa producer in the world (Allen and Donnithorne, 1957). It was in the early 1970s that the company experienced phenomenal expansion both geographically and sectorally. The expansion began with the purchase of China Engineers (Holdings) Limited, Harpers International Limited, and Amoy Canning Corporation (Hong Kong) Limited, all based in Hong Kong (United Nations, 1985). With Amoy Canning came the production of canned food, and with China Engineers came engineering, manufacturing, insurance and shipping activities. Harpers provided SD with the franchise for the distribution of Ford, BMW, and Mitsubishi automobiles (ibid).

In the United Kingdom, SD acquired Shaw and Co., a company engaged in investment, shipping, and trading with considerable investments in South Asia. SD also moved into discounting, broking and insurance with the acquisition of Clive Holding Ltd., Guy Butler and Robt Bradford and Co. Limited (United Nations, 1985). In Singapore, having been a market player since 1928, and the sole Caterpillar dealer in Malaysia for more than 70 years, SD, via Tractors, managed to penetrate the Singapore market. In fact, 95% of Sime's business in Singapore's heavy equipment sector comes from the sale of Caterpillar products. Nearer home, the company ventured into downstream processing activities with the purchase of Edible Products Ltd., a major vegetable oil refinery in Singapore.

Administratively, the group's international expansion can be divided into four main regions. Priority was given to neighbouring Asian countries with a similar culture. Like its domestic business activities, SD's international operations involved the group's five core areas: plantations, motors, heavy equipment, property and energy. Figure 1 lists the geographical locations of the group's international activities by region. SD acted on the assumption that the diversification of business based on geographical area would work well in reducing its business risks (Ragayah, 1997, 1999,; Kitchen and Ahmad, 2007).

Figure 1: Sime Darby Major Business Regions for International Activities

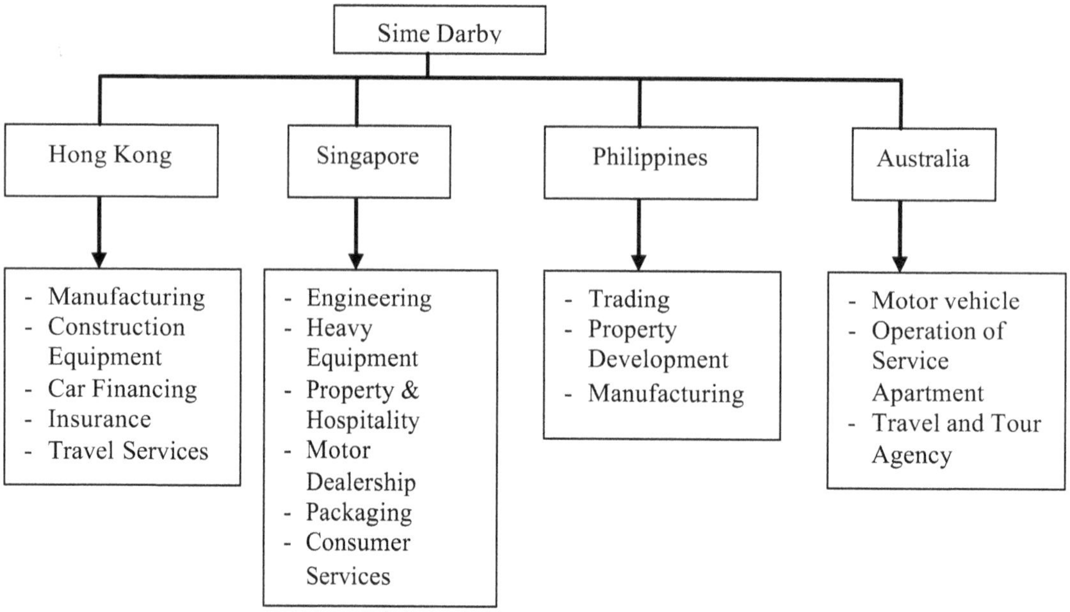

Source: Sime Darby

At the time of the study, the group had 185 subsidiaries and associated companies involved in various business activities in the Malaysian market. In its international operations, the group had 46 companies in Hong Kong, 72 in Singapore, 9 in the Philippines, 11 in Australia, 5 in Indonesia and 19 in other developing countries. In the developed countries, the group had 12 companies in the United Kingdom, 2 in the United States, and 15 in New Zealand (Sime, 2006). Sime Darby's major strength lies within the Southeast Asia region, with only limited coverage in other parts of Asia. Overseas operations accounted for about 60% and 35% respectively of the group's gross revenue and pre-tax profits for the past four years - with Malaysia, Hong Kong, Singapore and Australia collectively, holding the prize in posting revenues in excess of RM1 billion. By virtue of the fact that SD has operations in 20 countries, international business is one of the key sources of growth for the group. The next section explains how SD has built up its ownership advantages and business strategy.

6 OWNERSHIP ADVANTAGES

Strong Brand Name and Extensive Distribution Channels

With more than 95 years of corporate history and being involved in many avenues of diversified business, the group has built a strong reputation in trading domestically and internationally from recognisable brand products through its franchises and dealership agreements with various foreign parties. For instance, in the group's motor business, brands such as BMW, Ford, Land-Rover, Peugeot, Caterpillar and Kawasaki, to name but a few, are among the well-renowned brands to which the group holds primary distribution rights in several countries Through these and other recognisable brand names, SD has gained a reputation for the high level of quality and higher standards in its products typology.

The broad range of quality products offered by the group, has not only enhanced SD's market power but would also compensate for any declining revenues in specific highly competitive industries. For instance, in the automotive industry, the group suffered a setback when it lost its exclusive BMW automobile distribution franchise which was expected to have a significant effect on revenue. In June 2003, the German-based Bayerische Motoren Werke (BMW) group formed a 51:49 joint-venture company with Sime to take over wholesale distribution of BMW vehicles in the country. BMW invested about RM93 million in the venture (Malaysian Business, 1 September 2003). Losing its exclusive distributorship will have an impact on SD, as it was considered Sime's largest revenue contributor - at approximately 35-40% every year. It remains to be seen, however, as the group's diverse range of automotive brands seeks to minimise its investment risks.

SD has employed an acquisition strategy since its early establishment, with the purchase in 1929 of Sarawak Trading, which held the Caterpillar franchise. Benefiting from this acquisition until now, the group has the sole distribution rights for Caterpillar and this has contributed towards the growth of the group's business operations. As a result, SD enjoyed substantial advantages over newcomers, and consequently their industries became and remained oligopolistic.

In order to facilitate its marketing activities, the group continues to invest in the expansion of its distribution network and services facilities. With access to the group's marketing networks both domestically and internationally, customers do have confidence in accepting SD's products. In addition, recruiting its own staff to oversee day-to-day operations in all of its marketing networks ensures that quality meets international standards. This strategy has enabled the group to distinguish itself from other competitors in the same industry.

It would be too simplistic, however, to claim that the group's ownership advantage derived from its reputation in selecting quality brands and extensive distribution marketing channels alone. The SD group's competitive advantages domestically and internationally were also derived from several other sources which will be discussed next.

Strong Management-orientation and Financial Standing

Relying on brand name alone is no longer sufficient in the today highly competitive business environments. The group's competitive advantages in the domestic market were also derived from its strong management-orientation, sound financial standing and adoption of a conservative business strategy. Having the Malaysian government via its state agencies and trust funds such as Skim Amanah Saham Bumiputera, Employees Provident Fund, Permodalan Nasional Berhad (PNB), and Lembaga Tabung Haji (Pilgrims Fund Board) as its major shareholder made Sime Darby rather exclusive in the corporate scene. One expert expressed the opinion that "by virtue of its status as a Government-controlled Company, Sime is a professionally and well managed company that is transparent in its ways" (Quoted in Malaysian Business, 1 September 2003). A similar view was also acknowledged by its former CEO who stressed:

"In any organisation, you will find codes of conduct and procedures, but such rules and regulations cannot really be substitutes for basic honesty, integrity and common sense. Sime Darby could not have become the corporate giant it is today without being professional in whatever it does." (Nik Mohamed Yaacob, 1996)

Sime Darby's corporate strategy and management professionalism were guided by strong company values and its code of conduct. Hard work, honesty, integrity, professionalism, and entrepreneurship are some of the company's key principles, adopted by all levels of staff. The group's mission statement demonstrates attempts to the seriousness of its professionalism and commitment toward its image as a reputable Malaysian Corporation.

As well as its management orientation, Sime Darby's excellent financial standing was another source of advantage for group expansion. SD has been seen as among the wealthiest domestic corporation. The links of SD with the country's major trust funds and state agencies have contributed towards its domestic and international expansion. PNB, for instance, is among the country's leading investment institutions with total funds of more than RM49 billion and having a 40.82% interest in the group. This is followed by Employee Provident Funds (EPF) with 12.99% interest and Pilgrims Fund Board with 2.13%.

This has given the group an image and reputation for credibility that not many other Malaysian corporations have enjoyed. This privileged status made the group a preferred choice for foreign firms seeking a joint venture partner in the domestic market. Furthermore, SD's credibility also enhanced the group's relationships with financial institutions. SD has never had much difficulty in getting support to finance its operations and expansion.

However, links with the Permodalan National Berhad (PNB) do not necessarily bring benefits, especially for the group's business strategy; which is considered conservative and too methodical (Malaysian Business, 1 September 2003). The group's investment strategy is often described as 'conservative', focusing on exploiting incremental investment opportunities under the guidance of the holding company and its major shareholder. As an example, evidence of this was seen when the group took on a smaller player, IOI Corporation Berhad, in its bid to acquire Palmco Holdings Berhad in 2003, and lost its bid. For the record, Sime ended up with a 22% stake in Palmco and two board representatives, while IOI went to buy Loders Croklaan BV in the Netherlands (Malaysian Business, 1 September 2003). Many have suggested that with its huge cash pile, the group could have made better use of its money by acquiring Loders instead (ibid).

With regard to this, Nik Yaacob, a former group CEO, admitted in an interview that:

"I think it is true that people have the perception that we are conservative. But I would like to mention for the last six years or so, we have achieved very consistent growth." (Malaysian Business, 16 July 1993)

Despite attracting criticism, the 'conservative' business strategy adopted by the group, however, proved to be an advantage and helpful in minimising the impact from the Asian financial crisis in 1996/97. Like most Malaysian firms, SD was burdened with the problem of its foreign debts and losses on its financial account. The group were in the red with a loss before taxation of RM70.7 million in 1998. However, in 1999 and 2000, the group made profits of RM1,018.2 and RM1,199.1 respectively (Annual Report, 2000), thanks to its 'conservative' investment strategy. The next paragraphs discuss how internationalisation knowledge and experience became another source of the group's advantages.

International Knowledge and Experience

The group's ownership advantages were not only based on its management skills in managing the organisation, but also on its knowledge and experience in international trade, and knowledge about the regional market. The ability to understand how developing country markets work was another important advantage of SD. The group's past experience in dealing and managing an international project and trading business in the region provided a useful advantage for the group's international expansion. By focusing its business operations on the Asian market, segmenting its business operation into several product groups, and geographically spreading into five main regions, SD was able to take full advantage of its management know-how in plantations and other businesses to tap those markets without much competition from either local or foreign competitors. The group's skills and strength in plantations contributed to other business operations.

Although SD is known for its international investment in 20 countries worldwide, including Hong Kong, Singapore, Australia, New Zealand, Macau, China, Qatar, the Philippines, Papua New Guinea, Thailand, the United Kingdom, Egypt, Indonesia, Solomon Islands, and New Caledonia, the focus of its business is on exports and international trading activity. Sime Darby's interest in foreign direct investment only began in 1990s, when the domestic market was becoming saturated and internationalisation was another way to expand. Although the group's export markets were spreading to various developed countries such as the United Kingdom, European countries, and the United States, the group's destinations for foreign direct investment were still mainly concentrated in nearby Asean member countries and the Pacific Basin region.

Business Networking and Technological Capabilities

To cope with a diversified business activity, business networking is an important mechanism for a firm's growth (Chow et al., 1997). Networking with partners and other players in the industry may help a firm to acquire resources, market information and accessibility or business opportunity, domestically or internationally. Most businesses now rely on business alliances and networking as a strategy, and Sime Darby is no exception to this. With the group's diverse range of business activities, it was unlikely that the group could succeed without having assistance from other players.

With regard to this, close ties with PNB and (Employee Provision Fund) EPF certainly benefited the group's expansion. The group's close links with government trust agencies have been a source of its ownership advantage. Widely known as the first multinational in the country, the fact that Sime Darby enjoyed close links with the government cannot be denied. Because of its strategic value and status as a national company, it was given access to the right places, since any failure could have negative implications for the economy and government (Malaysian Business, 1 September 2003). Links with the PNB gave Sime Darby a remarkable advantage, in accessing investment opportunities to which other industrialists did not have access. In addition to these connections, SD's close links with the government can be seen since its early establishment, inviting top-management officials in the civil service with extensive experience to join the group as advisors or even as full-time employees. These included a former Minister of Finance (1959-1974), Tun Tan Siew Sin, as the first SD chairman from 1976-1988; a former Bank Negara governor (1962-1980), Tun Ismail Mohamed Ali as the second chairman from 1988-1998; and a former Chief Secretary to the Government as the third chairman (1998-present) (Malaysian Business, 16 October 2002; Annual Report, 2005).

Links with the government alone were not enough for the group's development, however. The second necessary sources of the group's connections were joint ventures with domestic and foreign partners. Because the technological sophistication of developing country MNCs tends to be insufficiently advanced, a developing country's firms need to accumulate technological capabilities from suitable foreign partners (Bell and Pavitt, 1997). In the case of SD, the group was able to form joint ventures and learn from its established partners in their respective industries in order to accumulate technological competencies. For instance, when the group decided to embark on entry into the petroleum industry, SD made an acquisition of 60% of C. E Crest Engineering (M) Company, which provided engineering and construction services to the petroleum industry. The group's expansion into agro-genetic engineering is another example where it decided to team up with a California-based company, International Plant Research Institute, which specialised in the research application of genetic technology to tropical crops (United Nations, 1985). A similar case was the group's decision to diversify into petroleum retailing, when it formed a joint partnership with the Houston-based Conoco Corporation (Business Times, 6 December 2001). Table 1 shows some of the group's current technological partners.

Table 1: Some of Sime Darby's Technology Partners

Foreign Partners	Country of Origin	Activity	Form of Contract
1. Aero-Green Technology	Singapore	Aeroponic Farming	Joint venture
1. Caterpillar	USA	Heavy Equipment Distribution	Joint venture
1. Caterpillar Financial Services Corporation 2. Diamond Lease and The Bank of Tokyo-Mitsubishi	USA Japan	Hire Purchase and Leasing	Joint venture
1. Sembcorp Engineering	Singapore	Oil and Gas	Joint venture
1. BMW 2. Ford 3. Mitsubishi 4. Alfa Romeo 5. Suzuki 6. Land-Rover	Germany USA Japan Italy Japan United Kingdom	Motor Franchises	Joint venture
1. Rengo	Japan	Packaging	Joint venture
1. Kansai Paints Co Ltd 2. W & J Leigh Co	Japan United Kingdom	Paint	Joint venture
1. Inax	Japan	Sanitaryware	Joint venture
1. B.F. Goodrich Philippines	Philippines	Rubber	Acquisition
1. Amston Equipment Pte Ltd	Singapore	Filter Presses	Acquisition
1. National Oil Services Company of Vietnam	Vietnam	Bituminous products and electrical control panels	Joint venture
1. Tesco Limited	United Kingdom	Retailing	Joint venture

Source: Sime Darby

As observed from the SD case, forming joint partnership with established foreign counterparts enabled the group to learn and accumulate technological skills. The group then made the effort to add more value and modify acquired technologies and needs. SD interviewees claimed that gaining technological competence enabled the group to expand its operations in foreign countries.

In sum, the domestic and international growth of SD was achieved through a mixture of the factors discussed above. With a strong business reputation and track record, the company has managed to grow from a company offering a single product and service in one country into a strong and dynamic international group with a comprehensive range of business activities domestically and internationally. The business networks of the group come not only from its early and ongoing connections with the government, but also from joint ventures and alliances with foreign partners. The limitations of its internationalisation knowledge were compensated for by its relationship with various parties for the group's expansion. The next section analyses the group's internationalisation pattern and process and entry mode strategy.

7 DISCUSSION: AN ANALYSIS OF SIME DARBY INTERNATIONAL EXPANSION

Conventionally, a firm becomes multinational by going through three stages: it begins as a domestic firm and through the normal process of development acquires technological, management and marketing capabilities to become a domestic leader. Limitation of the domestic market forces motivates the firm to begin to export abroad in order to increase revenue. Finally, when exports are threatened by tariff protection or competition, it uses its competitive advantage to produce products abroad and is then involved in direct investment (United Nations, 1985; Johanson and Vahlne, 2003).

Following this view, a closer look at the development of SD as a national MNC, reveals that the company was internationalised prior to its emergence as a Malaysian conglomerate. The group became a Malaysian MNC overnight through the acquisition of a British firm operating in the country. Sime Darby was a British-controlled corporation until the company's domicile was transferred from the United Kingdom to Malaysia in 1979. In line with the New Economic Policy (NEP) to increase Malay equity, the Malaysian government, after consulting investment bankers Rothschild and through its state trading arm Pernas, bought a number of Sime shares on the London Stock Market.

Through the efforts of Tradewinds (M) Sendirian Berhad, a Pernas subsidiary, Sime's equity became Malaysian-owned in 1977. Prior to its establishment as a Malaysian MNC, SD had international business in several foreign countries, and this included having offices in London and Singapore to support its international trading operations.

The argument proposed here is that the techniques employed by the Malaysian government through its state agencies, which allowed a massive acquisition drive, signified a new era in the method of internationalisation and thus went well beyond traditional theories of FDI as suggested by most scholars. However, it could be argued that the company possessed significant internal and ownership advantages created by nationalisation and favourable treatment by the Malaysian government as had been noted by Dunning's OLI theory (Dunning, 1993, 1995). Nonetheless such advantages had to be accompanied by strategic initiatives within the context initially of a regionally located competitive scenario. Nonetheless, the experience of SD presents an interesting and appealing alternative to companies attempting to become international by acquiring an existing MNC. Government intervention and nationalisation are, however, unlikely to happen in all situations, but sometimes government can augment or underpin MNC development in different ways as in the case in companies arising from the ex-Comecon countries. Further, the emergence of SD as a Malaysian MNC, however, supports the theory raised by Oviatt and McDougall that the firm can be internationalised from its inception. Oviatt and McDougall (1994) argued – for example – that firms need not to follow slavishly well-established steps to internationalisation. They may, instead, begin their international involvement directly from inception. Nonetheless, this theory stresses that such firms have ownership advantages prior to their establishment.

In its international expansion programme, although the group's expansion seemed to commence as an international trading company, especially in its commodity products, those trading businesses were expanded through the acquisition of firms in domestic and international markets. For instance, about two years after the coming home of the firm, SD acquired BF Goodrich Pilipinas in 1981, and started its tyre business with the setting up of Sime Darby International Tyre Company (SIDITCO), which also invested in rubber, coconut, cocoa and coffee plantations. SIDITCO in 1988 changed its name to Sime Darby Pilipinas Incorporated to reflect the company's growth from a pure tyre and tube manufacturing concern to a diversified company with tyre manufacturing, agriculture and agri-equipment businesses (United Nations, 1985). In the United Kingdom, the group bought Carboxyl Chemical Ltd, which manufactures metallic stearates, wires, lubricants and defoaments.

Evidently, the international expansion of the SD group poses issues and challenges to the internationalisation literature, which suggests that firms may minimise the risk of involvement when they first enter the international market and that, as the firm acquires more internationalisation knowledge and experience, it will assume a higher degree of involvement and resource commitment. However, the group's frequent use of equity participation through acquisition of firms operating in the country and abroad seems contradictory to that proposition. This contradiction may result from narrow assumptions about developing country firms which have been portrayed as small, having limited resources and lacking in management capabilities (Yeung, 1994).

Joint venture with foreign partners is another alternative arrangement available for SD's participation in international expansion. In some countries, the group chose to set up joint ventures with local partners in the host countries, to the mutual benefit of both parties. There are many reasons for SD to expand internationally and choose a particular country to be the recipient of its investments. In general, these may be classified as 'push' or 'pull' factors such as finding new markets, diversifying risks, home government disincentives, higher returns on investment, cheap and abundant resources, overcoming import restrictions, competition to enter new markets and to exploit technological innovations and the production process better. As with these views, SD's international expansion was driven by its goal to seek growth constantly through entry into new markets abroad and to facilitate the export of products to another country, especially in other developing countries. This was the reason for the group setting up regional divisions in countries like Hong Kong, Singapore, the Philippines and Australia, to support its business. This is because the developing countries not only offered opportunities for growth but also shared some similar features with which the group were familiar.

Specifically, from the interviews of key executives in the company, three primary reasons appear to be important reasons for SD to invest abroad. The first is to take advantage of market opportunities, that is, regionalising to key markets and access growing consumer demand in the region. The second is to diversify risks. And, the third is related to motivations which invariably revolve around diversification to escape high costs, labour, and other resource constraints in Malaysia. An equally important factor is the familiarity of the countries where the investment is directed, in the sense of common or shared experiences in history, culture, economics and even politics. From the point of view of location strategy, familiarity with the country and closeness to Malaysia will be the main criteria.

Diversifying risk is also an important determinant of the choice of overseas location. SD emphasises that the very nature of its organisation is to diversify risk by having a spread of products or geographically located businesses. The diversification strategy has worked for the group, since it may be that one business is declining but that it will be compensated for by the other businesses. The group's strategy in its investment is to be a long term player and try to make business work in every economic condition. In some countries, the group's business strategy was to start in trading; this then provided a window on opportunities, enabling SD to identify both new businesses and partners for establishing joint ventures.

With regard to its long-term strategy, SD wants to strengthen its position in the Asian regional market, and then the next logical step for SD is to be truly global. For this, it has to aim at inclusion in the Fortune 500 companies and thus must strengthen its presence in the European Community and the North American markets. Although it has set up subsidiaries, joint ventures and acquisitions in the United Kingdom and the United States, these are still inadequate. Moreover, it needs to be rather more aggressive about growing the business that it already has, as well as establishing new ones (ibid).

Managerially, there are many lessons to be drawn from the case analysis. They include the following:

a) managers need to avoid narrow or parochial views with regard to potential MNC development. There are many and diverse routes to such.

b) strategic initiatives – such as joint venture – are not purely dependent on cultural criteria, but on competitive circumstances, government support or lack of it, technological innovation, capitalisation, and managerial skills and know-how.

c) the rationale for 'going abroad' relies on opportunism, risk aversion, and managerial motivation.

d) strategies for entry will vary based on individual country criteria coupled with the three items mentioned above.

With regard to relevance and transferability to other Asian, national, company or cultural contexts, undoubtedly, new and old business models and modelling processes for FDI and internationalisation processes abound. Few, however, have concerned Malaysian-owned, Malaysian-managed MNC's. While SDB represents a somewhat unique case, several elements have been identified as relevant to the future development of nascent MNC's in Malaysia, other developing economies, and indeed emergent MNC's from developed economies. Thus, while there is no one straight road or approved path for this process, lessons learned from this case, may facilitate more strategic thinking than would otherwise be the case.

8 CONCLUSION

This paper has discussed the domestic and international expansion of the Sime Darby group, one of the largest Malaysian multinational conglomerates. Being internationalised from its inception through the reverse takeover of foreign companies operating in the country, SD can be viewed as a new model for the internationalisation process. The group's growth was achieved through a combination of its expanding its capacity as a diversified corporation. Its ownership advantages were derived from various internal and external sources, such as strong brand names, extensive marketing and support networks, strong financial standing, good management capabilities, international knowledge and experience, and business networks with various parties. SD's unique ties with the Malaysian government through its trust and state agencies helped the development of the group, and gave the group a formidable image of credibility and reliability. Its relationships with foreign partners in developing its technological capabilities also played a significant part in its domestic and international expansion.

SD is at the vanguard of Malaysia's thrust into the international arena as one of Asia's leading conglomerates. The Asia Pacific region is SD's stamping ground and its energy has largely been directed to this area, but ventures have also been made further afield for some of its investment, notably in the United States, the United Kingdom, South Africa and Egypt. To Sime Darby's way of thinking, it has grown beyond the boundaries of the region and will continue to broaden its horizons in future FDI. The group plans to grow using internal resources as well as to expand via acquisitions.

Having recognised the need to adapt to the challenges of globalisation, the group has outlined the broad strategies that it believes are vital for it to compete effectively in the international arena. Among these are:

a) a renewed focus on core competencies. This extends beyond the rationalisation of business units to leveraging the group's underlying strengths to build market leadership,

b) aiming for continuous growth in synergistic, related businesses through horizontal and vertical integration

c) fostering a learning culture which encourages the sharing of knowledge across organisational boundaries and geographical divides.

d) SD's overall strategy is to maintain its reputation as Malaysia's leading and most geographically diverse conglomerate, focusing primarily on the growth of the Asia Pacific region through products and services of impeccable quality.

From the experience of Sime Darby, three primary insights can be drawn. First, the acquisition method used by the Malaysian Government to acquire MNCs seems to portray a new dynamic in the extant patterns or modes of internationalisation. Second, although Sime Darby can now be considered as an established and successful MNC, without the proper investment strategy and skills required for its diverse activities, SD would have faced difficulties in expansion and this would ultimately have led to potential losses in their investments at home and abroad. Finally, in terms of international expansion, the group can now further capitalise upon its knowledge on international business in order to further augment its international prominence in the future.

REFERENCES

Adrian T. E., (2002), 'The international expansion of Singapore's largest banks', *Journal of Asian Business*, Vol. 18 (1), pp. 1-35.

Allen G. C., and Donnithorne A. G., (1957), *Western Enterprise in Indonesia and Malaya: A Study in Economic Development*, Allan and Unwin, London.

Anderson O., (1993), 'On the internationalisation process of firms: a critical analysis', *Journal of International Business Studies*, Vol. 24 (2), pp. 209-31.

Beamish P. W., (1990), 'The internationalisation process for smaller Ontario firms: a research agenda', in Rusman A., (eds.), *Research in Global Strategic Management*, J.A.I Press, Greenwich, Connecticut.

Bell M., and Pavitt K., (1997), 'Technological accumulation and industrial growth: contrasts between developed and developing countries' in Archibugi D., and Michie J., (eds.) *Technology, globalization and economic performance,* Cambridge University Press, Cambridge.

Blomstermo A., and Sharma D. D., (2003a), 'Three decades of research on the internationalisation process of firms' in Blomstermo A., and Sharma D. D., (eds.),

Learning in the Internationalistaion Process of Firms, Edward Elgar Publishing Limited, Cheltenham, United Kingdom.

Blomstermo A., and Sharma D. D., (2003b), *Learning in the Internationalisation Process of Firms*, New Horizons in International Business, Edward Elgar, United Kingdom.

Calof J. L., and Beamish P. W., (1994), 'Adapting to foreign markets: explaining internationalisation', *International Business Review*, Vol. 4 (2), pp 115-31.

Cantwell J. A., (1997), 'Globalisation and development in Africa', in Dunning J. H., and Hamdani K. A., (eds.), *The New Globalism and Developing Countries*, United Nations University Press: Tokyo and New York.

Cheong S., (1989), 'Sime Darby: after the coming home', in Cheong S., (ed.), *Corporate Groupings in the KLSE*, Bukmas Sdn Bhd, Petaling Jaya, Selangor, Malaysia.

Chow I., Holbert N., Kelly L., and Yu J., (1997), *Business Strategy: An Asia-Pacific Focus*, Prentice Hall, London.

Dunning J. H., (1981), *International Production and the Multinational Enterprise*, Allen G. and Unwin H: London.

Dunning J. H., (1986), 'The investment development cycle and Third World multinationals', in Khan K. M., (ed.), *Multinationals from the South: New Actors in the International Economy*, Printer Publishers: London.

Dunning J. H., (1993), *Multinational Enterprises and the Global Economy*, Addison- Wesley: Harlow, England.

Dunning J. H., (1995), 'Reappraising the eclectic paradigm in an age of alliance capitalism', *Journal of International Business Studies*, Vol. 26 (3), pp. 461-92.

Dunning J. H., Van Hoesel R., and Narula R., (1997), *Third World Multinationals Revisited: New Developments and Theoretical Implications*, in Discussion Papers in International Investment and Management Series B, No. 227, University of Reading; Reading.

Eisenhardt K. M., (1989), 'Building theories from case study research', *Academy of Management Review*, Vol. 14 (4), pp. 532-50.

Eriksson K., Johanson J., Majkgard A., and Sharma D. D., (1997), 'Experiential knowledge and cost in the internationalization process', *Journal of International Business Studies*, Vol. 28 (2), pp. 337-60.

Erramilli K. M., Srivastava R., and Kim Seong-Soo, (1999), 'Internationalisation theory and Korean multinationals', *Asia Pacific Journal of Management*, Vol. 16 (1), pp. 29-45.

Gummesson E., (1991), *Qualitative Methods in Management Research: Revisited Edition*, Sage Publications: London.

Ibeh K., Young S., and Lin H-C., (2004), 'Information technology and electronics firms from Taiwan Province of China in the United Kingdom emerging trends and implication', *Transnational Corporations*, Vol. 13 (3), pp. 21-52.

Johanson J., and Vahlne J-E, (1977), 'The internationalization process of the firm – a model of knowledge development and increasing foreign market commitments', *Journal of International Business Studies*, Vol. 8, Spring/Summer, pp. 23-32.

Johanson J., and Vahlne J-E, (2003), 'Building a model of firm internationalisation', in Blomstermo A., and Sharma D. D., (eds), *Learning in the Internationalisation Process of Firms*, New Horizons in International Business, Edward Elgar, United Kingdom.

Johanson J., and Wiedersheim-Paul F., (1975), 'The internationalization of the firm: four Swedish cases', *Journal of Management Studies*, Vol. 12 (3), pp. 305-22.

Kitchen P. J. and Ahmad S. Z., (2007), 'Outward investments by developing country firms: the case of emerging Malaysian corporations, *International Journal of Business and Management*, Vol. 2 (4), pp. 122-35.

Luo Y., (1999), 'Dimensions of knowledge: comparing Asian and Western MNEs in China', *Asia Pacific Journal of Management*, Vol. 16 (1), pp. 75-93.

Mathews J. A., (2000), *Accelerated Internationalisation for the Periphery*, Paper Read at European International Business Association Annual Conference, Maastricht in September 2000.

Mirza H., (2000), 'The globalisation of business and East Asian Developing-country multinationals', in Hood N., and Young S., (eds.), *The Globalisation of Multinational Enterprise Activity and Economic Development*, Macmillan: London.

Oviatt B. M., and McDougall P. P., (1994), 'Toward a theory of international new ventures', *Journal of International Business Studies*, Vol. 25 (1), pp. 45-64.

Pananond P., and Zeitaml C. P., (1998), 'The international expansion process of MNEs from Developing Countries: a case study of Thailand's CP group', *Asia Pacific Journal of Management*, Vol. 15 (2), pp. 169-84.

Punch K. F., (1998), *Introduction to Social Research: Quantitative and Qualitative Approach*, SAGE Publications.

Ragayah M. Z., (1999), 'Malaysian reverse investments: trends and strategies', *Asia Pacific Journal of Management*, Vol. 16 (3), pp. 469-96.

Ragayah M. Z., Mohammad A., and Habibah S., (1997), *Malaysia's Investment Abroad*, Paper Presented at Razak Conference 1997: Industrialisation and Development in Southeast Asia, Ohio University, Athens, U.S.A.

Ramamurti R., (2004), 'Developing Countries and MNEs: extending and enriching the research agenda', *Journal of International Business Studies*, Vol. 35, pp. 277-283.

Sim, A. B., (2005), 'An exploratory study of internationalization strategies of emerging Malaysian multinational enterprises' *Journal of Asia Pacific Business 6(1), 33-57*.

Sim A. B., and Pandian R. J., (2003), 'Emerging Asian MNEs and their internationalisation strategies: case study evidence on Taiwanese and Singaporean firms', *Asia Pacific Journal of Management*, Vol. 20 (1), pp. 27-50.

Tolentino P. E. E., (1993), *Technological Innovation and Third World Multinationals*, Routledge: London and New York.

Tolentino P. E. E., (1999), 'Globalisation, FDI and technology transfers: impacts on and prospects for Developing Countries', Book Review of Nagesh K., in collaboration with Dunning J. H., Lipsey R. E., Agarwal J. P., and Urata S., Routledge: London and New York in association with the United Nations University Press, 1998, *Transnational Corporations*, Vol. 8 (1), pp. 191-99.

Tolentino P. E. E., (2000), *Multinational Corporations: Emergence and Evolution*, Routledge Studies in International Business and the World Economy, Routledge: London.

United Nations Conference on Trade and Development (UNCTAD) (2005), *World Investment Report 2005: Transnational Corporations and the Internationalization of R&D*, United Nation Publication: New York.

United Nations (1985), *Transnational Corporations from Developing Asian Economies*, ESCAP/UNCTC Publication Series B, No. 7, ESCAP/UNCTC Joint Unit on Transnational Corporations Economic and Social Commission for Asia and the Pacific, Bangkok, Thailand.

Utrecht E., (1981), 'Foreign investment in Malaysia', in Utrecht E., (ed.), *Transnational Corporations in South East Asia and the Pacific: Volume III*, Transnational Corporations Research Project, University of Sydney, Sydney, Australia.

Van Hoesel R., (1997a), *Beyond Export-led Growth: The Emergence of New Multinational Enterprises from Korea and Taiwan*, Erasmus University, Rotterdam.

Van Hoesel R., (1997b), 'The emergence of Korean and Taiwanese multinationals in Europe: prospects and limitations', *Asia Pacific Business Review*, Vol. 4 (2/3), pp. 109-29.

Van Hoesel R., (1999), *New Multinational Enterprises from Korea and Taiwan: Beyond Export-led Growth*, Routledge Studies in International Business and the World Economy, Routledge: London and New York.

Vernon R., (1966), 'International investment and international trade in product cycle', *The Quarterly Journal of Economic*, Vol. 8 (2), pp. 190-207.

Vernon R., (1979), 'The product cycle hypothesis in a new international environment', *Oxford Bulletin of Economics and Statistics*, November, Vol. 41 (4), pp. 255-67.

Welch L. S., and Luostarinen R. K., (1988), 'Internationalisation: evolution of a concept', Journal of General Management, Vol. 14 (2), pp. 34-55.

Wells L. T., Jr., (1983), *Third World Multinationals: The Rise of Foreign Direct Investment from Developing Countries*, The M.I.T Press, Cambridge, Massachusetts.

Yeung H. W-C., (1994), 'Third World multinational revisited: a research critique and future agenda', *Third World Quarterly*, Vol. 15 (2), pp. 297-317.

Yeung H. W-C., (1997), 'Business networks and transnational corporations: a study of Hong Kong firms in the ASEAN region', *Economic Geography*, Vol. 73 (1), pp. 1-25.

Yeung H. W-C., (1998a), 'The political economy of transnational corporations: a study of the regionalisation of Singaporean firms', *Political Geography*, Vol. 17 (4), pp. 389-416.

Yeung H. W-C., (1998b), *Transnational Corporations and Business Networks: Hong Kong Firms in the ASEAN Region*, Routledge Advances in Asia – Pacific Business: London and New York: Routledge.

Yeung H. W-C., (1998c), 'Transnational economic synergy and business networks: the case of two-way investment between Malaysia and Singapore', *Regional Studies Association*, Vol. 32 (8), pp. 687-706.

Yin R. K., (1994), *Case Study Research: Design and Methods*, Second Edition, SAGE Publications, London: United Kingdom.

13

SMEs, electronically-mediated working and data security: cause for concern?

Fintan Clear, Brunel University
Brunel Business School
Elliott Jaques Building, Uxbridge, Middlesex, UB8 3PH, UK

Email: Fintan.Clear@brunel.ac.uk

Abstract

Security of data is critical to the operations of firms. Without the ability to store, process and transmit data securely, operations may be compromised, with the potential for serious consequences to trading integrity. Thus the role that electronically-mediated working plays in business today and its dependency on data security is of critical interest, especially in light of the fact that much of this communication is based on the use of open networks (i.e. the Internet). This paper discusses findings from a 'WestFocus' survey on electronically-mediated working and telework amongst a sample of SMEs located in West London and adjacent counties in South-Eastern England in order to highlight the problems that such practice raises in terms of data security. Data collection involved a telephone survey undertaken in early 2006 of 378 firms classified into four industrial sectors ('Media', 'Logistics', 'Internet Services' and 'Food Processing'). After establishing how ICTs and the Internet are being exploited as business applications for small firms, data security practice is explored on the basis of sector and size with a focus on telework. The paper goes on to highlight areas of concern in terms of data security policy and training practice. Findings show some sector and size influences.

Keywords: data security, small firms, ICT adoption behaviour, electronically-mediated working, telework, security policy, security training, sector, firm size

Acknowledgement: The author would like to acknowledge the financial support provided by WestFocus* under the Higher Education Innovation Fund (HEIF 2) and the contributions of the other project team members: David Barnes, Romano Dyerson, G. Harindranath and Wendy Gerrish (all Royal Holloway University of London), Keith Dickson and Lisa Harris (Brunel University), Paul Wallin (Kingston University) and Alan Rae (Ai Consultants). (*WestFocus is a partnership between universities, SMEs and community groups in South and West London and the Thames Valley, UK.)

1 INTRODUCTION

One particular consideration that firms must account for whilst engaged in electronically-mediated working is the security of data. Any standard text will argue that a security system can only be as strong as its weakest link. In a field that is notoriously difficult to obtain authoritative data, the WestFocus research project 'ICT adoption and use by SMEs' reported on in this paper attempted to gain empirical evidence *inter alia* on the manner in which SMEs balance security considerations with networked working and trading.

Data security was defined in 1992 by NISS as the "protection of data from unauthorized (accidental or intentional) modification, destruction, or disclosure". McLeod and Schell (1997) maintain that data security requires three aspects to be maintained: integrity (i.e. providing an accurate representation of the physical reality that data represents); availability (i.e. allowing those authorised to have access to data); and confidentiality (i.e the protection of data and information from disclosure to unauthorised persons). Without the ability to store, process and transmit data securely, operations may be compromised for which there can be very detrimental consequences for trading. Thus the role that electronic communications play in business today and its dependency on data security is of critical interest. Much of this communication uses open network protocols on an Internet whose underpinning technology was originally designed for sharing data in research projects rather than for the purposes of e-commerce (Ratnasingham, 1998). Given typical assertions that to retain competitive edge firms must develop e-business processes that span more than one organisation (Nah *et al.*, 2004), then firms so minded are obliged to exercise some level of oversight for data handling across electronically-enabled communications domains that extend beyond the internal. However apart from purely working with primary suppliers and customers in electronic alliance, firms are increasingly outsourcing tasks such as network support to 'third parties' (Gupta and Hammond, 2005) in electronic networks that may demand 'flexible workers' to have ubiquitous access (i.e. at any place and at any time using fixed and/or mobile modes) to both their own information systems and those of trading partners. With Spinellis *et al.* (1999) arguing that advanced technology has in many cases outpaced the development of 'control practice and employee knowledge', it is clear that the greater use of electronically-enabled communications may pose complex challenges for data security.

While much of the academic literature focuses on large firms, much less is evident on the experiences of SMEs in terms of ICT usage (Martin and Matlay, 2001; Dixon *et al.*, 2002) or on the emergence of networked trading which proponents such as Straub (2002) argue is becoming the dominant commercial paradigm. Clear and objective evidence on how small and medium-sized enterprises (SMEs) exploit ICTs and the Internet and the concommitant threats to data security need to be continually updated if policy makers, small firms and the technology providers that supply them are to work with the world as it really is, rather than as it may be portrayed on occasion by some technology providers. According to Simpson and Docherty (2004), distrust felt by owner/managers in the effectiveness of government-sponsored business support mechanisms conspires to add to a problem whereby small firms' ignorance of new technologies and systems makes them capable of their being exploited by technology providers. So in the absence of authoratative and objective voices informing small firms of market realities, unchecked commercial imperatives felt by organisations supplying the market with ICT-related tools may lead them to overstate threats in order to sell their wares, perhaps causing "firms (to) continue to choose technologies which may not be very effective for their environment" (Gupta and Hammond, 2005, p. 307). In findings from case studies of eight firms (of various sizes), Nathan *et al.* (2003) note poor ICT procurement practice whereby senior management purchase information systems that they do not fully comprehend, to then foist on an untrained staff which results in the sub-optimal use of those systems and what they call 'low-tech equilibrium'. Such a backdrop may do little to establish clarity for firms trying to work in a digital realm, and in all likelihood may conspire to confuse and hence to compromise data security policy and practice. Arguably, this constitutes a market failure.

There are over 4 million enterprises in the UK (DTI, 2003). The majority of these - nearly 3 million – are 'one-man-bands' (i.e they have no employees) leaving around 1.1 million which have employees. Further breakdown shows that 960,000 have between one and nine employees (constituting 'micro firms'), 160,600 have between 10 and 49 employees ('small firms'), 26,000 have between 50 and 249 employees ('medium-sized firms') and just over 6,000 have 250 employees and above ('large firms'). Thus SMEs – firms with between 0 and 249 employees - account for over 99 percent of all businesses in the UK, and thus have a significant role to play in the UK economy (Beaver, 2002). For the purposes of this study however, firms with no employees (i.e. single operators or 'one-man-bands') have been excluded. Exploration of sector and size differences will be undertaken therefore on the basis of firms with employees only.

The paper begins with a review of the literature, followed by an introduction of the WestFocus research project and methodology. Next research findings are set out, beginning with data on how ICTs and the Internet are being exploited by the SME sample in inter-firm trading. After setting out the general e-trading background for the sample as a whole, the discussion moves on to consider 'offsite working' or 'telework' with sector and firm size comparisons, followed by consideration of security policy and practice, again based on sector and size data. Then come concluding remarks.

2 LITERATURE REVIEW

There is a small but growing literature on e-business adoption taking a small firm perspective, some of which contains discussion on security risks. One focus whilst looking at adoption is on drivers, promoters or advantages of e-business (Poon and Swatman, 1999; Riemenscheider and McKinney, 2001; Shiels et al., 2003; Simpson and Docherty, 2004; Fillis et al., 2004; Stockdale and Standing, 2004 & 2006; MacGregor and Vrazalic, 2005) and barriers, hurdles or inhibitors (Riemenscheider and McKinney, 2001; Levy and Powell, 2003; Simpson and Docherty, 2004; Fillis et al., 2004; Stockdale and Standing, 2004 & 2006; Taylor and Murphy, 2004; MacGregor and Vrazalic, 2005). In a 2002 literature review of the area Dixon et al. (2002) identify common aspects found in relation to e-business adoption barriers for SMEs. Concerns for security and privacy is one such in a list that also contains a generalised lack of awareness of the potential of ICT, a lack of an IT skills base, concerns for high initial set-up costs, and a lack of staff to implement ICT. The general depth of discussion on security issues however in this literature is limited as noted in Appendix 1. Thus some authors spend a paragraph discussing the subject while others do little more than mention it. So while the subject of security is often raised in this literature, it lacks in-depth examination.

Researchers note the heterogeneity of SMEs (Martin and Matlay, 2001; Dixon et al., 2002; Taylor and Murphy, 2004), and sector and size examinations have been made of SME ICT and e-business adoption. Results are conflicting in places. Simpson and Docherty (2004) find sector to be a significant factor in e-business adoption and Martin and Matlay (2001) add that a micro-business focusing on business services is more likely to adopt ICT than a similar-sized manufacturing firm. Levy and Powell (2003) on the other hand find little evidence on the basis of sector for differential patterns in ICT adoption. Similarly, Van Beveren and Thompson (2002), MacGregor and Vrazalic (2005) and Levenburg (2005), argue that firm size is a significant factor in e-business adoption while Levy and Powell (2003) argue, in relation to ICT adoption, that size is not significant.

Another focus in this literature is on adoption models with a number being critical of stage models (which include the 'DTI Adoption Model') (Martin and Matlay, 2001; Levy and Powell, 2003; Fillis et al., 2004; Taylor and Murphy, 2004) on which UK business support has been based. These authors see stage models as prescriptive and ill-fitting of actual small firm adoption behavior. Simpson and Docherty (2004) are particularly critical of some business support mechanisms as delivered on the ground and based on the stage model paradigm; Levy and Powell (2003) argue for a 'contingent' approach in which adoption behavior is seen to be based more on apparent business need than on a linear and apparently seamless progression towards some vaguely-defined 'digital nirvana' where pervasive and integrated operations are transacted between and amongst firms. Ill-fitting policy can help contribute to distrust of government support agencies by small firms as Simpson and Docherty (2004) note with the potential effect of inhibiting small firms from seeking what should be 'disinterested' advice on critical issues such as data security. However MacGregor and Vrazalic (2005) find some taxonomies 'manufactured' (p. 511) and reflections of research design rather than reality on the ground. Citing Watson et al. (2000), Fillis et al. (2004) appear highly critical of the academic literature by warning of "the continued belief by many researchers in the sole value of formalised, structured, prescriptive ways of conceptualising business behavior despite the realities of non-linear, sometimes chaotic behavior" (p.350).

From an intra-firm 'distributed working' or 'telework' perspective, there is still however a paucity of in-depth academic research that looks into data security per se let alone one taking a small firm perspective. Aside from arguments on its efficacy, much writing on telework examines management issues raised by telework or, as for e-business, examines barriers inhibiting its adoption. So Lim and Teo (2000) in a commentary on ICT use in teleworking spend one paragraph discussing the risk of confidential data loss. Authors who take a more distinct focus on data security include Gupta and Hammond (2005) who examine IS security issues in small businesses. Echoing Spinellis et al. (1999) they go on to highlight resources as an issue for small firms where data security is concerned, and observe that 49% of organisations in the U.K see budget constraints as having some prime influence on 'computer security implementations'. They detail constraints felt by small firms in relation to security as: lack of staff with security expertise; lack of financial resources to hire expert help or to provide training; lack of understanding of risks or being dismissive of them; inability to focus upon security due to other business priorities (Gupta and Hammond, 2005).

Authors directly examining telework and data security issues however are Sturgeon (1996) and Spinellis *et al.* (1999). Sturgeon identifies risks such as individual teleworkers handling sensitive data from home; Spinellis *et al.* who compare home office security threats with those of small firms examine the use of networked information systems (IS) within small businesses and home offices. They go on to argue that each shares a similar lack of technical expertise and resources by which to create and maintain a security posture adequate to apparent threat. Both studies argue for use of risk assessment procedures to minimise such threats. Amongst sometimes dated recommendations, Nilles (1998) argues for strong methods of user authentication and for network design principles that reflect a heterogeneity of access modes. Rikitake *et al.* (2001, 2002a, 2002b) examine data security issues raised by technologies such as WLANs, teleconferencing, P2P and VoIP in telework. They point, for example, to the risk of other family members using the same home PC and accessing, perhaps, Peer-to-Peer (P2P) networks which are known to be risky due to the possibility, they imply, of picking up computer viruses and other malware (2001). A US government-sponsored study (Kuhn *et al.*, 2002) on telecommuting points to vulnerabilities in, amongst others, wireless networking, web browsers and printing software.

More typical of the literature are telework studies which have distinct foci other than security, but which note data security vulnerabilities as part of their examinations. Thus Clear and Dickson (2005) in a study on how management attitudes and levels of worker autonomy shape telework adoption in small firms discuss risks to data security in terms of its being a major disadvantage to the adoption of telework. Fulton *et al.* (2001) in a study on 'home-based e-work' that examines the blurring of home and work boundaries identify the shared use of home PCs as being a source of risk for data security. Tremblay (2002) explores work-life balance issues, but points to the dissatisfaction expressed by teleworkers of cumbersome security procedures. An Australian study (Standen and Sinclair-Jones, 2003) notes security issues raised by outsourcing and the development of a globalised service sector workforce. They go on to promote the use of 'ethical hackers' who can be employed to test network defences. Illegems and Verbeke (2003) argue that one of the factors militating against telework adoption is that it 'hinders the security of internal data' (p. 79) with two possible forms of unauthorised access defined: industrial espionage and intrusion by employees. They also argue that any form of telework implementation that leads to employees becoming self-employed freelancers will raise the level of risk to internal data as loyalty to their firm will diminish. Tran and Atkinson (2002) argue that privacy and security processes are required for multinational firms transferring data across international borders. Given the complexities of the issues inherent in the protection of data security, Lohmeyer *et al.* (2002) argue that IT departments should employ managed security providers (MSPs) to help them face security challenges online.

There are a number of guides offering advice on 'good practice' in relation to data security when working in a distributed and electronically-mediated manner and three are noted here. Huws and Podro (1995) argue that teleworkers should be trained to protect data security through anti-virus software, password use and taking back-ups of work-in-progress; if such training were not forthcoming, then teleworkers should not be held responsible for losses of data. The 'UK Online for Business' publication 'Working Anywhere' (2000) points out that safe data handling is dependant not just on technical measures and procedures but also on having reliable and vetted staff. Kuhn *et al.* (2002) argue that telecommuting staff working for US federal bodies should be given guidance on selecting appropriate technology, software packages and tools in order for best practice in data security to be followed.

However most of these authors are not reporting on small firms *per se*, and thus there is a hole in the literature given small businesses are not simply 'scaled-down versions' of large businesses (Quayle, 2004; MacGregor and Vrazalic, 2005). Numerous writers note that small firms face resource constraints not necessarily faced by large firms (Poon and Swatman, 1999; Levy and Powell, 2003; Simpson and Docherty, 2004; Fillis *et al.*, 2004; Gupta and Hammond, 2005. Smith and Rupp (2002) (cited in Gupta and Hammond, 2005) note that that smaller organisations may place a more limited value on information and its security than larger ones. So though Walden (2005) echoes assertions by Schneier (2000, 2003) that data security issues are not properly understood or given adequate attention in many organisations – i.e. irrespective of size - for theory on SMEs to be relevant, consideration of their "motivations, constraints and uncertainties" (p. 18) must be made which are different in comparison to their larger cousins (Westhead aand Storey, 1996).

Questions of data security are raised amongst other aspects by differing modes of access (fixed versus wireless) and in terms of the variegation of devices (including PCs, personal digital assistants (PDAs) and mobile phones/cell phones) with writers such as Ghosh and Swaminatha (2001) arguing that mobile commerce raises new security and privacy risks. Nevertheless, whatever the technologies and use of protocols that may protect data security whilst in transit across electronic networks, Gordon (2004) tempers any technology obsession by arguing that "If employees can walk out of the door of those organizations with reports, drawings, diskettes, files, and anything else in their pockets or briefcases (as they almost always can), then it's incorrect to say that telecommuting presents a new and different risk". Apart from deliberate intent by individuals to compromise the security of data, Lundegaard argues that "Disruptions of information systems are mostly a result of human error, ranging from system integration mistakes to accidental cutting of fibre optic cables, and natural disasters..." (Lundegaard, 1997). Whatever the source of risk, Reuvid (2004) argues that management controls and processes overseeing security are critical factors for firm survival. Thus Higgins (1999) observes, "a policy is the start of security management" (p. 217) and that "Effective security management ... is based on the systematic concept, dissemination and operation of an information security policy". In the absence of such a policy, businesses may be seen as vulnerable, whether as the result of accident or malevolence. So a firm having a policy suggests that at least some appraisal has been made of potential security threats, however imperfect.

In sum, there are a limited number of studies taking a small firm perspective that focus on security issues raised by electronically-mediated working. As a whole the SME literature offers a sketchy view of security risks faced by small firms in a virtual domain. Amongst a growing volume of studies looking at ICT and e-Business adoption that account for SME experience, a number focus on the 'drivers' and 'barriers' to adoption and/or adoption models, sometimes with sector and firm size consideration. Often security is noted in taxonomies of barriers, but the depth of analysis is such that in many parts the subject appears more mentioned than discussed. A strong critique is made of stage models and in particular the ICT adoption model used by the DTI to underpin UK business support policy. Discussion on the impact of such policy on data security issues however is not very apparent in this literature. A number of writers argue for small firms to start to use risk management methods by which to face up to e-Business security challenges. Nevertheless a persistent reminder in this literature is that a small firm perspective requires consideration of resource constraints. So the literature individuating telework that examines data security is limited Thus other studies, some taking a small firm perspective and some not, need to be sought out for relevant analysis on data security issues within virtual domains.

3 METHODOLOGY

The research findings discussed in this paper are derived from a telephone survey of 378 firms located in a region bounded by West London boroughs and adjacent counties. This involved use of a structured questionnaire of 51 questions which collected data on a broad range of company activities related to ICT adoption and use, including ICT strategy, implementation, investment, training and security policy. As part of a collaborative effort by researchers from Royal Holloway, Kingston and Brunel universities, the target for this phase of a WestFocus project examining 'ICT adoption and use by SMEs' was for 400 completed interviews on the basis of 100 firms each from four industry sectors. These sectors are 'Media', 'Logistics', 'Internet Services', and 'Food Processing', all seen as making significant economic contributions to the study region. Listings of firms for the sectors were obtained from a commercial database provider, and these were sampled until the survey team obtained 100 interviews per sector. The telephone survey took between 20 to 30 minutes to complete, and was undertaken between January and March 2006. Upon completion of the survey, detailed examination of the data by the analysis team led to a certain number of interviews being removed to create a final sample of 378 interviews.

Univariate analysis using SPSS was undertaken of the WestFocus dataset by use of frequency distributions for the whole dataset and by use of cross-tabulations of data by sector and size and other variables. The Chi-square test is applied to these cross-tabulations, and the significance measure is displayed in footnotes. If the Chi-square test shows a lack of significance, then such data is ignored.

According to an European Commission (2002) definition, a Small and Medium-sized Enterprise (SME) has between zero and 249 employees, has a turnover of less than 50 million Euros, and is no more than 25% owned by a non-SME (not including banks or venture capitalists). Due to difficulties in establishing ownership patterns, and getting accurate turnover data, one limitation of the empirical work in this paper is that data has been gathered on firms on the basis of employee numbers only.

As can be seen in Table 1 which shows breakdown of the survey sample by size and sector, the sample is composed of 100 firms from the 'Logistics' and 'Food Processing' sectors, 90 firms from the 'Media' sector, and 88 firms from the 'Internet Services' sector, making 378 firms in the dataset as a whole. By size the sample is composed of 205 'micro firms' (1-9 employees), 140 'small firms' (10-49 employees) and 33 'medium-sized firms' (50-249 employees). The comparatively low number of medium-sized firms in the WestFocus sample overall and the relatively low number of 'Media' (3) and 'Internet Services' (5) firms in this size category act as research limitations. Apart from other considerations, any cell with frequency data lower than five invalidates the Chi-square significance test. Any data in cross-tabular analysis that fails this test is ignored. Thus findings shown in this paper are sometimes constrained to present only partial representations of size and sector data.

Table 1: Survey Sample Breakdown by Size and Sector

		Firm Size			
		Micro	**Small**	**Medium**	**Total**
Sector	**Media**	60	27	3	90
	Logistics	49	38	13	100
	Internet Services	49	34	5	88
	Food Processing	47	41	12	100
	Total	205	140	33	378

4 FINDINGS

The data examined in this section show various findings from the survey. Some of the data is shown on the basis of the whole sample, while other data is shown with breakdown by sector and size. The first findings examined are related to technology use, and this is followed by an examination of 'offsite working' and security policy and practice.

Table 2: Technology Use for Whole Sample

Technology	**%**
Email	99%
Internet	99%
Anti-virus software	96%
Firewall	93%
Own computer network (LAN/WAN)	86%
Broadband	84%
Company Website	84%
Wireless access	53%
Intranet	40%
Extranet/EDI	31%
Video/audio-conferencing	27%
Groupware	23%

Table 2 shows frequency data for a series of technologies and their use by the whole sample. Email (99%) and Internet (99%) use are practically ubiquitous, followed closely by anti-virus software (96%) and firewalls (93%). Own computer network (86%), use of broadband (84%) and company websites (also 84%) also have relatively high levels of adoption. Wireless access is used by 53% of firms, a notable level of adoption given the amount of time that such access has become available. 40% of the sample use intranets and 31% use extranet/EDI technology. Video/audio-conferencing (27%) and Groupware (23%) are the least pervasive technologies in the list.

Levels of use of anti-virus software and firewalls almost mirror email and Internet ubiquity, and taken together suggest that firms are aware of Internet-borne threats and thus take measures to protect themselves. While each of these firms can demonstrate apparent intention, whether their infrastructures are actually secure (to some nominal 99.9% level) is not clear. So a limitation of the data is that evidence that might contradict this picture such as whether firewalls are mis-configured and the level of currency of anti-virus software (i.e. how up-to-date it is) was not obtained as part of the survey. Additionally this data is obviously based at the level of the firm and does not account for practice by individual employees. That said, other technologies of note in terms of distributed working are video/audioconferencing – used by 27% of the sample – and groupware – used by 23%.

Table 3 shows frequency of response to the question, "Do you use the Internet to...?" (and individual options shown in the table) for the sample as a whole. According to these figures it is arguable that 'networked trading' is an established phenomenon in supply chains with customer-facing (downstream) use being more prevalent than supplier-facing (upstream) use. Figures for trading are 58% and 50% respectively in terms of customers and suppliers. A surprising finding is the relatively high level of the use of the Internet to make payments, with 61% of firms receiving payment from customers and 56% of firms making payment to suppliers. Notably 44% of firms use the Internet to work with other firms on collaborative ventures.

Table 3: Use of Internet for Trading Purposes

Trading Purpose	%
Receive payments from customers	61%
Trade with customers	58%
Make payments to suppliers	56%
Trade with suppliers	50%
Work with other firms on collaborative ventures	44%

As numerous commentators including Ratnasingham (1998) argue, trust is a vital element in the take-up of electronically-mediated trading. Allowing access by trading partners to a firm's systems requires, arguably, a high level of trust on the part of the 'provider' to the 'user' (Straub, 2002). Table 4 shows frequency of response to the question "Do you allow remote access to your systems / databases by customers / suppliers / joint venture partners?". Only 11% of the sample allow customers remote access with 6% allowing such access by suppliers and 5% doing so by joint venture partners. The figures are too low for meaningful statistical examination by size or sector. Thus the overwhelming majority of firms in the survey sample do not allow trading partners, whether customers, suppliers or joint venture partners, to have remote access to their systems. While these findings do not in themselves shed light on the issue of trust and any inherent data security risks whilst working in an electronic realm, or, for that matter, on the availability or otherwise of appropriate and cost-effective technology, this data does suggest that close electronic working across supply chains is still rare amongst SMEs.

Table 4: Remote Access to a firm's systems / databases by trading partner

Trading partner	%
Customers	11%
Suppliers	6%
Joint venture partners	5%

Attention now shifts to challenges faced by firms undertaking electronically-mediated trading. Table 5 shows frequency of response for the whole sample to the question "Have you experienced any of the following challenges in developing e-commerce for your business?" As surveyed firms could respond to more than one of the options offered, the data is not mutually exclusive. Of greatest relevance to the concept of 'distributed trading/working' are the responses 'Customers do not want to change' (19%), 'Suppliers are not ready for electronic business' (10%) and 'Difficulties with information sharing in collaborative ventures' (8%). For those promoting the greater use of electronically-mediated trading, such data must offer succour given the relatively low response rate for these challenges as a whole. From the data security perspective, the responses 'Security failures / problems' (6%) and 'Internet fraud' (8%) are most relevant. Though not identical in description, this latter finding chimes with the "Theft or fraud involving computers" finding from the DTI security breaches survey of 8% (DTI, 2006). Again such findings will offer succour to promoters of electronically-mediated trading. However, getting reliable statistics on security issues is difficult (Smith *et al.* 2002 cited in Walden, 2005), therefore figures on the subject should always be approached with caution.

Table 5: E-commerce challenges

E-commerce challenge	%
Customers do not want to change	19%
Difficulty in getting good technical advice from outside	15%
High costs to develop / maintain the web site	14%
Difficulty in hiring staff with appropriate IT skills	13%
Suppliers are not ready for electronic business	10%
High connection costs	8%
Difficulties with information sharing in collaborative ventures	8%
Internet fraud	8%
Security failures / problems	6%

Moving on to a sectoral examination of technology use, data failing the Chi-square 0.05% significance test was removed from consideration. Thus Internet, email, firewall and anti-virus software – all of near-ubiquitous use – are ignored for further analysis. Technologies explored in Table 6 therefore are 'Broadband' (84% adoption rate for the whole sample), 'Wireless Access' (53%) 'Intranet' (40%), 'Extranet/EDI' (31%) and 'Video/Audio-conferencing' (27%). Within the 84% overall adoption rate for Broadband, there is a high of 94% for 'Media' and a low of 81% for 'Food Processing'. This is the only case in which 'Internet Services' (84%) is not the lead adopting sector. So while 81% of the 'Internet Services' sample has wireless access, a notably high figure, the other three sectors show rates of 50% and less. This pattern of adoption is repeated for the three remaining technologies with 'Internet Services' firms running ahead of 'Media', 'Logistics' and 'Food Processing' at adoption rates that are significantly greater. So while 68% of the 'Internet Services' sample uses an intranet, the other three sectors' figures are 38% and less; while 50% of 'Internet Services' uses 'Extranet/EDI', the other three sectors' figures are 34% and less; and while 56% of 'Internet Services' uses 'Video/Audio-conferencing', the other three sectors' figures are 32% and less. Though the figures for the other three sectors are much more bunched, 'Logistics' is shown to be the least-adopting sector for four out of the five technologies. 'Media' appears to slightly lead 'Food Processing' in overall adoption rates for the five technologies which are not much greater than 'Logistics'.

While the data shown here does not show relative use of the technologies by firms in the sample, nevertheless they suggest that electronically-mediated working is practised to relatively high levels by the sample as a whole, and particularly by 'Internet Services'. Even if it may come as no surprise that this sector leads the pack given the nature of their business, it is still sobering to recall that the Internet as a business tool emerged little over 10 years ago.

Table 6: Technology Subset Use by Sector

Technology	Media	Logistics	Internet Services	Food Processing
Broadband	94%[1]	78%	84%	81%
Wireless access	48%	35%	81%	50%
Intranet	38%	36%	68%	28%
Extranet/EDI	21%	20%	50%	34%
Video/Audio conferencing	32%	14%	56%	16%

Having established some ICT adoption and use patterns for the sample as a whole and by sector, attention is now drawn to the firms' use of 'offsite working' and security policy and practice. While there are other measures that can be used to evaluate apparent preparedness in data security terms (e.g. policy noted in a staff handbook or employee contract or as part of an induction process), due to the necessity for economy in the survey, two questions were put that were adjudged to be more revealing in these terms. These are "Does your company have a written security policy for employee use of IT?" (referred to in Table 7 as 'Written security policy') and "Do your employees get training to make them aware of IT security issues?" (referred to in Table 7 as 'Security Training'). The other question "Do any of your company's personnel work offsite with access to your information systems (or

---

[1] Missing data for 1 firm

'telework')?" is referred to in Table 7 as 'Offsite working'. This latter question was so framed in order to avoid possible confusion over sole use of the term 'telework' which the author had experienced in previous research on the subject (Dickson and Clear, 2003). Arguably working offsite '….with access to your information systems' is a reasonable synonym for 'telework' in any event. For the sample as a whole, 51% responded in the affirmative to the question on 'Offsite working'. However when cross-tabulating with 'sector', for three of the four ('Media', 'Logistics' and 'Food Processing') the proportion of firms denying having 'offsite working' in these terms was greater than those having it, with responses of 45%, 37% and 43% respectively. Only 'Internet Services' had a greater proportion of 'offsite working' (82%) than not.

Table 7: 'Offsite working', 'Written security policy' and 'Security training' by Sector

	Sector			
	Media	**Logistics**	**Internet Services**	**Food Processing**
'Offsite working'[2]	45%	37%	82%	43%
Written security policy[3]	30%	32%	53%	45%
Security training[4]	46%	40%	79%	51%

In terms of security policy, as noted above, if management controls and processes are important for a firm's survival (Reuvid, 2004), then to manage data security some form of policy will be required (Higgins, 1999). Policies can be formal or informal, but in order to gather definitive data on the issue, a focus was placed on whether firms had a written and therefore formal security policy or not. With 40% of the whole sample answering 'yes' to this question, breakdown by sector shows that only 'Internet Services' (53%) had a greater proportion of those with a written security policy than not. This suggests that 'Internet Services' firms are generally more aware of the need for data security than the other sectors though 'Food Processing' (45%) is not far behind. However, that said, it may be surprising given the nature of their business that the proportion of 'Internet Services' firms having a formal policy is not even higher.

If having a written security policy demonstrates management commitment to data security in theoretical terms, then devoting time and effort to awareness training of staff on IT security issues may be seen as putting theory into practice to some extent. Across the whole sample, 53% answered 'yes' to the question on security training. 'Internet Services' and 'Food Processing' have a greater proportion providing such training than not, with the converse true for 'Media' and 'Logistics'. 'Internet Services' (79%) firms provide much more training than 'Food Processing' (51%), 'Media' (46%) and 'Logistics' (40%). All sectors show greater levels of 'security training' than 'Written security policy' use. However sector heterogeneity is shown elsewhere: figures for 'offsite working' are greater than 'written security policy' for 'Internet Services', 'Media' and 'Logistics' while for 'Food Processing' the opposite is true; figures for 'offsite working' and 'security training' are similar (+/- 1% and 3%) for the same three sectors with the least similar being for 'Food Processing' (where 'security training' exceeds 'offsite working' by 8%). So arguably the 'Food Processing' sector shows some different adoption behavior here from the other three.

Table 8: 'Offsite Working', 'Written security policy' and 'Security training' by Firm Size

	Size		
	Micro	**Small**	**Medium**
'Offsite working'[5]	42%	57%	84%
Written security policy[6]	26%	53%	74%
Security training[7]	46%	60%	64%

Table 8 shows cross-tabulations between frequency of response to the same three questions as noted above for Table 7 but on the basis of firm size. As noted, the overall number of 'medium-sized

---

[2] Missing: 11 ('Media': 2; 'Logistics': 1; 'Internet Services': 4; 'Food Processing': 4); Chi-square significance: .000
[3] Missing: 6 ('Media': 1; 'Logistics': 1; 'Internet Services': 2; 'Food Processing': 2); Chi-square significance: .004
[4] Missing: 7 ('Media': 1; 'Internet Services': 4; 'Food Processing': 2); Chi-square significance: .000
[5] Missing: 11 (Micro: 5; Small: 4; Medium: 2); Chi-square significance: .000
[6] Missing: 6 (Micro: 5; Small: 1); Chi-square significance: .000
[7] Missing: 7 (Micro: 5; Small: 2); Chi-square significance: .016

firms' in the whole sample (33) is much smaller than 'small firms' (140) and 'micro firms' (205). If we can accept this as a limitation, then there is an evident size effect in the data for the three questions. Responses to the question on 'offsite working' show affirmative figures of 42% for 'micro firms', 57% for 'small firms' and 84% for 'medium-sized firms'. Responses to the question on 'written security policy' show that 26% of 'micro firms', 53% of 'small firms' and 74% of 'medium firms' have written security policies. This finding chimes with DTI (2006) findings (commented on below) which found that "larger companies remain more likely to have a security policy" (p. 7) with 60% of UK businesses having no formal security policy (Walden, 2005). The final question on 'security training' shows that more 'small firms' and 'medium-sized firms' offer such training than not, with 'micro firms' showing the converse: 64% of 'medium-sized firms' and 60% of 'small firms' offer this training while only 46% of 'micro firms' do so. A 'switchover' is evident in this size data: higher rates of training is recorded than use of a formal security policy for 'micro' and 'small' firms but this is in the reverse for 'medium' firms.

Table 9: Training for Awareness of IT Security Issues v 'Offsite Working'

		'Offsite Working'?		
		Yes	No	Total
Training for awareness of IT security issues?[8]	Yes	32%	21%	53%
	No	19%	28%	47%
	Total	51%	49%	100%

At this point, consideration is turned to direct comparison between levels of training on IT security awareness and 'offsite working' (or 'telework') on the basis of the whole sample. Table 9 shows a cross-tabulation of frequency of response to the questions "Do any of your company's personnel work offsite with access to your information systems (or 'telework')?" and "Do your employees get training to make them aware of IT security issues?". Proportions shown are noted for a total sample of 364 responses[9]. The table shows that 51% of the total sample have 'offsite working' and 49% not with 53% of the total sample having training on IT security awareness and 47% not. Cross-tabulating these two variables shows that 32% of the sample have both 'offsite working' *and* training on IT security awareness while 19% have 'offsite working' *and no* security training. Put another way, 37% of the firms with 'offsite working' do not have security training.

Table 10: Written Security Policy v 'Offsite Working'

		'Offsite Working'?		
		Yes	No	Total
Written Security Policy?[10]	Yes	28%	12%	40%
	No	23%	36%	60%
	Total	51%	49%	100%

Table 10 shows a cross-tabulation of frequency of response to the questions "Do any of your company's personnel work offsite with access to your information systems (or 'telework')?" and "Does your firm have a written security policy for employee IT use?" 28% of the responses show firms with both 'offsite working' and a written security policy, but 23% of those firms having 'offsite working' do not have a written security policy. Put another way, 45% of the firms that have 'offsite working' have no formal security policy.

---

[8] Missing: 12; Chi-square significance: .000

[9] On a methodological note, from this point findings for total numbers of responses may differ with those cited in sections above. So whereas the number of those having 'offsite working' noted above is 367 (with missing data for 11 firms), and the equivalent number for 'training for awareness of IT security issues' is 371 (with missing data for 7 firms), the confluence of data for these two responses produces a total of 364. If data is missing for either question, then that case will be ignored for analysis purposes. Variability of totals for the same question between different cross-tabulations is explained by the fact that missing data can be mutually exclusive (i.e. where data is missing for one question only) or mutually inclusive (i.e. where data is missing for both questions).

[10] Missing: 13; Chi-square significance: .000

Now cross-tabulation of the data is attempted using three variables. However a lack of statistical significance reported by SPSS for the Chi-square test renders some cross-tabulations invalid. Cross-tabulating the training variable with formal policy and 'offsite working' variables is one such enquiry, so is ignored from further consideration. Therefore attention is drawn to use of a formal security policy and 'offsite working' by size and sector, though here too there are limitations. Failure of the Chi-square significance test is also the case for 'medium' firms so cross-tabulation of 'written security policy' and 'offsite working' data (as shown in Table 10) by firm is restricted to 'micro' (Table 11) and 'small' (Table 12) views. Table 11 shows that 42% of the total of 196 micro firms have 'offsite working' with 14% having a written security policy and 28% not. Table 12 shows that 57% of small firms have 'offsite working' with 39% having a written security policy and 18% not. This shows an apparent size effect: the smaller the firm the less likely they are to have 'offsite working' or a written security policy.

Table 11: Written Security Policy v 'Offsite Working' v Firm Size: Micro Firms

		Offsite Working'?		
		Yes	No	Total
Written Security Policy?[11]	Yes	14%	12%	26%
	No	28%	46%	74%
	Total	42%	58%	100%

Table 12: Written Security Policy v 'Offsite Working' v Firm Size: Small Firms

		Offsite Working'?		
		Yes	No	Total
Written Security Policy?[12]	Yes	39%	13%	52%
	No	18%	29%	48%
	Total	57%	43%	100%

To view sector influences, 'written security policy' and 'offsite working' data in Table 10 is further cross-tabulated by sector and results are shown in Tables 13 & 14. However data for the 'Internet Services' and 'Media' sectors failed the Ch-square test so only data for 'Logistics' and 'Food Processing' is shown. Table 13 shows that 38% of 'Logistics' firms have 'offsite working' with 21% having a 'written security policy' and 17% not. Table 14 shows that 42% of 'Food Processing' firms have 'offsite working' with 27% having a written security policy and 17% not. So while 'Food Processing' shows significantly more firms having 'offsite working' than 'Logistics', this is not the case for use of a 'written security policy' where 'Logistics' has a slightly higher rate of adoption than 'Food Processing'.

Table 13: Written Security Policy v 'Offsite Working' v Sector: Logistics

		Offsite Working'?		
		Yes	No	Total
Written Security Policy?[13]	Yes	21%	12%	33%
	No	17%	50%	67%
	Total	38%	62%	100%

Table 14: Written Security Policy v 'Offsite Working' v Sector: Food Processing

		Offsite Working'?		
		Yes	No	Total
Written Security Policy?[14]	Yes	27%	17%	45%
	No	15%	40%	55%
	Total	42%	58%	100%

---

[11] Missing: 9; Chi-square significance: .041
[12] Missing: 4; Chi-square significance: .000
[13] Missing: 2; Chi-square significance: .000
[14] Missing: 6; Chi-square significance: .001

5 DISCUSSION

To give some perspective to data in the whole WestFocus sample, some analysis from the bi-annual DTI Information Security Breaches Surveys of 2004 and 2006 is included in Table 15 which shows the level of threat faced by firms working in an electronic realm. The DTI data is based on a sample of 1,001 firms of all firm sizes (i.e. including large firms) so comparison with WestFocus SME data cannot be wholly valid. Nevertheless, given the paucity of empirical data on security risks faced by small firms, the DTI data acts as a benchmark here. The evidence from these surveys highlight a relatively variegated picture of some of the threats to data security: 'virus infection and disruptive software' and 'theft and fraud involving computers' have decreased in incidence after a hiatus in 2004; 'staff misuse of information systems', and 'unauthorized access by outsiders (including hacking attempts)' increased from 2002 to 2004 but have more-or-less plateaued after this; and 'systems failure or data corruption' have increased in incidence (given there is missing data for 2002).

Table 15: Type of Security breach suffered by UK businesses in 2002, 2004 & 2006 Surveys

Type of Breach	*2002*	*2004*	*2006*
Virus infection and disruptive software	41%	50%	35%
Staff misuse of information systems	11%	22%	21%
Unauthorised access by outsiders (including hacking attempts)	14%	17%	17%
Theft or fraud involving computers	6%	11%	8%
Systems failure or data corruption	N/A	27%	29%

Source: Compilation from DTI Information Security Breaches Surveys 2004 and 2006

The DTI typology does not yield exact equivalents for WestFocus data, but two comparisons are made here as a means of exploring the data. A WestFocus rate of 8% for 'Internet fraud' is exactly the same as the 2006 DTI figure for 'Theft or fraud involving computers'. However 'Security failures / problems' at 6% in WestFocus data is significantly different from the 2006 DTI figure for the nearest equivalent term 'Systems failure or data corruption' of 29%. Whatever the quality of these comparisons, and with caution extended to the value of self-revealed data on sensitive issues such as data security, the WestFocus figures do not make a case for overbearing levels of risk faced by small firms trading online. Certainly the high levels of electronically-mediated trading evident in the WestFocus data - which chime with general year-on-year volume growth in electronically-mediated trading as a whole (Fulford and Doherty, 2003) – can be set favourably against the relatively low figures for security incidents.

Further comparison between the two sets of data can be made in terms of 'security policy' and 'security training'. A figure of 40% is shared by WestFocus 'written security policy' data and the DTI 'formally defined and documented information security policy' data (2006). However, given that the 'large firms' component for the DTI finding is noted as 73%, the true figure for SME security policy in the DTI data must be lower than 40%. In terms of training WestFocus data shows a figure of 53% for the 'training for awareness of IT security issues' while DTI figures show that 35% of the sample overall undertake 'training and presentations' as one means by which firms 'make their staff aware of their obligations regarding security issues' (DTI, 2006). Further, a DTI figure of 40% for large firms implies that the figure for SMEs in the DTI sample must be lower than 35%. Accepting the inherent limitations of both of these comparisons, this analysis again reflects favourably on the WestFocus sample.

From a technological perspective, the use of Internet-related technologies found in this study shows that a basic electronic communications infrastructure (composed of Internet, email, firewalls and anti-virus software) is in place for the WestFocus sample as a whole. While the almost ubiquitous use of these technologies makes sector and firm size considerations irrelevant, sector influence is evident for a subset of other technologies examined ('wireless access', 'intranet', 'extranet/EDI' and 'video/audio conferencing') which have lower general levels of take up in comparison with the 'basic infrastructure' technologies. Greatest adoption rates – by some margin – are for 'Internet Services', with a notable high of 81% for 'wireless access'. 'Broadband' bucks the adoption-by-sector trend in that 'Media' firms are its greatest adopters, but this can be tempered by the very high levels of its adoption overall. At the level of the whole sample, the relatively high levels of Internet use for commercial purposes (such as receiving payment from customers) suggest that 'networked trading' may be entrenched in places. If sector adoption behavior established for ICT holds true for commercial uses, then assertions made by Nah *et al.* (2004) - that firms need to develop e-business processes spanning more than one organisation in order to maintain a competitive edge – would appear most keenly matched, unsurprisingly perhaps, by the 'Internet Services' sector. Some way behind in terms of technology adoption come 'Media' and 'Food Processing', with 'Logistics' as the slight laggard. The WestFocus data does not identify high relative levels of e-commerce challenges for firms in the sample as a whole. To what extent use of a such an infrastructure guarantees secure distributed working and electronically-mediated trading for firms is by definition difficult to measure, even if some general perspective on security threat has been garnered. Nevertheless the comparatively low levels of remote access accorded by the whole sample to trading partners suggests that the majority of SMEs are not ready for and/or do not have the high levels of trust necessary for the kind of integrated trading along their supply chains propounded by writers such as Straub (2002). Certainly DTI figures add a threatening backdrop in that firms that allow remote access are twice as likely to have their networks penetrated (2006).

Mirroring work on e-commerce adoption (Martin and Matlay, 2001; Simpson and Docherty, 2004), evidence was found for differences in 'offsite working' (i.e. teleworking) on the basis of sector, and for data security practices on the basis of both sector and size. In terms of sector, 'Internet Services' demonstrated greatest attention to data security risks in terms of written security policies and provision of training for IT security awareness. As with levels of technology adoption, overall the other sectors ('Food Processing', 'Media' and 'Logistics') come some way behind in these terms. A common adoption pattern for these three sectors shows that 'security training' levels were slightly greater than 'offsite working' with 'written security policy' trailing somewhat. 'Internet Services' had a slightly higher level of 'offsite working' than 'security training' to buck the trend, but the much higher levels of technology adoption and use of 'offsite working', 'written security policy' and 'security training' mark the sector out as different to the rest. Nevertheless in all four sectors, use of a formal security policy came in third place. However additional sector level data for 'Logistics' and 'Food Processing' points to further differences in behavior with 'Food Processing' firms enjoying higher levels of 'offsite working' though lower levels of formal security policy. Suggestions that 'Food Processing' firms are more promiscuous than 'Logistics' firms in security terms should be tempered however with evidence that 'Food Processing' as a sector has more awareness training on security issues for employees than 'Logistics'.

In regard to size, generally the larger the firm, the greater the levels of written security policies and training in evidence, which chimes with work on e-commerce adoption (MacGregor and Vrazalic, 2005; Levenburg, 2005; Van Beveren and Thompson, 2002). In the WestFocus data, different behavior is apparent between 'written security policy' and 'security training' by firm size. So while response rates for 'micro' and 'small' firms show higher response rates for security training than formal security policy, the converse is true for 'medium' firms where response rates for formal security policy exceed those for security training. In the absence of additional analysis using the training variable, direct comparison between 'offsite working' and 'written security policy' for 'micro' and 'small' firms shows higher proportionate use of policy by 'small' firms than 'micro' firms.

There is a trade-off between the apparent robustness of measures taken to protect data security and the ability to trade or work with information systems. Obviously a security interface that is overly robust can stymie attempts to work remotely. As Nilles (1998) argues, tongue-in-cheek, "sensitive company information is easiest to protect from outside intruders if it is kept securely locked in the company's vaulted, main office computers with no access allowed from the outside" (p. 83). In a networked electronic world of course such a stance would be untenable, with telework by definition impossible. The ability to telework at its simplest functional level requires a PC, a telephone line, an ISP (internet service provider) account and an email agent. Then, where electronic communication is restricted to email use only between remote worker and colleagues at a central location, arguably the level of controls required to handle data safely would be relatively minimal, all things considered; similarly the ability to interrupt workflow when systems are offline may be relatively minimal. If on the other hand such 'offsite working' required direct access to a firm's systems by a mobile worker exploiting wireless technology, then additional controls may be required to provide a similar level of apparent data security. Such additional controls may bring in their train some greater potential to interrupt workflow. Thus drawing the balance between the robustness of a firm's security system and an ability to work or trade whilst offsite requires management consideration.

In a dynamic and fast-moving marketplace, wireless communications, for example, is noted as one technology posing threats to secure teleworking (Rikitake, 2002a). Adoption of 'wireless access' does not by definition imply 'remote' or 'offsite access' necessarily as wireless technologies such as Bluetooth are designed for short-distance transmissions amongst local devices and a teleworker is notionally some 'non-local' distance away from co-workers. Nevertheless it is possible to conjecture scenarios in which teleworkers in the sample firms access systems remotely using wireless means. If critical and sensitive data were to be handled in these scenarios, then the 2006 DTI survey (whose limitations as a comparator for this study are noted above) might raise questions in data security terms when it observes that 60% of firms that allow remote access, and 40% of firms that allow staff to connect via public wireless (WiFi) hotspots), do not encrypt their transmissions. While technological solutions should be seen only as part of meeting challenges to data security, encryption, where desired, implies more complex data handling processes and working practices for firms, and hence higher costs. Given observations on resource constraints faced by small firms (Poon and Swatman, 1999; Levy and Powell, 2003; Simpson and Docherty, 2004; Fillis *et al.*, 2004; Gupta and Hammond, 2005) the ability for firms to accommodate users whether 'onsite' or 'offsite' using fixed and mobile (wireless) modes and perhaps via a multiplicity of devices (e.g. PC, mobile phone) in an apparently secure extended electronic network may be beyond the level of skills, knowledge and financial resources that some smaller firms in the WestFocus sample possess. The fact that technology adoption patterns by the WestFocus sample as a whole are generally higher than relative levels of 'written security policy' use and 'awareness training for IT security issues', added to apparent resource constraints, may indicate that claims by Spinellis *et al.* (1999) that advanced technology outpaces the development of 'control practice and employee knowledge' have validity. Given that smaller firms are less likely to have a formal security policy than their larger equivalents, then it is possible to speculate further that smaller firms are more likely to have unsafe handling practices than larger firms.

If technology providers fail to meet the needs of firms as Nathan *et al.* (2003) imply, then there is a role for government agencies to step into the market gap to help ensure firms handle data securely safely. Martin amd Matlay (2001) however assert that 'there is an acute lack of engagement on behalf of small business owner/managers who are largely suspicious of government interference in industry'. Thus traditional business support mechanisms through which small firms can learn about security policy formation and safe data handling practice may fall short as a desired policy goal, as Simpson and Docherty (2004) intimate. The 'cat-and-mouse' struggles between those responsible for system security and those intent on exploiting security flaws, whether with criminal intent or otherwise, supports the case advocated by Standen and Sinclair-Jones (2003) for the use of 'ethical hackers' (i.e. trusted individuals and agencies who seek to test the security of systems in order to reveal security flaws to a target firm) by which firms can check their security posture. This is not a simple task given the variegation of devices and loci noted by which to access firms' systems, and the 'motivations, constraints and uncertainties' (Westhead and Storey, 1996: p.18) experienced by small firms that includes 'non-linear (and) sometimes chaotic behavior' (Fillis *et al.* 2004). Thus, amongst other enquiries, such an initiative would require answers to the following questions:

a) Can small firms afford such support, and if so, can they then be persuaded to make such an investment (especially those firms that may be in great need of such an offering but which show little inclination to seek out business support interventions)?

b)   How can small firms be sure of the *bona fides* of such individuals and agencies?

c)   How can small firms be persuaded that such individuals and agencies themselves are secure?

Given the existing legal and administrative burdens already felt by SMEs struggling to survive in an increasingly competitive marketplace, there may be little apparent enthusiasm for yet another state-sponsored instrument. Thus there may be a role for policy makers working with stakeholders to facilitate the development of an appropriate mechanism. Use of some form of licensed 'honest broker' that enjoyed a level of independence from government would likely be required.

6 CONCLUSION

This paper attempts to help fill a gap in the academic literature on data security issues in relation to electronically-mediated working by SMEs. Based on a telephone survey of 378 firms in West London and surrounding counties in early 2006 and managed by a WestFocus project team composed of researchers from Royal Holloway, Kingston and Brunel universities, this analysis attempts to explore technology adoption and threats to data security on the basis of the whole sample, and where possible on the basis of four industry sectors ('Media', 'Logistics', 'Internet Services' and 'Food Processing') and three firm sizes ('Micro', 'Small', and 'Medium') of SME. The small firms literature shows that data security is a subject mainly examined in combination with some other issue(s), and that there are few studies dedicated to security issues raised by telework *per se*. General findings on Internet-related technologies show that the basic infrastructure for secure distributed working and electronically-mediated trading is in place for the sample as a whole, even if the quality (or otherwise) of such an infrastructure cannot be ascertained.

Mirroring work on e-commerce adoption, evidence was found for differences in 'offsite working' on the basis of sector, and for data security practices on the basis of both sector and size. In terms of sector, 'Internet Services' demonstrated greatest attention to data security risks in terms of written security policies and provision of training for IT security awareness. Overall the other three sectors ('Food Processing', 'Media' and 'Logistics') came some way behind in these terms. Further sector behavior shows that 'Food Processing' firms appear to display different adoption behavior from the other sectors in regard to the relative balance between 'offsite working', use of a formal security policy and security training for employees. In terms of size, generally the smaller the firm, the lower the levels of written security policies and training in evidence, which chimes with work on e-commerce adoption. An apparent market failure allied with small firms' distrust of state-sponsored business support mechanisms begs for new approaches in the promotion of data security. Use of 'ethical hackers' by 'honest brokers' may be one approach deserving policy attention therefore. Nevertheless, whatever the relative merits and demerits of such a proposal, if teleworking and mobile working in general are to flourish amongst small firms, then greater research effort needs to be devoted to data security issues in the virtual domain that takes a small firm perspective.

APPENDIX 1: Selected review of studies examining ICT adoption that highlights the relative level of discussion on security issues

Author(s)	Description	Empirical Data	Security
Clear and Dickson (2005)	UK study examining how adoption of telework is influenced more by management attitudes, levels of worker autonomy and employment flexibility than technology provision	303 SME survey; 58 face-to-face interviews	Data security discussed only in terms of its being 'a major disadvantage to the adoption of telework'
Dixon et al. (2002)	Literature review providing a critique of research into ICT use by SMEs; examines UK policy and ICT targets; highlights UK regional and international differences in ICT adoption; maintains that influences of sector, age and firm size on ICT adoption is under-researched	Reviews papers that use empirical data but no primary empirical data	'Security/privacy issues' noted as one of a number of barriers to ICT adoption
Fillis et al. (2004)	UK study that examines factors promoting and inhibiting adoption of e-business; critiques stage models of adoption; findings show that sector has an important influence on e-business development	21 SMEs; 18 face-to-face interviews; 3 phone interviews	'Security issues' mentioned as a possible impediment to future business development
Gupta and Hammond (2005)	US study examining information systems (including Internet technologies) security issues for 'small businesses'	138 small business survey using US definition of SME (1-499 employees) though only 6 responses > 200	Identifies security risks as perceived by small business owners, security incidents experienced by the sample and measures taken to guard against security threats; findings raised doubts about the effectiveness of security measures
Levenburg (2005)	US study examining how small firms use a range of 'e-business' tools in their supply chains; finds more extensive use of ICT tools in the supply chains of 'small' and 'medium-sized' firms rather than in 'micro' firms, though when a 'micro' firm adopts 'e-SCM', 'benefits are more pronounced'; finds that 'micro' firms show different use behavior from 'small' and 'medium' firms	395 SME survey	No mention of security
Levy and Powell (2003)	UK study that critiques stage adoption models; argues for an alternative 'transporter' model which recognises the fact that at adoption behavior is contingent on perceived	12 SME case studies	Brief discussion that highlights the experience felt by one firm whose customers failed to use their web site due to a perceived security risk

	business need; highlights owner attitude as instrumental in adoption decisions; identifies sector adoption behavior of firms		
MacGregor & Vrazalic (2005)	Examines e-commerce adoption barriers amongst small firms in regions in Sweden and Australia; uses statistical methods by which to derive two fundamental factors affecting adoption: either firms find e-commerce 'too difficult,' or 'unsuitable' for their business, or both	477 small firms survey	'Security' seen as a barrier but its discussion is limited; discussed mostly in terms of its being a statistically-divergent artifact for Australian and Swedish adoption practice in the two factor model
Martin and Matlay (2001)	UK study that critiques government policy based on use of the DTI five-stage ICT adoption model (developed by Cisco); seen as deficient due to its 'one-size-fits-all' underpinning that is based on wholly linear progression and that ignores key influences such as sector, size, ethnicity, gender, human & financial resources, customer base and internationalisation	No empirical data	'Security systems' mentioned as part of a discussion on business support requirements for small firms
Poon and Swatman (1999)	Australian study that examines the benefits of 'small business Internet commerce'; strong interest in email detected in firms but almost no integration between firms' Internet use and internal systems found; highlights some sector influences	23 small firms	No mention of 'security'
Quayle (2002)	UK study that examines levels of awareness about e-commerce and levels of e-commerce adoption amongst SMEs	298 small firms survey	Mentions security in the literature review as one of a number of 'hurdles' to e-commerce adoption
Riemenschneider and McKinney (2002)	Brief article reporting on a US study examining advantages and disadvantages of e-commerce adoption by adopting and non-adopting firms	27 telephone interviews and 184 firm survey	'Lack of security regarding important information' seen as one of four reported disadvantages, and a predominant concern for non-adopters
Shiels et al. (2003)	UK study examining ICT adoption in firms in four sectors using an 'ICT Exploitation and Integration Model' which posits four levels of ICT sophistication: 'technical integration', 'operational integration', 'inter-organisational integration' and 'strategic integration'.	24 SME case studies	Mentions network security and security of back-ups in discussion of 'technical integration'
Simpson and Docherty (2004)	UK study examining barriers and drivers for e-commerce adoption; critical of UK business support mechanisms; argues SME distrust of government business support may allow third party vendors to exploit SME ignorance	Small number (undefined) of interviews with owner-managers	Security concerns noted as one of a number of barriers to e-commerce adoption
Spinellis et al. (1999)	Conceptual study that examines security requirements for the 'small enterprise' and 'home-office environments'; argues for use of risk analysis methodologies and uses two scenarios as exemplars by which to illustrate security threats; makes a series of recommendations for potential solutions to threats.	No empirical data	Focuses on security issues related to 'small enterprises' and home offices and notes that these can suffer serious security problems as they typically lack the technical expertise to create and maintain a suitable level of security. Finds that SMES and home offices face similar levels of risk.

Stockdale and Standing (2004)	Australian study that identifies SME benefits and barriers to e-commerce	No empirical data	Security not mentioned
Stockdale and Standing (2006)	Australian study examining drivers and barriers for e-commerce adoption; draws up a typology of SME adopters	Combination of secondary case study data and 'interactions' with stakeholders	'Security and worries about fraud' noted in a brief discussion on security issues
Sturgeon (1996)	US study that examines drivers for telework and the security threats and risks that it poses for firms (i.e. it does not focus on small firms *per se*), especially in terms of sensitive data. Written before wireless modes of communication became common though measures to manage risks appear valid still	Uses small number of anonymised case studies to highlight vulnerabilities	Focuses on threats to data security raised by telework under a taxonomy that includes 'disclosure', 'interruption', 'modification', 'destruction' and 'removal'; argues for risk assessment; recommends various types of measure to manage threats
Taylor and Murphy (2004)	UK study that critiques DTI adoption model echoing Martin and Matlay (2001) and argues for the use of the PITs model (Foley and Ram, 2002); discusses barriers to adoption and tries to identify factors that promote 'successful adoption of e-business technologies'	Discusses empirical data provided by other researchers	As a barrier to entry into the digital economy, notes there are perceptions of unresolved security and privacy issues which most acutely identifies online payment and which discourage small firm adoption of 'this technology' and e-business
Van Beveren and Thomson (2002)	Brief paper reporting on an Australian study that highlights firm size as a factor that influences e-commerce adoption	179 SME survey of manufacturers	No mention of 'security'

REFERENCES

Beaver, G. (2002), Small Business and Enterprise Development, Prentice Hall

Clear and Dickson (2005), Teleworking practice in small and medium-sized firms: management style and worker autonomy, New Technology, Work and Employment, Vol. 20(3), pp. 218-233

Dickson, K. and Clear, F. (2003), Transnational Report of the Qualitative Research Phase: A Comparative Analysis of Regional Findings, IST project 'eGap' (IST-2001-35179) www.egap-eu.com (accessed 10-07-06)

Dixon, T., Thompson, B. and McAllister, P. (2002), The Value of ICT for SMEs in the UK: A Critical Review of Literature, Report for the Small Business Service Research Programme, The College of Estate Management, Reading.

DTI (2003), Small Business Service Excel Tables - SME Statistics UK 2003, Table 1: UK Whole Economy, http://www.sbs.gov.uk/default.php?page=/analytical/statistics/smestats.php (accessed 10-07-06)

DTI (2004), Information Security Breaches Survey 2004 Technical Report, HMSO

DTI (2006), Information Security Breaches Survey 2006 Technical Report, HMSO

European Commission (2002), Benchmarking National and Regional E-business Policies for SMEs, final report of the Ebusiness Policy Group of the European Union, Brussels, 28 June.

Fillis, I., Johansson U. and Wagner, B. (2004), A qualitative investigation of smaller firm e-business development, Journal of Small Business and Enterprise Development, Vol. 11(3), pp. 349-361

Fulford. H. and Doherty, N (2003), The application of information security policies in large UK-based organizations: an exploratory investigation, Information Management & Computer Security, Vol. 11, No. 3, pp. 106-114

Fulton, C., Haplin, E. and Walker, S. (2001), Privacy Meets Home-based eWork, Proceedings of the Eighth International Assembly on Telework, Helsinki, September 12th-14th
http://www.telework2001.fi/FultonHalpinWalker.pdf (accessed 10-07-06)

Ghosh, A. and Swaminatha, T. (2001), Software Security and Privacy Risks in Mobile E-Commerce, Communications of the ACM, Vol. 44(2), February

Gordon, G (2004) Administration and General Info FAQ. What about the security or confidentiality concerns for telecommuting?   www.gilgordon.com/telecommuting/adminfaq/admin10.htm (accessed 10-07-06)

Gupta, A. and Hammond, R. (2005), Information systems security issues and decisions for small businesses. An empirical examination, Information Management & Computer Security, Vol. 13(4), pp. 297-310.

Higgins, H. (1999), Corporate system security: towards an integrated management approach, Information Management & Computer Security, Vol. 7 No. 5, pp. 217 - 222

Huws, U. and Prodo, S. (1995), Employment of homeworkers: Examples of good practice, ILO: Geneva

Illegems, V. and Verbeke, A. (2003), Moving Towards the Virtual Workplace, Edward Elgar: Cheltenham

Kuhn, D, Tracy, M. and Frankel, S. (2002), Security for Telecommuting and Broadband Communications: Recommendations of the National Institute of Standards and Technology, National Institute of Standards and Technology, Gaithersburg, MD

Levenberg, N. (2005), Does Size matter? Small Firms' Use of E-Business Tools in the Supply Chain, Electronic markets, Vo. 15(2), pp. 94-105

Levy, M. and Powell, P. (2003), Exploring SME Internet Adoption: Towards a Contingent Model, Electronic Markets, Vol. 13(2), pp. 173-181

Lim, V., and Teo, T. (2000), To work or not to work at home - An empirical investigation of factors affecting attitudes towards teleworking, Journal of Managerial Psychology, Vol. 15, No. 6, pp. 560-586

Lohmeyer D., Mcory, J and Pogreb, S. (2002) "Managing information security, McKinsey Quarterly.

Lundegaard, K (1997). Telecommuting issues. What to consider if you're an employer, Washington Business Journal, July 7th.
http://Washington.bizjournals.com/Washington/stories/1997/07/07/focus2.html (accessed 10-07-06)

Martin, L. and Matlay, H. (2001), "Blanket" Approaches to Promoting ICT in Small Firms: Some Lessons from the DTI Adoption Model in the UK, Internet Research: Electronic Networking Applications and Policy, Vol. 11, No. 5, pp. 399-410

MacGregor, R. and Vrazalic, L. (2005), A basic model of electronic commerce adoption barriers. A study of regional small businesses in Sweden and Australia, Journal of Small Business and Enterprise Development, Vol. 12, No. 4 pp. 510-527

McLeod, R., and Schell, G. (1997), Management Information Systems, Prentice-Hall

Nah, F., Rosemann, M., and Watson, E. (2004), E-Business Process Management, Business Process Management Journal, 10(1)

Nathan, M., Carpenter, G., Roberts, S., Ferguson, L. and Knox, H. (2003), Getting by, Not Getting On: Technology in UK Workplaces, The Work Foundation: London

Nilles, J. (1998), Managing Telework, Strategies for Managing the Virtual Workforce, John Wiley: New York

NISS (National Information Systems Security) (1992), INFOSEC Glossary, NSTISSI No. 4009, June 5, 1992, National Security Telecommunications and Information Systems Security Committee, NSA, Ft. Meade, MD 20755-6000

Poon S. and Swatman P. (1999), An Exploratory Study of Small Business Internet Commerce Issues, Information and Management, Vol. 35, No. 1, pp. 9-18.

Quayle, M. (2004) E-commerce the challenge for UK SMEs in the Twenty-First Century, Journal of Operations and Production Management. Vol. 22, No. 10, pp. 1148-1161

Ratnasingham, P. (1998), Trust in web-based electronic commerce security, Information Management & Computer Security, Vol. 6, No. 4, pp. 162-166

Reimenscheider, C. and McKinney, V. (2001), Assessing Beliefs in Small Business Adopters and Non-Adopters of Web-Based E-Commerce, Journal of Computer Information Systems, Vol. 42, No. 2, pp. 101-107

Reuvid, J. (2004). The secure online business handbook: E-commerce, IT functionality and business continuity (2nd ed.), Kogan Page: London.

Rikitake, K., Kikuchi, T., Nagata, H., Hamai, T. and Asami, T (2001), Security Issues on Home Teleworking over Internet, IEICE Technical Report IA2001-20, Vol. 101, No. 440, pp. 9-16

Rikitake, K., Kikuchi, T., Nagata, H., Hamai, T. and Asami, T (2002a), Secure Teleworking over Wireless Internet, IEICE General Conference Symposium, SB-12-3, IEICE

Rikitake, K., Kikuchi, T., Nagata, H., Hamai, T. and Asami, T. (2002b), Secure Gateway System Design for Home Teleworking, IPSJ SIG Notes 2002-CSEC-17, Vol. 2002, pp. 1-6

Schneier, B (2000), Secrets and Lies: Digital Security in a Networked World, John Wiley: New York

Schneier, B (2003), Beyond Fear: Thinking Sensibly about Security in an Uncertain World, Springer-Verlag

Shiels, H., McIvor, R. and O'Reilly, D. (2003), Understanding the implications of ICT adoption: insights from SMEs, Logistics Information Management, Vol. 16(5), pp. 312 – 326

Simpson, M. and Docherty, A. (2004), E-commerce adoption support and advice for UK SMEs, Journal of Small Business and Enterprise Development, Vol. 11, No. 3, pp. 315-328

Smith, A. and Rupp, W. (2002), Issues in cybersecurity; understanding the potential risks associated with hackers/crackers, Information Management & Computer Security, Vol. 10(4), pp. 178-183

Smith, G. (1998), An Electronic Pearl harbour? Not Likely!, Issues on Science and Technology, 15, pp. 68-73

Spinellis, D., Kokolakis, S., Gritzalis, S. (1999), Security requirements, risks and recommendations for small enterprise and home-office environments, Information Management and Computer Security, Vol. 7 No. 3, pp. 121-128

Standen, P. and Sinclair-Jones, J. (2003) eWork in Regional Australia, Industries Research and Development Corporation, Australian Government.
http://www.rirdc.gov.au/reports/HCC/04-045.pdf (Accessed 10-07-06)

Stockdale, R. and Standing, C. (2004), Benefits and barriers of electronic marketplace participation: an SME perspective, Journal of Enterprise Information Management, Vol. 17(4), pp. 301-311

Stockdale, R. and Standing, C. (2006), A Classification Model to Support E-Commerce Adoption Initiatives, Journal of Small Business Enterprise and Development, Vol. 13(3), pp. 381-394

Straub, D (2002), Foundations of Net-Enhanced Organizations , Wiley

Sturgeon, A. (1996). Telework: threats, risks and solutions, Information Management and Computer Security, 4(2), 27-38.

Taylor, M and Murphy, A (2004), SMEs and e-business, Journal of Small Business and Enterprise Development, Vol. 11, No. 3, pp. 280-289

Tran, E. and Atkinson M. (2002), Security of personal data across national borders, Information Management & Computer Security, Vol. 10, No. 5, pp. 237-241

Tremblay, D (2002), Balancing work and family with telework? Organizational issues and challenges for women and managers, Women in Management Review, Vol. 17, No. 3-4, pp.

UK online for business (2000), Working Anywhere. Explaining telework for individuals and organisations, DfEE / DTI / DETR

Van Beveren, J. and Thompson, H. (2002), The use of electronic commerce by SMEs in Victoria, Australia, Journal of Small Business Management, Vol. 40, No. 3, pp. 250-253

Walden, I. (2005), Crime and Security in Cyberspace, Cambridge Review of International Affairs, Vol. 18, No. 1, pp. 51-68

Watson, R., Berthon, P., Pitt, L. and Kinkhan, G. (2000), Electronic Commerce: The Strategic Perspective, Dryden Press: Orlando, Florida

Westhead, P. and Storey, D. (1996), Management Training and Small Firm Performance: Why is the Link so Weak?, International Small Business Journal, Vol. 14, No. 4, pp. 13-24

eBusiness Maturity and Regional Development

Paul Beynon-Davies
eCommerce Innovation Centre, Cardiff Business School, Cardiff University
Aberconay Building, Colum Drive, Cardiff, CF10 3EU, United Kingdom
Tel: +44 (0)29 2087 6013
Fax: +44 (0)29 2087 4419
Email: beynon-daviesp@cardiff.ac.uk

Abstract

This paper describes the experience of a major research centre supporting knowledge transfer in the area of eCommerce to SMEs. It debates with issues surrounding the integration of academic research with practical support to the SME community. For this purpose the use of an eBusiness framework as a platform for eBusiness maturity assessment is proposed. These devices are seen as key to the work of research centres such as ours in addressing the future challenges for smeeBusiness.

Keywords: ebusiness, maturity assessment, regional development

Acknowledgements: We wish to acknowledge funding support for the work described in this paper from the European Regional Development Fund under the Opportunity Wales programme. Note the opinions expressed in the paper are those of the author and not the Opportunity Wales programme.

1 INTRODUCTION

The author is currently head of a research centre based within the Cardiff Business School. This research centre has built a substantial amount of experience in knowledge transfer work in the area of eCommerce with SMEs. As we come to the end of current project work in this area we have been evaluating our experience of this activity with the overall objective of formulating what we see to be the future of support in this area amongst the SME community in a regional context. This paper documents some of our initial thinking and has the following key aims:

- To discuss the relationship between eBusiness and regional development
- To consider some of the relationship between university Innovation and Engagement (third mission) work and the concept of eBusiness growth
- To highlight the importance of assessing the maturity of eBusiness amongst companies to the process of effective knowledge transfer
- To consider the meaning of maturity in the context of eBusiness
- To discuss whether eBusiness for SMEs is different from eBusiness generally
- To describe what we see to be the challenges for smeeBusiness over the next decade

2 REGIONAL DEVELOPMENT AND EBUSINESS

Over the last decade much European, national and regional funding has been used to promote the adoption of ICT amongst SMEs (ECb 2002; ECa 2005). The rationale for making investment in this way is normally portrayed in the following terms. Greater adoption of ICT is seen to lead to clear business benefit such as greater business competitiveness. For example, ICT adoption is seen to facilitate the location independence of business while also permitting small business to access global as well as local markets. In other words, ICT adoption allows small business to 'level the playing field' with large business in many areas. In turn, since SMEs form the vast majority of businesses and SMEs are typically also seen as the growth agents within economies, overall investment in improving rates of ICT adoption amongst the SME community is seen as a major catalyst for regional development in terms of measures such as increased GDP and increased levels of employment .

Small and medium-sized enterprises (SMEs), defined as firms employing fewer than 250 people (ECc 2005), play a central role in the economy and are an essential source of employment, innovation, entrepreneurship and growth. In the UK as a whole, SMEs make up 99.9% of all enterprises and account for more than half (58.5%) of the private sector workforce and over half (51.3%) of UK turnover (SBSa 2005). In Wales small businesses also represent more than 99% of all businesses and are both socially and economically vital, accounting for approximately 60% of all Welsh private sector employment and over 40% of business turnover (SBSb 2004).

Typically the notion of ICT adoption has been bundled over the last decade amongst many European regions in terms of electronic commerce (eCommerce). More recently discourse in this area has expanded the notion of ICT adoption to that of electronic business (eBusiness).

Business can either be considered as an entity or as the set of activities associated with a commercial organisation. Electronic business or e-Business might be defined as the utilisation of information and communication technologies to support all the activities of business. Commerce constitutes the exchange of products and services between businesses, groups and individuals. Commerce or trade can hence be seen as one of the essential activities of any business. E-Commerce focuses on the use of ICT to enable the external activities and relationships of the business with individuals, groups and other businesses. The distinction between these two concepts will be elaborated further below and will be critical to the argument we wish to promote in relation to the future of knowledge transfer work as far as ICT is concerned in the future.

The problem with this association between ICT adoption, uptake of eCommerce or eBusiness, increased business competitiveness and better regional development is that it is difficult to measure linkage effects. Our experience tells us, for instance, that it is critically difficult to evaluate the impact of eCommerce at the regional level. A key problem is that companies (particularly SMEs) do not evaluate their ICT investments effectively. In other words, SMEs do not and frequently cannot systematically trace the impact that something like an investment in a customer web-site has for their business. To cite a more specific example, many small businesses within Wales cannot distinguish sales they have taken face-to-face, over the phone or through their web-site. It is therefore impossible for them to estimate something like their on-line revenue contribution (Beynon-Davies 2004). Without this it is difficult to estimate aggregate regional development impact, except in the sense of profiling adopters against non-adopters as has been done under the *Opportunity Wales* programme which is discussed below.

3 INNOVATION AND ENGAGEMENT AND RESEARCH

Universities as organisations traditionally fulfil a number of different roles within the society, economy and polity of a country. At least as far as UK universities are concerned it is conventional to divide up the competences of a university in terms of three main areas of mission:

- The first mission of a UK university, particularly those within the top rank, is research which we might define very broadly as that activity devoted to the generation or production of new knowledge.
- Universities are traditionally seen as knowledge repositories, accrued through academic research but also through academic scholarship. The expectation is that universities must seek to transfer this knowledge in some way into the wider community. The normal route through which this occurs is through various forms of teaching to students. This is the second mission activity or competence of a university.
- The third mission of a university is now typically conceived in terms of innovation and engagement. There is a growing imperative both from government and industry for universities to be involved in both the transfer of knowledge to the wider world but also the engagement with this wider world in terms of 'leveraging' local economies, engaging with the broader society and helping to shape the actions of the polity.

However, there are difficult junctures between the 1st and 2nd missions of universities and 3rd mission work. For instance, because of the ways in which third mission work is both funded and operated it is particularly difficult to marry the demands of Innovation and Engagement work with good academic research. By good academic research we normally mean investigation which is both conducted and reported upon in a rigorous manner, the notion of rigour typically defined by the overarching academic discipline within which the research is conducted. In contrast, Innovation and Engagement work may be driven by alternative imperatives of timeliness and relevance.

A focus on eCommerce and eBusiness exacerbates some of these junctures. It is argued below that eBusiness is by its very nature a socio-technical phenomenon. By this we mean it exists at the interaction between technology and human activity. As such, it is by its nature inter-disciplinary. This frequently does not marry with the divisions of traditional academic structures. The area is also applied in the sense that it is interested in the practical application of technology. This leads to the problem of managing and disseminating the knowledge concerned with the application of a fast-changing technology. This means that what is relevant for business in terms of the application of ICT may have a relatively short time-frame (months) as compared to the typical time-frame of academic research (years).

4 ECOMMERCE INNOVATION CENTRE

The eCommerce Innovation Centre (eCIC) has been in existence for over 10 years as part of Cardiff University and more recently as part of the Cardiff Business School. The author has recently taken over as director of the centre. The expertise of the centre historically as its name suggests has been located primarily in the application of eCommerce amongst SMEs. With the new leadership this remit is expanding to include an interest in all matters concerned with organisational informatics (Beynon-Davies 2002). Organisational informatics is concerned particularly with the application of ICT to improve organisational performance. However, this does not mean that the focus of concern can and should stay merely within the organisational domain.

We would argue that by its very nature ICT is a systemic issue. In other words, ICT is embedded within modern society, economy and polity. Hence the issue of organisational performance is impacted upon by ICT developments in the wider environment. For example, concern has been continuously expressed over the issue of the digital divide. In broad terms this is the social phenomenon concerned with differential rates of awareness, interest, skills and access to ICT throughout society. This has and is likely to continue to have an effect on eBusiness. For instance, certain customer segments are more likely to be eLiterate and have the preference to shop for goods and services online than others. This is likely to help direct eBusiness strategy for many companies into the future. Also, aspects of the polity such as eGovernment, particularly in the area of eProcurement can be a significant lever for eBusiness (particularly amongst SMEs). With the drive for greater public sector efficiency many government organisations will mandate online links with suppliers in the future for most of their procurement. This has particular implications for those SMEs which conduct a significant part of their trade with government.

eCIC is the site for three major projects currently:

- The *Broadband Wales Observatory* is an integral element of the five year, multi-million pound, Broadband Wales Programme. Launched in 2002, the programme is designed to improve the availability and take-up of broadband across Wales and, ultimately, to help underpin the achievement of economic development objectives. The aim of the Observatory is to track developments in the broadband marketplace and to identify best practice in relation to the roll-out and usage of high speed networks by individuals, businesses, industry sectors and public sector organisations.
- The *ePROC* project is a collaborative European project funded by INTERREG IIIB NWE with partners from Germany, Holland, Ireland and Wales. The aim of the project is to investigate the adoption of new procurement processes and tools by SMEs in more rural areas who might find themselves disadvantaged as a result of new eProcurement systems adopted by local authorities.
- eCIC acts as the centre of excellence for the *Opportunity Wales Programme* (OW). We particularly focus on describing some of the features of the OW programme because of its relevance to the themes of this paper.

5 THE OPPORTUNITY WALES PROGRAMME

The Opportunity Wales programme is funded under the European Regional Development fund and aims to provide SMEs with advice and support in achieving the benefits of eCommerce. This support programme has involved:

- the establishment of a process of knowledge transfer from eCIC through accredited eCommerce advisors to SMEs
- general awareness raising of eCommerce benefits to SMEs through intensive marketing campaigns
- the establishment of a contact centre to coordinate client relationship management, adviser activity and management information
- the development of a Web site to provide a 24/7 online resource on eCommerce knowledge and information
- advisor support to encourage SMEs to introduce and enhance the use of eCommerce and to assist them to implement solutions
- client aid for appropriate eCommerce products and services.

The OW programme is considered an exemplar regional support programme by the European Commission. This is particularly because it is structured as a public/sector partnership, has developed and uses a clear delivery methodology including quality assurance and uses benchmarking to continually evaluate performance.

As of April 2006 Opportunity Wales has supported over 10,000 businesses within the objective 1 and 2 areas of Wales. Benchmarking data has been collected from 5,899 clients showing substantial growth since April 2001 with 3,150 new jobs being created and an increase in turnover of £295m. There is also a nucleus of over 120 trained and University accredited advisors, capable of supporting SMEs in future eCommerce activities.

6 THE STATE OF ECOMMERCE IN WALES

As part of the OW programme eCIC has conducted a large annual survey of the state of eCommerce adoption amongst SMEs in Wales (ECIC 2006). This survey, conducted since 2002 with over 2000 plus companies annually has used a variant of the original DTI adoption ladder to categorise companies' experience of eCommerce. This model describes the process of eCommerce adoption in terms of 7 key steps or stages represented in table 1.

Table 1: Stages of the eCommerce Adoption Ladder

Stage	Title	Definition
0	Have not started yet	The business does not have Internet access
1	Use eMail and the Web	The business does not have a web-site but accesses information and services on the Web and uses eMail. This step can be further divided into businesses using eMail only but not surfing the Web.
2	Have a basic Web site	The business has its own web-site which only included very basic information about the business; for more information customers have to contact the business.
3	Have an on-line brochure	Customers can access more detailed information about products/services from the web-site but cannot buy or pay on-line.
4	Have an on-line store	Customers can buy and pay for products/services from the web-site, but the web-site is not linked to internal systems and orders are processed manually.
5	Have integrated systems	The on-line 'store' is integrated with other business systems, e.g., order processing, fulfilment, accounts and/or marketing.
6	Use advanced eCommerce	Internet technology drives the business internally and externally, and is used to manage all processes end-to-end more effectively and efficiently.

As part of the annual survey we have plotted eCommerce adoption within Wales against this ladder. The latest data we have for 2005/2006 (see figure 1) indicates that across Wales eCommerce adoption has particularly focused on the basic utilisation of eCommerce such as the use of web-sites for marketing purposes. The majority of SMEs in Wales are in steps 1 and 2 of the ladder. Some SMEs are beginning to build web-sites that offer ordering and fewer are offering on-line payment as an option. Fewer still businesses are moving into advanced forms of eCommerce technologies such as CRM and fewer still are exploiting the integration and innovation opportunities of ICT. Worryingly, a substantial amount of SMEs in Wales are on step 0; they do not yet have an internet connection.

This sets us the vision for the next level of challenge in Wales and we suspect most regions within the UK. We can demonstrate in comparing the profile of OW clients against the general population that some impact has been made with this support programme. The profile of OW clients is generally much better. In other words, they tend to be further up the ladder with the majority at steps 3 and 4. However, the challenge for the next level of Innovation and Engagement in this area is to marry the still relevant needs of the 'mass market' with the need to further progress companies that have started the process of innovation with ICT.

Figure 1: The OW eCommerce Adoption Ladder and Adoption in Wales for 2005/2006

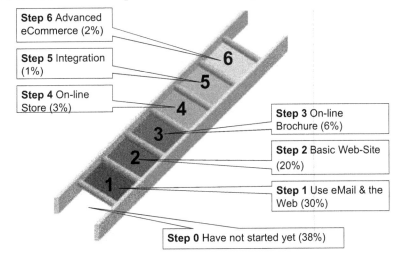

7 WHAT DO WE MEAN BY EBUSINESS MATURITY?

The eCommerce adoption ladder described in the previous section can be considered a very basic attempt to encapsulate the issue of eCommerce maturity. However, the ladder was developed as an Innovation and Engagement instrument, particularly for use as an explanatory tool with SMEs and as a tool for promoting the benefits of eCommerce to these companies. It was never intended as a research instrument and not surprisingly there are key problems with the ladder as an instrument in this sense.

First, the adoption ladder focuses on eCommerce and particularly B2C eCommerce to the detriment of other forms of eBusiness such as internal, B2B, C2C and P2P eBusiness (see below). Second, the definitions of the steps of the ladder are somewhat vague, particularly for steps 5 and 6. In practice, for instance, it is unclear what is meant by the definition used for step 6 - *the use of Internet technology to better manage end-to-end processes*. Third, in our SOTN survey companies have been asked in the past to place themselves against this framework. This introduces potential mis-measurement as respondents may over-rank themselves against the ladder.

Hence, we have been re-working our ideas both in terms of Innovation and Engagement and research work around a more sophisticated and hopefully more useful instrument. This instrument is grounded in an assessment of eBusiness maturity and specifically linked to a vision of how we envisage SME support in the future. In other words, we are attempting to delineate the major shape of what we might call smeeBusiness for the next five years or so.

8 VISION FOR SMEEBUSINESS

As a centre, we see the vision for smeeBusiness as expressed in a series of succinct statements that form the essence of the message we feel needs to be promoted in the next generation of Innovation and Engagement work in this area.

Move from eCommerce to eBusiness

eCommerce was the banner around which support work was built in the past. It must be acknowledged that eBusiness is now the more accepted term and is generally used as more encompassing term to include eCommerce within its domain. The term eBusiness emphasises both an external and internal focus. It also emphasises the use of technology both for competition and collaboration (Beynon-Davies 2004).

Next level of leverage will come from promoting eBusiness across the value-chain

The value-chain concept has been much promoted and has come under some criticism from certain quarters. Nevertheless the value-chain idea is useful to emphasise that ICT is applicable across all business value-adding activities (supply-chain, internal value-chain, customer-chain and what we like to call the community chain). It will also become increasingly significant across partnership networks. Hence, the key assumption is that the next level of competitive advantage will come from integrating ICT systems across the value-network (see below).

Process innovation through application of a new range of technologies across the value-chain

We would argue that the focus on organisational processes is the key to transition in the SME sector. The first generation of adoption of ICT has generally been to support existing processes (particularly through efficiency gain) or replace processes through automation. The second generation adoption of ICT will be to innovate new ways of doing things (new processes). For instance, a new range of technologies (such as CRM systems) allow the SME to process innovate in ways previously only available to the large company.

These three levers suggest a more encompassing model of ICT adoption amongst SMEs, an issue which will be elaborated upon in the next sections. In so doing, the paper will attempt to highlight some of the likely 'developments' in the area of smeeBusiness.

9 THE CONCEPT OF EBUSINESS

To produce an effective eBusiness maturity assessment we need a clear conception of eBusiness - an eBusiness framework. Within our research centre we are in the process of developing such a framework based upon a distinct conception of eBusiness first elaborated in my textbook (Beynon-Davies 2004). This acts as what you might call an ideal-type of the eBusiness based around the platform of the value-chain concept.

The framework is based in the conception of a business as a value-creating system based within a value-network. The original Porter value-chain model (Porter 1985) has proven useful as a generic 'business model' for understanding the place of ICT in the business. More recently the value-chain idea has progressed into the idea of the value-network (Kalakota and Robinson 1999). The value-network concept is useful as a means particularly of distinguishing between eCommerce and eBusiness. It also allows us to place some of the newer application areas for eBusiness in relation to some of the more established areas of eBusiness.

The traditional view of eCommerce mapped onto the value-network is expressed in figure 2. Here, eCommerce is conceived of as the use of ICT to support the external activities/relationships of business – 'trade' – with two major stakeholder groups: suppliers and customers.

Business to consumer e-Commerce is sometimes called sell-side e-Commerce and concerns the enablement of the customer chain with ICT. Customers or consumers will typically be individuals, sometimes other organisations. Business to business e-Commerce is sometimes called buy-side e-Commerce and involves supporting the supply chain with ICT. B2B commerce is clearly between organisational actors - public and/or private sector organisations.

Figure 2: Forms of eCommerce

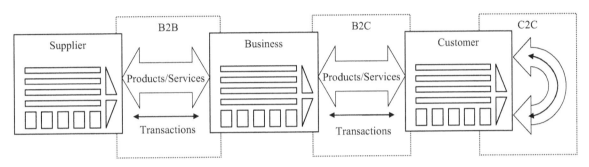

C2C or Consumer to Consumer eCommerce also has a place within this model. C2C eCommerce is a developing form of eCommerce particularly and recently linked to 'new media' services. We would argue that this is potentially the most radical form of eCommerce since it overlaps with non-commercial activity in the area of community. C2C eCommerce therefore exists in the 'community' chain and a new range of business opportunities emerge within virtual networking as a phenomenon driving new levels of content and services.

However, the traditional interest in eCommerce has tended to devalue the importance of ICT to internal operations. We would argue that the notion of eBusiness resurrects this internal focus in that eBusiness is as much about internal operations as it is about external relationships. The model in figure 2 is also useful because it emphasises integration between the internal and external focus across the value-chain.

Figure 3 represents a more encompassing model of eBusiness which includes two areas of critical development (see figure 3).

First, any contemporary model of eBusiness must address the range of critical issues associated with infrastructure issues in multi-part businesses spread geographically across the globe. The modern eBusiness is likely to be made up of numerous dispersed business elements some physically located, some mobile. A modern ICT infrastructure acts as a backbone to form the organisation.

Second any eBusiness framework must extend the notion of business cooperation and collaboration beyond that of the supply chain. Contemporary eBusiness is likely to be framed in a network of business partnerships of varying complexity. Hence, eBusiness involves cooperation as well as competition. Another business may actually fulfil a number of different roles in the business network at the same time – such as both a partner and a competitor. Some have referred to this phenomenon as cooptition.

At the level of technical infrastructure the idea of networks of business partners appears to have much in common with traditional notions of inter-organisational information systems (Barrette and Konsynski 1982). Facilitating partnership activity and information flow through common information systems or more generally through mutually enhancing electronic channels is critical to this phenomenon. However, it also seems to relate to the idea of building elements of a common informatics infrastructure for facilitating the value network.

Figure 3: Modern eBusiness

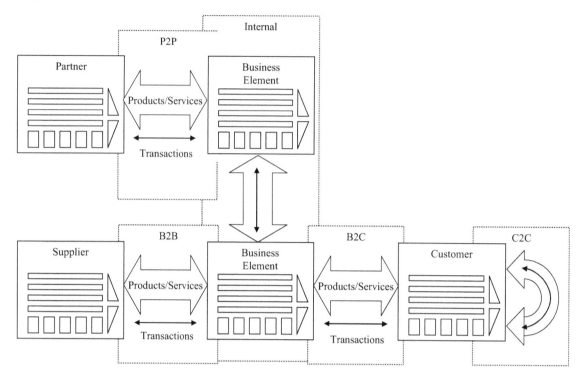

10 HOW DO WE OPERATIONALISE EBUSINESS MATURITY?

The eCommerce adoption ladder described in section 5 could be seen as a very simplistic stages of growth model for SME eCommerce.

In terms of the expressed deficiencies of this approach we want a model which embraces all the elements of eBusiness discussed in section 8. We also want to be able to assess a company's maturity in terms of such a model and believe that this constitutes a more sophisticated notion than traditional stages of growth ideas for ICT adoption.

Ideas of plotting stages of growth in relation to ICT adoption date back to at least the early paper of (Nolan 1990). A number of limitations are evident in such stages of growth models. First, they assume that companies adopt ICT and progress such adoption in a linear manner. Second, the assumption is that adoption is a uniform phenomenon; that one size of adoption fits all. In our experience both these assumptions are suspect in that they cannot deal with the complexity of the modern eBusiness.

However, we do believe in the benefits of maturity assessment. Maturity assessment is a well-used idea in other areas such as software process improvement. It is useful as a means of benchmarking individual companies against the general profile of adoption. It is also useful as a means of highlighting areas to input into strategy development.

We are aware of some but limited evidence of adoption of this idea, particularly within the Innovation and Engagement context. One of the most important examples include an early attempt to develop an eBusiness index at the DTI (DTI 2004). However, we have found little evidence of work which assesses the utilisation of this as a means both of managing research and for supporting/guiding Innovation and Engagement work.

11 WHAT DO WE MEAN BY AN EBUSINESS FRAMEWORK?

We see eBusiness maturity assessment as being formulated upon the platform of an eBusiness framework. By an eBusiness framework we mean an organised collection of key topics which help frame the eBusiness phenomenon. Our wish is to construct the framework in terms of what might be called knowledge packages – elements of ICT with a clear relevance to process innovation and linked to the idea of a value network. We expect the framework to be an active entity in the sense that we expect continuous revision of the framework to be required in order to reflect developments in technologies and processes.

As a research centre in eBusiness we want to use such an eBusiness framework as a tool for multiple purposes:

- As a mechanism for guiding and controlling the ongoing research of our research centre, particularly for suggesting research areas we need to develop
- To replace the eCommerce route map with eBusiness maturity assessment
- As a way of directing our knowledge transfer work in the sense of defining eBusiness knowledge of relevance to SMEs

We are in the early stages of constructing such a framework. Some of our preliminary thinking is described here.

Since eBusiness is a socio-technical phenomenon any framework must cover both the social and technical. We intend use of a value-chain approach for key processes and technologies (the technical). However, it is also important to include aspects of social infrastructure (capability/the social). We are particularly interested in the capacity of a company to engage in strategic eBusiness thinking and innovate processes.

Clearly any effective framework needs to provide answers to questions such as: what is eBusiness? What is it composed of? What elements of eBusiness relate to what other elements?

We are of the opinion that at a high-level we need some hierarchical and possibly graphical representation of topics/knowledge packages. We have begun experimenting with the idea of using a hierarchical set of kiviat diagrams as a means of graphically representing the knowledge packages and their relationships. Figure 4 represents a top-level view of the prototype elements from the current eBusiness framework.

Figure 4: A 'prototype' of the top-level elements of the eBusiness Framework

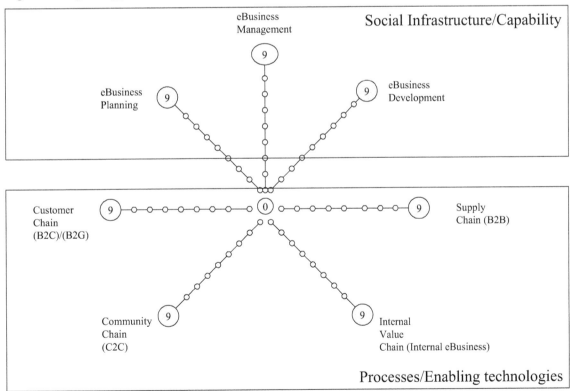

To turn the eBusiness framework into a maturity assessment tool we need some way of scoring a company's experience against a particular knowledge package. In other words, for each dimension on any particular kiviat diagram we will need some way of translating a company's experience of a technology/process mix into a score between 0 and 9. If this is feasible we may then aggregate 'scores' against topic areas. This will allow us to plot a profile for a particular company against the hierarchical set of kiviats; the profile being represented by the area under each polygon formed on a kiviat.

Figure 5 illustrates profiling of a particular company against the top-level kiviat diagram from the framework. A visual comparison with an aggregate profile produced for the industrial sector within which the company sits is illustrated. The diagram also presents an aggregate profile for the area of Wales in which the company does business and a gross aggregate profile for the whole of Welsh SMEs.

Figure 5: Profiling against the framework

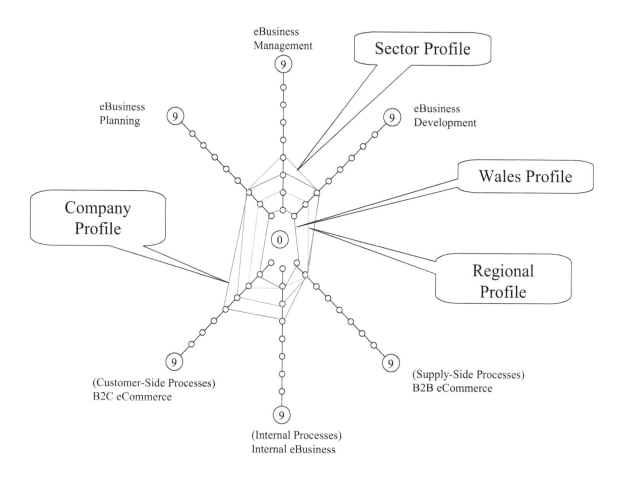

12 CHALLENGES FOR SMEEBUSINESS

From an evaluation of our own work in this area we know that there are a number of key challenges to achieving the vision expressed in section 7 as far as the future of smeeBusiness is concerned. These include:

The inertia of adoption

We know from our own research that the Opportunity Wales programme has skimmed the surface of adoption within Wales (10,000 out of a potential population of 90,000 SMEs in the region). We know from regular reviews we do of the sector that there is still a demand for and need for lower-level eBusiness support such as the basics of setting up an information web-site for companies. One of the key challenges for us is how do we marry this with a necessary wish to help the progressive companies grow further? How do we also marry this need with the wish to impart a greater/broader range of knowledge to the business community?

Segmentation of eBusiness

One of the key criticisms of traditional stages of growth models whether for ICT in general or eBusiness in particular is that they assume that one shape of eBusiness is likely to fit all. Our feeling is that we will probably need different eBusiness models for different 'customer segments'. For instance, the relevance of certain knowledge packages is likely to vary depending on the size of business/ business sector/age of business. Clearly we need to test to see whether the notion of maturity makes sense in such a context? For example, will the eBusiness model appropriate to the large company be relevant to the small company?

Managerial awareness and skills

Our previous research within eCIC has identified a key lack of strategic thinking re. eBusiness opportunity amongst leaders and managers of SMEs in Wales (ECIC 2006). This is perhaps a reflection of the way in which ICT is treated generally by many businesses, as an adjunct to business strategy and particularly focused merely on operational improvement.

eBusiness and Growth

Most of the companies we have dealt with do not evaluate their ICT investment. This makes it difficult for such companies to justify existing investment but more particularly it makes it difficult to demonstrate the potentiality in future eBusiness innovation. We feel that effective evaluation of ICT investment and the management of the benefits of ICT is critical to issues of growth in this area.

The technology/process mix

Electronic Business as we have mentioned a number of times above is a socio-technical phenomenon. The upshot of this is that value may not come in exploiting the most advanced technologies within business. Value may emerge from utilising mainstream technologies innovatively. However, there is a key disjuncture here in that I & E organisations may experience difficulty in funding 'mainstream' technologies.

13 CONCLUSION

At the start of this paper we set a number of objectives. In terms of the relationship between eBusiness and regional development, eCommerce has been seen as a major enabler of regional development in the past. We believe that eBusiness will be the next significant enabler within the SME sector over the next few years. University involvement in eBusiness support to SMEs is likely to be critical to success. But a balance has to be struck between the academic needs of rigorous research and the industrial need for relevant knowledge. As a centre, we have been starting work on using an eBusiness framework as a way of balancing the needs of research with that of knowledge transfer. Such a framework we feel is essential for also highlighting those aspects of eBusiness knowledge that are critical to particular segments of the SME sector. We further believe that building appropriate ways of assessing the maturity of SMEs in the eBusiness area is critical to achieving effective knowledge transfer. It is critical not only to helping us place companies currently but to highlight practical and effective strategies for innovation. These devices are means to help us meet the key challenge for smeeBusiness in the near future - to achieve a step-change in thinking. The sector needs to move from treating ICT as an add-on to an enabling and strategic technology for process innovation.

REFERENCES

Barrette, S. and B. R. Konsynski (1982). "Inter-Organisational Information Sharing Systems." MIS
    Quarterly(Fall).

Beynon-Davies, P. (2002). Information Systems: an introduction to informatics in organisations.
    Houndmills, Basingstoke, Palgrave.

Beynon-Davies, P. (2004). e-Business. Houndmills, Basingstoke, Palgrave.

DTI (2004). Business in the Information Age: International Benchmarking Study 2004. London,
    Department of Trade and Industry.

ECa (2005). i2010: A European Information Society for Growth and Employment, European
    Commission.

ECb (2002). eEurope 2005: an information society for all. Brussels, European Commission.

ECc (2005). Definition of Micro, Small and Medium-Sized Enterprises, European Commission.

ECIC (2006). eCommerce in Welsh SMEs: the state of the nation report 2004/2005. Cardiff.

Kalakota, R. and M. Robinson (1999). E-Business: roadmap for success. Reading, Mass, Addison-
    Wesley.

Nolan, R. L. (1990). Managing the Crisis in Data Processing. The Information Infrastructure. Cambridge, Mass., Harvard Business Review.

Porter, M. E. (1985). Competitive Advantage: creating and sustaining superior performance. New York, Free Press.

SBSa (2005). Statistical Press Release, Small Business Service.

SBSb (2004). Statistical Press Release 2004: Small and Medium-Sized Enterprise Statistics for the Regions, Small Business Service.

15

Biting the hand that feeds: Social identity and resistance in restaurant teams

James Richards
School of Management & Languages, Heriot-Watt University
Edinburgh, EH14 4AS, United Kingdom

Email: j.richards@hw.ac.uk

Abigail Marks
School of Management & Languages, Heriot-Watt University
Edinburgh, EH14 4AS, United Kingdom

Email: a.marks@hw.ac.uk

Abstract

The aim of this paper is to engage with, and develop the literature on teamwork and employee resistance by examining the use of teamwork as a means of work organisation and as a distinctive forum for employee resistance. We emphasise how employees, at times of heightened conflict, first of all re-evaluate their group memberships and group loyalties (including membership of teams and other competing groups and sub-groups), and second, take action in line with the groups most suitable to helping them attain beneficial outcomes. Drawing on an ethnographical mode of inquiry, we explored what turned out to be an incompatible application of teamworking to counter the typically busy and chaotic nature of front-line hotel restaurant employment. The resistance that emerged varied from individual forms of resistance and misbehaviour to overt collective forms involving the joined up efforts of team members and team leaders. Subsequent analysis confirmed the value of using a social identity approach as a means to explain workplace behaviour. However, additional work is required in considering a broader range of research methods and team-related variables in order to verify these insights and develop knowledge on teams and resistance.

Keywords: social identity approach, labour process, resistance, teamwork, ethnography, hotel and catering

1 INTRODUCTION

Groups and teams have been a major focal point of psychological and sociological theory and research. An understanding of groups is necessary for almost every analysis of social behaviour, including, leadership, majority-minority relations, status, role differentiation and socialisation (Levine and Moreland, 1998). Furthermore, small groups provide important contexts within which other behaviour occurs e.g. attraction, aggression and altruism (Geen 1998; Batson 1998). At a functional level, people spend much of their lives in collectives of some kind; e.g. families, school classes and sports teams, and these groups provide members with vital material and psychological resources.

Yet, the formal use of teams within organisations is a relatively recent phenomenon. Traditional work arrangements attempted to remove the power of the informal team and preferred a more individualised form of work organisation. Indeed, Cohen, Ledford and Spreitzer (1996) reported that nearly half of US organisations used self-managed work teams for at least some proportion of their workforce. Similarly, within the UK, the 1998 Workplace Employee Relations Survey (WERS) indicates that 65 per cent of workplaces report that they use some form of teamwork (Cully, Woodland, O'Reilly and Dix, 1999) and a review undertaken by the Institute of Work Psychology found team based working operating within 70 per cent of the organisations examined (Waterson, Clegg and Axtell, 1997).

The expansion in interest in teamwork has been seen as a response to increased competitive pressures, specifically as a mechanism for improving flexibility, responsiveness and quality (Lloyd and Newell 2000). Groups and teams have been at the core of programmes to reform routine work within manufacturing – partly as a response to Human Relations theory in the 1930s, sociotechnical systems theory in the 1950s and Japanization and lean production in the 1980s. Indeed, managerialist and psychological accounts view teamwork as the answer to all organisational ills, as it not only enhances productivity, flexibility and efficiency, but also improves employee satisfaction, motivation and commitment to the organisation (e.g. Jackson, Sprigg and Parker, 2000; Wall and Jackson, 1995). Moreover, organisations such as call centres, where the work is organised in a manner that would not logically adapt to teamwork are, nevertheless adopting teams and teamwork (van den Broek, Callaghan and Thompson, 2004). This has in part led to more critical writers viewing teamworking as the latest in a succession of management fads or as covert mechanism by which management intensify their control over labour (e.g. Barker, 1993; Sinclair, 1992).

Accordingly, one of the mainstays of the labour process debate, the countering of managerial control by resistance behaviour (Edwards, 1986) has only been given limited analysis at a team level (e.g. Bacon and Blyton, 2005; Barker, 1993; McKinlay and Taylor, 1996a and 1996b). The very nature of the team system, which cultivates patterns of commonality and mutual support, provides the ideal domain for employees to contextualised and reinterpret managerial interventions. In one sense the team is providing employees with organisational resources that can be used to develop resistance behaviour (Vallas, 2003).

We suggest that in order to further detail resistance within teams it is of value to take account of, at least some of the principles of the social identity approach (Haslam, 2004). Social identity theory (SIT) purposely examines the methods by which collections of individuals interpret and behave towards their own group and other important groups (Tyler and Blader, 2001; Turner and Oakes, 1997; van Knippenberg and van Schie, 2000). Importantly, SIT not only recognises that dimensions of identity derive from self-enhancement strategies, but also from the groups that we belong to and the significance that we place on those groups. Indeed, the emphasis of SIT is on the processes through which groups chose to what extent they wish to share beliefs regarding their self-definitions, i.e. SIT is likely to aid our understating on how the relationship within the group and between the group and the organisation or management body will impact on resistance behaviour.

As such, the main aim of this article is to demonstrate that by using a social identity approach we can begin to explain how the processes within teams and between the team and the organisation lead to resistance behaviour. We draw on empirical evidence from a detailed ethnographic study of the restaurant in Hotelcorp – a branch of a large hotel chain, to illustrate and further explain the relationships between team identity and resistance. We start by looking at some of the existing work on resistance and specifically resistance within teams. Our following discussion concerns the social identity approach. However, the social identity approach is considerable (see Haslam, 2004 for a review) and only some dimensions are relevant to the current discussion. Following a summary of the social identity approach, we present our research methods and then examine the interplay between identity and resistance for the teams within our sample. We conclude this paper with a more detailed evaluation of how this work contributes to existing theorising within the area and make suggestions for further study.

2 TEAMWORK AND EMPLOYEE RESISTANCE

Edwards and Scullion (1982) refer to resistance as overt action taken to express recognition of conflict. As such, resistance equates first and foremost with attempts to subvert management demands. The basis for understanding resistance, however, is far more contentious. Despite having some noteworthy strengths and many supporters at both management and governmental level; both a unitary and a pluralist approach are viewed as being inadequate analyses for the basis of industrial conflict (Edwards, 1986). Moreover, whilst the Marxist perspective emphasises the central importance of the division between those who own the means of production and those who merely have their labour to sell, many Marxist concepts have often proven to be somewhat blunt instruments for analysts seeking to understand the nature of employment relations within different work contexts (Blyton and Turnbull, 2004). Indeed, a further dilemma is put forward by Foucauldian writers (e.g. Jermier, Knights and Nord, 1994) who believe that the most prevalent way of analysing resistance - a reactive process where agents embedded in power relations actively oppose initiatives by other agents - is associated with an overly simplistic view of who resists and how and why they do so. This is despite the fact that actual accounts of resistance can rarely be found in such studies (Ackroyd and Thompson, 1999).

This work is not for the purpose of taking sides in the orthodox versus Foucauldian labour process debate – in particular, the rather adversarial debates over 'subjectivity' or 'self-identity'. In actuality, we are responding to an inherent problem in labour process theory outlined by Thompson (1989). That is the limited focus within existing work on the role of individual and social identity within the conceptual structure for explaining the labour process. Following Thompson (1989) and Thompson and McHugh (2002), we make the case for (and ultimately wish to demonstrate) the use of a critical psychology to inform our understandings of the labour process. Namely, how resistance is engendered as much by the indeterminate social identity of employees as it is by the subjectivity associated with dominating forms of work organisation.

However, for this particular analysis of team-related resistance, we correspond with the materialist approach advocated by Edwards (1986). This is because an analysis based on Edward's position, where an omnipresent 'structured antagonism' leads to the subjection of workers to the authority of management and the need to plan production with the needs of a capitalist market, is likely to be accepted in principle by people committed to the capitalist system, yet at the same time allow us to develop genuinely objective concepts of resistance.

Indeed, many of the first accounts of teams as a potential source of resistance centred very much on Edward's materialist approach and established that resistance could actually flourish in what many believed to be inhospitable circumstances. For example, McKinlay and Taylor (1996a and 1996b) gave detailed accounts of informal team-based peer review processes and how tacit trading of scoring team members were said to nullify its disciplinary content. There were also chronicles of other ways in which teams gradually withdrew from their disciplinary role, 'silent strikes', and, a three-week go-slow. Moreover, Palmer (1996) reported on young employees who turned out to be far less malleable than initially imagined to be by management. This was evidenced in poor attendance and high turnover that persisted despite threats of disciplinary action. As a result, management was forced into making formal and informal concessions to their lowest level and least skilled workers. However, not all reports of team activity pointed towards spirited expressions of conflict and unplanned management accommodation. For instance, Delbridge (1995) suggested that whilst worker resistance and 'misbehaviour' may persist in such circumstances, it would be in ways that are increasingly fragmentary and marginal. Similarly, Knights and McCabe (1998 and 2000) outlined arguably weak and typically individual forms of team-based resistance. These included call operatives 'mouthing words' as a means to have a rest and engaging in fiddles to avoid being disciplined.

Other research on team based resistance has focused on more detailed accounts of the process. For instance, Griffiths (1998) suggest that team-based resistance (mostly in the form of humour) can be attributed to leadership styles. More specifically, humour allowed team members to put pressure on the team leader to listen more carefully to their concerns. What is more, a series of articles lead by Kirkman (i.e. Kirkman and Shapiro, 1997; Kirkman, Jones and Shapiro, 2000; Kirkman and Shapiro, 2001) suggested 'cultural values' were a problematic reality when implementing teams as a new form of work organisation. In effect, enduring cultural values were said to seriously conflict with the main objectives of self-managed work teams - setting goals, self-monitoring, self-evaluation, self-reward and self-punishment. It was also suggested that low levels of trust, low tolerance of change, or even a disdain for making sacrifices for others were key determinates in team-based resistance.

Recent work has started to move towards more detailed explanations of the micro-social processes that lead to resistance in teams, or at least points to why this level of analysis is necessary. For example, Vallas (2003) outlines why teams could be said to be a particularly suitable forum for resistance. Despite his admission that teamworking clearly heightened lateral tensions between team members, he argued that 'team systems' fostered new ways of resistance by providing workers with a rhetorical framework that enables them to negotiate boundaries of managerial authority. Teams are also said to enable workers to contest or recast managerial initiatives. Teams provide workers with organisational resources that can be used to claim discretionary powers that may have been previously been denied, the contradictions of control and reality of teams (essentially a re-engineered) authoritarian practices rekindled oppositional consciousness amongst workers, and, team systems essentially encourage collectivism in an environment where unions may fail to do so. However, Vallas point to a need for further research to disentangle the micro-social processes involved in team systems, yet other than the apparently paradoxical features of teamworking philosophies and teamworking realities, what are the more explicit or localised conditions that cause team members to bite the hand that feeds?

3 APPLYING A SOCIAL IDENTITY APPROACH

This section is essentially guided by what we view as being the most appropriate method or theoretical framework for unravelling the micro-social processes implicated in team level resistance. Whilst a labour process perspective (e.g. Bain and Taylor, 2000) provides a sophisticated socio-economic explanation of the structural causes of resistance, it fails to 'get to grips' with the actual phenomenon that occurs in terms of the interactions within a group that lead to and promote resistance behaviour. On the other hand, by adopting a traditional psychological approach to team resistance (e.g. Kirkman and Shapiro, 1997; Kirkman, Jones and Shapiro, 2000), the focus on the minutiae of variations in personality profiles, team size and diversity perversely ignores any impact of structure or broader context on the resistance process. In effect, we are rejecting what is commonly referred to as 'methodological individualism' (Jenkins, 1999) For these reasons, there needs to be a focus on the social psychological processes that not only explain the course of resistance within the team, but also what triggers the responses that lead to that resistance occurring.

Hence, it is proposed that by adopting a social identity approach (Tajfel, 1978; Haslam, 2004), it is possible to start to explain and refine understandings of the experience of team level resistance. Indeed, SIT has been described as being a concept that lies at the intersection of social psychology, sociology and political science, and is rapidly gaining prominence within all these fields (Sanchez-Mazas and Klein, 2003). Although SIT (e.g. Turner, 1978) was established as a distinct theory as opposed to a theoretical perspective or paradigm, it has been argued by Haslam (2001: 26) that SIT can 'lay the foundation for an alternative way of approaching' the study of behaviour within organisations, in that the psychology of the individual can not be separated from the psychological and social reality of the groups. Social identity therefore affords a mechanism for examining behaviour at both an individual and group level.

An examination of identity enables the understanding of how social interaction is bound up with individuals' social identities, i.e. their definition of themselves in terms of group memberships, as opposed to just studying individuals as individual (Haslam, 2001). Specifically, this perspective not only recognises how dimensions of the self and identity derive from individual self-enhancement strategies, but also from membership of groups and the relationship between these groups and other groups. The weight that social identity theory puts on the process by which team members acquire shared beliefs, assist in the understanding of why some groups will resist organisational control, whilst other groups subscribe to the company's ideology.

Importantly, we need to understand the interplay between social identity processes and organisational control mechanisms and how this leads to a collective notion of resistance within a team. Let us start with the knowledge that even when placed within a team, individuals do not always operate as a collective. This is accepted within the social identity approach in terms of opposite poles of social behaviour (Tajfel, 1974). At one extreme can be found interactions that are wholly determined by interpersonal relations and individual characteristics and not by the groups and categories to which they belong (Deschamps and Devos, 1998). At the opposite pole are interactions between groups of individuals that are entirely determined by their respective membership of different groups and are not affected by inter individual relations among the relevant persons (Tajfel and Turner, 1979).

These extremes of behaviour are in practice hypothetical, as membership of a social group or social category always plays some role in shaping interaction. Tajfel (1974) alleged that social identity processes start to be performed; the further behaviour is defined at the intergroup extreme of this continuum. Namely, individuals define themselves in terms of their group membership when the context in which they find themselves is defined along group-based lines. For instance, if two departments within an organisation merge, each employee is more likely to define themselves in terms of one department or the other rather than as an individual.

Consequently, Tajfel (1978) developed an important premise, that the more that behaviour becomes defined in intergroup terms, the more that members of the group would react in a similar way to members of the outgroup. A number of other writers have supported this premise, specifically that heightened group salience is associated with an increase in perceptions that of homogeneity of the group and heterogeneity of the outgroup (Haslam, Turner, Oakes, McGarty and Reynolds, 1998). David and Turner (1999) found the extreme ingroup members were more likely to influence more moderate group members in an intergroup situation as opposed to an intragroup situation. Similarly, Abrams, Marques, Brown and Henson (2000), suggested that intergroup context is an important mechanism for conveying that the ingroup is distinct from the outgroup. Other group members evaluate group members that deviate from the group norm more negatively. This premise concurs precisely with traditional psychological theory, that individuals are attracted to people who hold similar views and beliefs (Horowitz and Bordens, 1995). Moreover, recent research has found that teams where members perceive themselves as 'being similar', have highly salient social identities regardless of whether there is the perception of the existence of an outgroup or not (Marks, 2005).

However, from an organisational perspective, there is one factor missing from the ingroup/outgroup equation. There is an assumption from SIT that by making the ingroup/outgroup comparison that there is some congruity in terms of size and structure between the two groups (Haslam, 2004). That is the ingroup and outgroup are two departments within the same organisation or two teams working within the same plant. The reality however, could be very different. The organisation itself could be viewed as the outgroup and the team the ingroup. Moreover, if this is the case, there is evidence from some writers that a highly salient team social identity is not always the product of viewing the outgroup as fundamentally different to the ingroup, it may also be a product of viewing the outgroup as similar to the team or ingroup. Jenkins (2000) argues that if an external body, such as an organisation is viewed as being legitimate in the eyes of a group, that this implies some shared beliefs and understandings of authority. As such, there will be a strong identification with both the organisation and the team. That is, if the role of the team is seen as being legitimate and team members accept the structures of control within the organisation the team will have a highly salient identity as a team or members of a team. However, Jenkins (2000) also argues that if the definition as a team results from an imposition of power or that the form of control that the organisation has or uses is not seem as legitimate the members of the team (or in Jenkins' terms the categorised) will resist.

Yet, this resistance and striving for autonomy of self-identification may in itself lead to an internalisation of the notion of the team and paradoxically, in this case, we may also find a highly salient team social identity. This notion is compatible with the work of Bacon and Blyton (2005), who explore how workers respond to teamworking and look at employee attributions of management motives for teamworking. Bacon and Blyton classify employee views of management by four main types: economic, political, institutional and cultural. What this reveals is not so much directly related to resistance strategies, it relates to the idea that workers are very much attuned with management motives for teamworking. Crucially, the evidence from this research suggests that these workers were able to distinguish both unfavourable and beneficial aspects of new methods of organising work and at the same time scrutinise every motive management had in implementing them. As such they make informed decisions as to whether they accept teamwork both in terms of their day to day work activities and the control mechanisms associated with it.

However, as per the norm, the story is not that straightforward. It is important to understand why a highly salient team identity will embrace group members into resisting a team rather than exiting from a situation that they feel dissatisfied with. Tajfel (1975), believed that one of the fundamental components of the social identity perspective, are an individual's belief structures which also lie on a continuum from a philosophy of social mobility on the one hand to social change on the other. As long as membership of a group enhances one's self-esteem, one will remain a member of that group. But, Tajfel argues (1978), if the group fails to satisfy this requirement, the individual may try to change the structure of the group (social change); seek a new way of comparison which would favour his/her group, and hence, reinforce his/her social identity (social creativity); or leave/abandon the group with the desire to join the 'better' one (social mobility). For those with high social change beliefs, and hence high social identity salience, there is the belief that the only way to improve negative conditions lies in group action. Within an organisation, this may relate to forms of collective action such as through trade union membership, which actively presses forward for the cause of the ingroup. Hence, strong identity salience is underpinned by a supposition that that is not possible to escape one's group for self-advancement (in part due to the benefits of team membership to individual's self-esteem). In this case we are likely to see collective examples of resistance as a means of improving unfavourable conditions. On the other hand, social mobility beliefs are likely to result in individual action as individual team members sense they are free to move between groups in order to improve or maintain their social standing. In short, we argue that in a situation where a team could be said to have a strong social identity, we are likely to witness social change beliefs as the key to explaining resistance strategies. In the absence of a strong social identity salience, it is doubtful whether resistance will take a collective form.

4 METHODS

Hotelrest was the subject of 12 weeks of intensive data collection. The methodologies used are essentially ethnographic by nature and supplemented by recognition of company documentation. Unobtrusive participant observation was considered to be the most appropriate method of investigating this form of organisational behaviour (Analoui, 1995; Analoui and Kakabadse, 1989). The data collection was undertaken by the lead author who accessed Hotelcorp by gaining paid employment and assuming the dual role of employee and research data collector.

This method of data collection has been undertaken by many other researchers (e.g. Roy, 1952; Bradney, 1957; Analoui and Kakabadse, 1989; Graham, 1995; Calvey, 2000) and helps overcomes the unwillingness of management to let academics research the phenomenon as well as the reluctance of employees to divulge information regarding the trend under investigation. Observations are efficient because it reveals behaviour that people usually prefer not to report and the researcher has greater opportunity to identify manifestations without attempts to conceal or distort them. Furthermore, longitudinal studies may reveal causal relationships. Other than documentary information in the form of corporate literature, the vast majority of data was collected in the form of daily journal entries based on observed activities, guided discussions and regular reflective accounts of emerging patterns in team activity. To demonstrate this point and commitment to the research method, the final diary of events at Hotelrest was comprised of over 30,000 words.

The daily journal entries and company data were then analysed for keywords and phrases and themes. Both authors coded data independently. They then conferred before determining final categories and codes. This is a form of content analysis, a technique social psychologists have traditionally used to deal with qualitative data (Holsti, 1968; Babbie, 2001). Although the generation of categories and themes implicit in content analysis may not be ideal for understanding some of the subtleties of the discourse in the interviews, for analysing diary data the method provides an effective portrayal of the broader culture and work structures in the organisation. Descriptions of the work process are based on the report and experience of the researcher, who only worked the day shift. Extracts from the diary are inserted when appropriate.

Unsurprisingly, the method chosen to research the reality of teamworking in the hospitality industry comes with a range of limitations and ethical issues. For instance, commenting on unobtrusive participation observation Analoui and Kakabadse (1989) believe such methods can be a 'long, laborious and often dangerous process, with the danger of "getting sacked", one's cover "being blown" or being made "redundant" ever present' (1989, p. 13). Beyond the practicalities, however, lies a range of procedural obstacles. Indeed, it is believed that the nature of being "hidden" increases the chances of the researcher becoming passive to what is going on around him or herself (Riecken, 1967) and being (hypothetically) less free than an overt observer decreases the chances of access to wider social interaction (Dean, Eichhorn and Dean, 1967). What is more, a further consideration is of knowing when to withdraw from the research site (Viditch, 1969).

Whilst it is necessary to point out that covert data collection is a surprisingly common and efficient research method (Reynolds, 1979), we cannot ignore the lack of informed consent that comes with unobtrusive methods (Bulmer, 1982). Indeed, as the *British Sociological Association* (2004) points out, covert methods should only be considered, 'where it is impossible to use other methods to obtain essential data' (2004, p. 5). We believe the nature of what is being researched – the reality of social interaction in a busy and highly conflictual environment combined with management unlikely to grant full access to an outsider in such situations – does not allow the use of open methods of collecting data. More importantly though, we also believe no other method is likely to allow the researcher to gain acceptance from both co-workers *and* management (Hodson and Sullivan, 1990).

5 HOTELREST AND HOTELCORP

Hotelrest is the catering facility of a Hotel which is part of the Hotelcorp chain. Hotelcorp describes itself as a 'global hotel' and employs over 10,000 people in the UK alone. Its most recent management initiative is the introduction of '[Service] Standards', or in Hotelcorp's own words: 'maintaining corporate standards through brand identity, brand position supported by behaviour, attitude, product consistency and performance'. Service Standards involve the regulation and routinisation of all dimensions of work which are clearly documented and disseminated to employees through formal documentation, team meetings and training sessions.

At the research site, Hotelcorp employs around 250 employees. The hotel's restaurant takes up to 230 'covers' a day. However, there are significant retention problems for the 60 employees that work in Hotelrest. The aggregate turnover at Hotelrest is over 50 per cent despite Hotelcorp's strategy of compulsory training and development programme focusing on 'Job-related Skills' (anonymised and JRS for short). The JRS programme has a strong emphasis on teamwork. Completing JRS training can, supposedly, be up-dated to a nationally recognised vocational qualification (NVQ level II for waiting staff and level III for supervisory staff). Moreover, completion of training entitles each employee to what Hotelcorp promotes as being a lucrative hotel-related package of benefits. This includes greatly reduced admission to the adjacent health club and highly discounted room rates throughout Hotelcorp's chain of hotels. However, JRS was not viewed as particularly effective at either engendering loyalty or retaining employees. One full time member of the waiting staff, James, explained how it had taken nearly a year to complete the JRS training and nearly two years later he was still awaiting his health club membership. Some members of staff had been with the company over a month and had, to date, received no JRS training. At team meetings employees frequently complained about waiting for their card entitling them to the benefits package. Although one employee, when commenting on the discounted room rates noted, 'you get the smallest and smelliest room that they probably couldn't sell anyway.'

Hotelrest serving staff work in groups of approximately 10 employees. The composition of the shift varies day to day dependant on scheduling. Each shift team is frequently augmented with agency workers. As well as the serving staff there are about 10 individuals working in the kitchen as chefs and kitchen porters. The hotel classifies both serving and kitchen staff as members of the Hotelrest team, however there is a clear separation between the waiting and kitchen staff. Importantly, as the fieldwork was carried out in the restaurant rather than the kitchen this is the main focus of the research.

The Hotelrest serving staff are an even mixture of waiters and waitresses, the rest are supervisors, 'hosts' or team leaders (six), two assistant managers, and one restaurant manager. All supervisory staff and assistant managers have been promoted from within; quite rapidly in some cases. However, the restaurant manager was recruited from outwith the company. There is also a dedicated trainer who works approximately 25-30 hours per week. Pay for waiting is low with those aged 22 and over receiving an hourly rate on a par with the national minimum wage (NMW). Waiters and waitresses aged 21 years or below (the majority of the waiting group) earn less than their older counterparts, but higher than the NMW for this category. Supervisors earn about ten per cent over the NMW.

6 HOTELREST AND TEAMWORKING

Hotelcorp presents the face of an organisation with a generous commitment to teamwork. This commitment is most acute for those who are front-line staff in the restaurant. For instance, potential Hotelrest employees are subjected to a mock team-based selling exercise during the selection procedure. During the day-long induction, new recruits are provided with an induction handbook with significant reference to the principles of teamworking. The most explicit representation to the devotion to teamworking is the compulsory and lengthy monthly team meeting. Furthermore, the upholding of Service Standards included in JRS training are based on teamworking and team communication processes, a typical eight-hour shift involves a minimum of three team briefings - immediately before serving starts, after serving ends and before re-organising restaurant for next setting, and prior to start of second period of service. As a final point, indiscipline is often confronted with team-based chastisements such as widely broadcast humiliations, e.g. team leaders regularly admonish front-line employees for neglecting their team-based loyalties and responsibilities. The lengths that Hotelrest go to in attempting to infuse a teamworking attitude amongst waiters and waitresses are epitomised during the monthly team meeting. The first team meeting during the research period lasted for just over three hours and included a presentation on teamworking as means of increasing sales.

Superficially at least, Hotelcorp looked as if its policy on the promotion of team based work was functioning effectively. When the hotel was closed or during quiet periods, and when the number of waiting staff exceeded the requirement of the number of guests dining, employees appeared to co-operate with one another and with team leaders. During these periods, this co-operation was interjected by relatively open, yet playful acts of what Ackroyd and Thompson (1999) call misbehaviour or irresponsible autonomy. These acts included waiting staff engaging in a variety of horseplay, flirting rituals and playful humour. Nevertheless, this did not tend to be at the expense of the achievement of allocated work to an acceptable standard.

Yet, the reality of teamwork for most employees was inconsistent with the rhetoric presented by the organisation. Teamwork was only really implemented as a managerial ideology aimed at tightly controlling and determining a wide range of employee behaviour and activity. Despite a clear rationale by management for teamwork - as a mechanism to implement good customer service in the guise of Service Standards - the Taylorised nature of Service Standards made the performance of any teamwork behaviour, especially under stressful conditions, impracticable. Whilst the catering group were defined as a team for the undertaking of work, there was no joint nature to the technical division of work and no collective responsibility or indeed flexibility in terms of work organisation. This is demonstrated clearly in the following sections.

7 TEAMS, COLLECTIVE AND INDIVIDUAL RESISTANCE STRATEGIES

As with the current work, other research on teams in the service sector found tight control, high commitment management and low value incentives (e.g. Kinnie, Hutchinson and Purcell, 2000). We also found teamwork to be unworkable due to the size and nature of supervision of the team. Teams were so poorly defined that this form of work organisation ultimately caused great conflict between groups of employees rather than harmony. The size and structure of the teams fashioned a situation which was entirely in opposition to the unitarist ideology espoused by the firm. Even the weak or diluted form of teamwork identified by other researchers failed to materialise (e.g. Batt, 1999; van den Broek, Callaghan, Thompson, 2004). There was no indication of collective learning or problem solving (apart from the odd example of employee resistance) and the only true function of teamwork appeared to be as a structure of control over employees and Service Standards.

Any authority with the objectives of teamwork was really only apparent in times of calm when employees had a high degree of control over their work. Consent broke down under a number of specific circumstances; work intensification, mobilisation of friendship groups and endorsement of individualised strategies of resistance by management.

The diary entries detailed below demonstrate the emergence of chaos and the collapse of teamworking initiatives and other formal working policies and practices, when work conditions suddenly intensify.

> The shift itself was a bit of a disaster, i.e. from the views of the customer and the employees. For example, the use of Service Standards broke down with tables used and not re-set, remains of meals were left on tables, long queues developed, and few if any guests got their orders on time. The team suddenly appeared to lack a will to co-operate and waiters and waitresses just looked after their own immediate concerns. This was despite the close presence of two assistant managers who were themselves put under enormous strain at this particular time of the working day. It was also apparent that Hotelcorp-employed waiters made even less effort to help the agency staff brought into deal with staff shortages (Field notes, 18 September).

> Today was a living nightmare. We were stretched well beyond our limits with over 370 guests for breakfast in a restaurant that has a capacity of 230, and therefore requires around 140 resets. The support I had at the beginning of the shift soon dissipated as the queue lengthened by the minute and the disquiet amongst the queuing customers increased (Field notes, 14 October).

With no holds barred, consent and compliance with team-based values and Service Standards collapsed the moment the pace of work intensified. An increase in pace triggered a widespread inability to cope with the pressures of carrying work out in a strict and arguably unsustainable style, which occurred on an almost daily basis, but always at the weekend when customer levels were nearly always close to or at hotel capacity. It also transpired when staffing levels dropped due to unauthorised absence and high turnover of labour. When consent broke down the behaviour that ensued varied quite dramatically. Some waiters and waitresses worked on regardless and did whatever they could to satisfy the typically understanding and tolerant customers, whilst an equal number of waiters and waitresses avoided work to some degree as a result of these pressures. Importantly, under times of work pressure, friendship groups began to mobilise and perform collective forms of resistance. For outgroup members – those not included in friendship cliques - there was an almost automatic default to individualistic forms of resistance strategies.

Field notes suggested that many individual acts of resistance were, in fact, undertaken with the tacit support of the team (these included pilfering of food, unsolicited smoking breaks, stretching the time for room service request, disposal or deliberate damage of company materials such as crockery or cutlery, and unauthorised absenteeism). In contrast, far more overt examples of collective resistance included waiters and waitresses making their fellow team members aware that they suspect a mystery guest had arrived on the premises. Waiters and waitresses increasingly shunned agency staff sent to 'help' them, and there was evidence of an organised slow down once customers left the restaurant or the next shift was imminent. Further examples of this order included a broad-based boycott of the new incentive scheme introduced at the beginning of the research, and waiting staff stopping work at their official finishing time even when offered discretionary incentives, the chance to be praised at the next team briefing or even team meeting or threatened with disciplinary action.

Informal teams or friendship groups - sub-sections of a larger team – were largely often difficult for management to identify, although the use of teamworking was certainly applied as a measure to divide these informal loyalties. Mostly as a result of the ignorance of informal activity *and* potent commercial and operational pressures, management could only make superficial attempts to unmake these collectives. In the example below, management made an explicit attempt to counteract the 'subversive' potential of friendship groups.

> Michelle [assistant manager] was setting up for the event. She had used the £40 or so tips from the last coach trippers to pay for large amounts of sweets, crisps, soft drinks, and some wine, etc. The meeting was in the McDonald suite and was set out with tables around the outside. The refreshments were in a small room to the side. From a quick head count there were about 25 waiters and six supervisors or management staff. As people came in, whether they were on duty or not, they sat with their friends. The supervisory staff sat on a table at the front of the room and looked like a panel. Dismayed that the room had been split up into cliques, Peter [one of the restaurant's 'hosts'] re-organised the waiters and waitresses in a random fashion in preparation for team activities (Field notes, 16 September).

On the other hand, many of the explicitly individualised examples of resistance were undertaken by established members of the organisation and were at least tacitly endorsed by management. For example, long tenure waiters or waitresses were allowed to 'opt out' of specific team roles or obligations, such as specialising in one favourable aspect of restaurant work when form rules disallowed this. There was also open collusion or authorisation over activities that clearly breached Service Standards.

8 CONTRADICTIONS IN PRACTICE

We would argue that the discussion above, in part, demonstrates cynicism towards the principles of teamwork. Although Hotelrest placed a strong emphasis on the team and the notion of teamwork, the nature of the work (highly individualised) and the nature of the teams (composed of core and peripheral members) contradict the principles of teamwork and this was picked up by team members, not only in terms of behaviour, but in the way that they reacted to the formal team briefing and team training sessions. Examples of this are provided in the two diary extracts below:

> After the final presentation and the room began to quiet down Jeanette [trainer] asked the team as a whole what they thought the task was *really* about. No one responded to this. However, Jeanette ignored the silence and went on talk about how it was a 'way of expressing yourself...exchanging ideas...working together...to give you more confidence...so you can pull together as a team'. She also asked the question 'do you think you could have done the task on your own?' In reply, a few tamely said no. Jeanette finished on the words 'we can't do it on our own', which is a phrase that I had already become increasingly familiar with (Field notes, 16 September).

> The feedback session was by far the most interesting section and lasted for approximately one hour and forty minutes. I have no doubt it would have gone on much longer as after 100 minutes we had only heard from about a third of the group as other waiters and waitresses kept interjecting and upsetting the round-the-table process. Of particular note was how the session started with most staff remaining silent or failing to say much if they were asked their opinion. However, when Susan [waitress on a working

holiday from Australia] began to speak out the tone of the event quickly changed. Specifically, most waiters and waitresses had clearly felt restrained until that point. Furthermore, her comments not only provoked others into action, the issues then on became increasingly critical of and specific to management (Field notes, 16 September).

It would seem that despite a high profile commitment to incorporating teamworking into the Hotelcorp's business and human resource strategy, the management at Hotelrest clearly has problems convincing the majority of restaurant employees of its merits. This was certainly the case when management arranged the opportunity for team-based feedback, i.e. the situation quickly turned from being a team bonding exercise into a forum for a range of responses that included passive silence and participation to a barrage of criticism.

However, this contradiction was unbearable for many and compelled many employees to leave Hotelcorp, in terms of the practice of what Thompson (2003) labels the externalisation of resistance. In other words, the high turnover of team members appears to be in part a result of the length that team members are prepared to tolerate both work intensification and incongruity in practice and policy. Whilst long term team members were less inclined to undertake informal resistance behaviour and sought solitude in favourable terms and conditions afforded by management, the behaviour was different for lower tenure employees. In the absence of robust forms of collectivism either in terms of the formal team or trade union representation, Hotelrest was typified by 'micro-collectivism' or cliques that were capable of transcending formal group boundaries and formal group hierarchies.

Teare, Ingram, Scheuing and Armistead (1997) noted that teams in the hospitality industry are characterised by inter-group conflict. This was confirmed by the findings of the current study. Not only were there tensions between young and old (the older members of staff thought that the younger employees were lazy), but also between the kitchen and the restaurant staff. On the 7th September the diary entry noted how there was a break time discussion about inter-group rivalry. One member of the waiting staff said 'chefs don't like us but we don't like them either'. This is a theme that was common in the field notes. Tensions arose when kitchen staff thought that waiting staff were not clearing up after themselves and therefore creating more work for the kitchen.

This division was re-enforced by kitchen staff not being invited to team meetings. Indeed, team meetings provided an arena for many other tensions in the group to be played out. This is illustrated in a diary entry dated 2nd of October:

> It is becoming obvious that the ideas of teamwork in the restaurant do not bring cohesion between waiters and supervisors/managers. What's more, it is clear and fair to say that the 'team' is in fact at least two groups (if not more), with teamworking limited to manageable tasks performed under ideal circumstances that are not typical to restaurant work. Where such occupational groups come together as a team appears to be on the basis of resisting higher-level commands and not concerning what the team *should* be doing (Fieldnotes, 2 October).

The disloyalty to the team, however, is not surprising as during the three months of research in the restaurant there was only one explicit attempt at a teambuilding exercise and even this was focused on customer relations and sales. Employees were placed into groups in a team meeting and asked to sell a number of items to other members of the meeting – these items included a high chair, a soup bowl, a toast rack, tomato juice and salt and pepper sachets. No one in the room appeared to take the exercise seriously apart from management.

Yet, despite very modest training activities and supervisors being on hand to reinforce team ideals, employees complained bitterly in the wider work setting that they never received help from other team members and one noted that 'it's not my problem' or 'I've not been told to do that' were phrases that were commonly heard on the shopfloor. Indeed, further conflicts between employees were mentioned in the diary on a daily basis. On the 2nd of October, one employee threatened to 'kick the butt' of another team member over the issue of re-using dirty dishes and cutlery. The more experienced of the two then started to quote teamworking propaganda to his colleague. His tirade was based on the ideas presented in the JRS handbook – focusing on the notion of 'letting other team members down' when an employee does not pull their weight. Despite being indoctrinated with teamwork principles and ideals, normative values of being a team player and cultural on cohesion were rarely put into practice. On the 17th October, one employee even stated, 'teamworking is really every man for himself'.

In a wider sense, it was not only teamworking that made employees cynical. For instance, most employees appeared unhappy with their work, as shown in this diary entry from 23rd September.

I spoke to a woman who started at the same time as I did. She came out of her way to say hello and asked me what I though of the job so far. I asked her and she said 'I'd rather be stacking shelves in Tesco' (Field notes, 23 September).

Comments such as this were common. However, there were a few employees who appeared a little happier with the work. This was often based on the advantage of the benefits package to them. A couple of female employees liked to travel round the country so made good use of the reduced rate hotel rooms. Another employee (28th October) spent a great deal of time explaining how pleased she was with her reward club membership. Although one of her colleagues stated, 'I see you are now a fully paid up member of the brainwashed club'.

9 A RE-EVALUATION OF TEAM RESISTANCE USING A SOCIAL IDENTITY APPROACH

Taking a very superficial analysis of events, it would appear that our findings concur with the basic premise of SIT, that by merely placing individuals within a collective that they will identify with the group (Tajfel, 1974; Tajfel, 1979). The waiting staff, in times of quiet, demonstrated communality in their work and compliance to the guiding principles of teamwork as presented by the organisation. However, when work intensified, in the terms of the labour process debate, this compliance, or in the terms of SIT, this identification with the team, dissipated, and led to a clear division in terms of both collective and resistance behaviour. This follows Jenkins' (2000) argument that suggests that if power and control mechanisms are not seen as legitimate, this may facilitate identity work. That is an individual response to pressure, which involves coping strategies that tend to be instrumentally derived tactics and accommodation to the dominant culture as well as different types of resistance (Thompson and McHugh, 2002). Instead of necessarily being controlled by the organisation, individuals are viewed as managing in the best fashion that they can, in the given circumstances and the 'form of response being determined in subjective terms by available scripts and what appears to work' (Thompson and McHugh, 2002: 346).

In this case, it was frequently at the point where work built up to potentially unmanageable levels that we started to observe the interplay in terms of behaviour between resistance and identity strategies. What is more, employees quickly sensed what was required was unreasonable, lacked legitimacy and went on to engage in behaviour to manage this situation. A social identity approach would suggest that the group as a whole would engage in behaviour to either resist or cope with the pressure. However, in the case of Hotelrest, behaviour was not that straightforward. Instead of employees' behaving in terms of the organisationally imposed idea of the team, any collective behaviour focused on illicit inter-occupational coalitions, friendship groups and cliques. Members of the team that were not part of the friendship group either failed to engage in any resistance behaviour and continued with their work or used highly individualised methods of coping. Except to continue working in an individualistic fashion made the team less efficient and likely to make committed team members cynical of teamworking. The friendship groups, in a classical correspondence with theories of group attractiveness and SIT (e.g. Horowitz and Bordens, 1995; Tajfel and Turner, 1979) resisted collectively.

Yet, contrary to the work of David and Turner (1999), who suggest that core group members define the behaviour of the entire group, these friendship groups or extreme ingroup members did not affect the behaviour of other group members. Hence, not only was there an ingroup-outgroup separation between managers and ingroup members on formal functional duties, there was a separation within the group between the cliques or friendship groups who resisted collectively and the other team members who resisted individually. Perceptions of homogeneity or attraction caused an identity affect but not throughout teams as a whole.

These group members or cliques who had a highly salient group identity when dissatisfied with the existing situation undertook resistance or misbehaviour as a group. Being a member of a subgroup or an alternative team-nurtured group served a valuable purpose in terms of self-esteem and getting work done. As such, having multiple group memberships allows in one sense alternative paths to being capable of coping with work and retaining a sense of dignity, but in another, highlights the crucial trigger for employees who in this instance are constantly faced with being members of an inferior and substandard group – that is, the team. Whereas the other members of the team, took what Tajfel (1978) would classify as a combination of a social creativity and social mobility response, that is appear to abandon the group (possibly the organisation as well) but also adapt the existing situation to a point which favours the individual. It is believed that the adopted research approach allowed such acute nuances to be observed and relayed to non-organisational members.

Although on the face of it this case demonstrates that the imposition of teamworking can lead to team-based forms of resistance, this is a highly simplified picture. As we have demonstrated there are some serious limitations or generalisations from the social identity approach, in the assumption that by labelling people as a group that they will behave collectively. However, one compensatory factor has been to promote and *not* neglect the deep-seated significance of asymmetrical employment relations in forming the basis of formal and informal group activity. Moreover, this study provides further insight into a recent trend of introducing teamworking initiatives to organisations where work at an even superficial level, is in reality highly individualised.

We moved beyond an analysis that focuses on the inappropriateness of the label and the transposition of teamwork to individualised work (e.g. van den Broek, Callaghan and Thompson, 2004). We have focused on the impact that this label the label of 'team' has had on the groups with Hotelrest. We believe that, in part, the organisation created a situation that has presented little benefit in terms of motivation or productivity but may have led to team based resistance for subgroups or cliques. For these subgroups, teamworking nurtures tacit counter collectivism, despite the fact that employees themselves were also fully aware of the contradictions that they were faced within in terms of the forced commitment to teamworking without the real opportunity to practice as a team. This conflict between ideology and practice and the reaction to it by employees was expressed most clearly within the forum of the monthly team meeting.

It could be argued that the scenarios of team based resistance within manufacturing settings which have a clearer infrastructure for collective behaviour would provide more simplified and lucid accounts of the relationship between the identity process and group level resistance (e.g. McKinlay and Taylor, 1996a and 1996b; Ezzamel and Willmott, 1998). However, the benefits of the teamwork paradox observed in this study, are that they allow for a more complex understanding of why teams fail to function as planned and why identity and resistance behaviour may grow or persist on such introductions. Moreover, further benefits of this particular case study (and methods) are that they allowed observation of behaviour that may not manifest so obviously or quickly elsewhere - that is, if the intolerable conditions at Hotelrest were apparent in a highly unionised context we may expect to see serious formal industrial action, on a regular basis, and the same time less informal resistance or group behaviour.

We suggest that this work needs to be interpreted in the context in which the data was collected. Hence, it is essential to account for, if only briefly, the strengths and weaknesses of the current study. Importantly, the work reported in this study is a single organisational case study, and as such the generalisability to other organisations maybe limited. Furthermore, one researcher using a single method collected the majority of the data. Although the method was highly rigorous and detailed there is still the potential for bias. Nevertheless, there were many interesting dynamics that have emerged from this analysis and support the propositions made earlier in the paper. This work develops existing studies and theorising regarding both SIT and resistance.

Further research is required to incorporate a greater variety of team structures, team sizes, and management approach to teams. Moreover, future research into team-related resistance must cater for unionisation, professional or occupational affiliation, or any other salient identities that are prone to manifestation in the context of the workplace. It should be acknowledged at this point, that most research on workplace identity looks at employees where occupation forms a core element of an individual's identity (e.g. Marks and Lockyer's 2005 study on software developers). It is unlikely that waiting staff embrace their occupation as a strong element of their identity, which is why friendship groups were of such importance and resistance strategies so overt. If the occupation in itself, rather than the social group in the workplace, had had a greater impact on identity we may have seen less resistance behaviour. Similarly, although we can look at tensions between formal requirements and the informal group, any examination of multiple workplace identities (e.g. the organisation and the profession) are problematic due to the weak ties with work based entities. Finally, additional work using a wider array and combinations of research methods is likely to shed further light on such strategies.

References

Abrams, D., Marques, J.M., Bown, N.J., and Henson, M. (2000). Pro-norm and anti-norm deviance within in-groups and out-groups. *Journal of Personality and Social Psychology, 12*(4), 906-912.

Ackroyd, S, and Thompson, P. (1999). *Organizational misbehaviour.* London: Sage.

Analoui, F. (1995). Workplace sabotage: Its styles, motives and management. *Journal of Management Development, 14*(7), 48-65.

Analoui, F, and Kakabadse, A. (1989). Defiance at work. *Employee Relations, 11*(3).

Babbie, E. (2001). *The practice of social research.* London: Wadsworth.

Bacon, N. and Blyton, P. (2005). Worker responses to teamworking: Exploring employee attributions of managerial motives. *International Journal of Human Resource Management, 16*(2), 238-255.

Bain, P. and Taylor, P. (2000). Entrapped by the 'electronic panopticon'? Worker resistance in the call centre. *New Technology, Work and Employment, 15*(1), 2-18.

Barker, J. (1993). Tightening the iron cage: Concertive control in self-managing teams. *Administrative Science Quarterly, 38,* 408-437.

Batson, D. (1998). Altruism and prosocial behavior. In D. Gilbert, S. Fiske & G. Lindzey (Eds.), *The handbook of social psychology* (pp. 282-316). Boston, MA: McGraw-Hill.

Batt, R (1999). Work organization, technology, and performance in customer service and sales. *Industrial and Labor Relations Review, 52*(4), 539-564.

Blyton, P. and Turnbull, P. (2004). *The dynamics of employee relations* (3rd ed.). Basingstoke: Palgrave Macmillan.

Bradney, P. (1957). The joking relationship in industry. *Human Relations, 10,* 179–187.

British Sociological Association (2004). *Statement of ethical practice for the British Sociological Association.* Durham: BSA.

Bulmer, M. (1982). The merits and demerits of covert participant observation. In M. Bulmer (Ed.), *Social research ethics: An examination of the merits of covert participant observation* (pp. 217-251). London: Macmillan.

Calvey, D. (2000). Getting in the door and staying there. A covert participant study of bouncers. In G. Lee-Treweek & S. Linkogle (Eds.), *Danger in the field: Risk and ethics in social research* (pp. 43-60). London: Routledge.

Cohen, S., Ledford, G. and Spreitzer, G. (1996). A predictive model of self-managing work team effectiveness. *Human Relations, 49,* 643-676.

Cully, M., Woodland, S., O'Reilly, A. and Dix, G. (1999). *Britain at work: As depicted by the 1998 Workplace Employee Relations Survey.* London: Routledge.

David, B. and Turner, J. (1999). Studies in self-categorization and minority conversion: The ingroup minority in intragroup and intergroup contexts. *British Journal of Social Psychology, 38,* 115-134.

Dean, J.P., Eichhorn, R.L. and Dean, L.R. (1969). Limitations and advantages of unstructured methods. In G.J. McCall & J.L. Simmons (Eds.), *Issues in participant observation: A text and reader* (pp. 19-24). London: Addison-Wesley.

Delbridge, R. (1995). Surviving JIT: Control and resistance in a Japanese transplant. *Journal of Management Studies, 32*(5), 803-817.

Deschamps, J.C., and Devos, T. (1998). Regarding the relationship between social identity and personal identity. In S. Worchel, J.F. Morales, D. Paez & J.C. Deschamps (Eds.), *Social identity: International perspectives* (pp. 1-12). London: Sage.

Edwards, P. (1986). *Conflict at work: A materialist analysis of workplace relations.* Oxford: Basil Blackwell.

Edwards, P. and Scullion, H. (1982). *The social organization of industrial conflict: Control and resistance in the workplace.* Oxford: Basil Blackwell.

Ezzamel, M. and Willmott, H. (1998). Accounting for teamwork: A critical study of group-based systems of organizational control. *Administrative Science Quarterly, 42*(2), 358-396.

Geen, R. (1998). Aggression and antisocial behavior. In D. Gilbert, S. Fiske & G. Lindzey (Eds.), *The handbook of social psychology* (pp. 317-356). Boston, MA: McGraw-Hill.

Graham, L. (1995). *On the line at Subaru-Isuzu. The Japanese model and the American worker.* New York, NY: Cornell University Press.

Griffiths, L. (1998). Humour as resistance to professional dominance in community mental health teams. *Sociology of Health and Illness, 20*(6), 874-895.

Haslam, A. (2001). *Psychology in organizations: The social identity approach.* London: Sage.

Haslam, A. (2004). *Psychology in organizations: The social identity approach* (2nd ed.). London: Sage.

Haslam, A., Turner, J., Oakes, C., McGarty, C. and Reynolds, K. (1998). The groups as a basis for emergent stereotype consensus. *European Review of Social Psychology, 9*, 203-239.

Hodson, R. and Sullivan, T. (1990). *The social organization of work.* London: Wadsworth.

Holsti O.R. (1969). *Content analysis for the social sciences and humanities.* London: Longman.

Horowitz, I. A., and Bordens, K. S. (1995). *Social psychology.* Mountain View, CA: Mayfield Publishing.

Jackson, P., Sprigg. C. and Parker, S. (2000). Interdependence as a key requirement for the successful introduction of team working: A case study. In S. Proctor & F. Muelle (Eds.), *Teamworking* (pp. 83-102). London: Macmillan.

Jenkins, R. (1999). *Social Identity.* London: Routledge.

Jenkins, R. (2000). Categorization: Identity, social process and epistemology. *Current Sociology, 48*(3), 7-25.

Jermier, J., Knights, D. and Nord, W. (1994). *Resistance and power in organizations.* London: Routledge.

Kinnie, N. Hutchinson, S. and Purcell, J. (2000). Fun and surveillance: The paradox of high commitment in call centres. *International Journal of Human Resource Management. 11*(5), 967-985.

Kirkman, B., Jones, R. and Shapiro, D. (2000). Why do employees resist teams? Examining the 'resistance barrier' to work team effectiveness. The International Journal of Conflict Management, 11(1), 74-92.

Kirkman, B. and Shapiro, D. (1997). The impact of cultural values on employee resistance to teams: Toward a model of globalised self-managing work team effectiveness. Academy of Management Review, 22(3), 730-757.

Kirkman, B. and Shapiro, D. (2001). The impact of cultural values on job satisfaction and organizational commitment in self-managing work teams: The mediating role of employee resistance. Academy of Management Journal, 44(3), 557-569.

Knights, D. and McCabe, D. (1998). 'What happens when the phone goes wild?': Stress and spaces for escape in a BPR telephone banking system work regime. *Journal of Management Studies, 35*(2), 163-194.

Knights, D. and McCabe, D. (2000). 'Ain't misbehavin'? Opportunities for resistance under new forms of 'quality' management. *Sociology, 34*(3), 421-436.

Levine, J., and Moreland, R. (1998). Small groups. In D. Gilbert, S. Fiske & G. Lindzey (Eds.), *The handbook of social psychology* (pp. 415-469). Boston, MA: McGraw-Hill.

Lloyd, C., and Newell, H. (2000). Selling teams to the sales force. Teamwork in the UK pharmaceutical industry. In S. Proctor & F. Mueller (Eds.), *Teamworking* (pp. 183-202). London: Macmillan.

Marks, A. (2005). *Reconciling competing debates within the teamwork literature. A social identity approach*. PhD Thesis. University of Strathclyde.

Marks, A., and Lockyer, C. (2005). Debugging the system: The impact of location on the identity of software team members. *International Journal of Human Resource Management, 16*(2), 219-237.

McKinlay, A. and Taylor, P. (1996a). Commitment and conflict: Worker resistance to HRM in the microelectronics industry. In B. Towers (Ed.), *The handbook of human resource management* (pp. 467-487). Oxford: Blackwell.

McKinlay, A. and Taylor, P. (1996b). Power, surveillance and resistance: Inside the 'factory of the future'. In P. Ackers, C. Smith & P. Smith. (Eds.), *The new workplace and trade unionism: Critical perspectives on work and organization* (pp. 279-300). London: Routledge.

Palmer, G. (1996). Reviving resistance: The Japanese factory floor in Britain. *Industrial Relations Journal, 27*(2), 129-142.

Reynolds, P.D. (1979). *Ethical dilemmas and social research. An analysis of moral issues confronting investigators in research using human participants*. London, Jossey-Bass.

Riecken, H.W. (1967). The unidentified interviewer. In G.J. McCall & J.L. Simmons (Eds.), *Issues in participant observation: A text and reader* (pp. 39-45). London: Addison-Wesley.

Roy, D. (1952). Quota restriction and goldbricking in a machine shop. American Journal of Sociology, *57(5), 427-442.*

Sanchez-Mazaz, M. and Klein, O. (2003). Social identity and citizenship: Introduction to the special issue. *Psychologica Belgica, 43*(1), 1-8.

Sinclair, A. (1992). The tyranny of a team ideology. *Organization Studies, 13*, 611-626.

Tajfel, H. (1974). Social identity and intergroup behaviour. *Social Science Information, 13*, 65-93.

Tajfel, H. (1975). The exit of social mobility and the voice of social change. Social Change Information, *14*, 101-118.

Tajfel, H. (1978). *Differentation between social Groups: Studies in the social psychological of intergroup relations.* London: Academic Press.

Tajfel, H. and Turner, J. (1979). An integrative theory of intergroup conflict. In W. Austin & S. Worchel (Eds.), *The social psychology of intergroup conflict* (pp. 33-47). Monterey, CA: Brooks/Cole.

Teare, R., Ingram, H., Scheuing, E. and Armistead, C. (1997). Organizational teamworking frameworks: evidence from UK and USA-based firms. *International Journal of Service Industry Management, 8*(3), 250 – 263.

Thompson, P. (1989). *The nature of work: An introduction to the debates on the labour process* (2nd ed.). London: Macmillan.

Thompson, P. (2003). Fantasy island: A labour process critique of the 'age of surveillance'. *Survey and Society, 1*(2), 138-151.

Thompson, P. and McHugh, D. (2002). *Work Organizations* (3rd ed.). London: Palgrave Macmillan.

Turner, J. (1978). Social comparison, similarity and ingroup favouritism. In H. Tajfel (Ed.), *Differentiation between social groups: Studies in the social psychology of intergroup relations.* European Monographs in Social Psychology 14, London: Academic Press.

Turner, J. and Oakes, P. (1997). The socially structured mind. In C. McGarty & A. Haslam (Eds.), *The message of social psychology* (pp. 355-373). London: Blackwell.

Tyler, T, and Blader, S. (2001). Identity and co-operative behaviour in groups. *Group Processes and Intergroup Relations, 4*(3), 207-226.

Vallas, S. (2003). The adventures of managerial hegemony: Teamwork, ideology, and worker resistance. *Social Problems, 50*(2), 204-225.

van den Broek, D., Callaghan, G. and Thompson, P. (2004). Teams without teamwork? Explaining the call centre paradox. *Economic and Industrial Democracy, 25*(2), 197-218.

van Knippenberg, D. and van Schie, E. (2000). Foci and correlates of organisational identification. *Journal of Occupational and Organisational Psychology, 73*(2), 137-147.

Viditch, A.J. (1969). Participant observation and the collection and interpretation of data in G.J. McCall, & J.L. Simmons (Eds.), *Issues in participant observation: A text and reader* (pp. 78-86). London: Addison-Wesley.

Wall, T, Jackson, P. (1995). New manufacturing initiatives and shopfloor job design. In A. Howard (Ed.), *The changing nature of work* (pp. 139-174). San Francisco, CA: Jossey Bass.

Waterson, P., Clegg, C. and Axtell, C. (1997). The dynamics of work organization, knowledge and technology during software development. *International Journal Human-Computer Studies, 46,* 79-101.

16

The Value of Virtual Assets – The Role of Game Characters in MMOGs

Tony Manninen
Game Design and Research Unit, University of Oulu
PO Box 3000, FIN-90014, Finland

Email: tony.manninen@oulu.fi

Tomi Kujanpää
Game Design and Research Unit, University of Oulu
PO Box 3000, FIN-90014, Finland

Email: tomi.kujanpaa@oulu.fi

Abstract

Game character, or avatar, acts as the nexus of virtual assets that the player collects and produces while exploring online game worlds. What is the value of this virtual identity in the online game community? Furthermore, what are the components of play that provide added-value to the players? The evolution of Massively Multiplayer Online Games (MMOGs) has been dramatic for the past 30 years. What has remained stable, however, is the role of game characters as the main channel for value growth and perception. In this paper, we apply game studies background in order to offer implications that would contribute to the field of business. By using the motivational framework with the game characters as focal point, we will point out the specific value structures that emerge in contemporary MMOGs.

Keywords: games, virtual worlds, virtual economies

1 INTRODUCTION

The seemingly virtual domains of massively multiplayer online games (MMOGs) have escaped the boundaries of cyberspace. Virtual economies, artificial currencies and intangible property are all inherent phenomena of contemporary virtual worlds that exist in the depths of the computer devices and networks. The likes of science fiction authors William Gibson (1984), with his *Cyberspace*, and Neal Stephenson (1992), who used the term *Metaverse*, have long ago predicted the future of networked online communities. While the society has perceived these as mere fictional playgrounds, the virtual worlds have slowly evolved to places and spaces of – at least – half-real assets.

There are numerous examples of cases that illustrate the shift and crossover between virtual and real. Making a profitable business by selling virtual property (Anshe Chung Studios 2006; BusinessWeek online 2006), running a 'gold farmer' company whose only aim is to collect and sell virtual resources (BBC News 2006; TheObserver 2005) and of course the wide spread auctioning of ones game characters (Washington Post Online 2005; BBC News 2005) are just but a few occurrences of future trends in economy. From the business point-of-view, these examples are far from the domain of 'playgrounds for kids'. The money involved is real money and these people make a living out in the cyberspace.

In this article we discuss the evolution of MMOGs by analysing the value of virtual assets in these non-physical realms. Since the central role of game characters as virtual asset 'warehouses' is the key, we align our approach to character-oriented study. We tackle the question of what is the value of ones virtual identity in the online game community. Furthermore, we delineate the motivation components of play, in relation to the perceived net worth of different aspects of character value. We approach the topic from the field of game studies, but we focus on the implications that would contribute to the field of business.

Before venturing into the intricacies of virtual assets, it is necessary to offer a rationale behind the evolution and success of MMOGs. We will start by defining the concept of MMOGs by outlining the most distinctive characteristics of these virtual worlds.

2 FEATURES OF MMOGS

MMOGs belong to a distinctive field of virtual worlds which are neither plain chat rooms nor traditional video games. Although MMOGs generally possess qualities and features from both of the aforementioned 'sisters', they have many properties that are unique in the domain of online systems and services.

According to Bartle (2003, 4), most of the MMOGs adhere to certain conventions that distinguish them from other virtual spaces. Table 1 outlines the most important of these conventions and describes the potential business implications of each of these.

Table 1: The conventions of MMOGs.

MMOG Convention	Potential Business Implication
The world has underlying, automated rules that enable players to effect changes to it.	There is a more or less dynamic physics model that allows, for example, construction of buildings, harvesting of resources, or other manipulation of the surrounding objects. → *construction of virtual goods, value-chain structures*
Players represent individuals in the world. This is their character and all interaction with the world and other players is channelled through characters.	The player has a proxy in the form of game character, which is the main instrument and interface for interacting with other players. Usually, only one acting character at any point of time is allowed, although the players may alternate among several. → *virtual identity, trust catalyst, transaction platform*
Interaction with the world takes place in real time. When you do something in the world, you can expect feedback almost immediately.	The MMOGs operate like simulations of artificial worlds where majority of the activity is executed by human participants who all add to the emergent nature of the system. → *consumers-producers, diverse motivations and needs*

The world is shared, so there are other participants that act and play in the virtual world.	'Massively multiplayer' means that the online games can have hundreds, or even thousands, of simultaneous players. The large number of users generally create interesting potential for virtual – and real – economies. → *markets, communities and trends*
The world is at least to some degree persistent, i.e., constantly up and running.	Since the MMOGs are usually persistent virtual worlds that stay on even if the player is not logged in, the worlds evolve and other players continue their activities 24/7 – there is no downtime, except during the maintenance breaks. → *long-term value, 'stable' investments, constant processes*

3 A BRIEF HISTORY OF MMOGS

While the history of MMOGs is by far too rich to be exhaustively discussed in this paper, we will provide a brief outline of the most influential developments by bridging the key issues with the potentially important implications for virtual and real economies. Figure 1 illustrates some of the key MMOGs that emerged during this 30-year period. The history of MMOGs starts in the late 70s with systems that hardly resemble the contemporary multimedia spectacles available on the today's Internet.

Figure 1: Development of MMOGs from MUD to World of Warcraft and Second Life.

MUDs – Multi-user Dungeons

The first multi-user dungeon, or *MUD1* as it was later dubbed, was programmed on a computer mainframe at Essex University, England, in the fall of 1978 by Roy Trubshaw. His work was then continued by Richard Bartle. The inspiration behind MUD came from single-player adventure games, like Crowther and Woods' *ADVENT* and Anderson, Blank, Daniels and Lebling's *ZORK*. (Bartle 2003, 5). The MMOG phenomenon, therefore, can be said to have started almost 30 years ago.

As an interesting side note about the evolution of MMOGs, the original text-based MUD (*MUD1*) had no formal currency whatsoever. Although the idea of putting money into MUD1 was suggested many times by its players, the designer resisted because of the fear of inflation in the virtual world. (Bartle 2003, 299). Had this tendency continued, the world of MMOGs would be quite different today.

From the 1985 onwards many of the MUDs went on to achieve commercial success as part of early online services. However, most of the evolution of these text-based virtual worlds occurred within the academic domains of universities. This spawned MUDs like *AberMUD, TinyMUD, LPMUD and DikuMUD* (Bartle 2003, 9). Of all these examples, it was *TinyMUD* that laid down a track that still has important consequences. Since *TinyMUD* was not actually a game, the players spent most of their time creating things and talking about their creations (Bartle 2003, 9). Naturally, all of these were textual representations stored within the memory banks of the computer network. Regardless of the media, the self-created virtual assets were valued as one of the most significant artefacts in the online domains. The likes of *Second Life* (Linden Lab, 2007) follow this path even today.

Finally, the big bang of virtual worlds emerged in the form of *LPMUD*. The author Lars Pensjö, having played both *AberMUD* and *TinyMUD*, decided to write his own game with the adventure of the former and the user extensibility of the latter. He developed an in-game programming language LPC that allowed players of sufficient experience to add not only objects, but also powerful functionality to the game as it ran. (Bartle 2003, 10). The era of user-created game content had begun.

Dawn of Graphical MMOGs

Although there are early examples of graphical MMOGs like *Oubliette* (1977), *Avatar* (1979 on PLATO), *NeverWinter Nights* (1991 on AOL) and *Shadows of Yserbius* (1992 on ImagiNation Network), the biggest impact was made by *Ultima Online* (1997) with its 100000 subscribers by the end of the first year of operations. From the start, *Ultima Online* was conceived to be a richer and deeper virtual world than a typical MUD, with an emphasis on community building, player-driven action, and the ability to accommodate different playing styles. (Bartle 2003, 17-22).

The innovative nature of *Ultima Online*, however, caused some interesting problems. For example, the means by which players were punished for attacking each other's characters was not effective. Furthermore, the detailed ecological model employed broke down when players rapidly killed everything that moved and, thus, the economy collapsed after a bug led to hyper-inflation. (Bartle 2003, 22). Nevertheless, *Ultima Online* was the benchmark MMOG for several years before its rivals could catch up.

While *Ultima Online* was a commercial success, the same cannot be said about *Meridian59* (1996). Launched a year ahead of *Ultima Online, Meridian59* was the first graphical virtual world, since the days of *Avatar,* to employ a first-person point-of-view. The reasons behind the failure of *Meridian59* are numerous, but the main reason for its only modest success was that it came to market a touch too soon. This, however, was not the case with *EverQuest* (1999). (Bartle 2003, 23-25).

Among the Big Ones

EverQuest was exactly in the right place at the right time. It was basically a *DikuMUD* with a graphical front-end (client) bolted on. But, on the contrary of its competitors, *EverQuest* was able to reach the critical mass of players. Actually, *EverQuest* was so successful that within two years of its launch, over a hundred of graphical virtual worlds had been announced as being in development. These include the likes of *Asheron's Call* (1999), *Anarchy Online* (2001), *Dark Age of Camelot* (2001), *Sims Online* (2002), *Star Wars Galaxies* (2002) and *Asheron's Call 2* (2002)

Outside the published success of the western MMOGs, there have been others that are even bigger in terms of number of subscribers and revenue collected. The first place would clearly go to *Lineage*, which was published in 1998 by NCSoft in Korea. Being a year ahead of *EverQuest* makes *Lineage* as one of the pioneering successes. Unfortunately, the 2001 launch in US did not produce as successful subscription rates, hence the western world seems to have ignored the massive number of customers *Lineage* was able to attract. (Mulligan & Patrovsky 2003, 327).

With all the preceding success stories and quiet failures, there is one MMOG that has risen above everything else. *World of Warcraft* (Blizzard Entertainment 2007), with its claimed 8+ million subscribers, dominates the field of virtual game worlds. What seems to be even more significant is the fact that *World of Warcraft* has been able to break the East-West boundaries of MMOGs. Naturally, all this means tough times for potential competitors. The sheer mass of players brings the impact and complexity of a virtual economy to a totally new level.

Finally, the recent years have witnessed another track on virtual worlds that essentially draw upon the likes of *TinyMUD*. The over 2 million registered users and numerous real businesses with virtual branches have made Linden Lab's *Second Life* (2007) as a truly interesting phenomenon. While gaming is not the main focus here, the modifiability and possibility to bring in your personal content have captivated the dwellers of virtual worlds. The free basic entry policy guarantees the influx of new members and, hence, attracts the businesses that produce added value. Being together is the key - with more users there are more possibilities for business and pleasure.

4 PLAYING TOGETHER IN MMOGS

Playing together is inherent to both animals and humans. Multiplayer games are by no means a new innovation. Football, ice hockey and numerous other games cater for multiple simultaneous players who jointly participate in creating the overall game experience. Playing together is as old as games themselves - people (and animals) have shared the play experience with their peers since the dawn of existence. There definitely is social function involved with games. To quote the words of Roger Caillois: "Play is not merely an individual pastime. It may not even be that as frequently as is supposed." (1961, 37) Actually, one of the seminal accounts on playful culture, discussed by Johan Huizinga (1950, 1), starts by illustrating the young puppies playing together and experiencing tremendous fun and enjoyment while doing so. Being together is more fun than being alone.

This pull towards social play activity can be seen as one of the driving forces behind the evolution of multiplayer online game worlds. As commented by Csikszentmihalyi (2002, 168), almost every activity is more enjoyable with other person around, and less so when one does it alone. People seem to be more happy, alert, and cheerful if there are others present, compared to how they feel alone. Based on this, it has been only a matter of time – and technological development – before the social togetherness transferred into the domain of virtual worlds.

If the digital game is played together with other people, the social interplay is enhanced by numerous traditions that are inherent in the interactions of physical world. The greatest advantage of these multiplayer games is that they transform computer games into truly social experiences. The social bonding can be so strong that it becomes one of the most important motivating factors for people to play games (Rouse 2000). Furthermore, the social presence of other human beings demands additional skills from the players. In most of the multi-player games, social skills are needed, or must be developed in order to succeed (Aarseth 2001). All these skills and actions need a platform where they are projected from. This is where the avatars, or game characters, come into the picture.

5 GAME CHARACTER AS A PROXY FOR INTERACTION

The main difference between virtual worlds and the physical one is the need for avatar, or game character, to act as a representation of your physical self. The character is player's representative in the game world and can generally take any form, shape, or a specific perspective (Friedl 2003, 172). Since this avatar is the proxy for most of the actions you do in the virtual world, without it you are nothing in MMOG – you do not exist and, hence, there is no value to be calculated. Without a character the player is just an invisible spectator who has no say in the happenings of the virtual world. The importance of game character originates from the early pen'n'paper role-playing games (e.g., Gygax & Arneson 1974) where your main aim was to execute adventurous quests and develop the stats of your character while doing so. The game character became a tool for player's actions. The role-playing, fighting, micro-management and all the other actions were channelled through game character.

Furthermore, a game character in MMOGs is also one's interface to other human players (Friedl 2003, 173). Game characters are constantly read and interpreted. The expressions and movements, performed by the players, are communicated through the characters into the game world. Players adjust their behaviour and decide their responses based on the cues they read from other characters. Moreover, besides being an interface between individual players or the player and the game world, player can form a relationship directly with the character. By giving the character a sense of personality, unique behaviour, intentions, and style, a player starts to form a relationship with the character. The player starts to understand the game character as a second self, as something to protect and worry about, as one's role in the virtual game world. (Friedl 2003, 185).

While the game worlds consist of other objects than just a collection of game characters, many of the actions revolve around these virtual proxies. There may be a possibility to buy a house (a home for the game character), collect better armour and weapons (protection for the game character), or just chat with your fellow players (words projected out of the game character). The game character, hence, is the focal point of all these virtual realms. While the games have evolved during the past 30 years, the importance of the avatars has remained.

6 ASPECTS OF GAME CHARACTER VALUE

Since game characters play essential part when participating in game activities, we will examine the elements that constitute a character's value to the player. As a framework for different character value components, we use Yee's (2006) categorisation for motivations of play in online games. Yee's model is formed through factor analytic approach utilising survey data collected from 3000 players on several different MMOGs (e.g. *EverQuest*, *Dark Age of Camelot*, *Ultima Online*, and *Star Wars Galaxies*). Yee (2006) divides motivations of play into three main categories: *achievement*, *social* and *immersion*. These categories are further divided into subcategories that depict the nature of each category in more detail (see Table 2). In our examination, we use the main categories to structure the discussion and point out examples that relate to the subcategories.

Table 2: Motivations of play in online games (Yee 2006, 774)

Achievement	Social	Immersion
Advancement Progress, Power, Accumulation, Status	**Socializing** Casual Chat, Helping Others, Making Friends	**Discovery** Exploration, Lore, Finding Hidden Things
Mechanics Numbers, Optimization, Templating, Analysis	**Relationship** Personal, Self-Disclosure, Find and Give Support	**Role-Playing** Story Line, Character History, Roles, Fantasy
Competition Challenging Others, Provocation, Domination	**Teamwork** Collaboration, Groups, Group Achievements	**Customization** Appearances, Accessories, Style, Color Schemes
		Escapism Relax, Escape from RL, Avoid RL Problems

7 ACHIEVEMENT VALUE OF A CHARACTER

Salen and Zimmerman (2004, 80) define game as *"a system in which players engage in an artificial conflict, defined by rules, that results in a quantifiable outcome."* Even though they criticise role-playing games having no final end game (i.e., final quantifiable outcome), they agree that session-to-session missions, or quests, may have quantifiable outcomes. Besides the quests, character development, as part of the game, has stages that can be seen as quantifiable outcomes. In MMOG, a player needs to invest time in learning how to play the character. Especially in the case of role-playing games, the player needs to invest time in improving the character's skills. Creating competent enough character for the challenging quests is a long and time consuming process. In the beginning, characters have only modest skill levels which need to be trained. Completing quests or missions, slaying beasts, crafting artefacts, or harvesting minerals gain experience points that, at times, result in levelling up. This means that the game character gains an amount of numerical points that the player can use to increase different skills the character possesses (e.g. weapon handling, healing, or magical abilities). In this manner the character advances periodically towards the chosen direction (e.g., becomes more skilful warrior, thief, bard or monk).

Completion of the quests and levelling up the character statistics (i.e., the quantifiable outcomes) are clearly achievements for the player who controls the character. According to Yee (2006), achievement is one of the thriving forces for playing an online game. Players get satisfaction from advancing, competing, and being self sufficient in the game. Players enjoy becoming better in achieving the chosen objectives and excelling over each other. From the business point-of-view, this indicates the potential of development structures that allow the players to increase the value of their virtual assets in concrete.

Achievement value of the character can, therefore, be seen as covering two main aspects: 1) the elements that constitute to the overall numerical competence of the character in the game world, and 2) the status achieved either through social dealings or through excellence in competing with other players or mighty non-player opponents. Elements constituting to the overall numerical competence of the character are the artefacts and wealth the player acquires for the character (such as weapons, armour, potions, gold, and even virtual property), as well as the improvements in the character's skilfulness (i.e., the character statistics). Artefacts and wealth can be collected by completing quests and executing other gameplay activities. The second aspect regarding the value of the status is harder to measure. However, it sums up in the admiration the player, or her character, receives from her fellow players. The greater the legend you become amongst your online friends, the better the feeling.

8 SOCIAL VALUE OF A CHARACTER

Most of the MMOGs cater for activities other than pure gameplay. This provides players a possibility to select goals of their personal liking, or to simply hang around in the game environment. The freedom allows players to share their experiences about the game but also strengthens the possibilities for the emergence of more permanent play-communities. As Huizinga (1955, 12) argues: *"A play-community generally tends to become permanent even after the game is over. Of course, not every game [...] leads to the founding of a club. But the feeling of being "apart together" in an exceptional situation, of sharing something important, of mutually withdrawing from the rest of the world and rejecting the usual norms, retains its magic beyond the duration of the individual game."* In the case of MMOGs, players may follow the built-in game structure, but they may as well choose their own game independent elements such as exploring the game world or taking part in social activities. Therefore, character's value is not only about how competent it has become game-wise, but also about the areas of social connections and experiences built during and after the gameplay.

Many of the quests in MMOGs are built to encourage teamwork. It is often really hard, or even impossible, to complete certain quests without teaming-up with a properly formed group (i.e., the group that has game characters with complementing skills) (Jakobsson & Taylor 2003, 83). Since the death of a game character often results in the loss of experience points and other virtual assets, the players generally feel the need to trust in each other. Your character's life is partly in the hands of your team players. If you do not manage to communicate properly, or, if your group members decide to flee and leave you in the midst of the raging battle, your character is most likely to die. After playing several quests within a same group, or after taking part in guild activities, the player and her character start to gain reputation. Some of the players/characters are known as trouble makers while others are known of their just behaviour and/or good playing skills (Jakobsson & Taylor 2003, 85-87).

Social value of the game character concerns aspects related to other players. The value can be considered from at least two perspectives: 1) meaningful social interaction with other players, and 2) the image of the player formed in the eyes of fellow players. The social value is, therefore, a resource for being able to form meaningful connections that, at their basic level, provide a possibility for casual communication and teamwork. On a deeper level the casual connections can turn into friendships, or even romantic relationships, in which the social value may well exceed the boundaries of a mere game. From the business point-of-view, the strong bonding of players offers interesting possibilities, for example, in the form of community services, trust-brokers, transaction mechanisms and reputation ladders. Many of the conventions of real world commerce apply to the MMOG societies. However, the ambiguous implementation of aspects, such as, identity, contracts and social-components of transaction procedures, makes it challenging to integrate traditional business models within the online games.

Finally, the image of the player comes into the picture especially in the organised forms of social play, such as, guilds and other consistent groups. It is not necessarily the other players that form the addictive component, but the image one gets of oneself from other players (Ducheneaut et al. 2006, 413). Furthermore, in guild activities concepts such as *trust* and *reputation* become essential as part of the player image (Jakobsson & Taylor 2003, 85-87). Some of the guilds require a certain amount of playing hours or certain percentage of attendance in guild activities, such as, meetings and raids. If you are willing to live up to your *responsibilities*, you may advance in the guild. If you fail to meet the requirements, you may be kicked out. Letting someone else to play your character could, therefore, potentially result in tremendous consequences.

9 IMMERSIVE VALUE OF A CHARACTER

Immersion into the MMOG can be achieved through many different elements. Yee's (2006) subcategories list elements, such as, discovery, role-playing, customisation and escapism. When considering immersion from the game character point-of-view it is obvious that some elements are more essential than others. What is elemental, however, is the need for the player to be able to identify with the game character. Sociologist Gary Alan Fine (1983, 214-215) discusses the importance of identifying with the character and comments that *"players must invest their character with meaning. [...] For identification, the character must have attributes that permit a player to esteem that persona."* Quite similarly, but from a bit different point-of-view, Friedl (2003, 185) argues that *"if a player has the possibility to give this avatar a sense of personality and contribute his unique behaviour, intentions, and style to the game world, he will establish an individual relationship with the character."*

MMOGs commonly provide game characters that have attributes such as distinctive appearance, changeable clothing, as well as, armour and weaponry that indicate the desired playing style. Furthermore, interaction with other players and the game world, through the game character, offers possibilities to develop and share a unique personality, story lines and character's history. This type of interaction enables the role-playing of the character. The role-playing may be about constructing and representing a fictive persona, or just an experimentation of the selected parts of players actual self (cf. Turkle 1999, 643-644). However, the persona of the game character does not form immediately. When playing a character for a long time, the player starts to identify with it and begins to feel what the character "feels" (Fine 1983, 217).

Based on the aforementioned theories, immersive value of the character deals with aspects that build up an image of the character and make establishment of individual relationship possible. A player may not be actively trying to role-play the character, but through discovering the world, taking part in quests, and socialising with other players, an image of the character starts to emerge. This image can be further altered through customisation of appearance and style of the character. Player invests her time and shares memorable adventures with her game character. If the player also empathises with the game character, it is possible to immerse into the character, as well as, to the world - through the character. The investment of time and the empathic approach to the character may also result in player wanting to think back the events shared with, and the qualities built for, the character. In this way the character gains sentimental value.

The immersion aspect of character value has mainly been ignored by the business applications. Although the games provide a platform for player immersion, there are no mechanisms that would directly support, or even increase, the construction of added-value. Personal records, virtual scrapbooks and other fan sites indicate the need of the players to both share and store their game experiences. User created content, in this form, could be integrated to the commercial game systems since the role of the content is mainly that of supporting to the overall gameplay experience.

10 OVERLAPPING VALUE ELEMENTS

Even though players may have clearly dominating motivations to play, it is common that the overall motivation arches over multiple elements from different subcategories (compare Yee, 2006). Most of the MMOGs have been built in a manner that requires most of the motivations to be pursued, at least to some extent, if the player wants to advance in the game. For example, it is hard to explore the world (immersion) without developing your character (achievement), since some areas have so powerful foes that the low-level character would not be able to survive. Similarly, as already noted earlier, many of the quests are built to encourage teamwork, hence character development and social communication are equally important. The overall value of the character cannot, thus, be measured by only basing it on a single value component.

The overall value of the character can be seen as a sum of the achievement, social and immersive components (see Figure 2). Depending on the case, one or more value components will be emphasised. By using this model, the game activities and player preferences can be analysed and their effects on the gaming community with potential business implications can be considered. For example, a player may dislike levelling up the character, but because of the immersive and/or social motivations he needs to pursue the achievement element. In this case, she might want to get a higher level game character without needing to go through the tedious achievement process. These types of opportunities can, however, have reflections on how other value components are viewed. The value of the character becomes evident only through the individual relationship formed via interaction between the player and her game character.

Figure 2: Different value components overlap and sum up as the overall value.

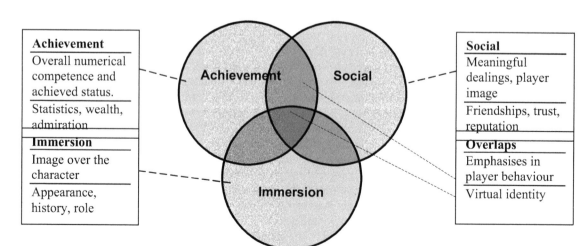

The relationship between a player and her game character forms during a period of time that can, for many players, be rather substantial. The players will generally go through most of the motivational forces - at least to try these out. Some parts of the game character may be more or less trivial for the player, but can nevertheless contribute to the overall image of the character. A player may, for example, purchase some additional levels for her game character, but this does not necessarily mean that the character's identity becomes different. It is the overall time the player invests in different value components that matters to the player. The interaction between the player and the character creates a *role* which becomes the *virtual identity* the player assumes while present in the game world. It is this virtual identity that holds the value of the game character in the online game worlds.

11 EXAMPLES OF VALUE PERCEPTION AND CONSTRUCTION

In this Section, we illustrate a series of empirical cases that offer insight into the various value constructing examples evident in MMOGs. The examples are organised according to the aforementioned player motivation model and each of the cases illustrate different approaches to perceived value of a game character.

Achievement Value

Achievements can generally be seen in the character. Level 60 character looks a lot different than level 10 character. High-level character's armour and weapons have become bigger and/or more fanciful. Experienced character possesses items that low-level characters have not even heard of. Veteran character has guts to attack powerful foes and it can spread tremendous damage. The progress made in game, thus, affects many of the aspects of the game characters. But what is the worth of all the experience levels? Basically everyone can reach high levels. MMOGs do not ask that much skill for playing. On the contrary, they are rather easy to play but ask a lot of time and patience - at least if concentrating on improving character statistics to high levels. This has made character, experience level, and item sales possible. Companies such as *Gamepal.com* buy and sell characters, levels, gold and other valuables that can be used in the game. The service includes many of the existing MMOGs, such as *World of Warcraft*, *Everquest 2* and *Star Wars Galaxies*. For example, a general price for a *World of Warcraft* account having 50-60 level character is ranging between $200 to $400 and power levelling of one's existing character costs about $20 to $300 depending on wanted levels. In this way, if a player finds levelling a tedious task, she can cut down the character development time and make a shortcut to the activities requiring higher character level.

The nature of achievement value cannot be measured only in selling or buying of ready made characters and levels. Value is also related to the advancement of the character itself. A player may receive sheer joy from the advancement as in: *"It gives me the illusion of progress, I know that. I hate the level of frustrated progress in the r/w so I play the game and lvl up instead. It is *crack* for the achievement center of the brain, like cocaine affects the pleasure center."* [M, 34] (Yee, 2005). Advancement is, however, also used to gain recognition from other players as clearly illustrated in: *"I basically play these games to become the most powerful force the game can allow. I want the best of the best items and people to truly respect my play style. I want to become a legend among players within the virtual mmorpg world!"* [M, 25] (Yee, 2005). But what happens to the value of the character when the player buys it from a shop instead of investing all her time in fine-tuning the character stats? Is the player still proud of her character? Or, more importantly, is the player having fun?

The boundaries between play and work seem to be immediately demolished when one thinks about the value of achievement. If the player decides to invest her time in advancing her game character, there is a great chance of playing turning into work. Or, as stated by a competitive player: *"My desire to stay competitive drives me to want to level fast, min-max, and gain rare drops. Those things in themselves aren't important to me, and I'd really rather it weren't important to the game, but if I intend to be competitive I've got to do the work to have the fun."* [M, 19] (Yee, 2005). The value of achievement, in this case, is so high that the player is voluntarily 'working' in order to reap the rewards in the form of occasional fun – and all of this in-game. Naturally, he could just purchase the laborious parts of the resource-gathering and invest his time on the more *ludic* activities. Value, as in all of these cases, is in the eye of the beholder.

Social Value

Players in MMOGs approach in-game relationships differently. Some regard them as being superficial while others value them similar to real life relationships (Yee, 2003a). The approach a player takes on the game will have an effect on relationship forming. One player comments the issue of meaningful relationships in MMOGs as follows: *"I've made many friends in games who become outside-of-game friends because we have a lot in common, same maturity level, looking for the same things in a friendship, and just click. I would call these very meaningful. But I also have many friends in games who are just sort of there to pass the time while I play... they're silly and fun to chat with... but I'd never want to deal with them outside of the game. Those relationships I would label as superficial"* [F, 22] (Yee, 2003a). According to the questionnaires collected by Yee in Daedalus Project (2003a), it is common to form lasting online friendships. The results reveal that 40% of the players feel that their online friends are comparable - or better - than their real life friends. This clearly suggests that the social role assumed in the virtual community adds immensely to the overall value of the game character. Many players have made good friends and some even got romantically involved through online relationships (Yee, 2003b). Players may try to be themselves or a fictive persona, but in both cases the relationships have been formed through the character.

Furthermore, MMOGs do not usually let you to change your identity (i.e., name and character appearance, excluding wearable items), which can greatly raise the value of your character. If a player would sell her account, she would potentially loose many of the formed relationships. A player could, in theory, build up these relationships by stating who she actually is, but this could be rather tedious task to perform. According to Yee (2003c) some evidence for this can be found from the results that over 50% of female players (who value relationships in game more than males) and more than 30% of males wouldn't sell their account for any price.

Guilds are rather common structure for organising play activities in MMOGs. The guilds offer an interface for getting in and familiar with gaming communities. Through a guild a player can find regular company to tackle different quests. Casual friends or even friendships formed through a guild activities are, however, not the only social value guilds have to offer. Since guilds are active communities arranging playable content, they need players on different levels to organise various tasks. By being active in guild organisation, a player can improve her social skills but also learn organising and leading skills. One player describes this as following: *"Last year, I was elected as the leader of the guild I'm part of when our old leader (a good RL friend) left. At first, I was a bit concerned about my ability to organize 100 some people from all over the world, but, as it turned out, I learned that I was much more organized that I had thought I would be, and ... that I had an uncanny knack for diplomacy and leadership. The experience made me feel very empowered, and good about myself [...]"* [F, 34] (Yee, 2002). This suggests that MMOGs can have life changing effects.

Perhaps the most interesting set of case examples considers the far reaching and intense effects of social values. For example, *"A Story About a Tree"* by Raph Koster is signifying the issue that MMOGs are not "just a game" (Bartle 2003, 209). In this case, a player named Karyn was found missing from the *LegendMUD* and after a quick check on her personal website, the community realised she had died two months ago. This started an immediate outpouring of grief in *LegendMUD*. There were numerous email consolidations, memorial service, and even a garden of remembrance with a tree bearing a plaque: "In memory of Karyn." (Bartle 2003, 209). Whether real stories or urban legends, the heart-breaking accounts of genuine sense of loss over someone the players have never actually met in real life, signify the uttermost personal value. The value of a player feeds the value of community, and *vice versa*.

Immersion Value

In terms of customisation, as part of the immersion component in the motivation model, the current value structures are more or less straightforward. You either invest your time in collecting personal gear, or, you pay extra to become more individual. The extra-payment scheme is actually a valid business model of the likes of *RuneScape* and *Habbo Hotel*. While the basic entry is free, you can purchase something extra with real money and, thus, become different from everybody else. For example, in *Second Life* you can spend your (real) dollars to customise your avatar. The science-fiction vision of Stephenson's (1992) *Metaverse,* with its budget-segregated avatars, seems to become more concrete year by year.

The final set of value cases is perhaps the most difficult to concretise since the concept of immersion – by nature – is highly psychological. There are, however, some typical trends in MMOGs that provide us clues about the potential value structures. Let us start with our personal expedition as *Gopher Tail Minstrels (or GTM)*. GTM was a group of adventurers in the world of *Asheron's Call 2* who, just out of curiosity and for the sake of fun, formed a party of troubadours. The main point here was not the public performances – although those occurred frequently and usually with keen crowds – but the role-playing of something that fell outside of the pure hack-and-slash pursue of points. After several months of gigs, numerous explorations to remote and desolate areas, and constant gathering of data (i.e., screenshots), the motivation to play faded. However, the memory of GTM never disappeared.

After a disastrous server crash, the only survived screenshot (Figure 3) remains as a testimonial of the days long-gone. The price tag for the additional images might easily become phenomenal, since there is no other concrete evidence of the life of GTM.

Figure 3: Gopher Tail Minstrels in action somewhere in the realm of Asheron's Call 2.

Actually, the case of Gopher Tail Minstrels is by no means unique. The loss of one's game character may well be more than just a loss of virtual artefact. And people may react very strongly in that kind of situation: *"On December 25th, 2006 I woke up to a big surprise. No, not a big pile of presents! I woke up to find my World of Warcraft character no longer existed. You may say, 'Sure it's just a video game, what's the big deal?' Oh, when you put 286 days of playtime in one character, it is a huge deal."* (My Crazy Blog 2006). This player, according to his own testimonial, was prepared to sue the guilty party with no expenses saved approach. He continues: *"Now, for the fun part. Finding a law firm that will pursue this case. I will be suing for the 286 days of life this man stole from me, and the $2000 it cost me to figure out everything about him."* The value, in this case, is not just memories. It can grow to become something even money cannot buy.

12 DISCUSSION

The aforementioned cases provide some practical implications to the field of business studies. While the roadmap from existing MMOG to a future business platform is not always clear, there are several key areas that could be harnessed. In essence, all the motivational components of play, form potential areas for commercial applications. This, however, should not result the players being charged more rigorously. Instead, the existing subscription-based business model, could be replaced with transaction-oriented mechanisms that offer ways for user-created content – and business. *Second Life* is a living example of value-adding procedures and virtual asset transaction.

The initial argument states that the more persistent the virtual world is, the greater the need for a formal economy (Bartle 2003, 299). This, however, is not the only approach in contemporary MMOGs. The spin-off businesses (e.g., auctions, gold farming, power-levelling, etc.) all add to the original economy model of the MMOGs. In addition, the concept of MMOG aggregators that integrate several different virtual worlds would make it possible to achieve true interconnectivity between the games. The virtual is not bound within the frames of formal computer systems. The cross-over to the real world has come to stay.

In their own field, MMOGs are rapidly advancing our shift towards game society. Basic ICT and Internet skills will not be enough since people need to master games and playing. Furthermore, people may need to master the business models and structures of virtual economies - with all the ripple effects to and from our real economies. The secondary markets with trading of virtual assets outside the MMOGs, and the novel but difficult to harness value chains provide interesting challenges for both researchers and practitioners.

Still, perhaps the strongest implication of the evolution of MMOGs might be the level of persistency these worlds possess. They currently do have a limited, yet substantial in duration, life span of 5-15 years. What will be the outcome if we truly have MMOG aggregators and systems that can keep your virtual property current year after year? When will the virtual become non-virtual? What is the threshold that needs to be crossed in order for us to start thinking these artefacts as real as the physical ones? Mobile phone life-cycle may be 1-2 years, average consumer products tend to 'last' less time than they did 10 years ago. The virtual home, built in *AlphaWorld* (nowadays *ActiveWorlds*), that is 20 years old cannot, by any means, be defined as quickly vanishing fad. Actually, it may have lasted longer than many real world houses.

Finally, the question of what is the value of ones virtual identity in the online game community remains a multifaceted problem. Since the perception of value differs greatly from one player to another, there is no concrete solution to the problem. However, through the motivational framework, and by illustrating the role of the game character as main tool to operate in MMOGs, we are able to point out the specific value structures that emerge. If the future business models are able to harness these basic value components, there may be room for development in MMOGs. With diversified added value mechanisms and clear option to select ones personal format of investment, the online games could truly become the *cyberspaces* and *metaverses* of tomorrow.

REFERENCES

Aarseth, E. (2001) Computer Game Studies, Year One. The International Journal of Computer Game Research (online) 1(1).

Anshe Chung Studios (2006) Anshe Chung Becomes First Virtual World Millionaire. (Referenced 27th of January, 2007). Online: http://www.anshechung.com

Bartle, R. (1996). Hearts, clubs, diamonds, spades: Players who suit MUDs. Journal of MUD Research 1, 1 (June 1996). (Referenced 27th of January, 2007) Online: http://www.mud.co.uk/richard/hcds.htm. Last referenced July 2nd 2006.

Bartle, R. (2003) Designing Virtual Worlds. Prentice Hall, p. 741

BBC News (2005) Fantasy fuels games with finances. (Referenced 27th January, 2007). Online: http://news.bbc.co.uk/2/hi/technology/4543212.stm

BBC News (2006) China's full-time computer gamers. (Referenced 27th January, 2007). Online: http://news.bbc.co.uk/2/hi/business/5151916.stm

Blizzard Entertainment (2007) World Of Warcraft Surpasses 8 Million Subscribers Worldwide. Press release from Jan 11, 2007. (Referenced 27th of January, 2007) Online: http://www.blizzard.com/press/070111.shtml

BusinessWeek online (2006) My Virtual Life – Virtual World, Real Money. (Referenced 17th January, 2007) Online: http://www.businessweek.com/magazine/content/06_18/b3982002.htm

Ducheneaut, N., Yee, N., Nickell, E., and Moore, R. (2006) "Alone Together?" Exploring the Social Dynamics of Massively Multiplayer Online Games. In Proceedings of CHI 20006 – Games and Performances. April 22-27, Montréal, Québec, Canada, pp. 407-416.

Fine, G. (1983) Shared Fantasy – Role-Playing Games as Social Worlds. The University of Chicago Press, USA.

Friedl, M. (2003) Online Game Interactivity Theory. Charles River Media, Inc, USA.

Gibson, W. (1984) Neuromancer. Victor Gollancz Ltd.

Gygax, G. & Arneson, D.L. (1974) Dungeons and Dragons [role playing game rulebooks]. TSR, Lake Geneva, WI.

Huizinga, Johan (1955) Homo Ludens: A Study of the Play-Element in Culture. Beacon Press.

Jakobson, M. and Taylor, T.L. (2003). The Sopranos Meets EverQuest: Social Networking in Massively Multiplayer Online Games. In Proceedings of the 2003 Digital Arts and Culture (DAC) conference, Melbourne, Australia, 81-90.

Linden Lab (2007) Second Life. Developed by Linden Lab / Linden Research Inc. (Referenced 27th January, 2007). Online: http://secondlife.com

Mulligan, J. & Patrovsky, B. (2003) Developing Online Games: Insiders Guide. Prentice Hall.

My Crazy Blog (2006) Some Bastard Hacked My World of Warcraft Account. (Refernced 29th of January, 2007). Online: http://www.fundular.com

TheObserver (2005). They play games for 10 hours - and earn £2.80 in a 'virtual sweatshop'. (Referenced 27th January, 2007). Online:

http://observer.guardian.co.uk/international/story/0,6903,1436411,00.html

Rouse, R. (2000) Game Design: Theory & Practice. Wordware Publishing, Inc., Plano, Texas.

Salen, K. and Zimmerman, E. (2004). Rules of Play - Game Design Fundamentals. Massachusetts Institute of Technology.

Stephenson, N. (1992) Snow Crash. Bantam Books, New York, NY.

Turkle, S. (1999). Cyberspace and Identity. Contemporary Sociology, Vol. 28, No. 6: 643-648.

Washington Post Online (2005). Virtual Gaming Economy. (Referenced 27th January, 2007). Online:
http://www.washingtonpost.com/wp-dyn/content/discussion/2005/09/13/DI2005091301150.html

Yee, N. (2002). " Growth and Transfer: Through the Looking Glass" from " Mosaic: Stories of Digital Lives and Identities" by Nick Yee. (Referenced 29th January, 2007). Online:
http://www.nickyee.com/mosaic/growth.html.

Yee, N. (2003a). "Are MMORPG Relationships Meaningless?" from "The Daedalus Project" by Nick Yee. (Referenced 29th January, 2007). Online:
http://www.nickyee.com/daedalus/archives/000632.php.

Yee, N. (2003b). "Inside Out" from "The Daedalus Project" by Nick Yee. (Referenced 24th January, 2007). Online: http://www.nickyee.com/daedalus/archives/000523.php.

Yee, N. (2003c). "How Much Would You Sell Your Account For?" from "The Daedalus Project" by Nick Yee. (Referenced 24th January, 2007). Online:
http://www.nickyee.com/daedalus/archives/000196.php.

Yee, N. (2005). "In Their Own Words: The Achievement Component" from "The Daedalus Project" by Nick Yee. (Referenced 29th January, 2007). Online:
http://www.nickyee.com/daedalus/archives/001300.php

Yee, N. (2006). Motivations of Play in Online Games. CyberPsychology and Behavior, Vol. 9, No. 6: 772-775.

Permissions

All chapters in this book were first published in IJBSAM, by International Journal of Business Science & Applied Management; hereby published with permission under the Creative Commons Attribution License or equivalent. Every chapter published in this book has been scrutinized by our experts. Their significance has been extensively debated. The topics covered herein carry significant findings which will fuel the growth of the discipline. They may even be implemented as practical applications or may be referred to as a beginning point for another development.

The contributors of this book come from diverse backgrounds, making this book a truly international effort. This book will bring forth new frontiers with its revolutionizing research information and detailed analysis of the nascent developments around the world.

We would like to thank all the contributing authors for lending their expertise to make the book truly unique. They have played a crucial role in the development of this book. Without their invaluable contributions this book wouldn't have been possible. They have made vital efforts to compile up to date information on the varied aspects of this subject to make this book a valuable addition to the collection of many professionals and students.

This book was conceptualized with the vision of imparting up-to-date information and advanced data in this field. To ensure the same, a matchless editorial board was set up. Every individual on the board went through rigorous rounds of assessment to prove their worth. After which they invested a large part of their time researching and compiling the most relevant data for our readers.

The editorial board has been involved in producing this book since its inception. They have spent rigorous hours researching and exploring the diverse topics which have resulted in the successful publishing of this book. They have passed on their knowledge of decades through this book. To expedite this challenging task, the publisher supported the team at every step. A small team of assistant editors was also appointed to further simplify the editing procedure and attain best results for the readers.

Apart from the editorial board, the designing team has also invested a significant amount of their time in understanding the subject and creating the most relevant covers. They scrutinized every image to scout for the most suitable representation of the subject and create an appropriate cover for the book.

The publishing team has been an ardent support to the editorial, designing and production team. Their endless efforts to recruit the best for this project, has resulted in the accomplishment of this book. They are a veteran in the field of academics and their pool of knowledge is as vast as their experience in printing. Their expertise and guidance has proved useful at every step. Their uncompromising quality standards have made this book an exceptional effort. Their encouragement from time to time has been an inspiration for everyone.

The publisher and the editorial board hope that this book will prove to be a valuable piece of knowledge for researchers, students, practitioners and scholars across the globe.

List of Contributors

Li-Wei Mai
University of Westminster Westminster Business School, University of Westminster, 35 Marylebone Rd, London NW1 5LS, UK

Mitchell R. Ness
Newcastle University School of Agriculture Food and Rural Development Newcastle University, Newcastle upon Tyne, NE1 7RU, UK

Juho Hamari and Vili Lehdonvirta
Helsinki Institute for Information Technology HIIT P.O. Box 9800, FI-02015 TKK, Finland

Talal Al-maghrabi and Charles Dennis
Brunel Business School, Brunel University West London, UB8 3PH, United Kingdom

Raed Algharabat and Charles Dennis
Brunel Business School, Marketing Department, Brunel University Elliot Jaques Building, Uxbridge, Middlesex, UB8 3PH, United Kingdom

Maria Leticia Santos-Vijande and Luis I. Alvarez-Gonzalez
Department of Business Administration, University of Oviedo Avda. del Cristo, s/n, 33071, Oviedo, Asturias. Spain

Alexis Barlow and Peter Duncan
Caledonian Business School, Glasgow Caledonian University Cowcaddens Road, Glasgow, Scotland, G4 0BA United Kingdom

Feng Li and Savvas Papagiannidis
Business School, Newcastle University Newcastle upon Tyne, NE1 7RU, UK

Bernt Krohn Solvang
Department of Work Life and Innovation, University of Agder Service box 509, 4898 Grimstad, Norway

Constantinos Coursaris
Department of Telecommunication, Information Studies, and Media Michigan State University, East Lansing, Michigan, U.S.A., 48824

Khaled Hassanein and Milena Head
DeGroote School of Business McMaster University, 1280 Main Street West, Hamilton, Ontario, Canada, L8S 4M4

Mohamed G. Aboelmaged
Ajman University of Science and Technology Po Box 346, Ajman, UAE

Abdallah M. Elamin
King Fahd University of Petroleum and Mineral (KFUPM) Po Box 488, Dhahran 31261, Saudi Arabia

James Cornford and Paul Richter
Centre for Social and Business Informatics, Newcastle University Newcastle upon Tyne, NE1 7RU, UK

Subrata Chakraborty and Shailja Agarwal
Jaipuria Institute of Management Vineet Khand, Gomti Nagar, Lucknow - 226010, India

Syed Zamberi Ahmad
Policy and Business Strategy Department, University of Malaya 50360 Kuala Lumpur, Malaysia

Philip J. Kitchen
The Business School, Hull University, Hull, HU6 7RX, United Kingdom

Fintan Clear
Brunel University Brunel Business School Elliott Jaques Building, Uxbridge, Middlesex, UB8 3PH, UK

Paul Beynon-Davies
eCommerce Innovation Centre, Cardiff Business School, Cardiff University Aberconay Building, Colum Drive, Cardiff, CF10 3EU, United Kingdom

James Richards and Abigail Marks
School of Management & Languages, Heriot-Watt University Edinburgh, EH14 4AS, United Kingdom

Tony Manninen and Tomi Kujanpää
Game Design and Research Unit, University of Oulu PO Box 3000, FIN-90014, Finland

Index

CPSIA information can be obtained
at www.ICGtesting.com
Printed in the USA
BVHW02*0436020218
506942BV00003B/147/P